Carriage by Air

Carriage by Air

Trevor Philipson QC, BA (Oxon), BCL (Oxon), Bencher of Middle Temple

Nicholas Underhill QC, MA (Oxon), Recorder, Bencher of Gray's Inn

Timothy Wormington, BA, BCL (Oxon), of Middle Temple, Barrister

Craig Orr, MA (Cantab), BCL (Oxon), of Middle Temple, Barrister

Bankim Thanki, MA (Oxon), Dip Law (City), of Middle Temple, Barrister

Akhil Shah, MA (Cantab), of Inner Temple, Barrister

Marcus Smith, MA (Oxon), BCL (Oxon), of Lincoln's Inn, Barrister

Veronique Buehrlen, MA (St Andrews), Dip Law (City), of Middle Temple, Barrister

John Taylor, MA (Cantab), of Middle Temple, Barrister

Adam Tolley, BA (Oxon), BCL (Oxon), of Inner Temple, Barrister

Louise Merrett, BA (Cantab), of Gray's Inn, Barrister

Paul Sinclair, MA (Cantab), LLM (Harvard), of Middle Temple, Barrister

Giles Wheeler, MA (Cantab), LLM (Cantab), of Lincoln's Inn, Barrister

Rosalind Phelps, BA (Oxon), BCL (Oxon), Dip French Law (University of Paris II), of Lincoln's Inn, Barrister

Butterworths
London, Edinburgh, Dublin
2001

United Kingdom	Butterworths, a Division of Reed Elsevier (UK) Ltd, Halsbury House, 35 Chancery Lane, London WC2A 1EL and 4 Hill Street, Edinburgh EH2 3JZ
Australia	Butterworths, a Division of Reed International Books Australia Pty Ltd, Chatswood, New South Wales
Canada	Butterworths Canada Ltd, Markham, Ontario
Hong Kong	Butterworths Hong Kong, a division of Reed Elsevier (Greater China) Ltd, Hong Kong
India	Butterworths India, New Delhi
Ireland	Butterworth (Ireland) Ltd, Dublin
Malaysia	Malayan Law Journal Sdn Bhd, Kuala Lumpur
New Zealand	Butterworths of New Zealand Ltd, Wellington
Singapore	Butterworths Asia, Singapore
South Africa	Butterworths Publishers (Pty) Ltd, Durban
USA	Lexis Law Publishing, Charlottesville, Virginia

© Trevor Philipson, Nicholas Underhill, Timothy Wormington, Craig Orr, Bankim Thanki, Akhil Shah, Marcus Smith, Veronique Buehrlen, John Taylor, Adam Tolley, Louise Merrett, Paul Sinclair, Giles Wheeler and Rosalind Phelps 2001

A CIP Catalogue record for this book is available from the British Library.

ISBN 0 406 02136 8

Typeset by M Rules, London
Printed in Great Britain by Antony Rowe Ltd, Chippenham, Wiltshire

Visit Butterworths LEXIS direct at: http://www.butterworths.com

Foreword

In large measure, international carriage by air is governed by international conventions which have been given the force of law in the United Kingdom by legislation. These conventions seek to create codes harmonising the liability of a carrier as regards the carriage of persons, baggage and cargo. The process began with the Warsaw Convention of 1929, which was revised by the Hague Protocol in 1955. Since then, the Warsaw/Hague regime has been supplemented by the Guadalajara Convention (1961), the Montreal Agreement (1966), the Guatemala Protocol (1971) and the Montreal Protocols (1975), which have been ratified in a piecemeal fashion by some, but by no means all, of the states signatory to the Warsaw or Warsaw/Hague Conventions. The result has been a fragmentation and confusion of the original Warsaw code. This, in turn, has led to a number of attempts (variously on the part of IATA, the European Union and ICAO) to reform the system, culminating in the Montreal Convention of 1999.

Members of Fountain Court Chambers have produced a lucid and scholarly book that deals specifically with this complex area. In doing so, they have performed an invaluable service for all those who have to consider, identify and deal with the difficult problems that carriage by air can give rise to.

Lord Justice Henry

November 2000

Preface

Although the law relating to the carriage of persons and goods by air is one that can justifiably be regarded as an area for the specialist, issues relating to carriage by air can, and regularly do, present themselves in a much broader context. This is scarcely surprising given the importance and pervasiveness of the aviation industry today. We have felt for some time that there is need for a book, in addition to the excellent *Shawcross & Beaumont*, that seeks to deal specifically with this particular aspect of aviation law.

This book seeks to explain the legal regimes governing carriage by air and their provisions, covering the various applicable international conventions, the provisions of European law and residual role of the common law. Although the law relating to carriage by air represents an effort to bring uniformity to rules that — because of the very nature of air transport — almost inevitably have an international dimension, such efforts are rarely completely successful. Inevitably, there is a national aspect. This book seeks to describe the regime regulating carriage by air from the standpoint of English law. Treaties such as the Warsaw-Hague Convention are described through the prism of the Acts that have made them applicable in English law, and foreign case law has been cited where it will assist the English lawyer.

The writing of this book has been a collegiate enterprise, involving a number of tenants of Fountain Court. We would like to thank family, friends and colleagues who have assisted and encouraged us during the time in which this book was written. We are also indebted to Sir Denis Henry for finding the time to write a Foreword on our behalf. Finally, we must express our considerable gratitude to the publishing team at Butterworths, not only for their support, but also their patience, throughout the preparation of the manuscript for publication.

We have sought to state the law on the basis of cases reported and legislation as it stood on or before 1 July 2000.

Fountain Court Chambers

2000

Contents

Note   References in bold are to paragraph number.

Abbreviations

AC	Law Reports, Appeal Cases, House of Lords and Privy Council, since 1890
AEA	Association of European Airlines
AJCL	American Journal of Comparative Law (US)
AL	Air Law (The Netherlands)
AL/ALR	Archiv fur Luftrecht (Germany)
All Ind Rep	All India Reporter
ALR	American Law Reports (Annotated)
Annals ASL	Annals of Air and Space Law (Canada)
App Div	Appellate Division Reports, New York Supreme Court, 1896–1955
App Div 2d	Appellate Division Reports, New York Supreme Court, Second Series, 1955–(current)
App/Apps	Appendix/Appendices
art	Article
ASLR	Australian Securities Law Reporter
Avi Cas	CCH Aviation Law Reporter, 1822–(current)
B & S	Best and Smith, Law Reports 1861–1870
Brod & B	Broderip and Bingham, Law Reports, 1819–1822
C & P	Carrington and Payne, Law Reports, 1823–1841
CA	English Court of Appeal
CAB	Civil Aeronautics Board
Camp	Campbell's reports, Nisi Prius, 1807–1816
Can YBIL	Canadian Yearbook of International Law
Carth	Carthew, Law Reports 1668–1701
Cass Civ 1re	Cour de Cassation première chambre civile
CB	Common Bench Reports, 1845–1856
CBNS	Common Bench Reports, New Series, 1856–1865
ch	Chapter
Chitty	Chitty on Contracts (28th edn, 1999)
CI & F	Clarke and Finelly, Law Reports, 1831–1846
CIDPA	Conférence Internationale de Droit Privé Aérien
CITEJA	Comité International Technique d'Experts Juridiques Aériens
CLR	Commonwealth Law Reports, 1903–(current)
Clerk & Lindsell	Clerk & Lindsell on Torts (Sweet and Maxwell)
Cmd	Command Paper

CMR	Convention on the Contract for International Carriage of Goods by Road
CP	Common Pleas
CPD	Law Reports, Common Pleas Division, 1875–1880
CRS	Computer Reservation Service
DC Colo	District Court, Colorado (US)
DCNY	District Court, New York (US)
DLR	Dominion Law Reports (Canada)
Doug	Douglas, Law Reports, 1778–1785
Drion	Drion *Limitation of liabilities in international air law* (Nijhoff, 1954)
E & B	Ellis and Blackburn, Law Reports, 1852–1858
East	East, Law Reports, 1800–1812
ECAC	European Civil Aviation Conference
ECR	European Court Reports, 1875–(current)
EDNY	Eastern District of New York
ESC	Economic and Social Committee
Esp	Espinasse, Law Reports, 1793–1810
Eur Tr L	European Transport Law
Ex	Exchequer Reports, 1847–1856
Ex D	Exchequer Division, Law Reports, 1875–1880
F	Federal Reporter (US), 1880–1924
F 2d	Federal Reporter (US), Second Series, 1924–(current)
F Supp	Federal Supplement (US), 1932–(current)
F Supp 2d	Federal Supplement (US), 1998–(current)
Giemulla/Schmid /Ehlers	Giemulla/Schmid/Ehlers *Warsaw Convention* (1992)
Goedhuis	Goedhuis *National air legislation and the Warsaw convention* (1937)
GSA	General Sales Agents
H & N	Hurlstone and Norman, Law Reports, 1856–1862
Harv LR	Harvard Law Reports
HL	House of Lords
IATA ACLR	International Air Traffic Association (Air Carriers Liability Reports)
IATA	International Air Traffic Association
ICAO	International Civil Aviation Association
ICLQ	International and Comparative Law Quarterly
ICR	Industrial Case Reports, 1972–(current)
IGIA	Interagency Group on International Aviation
Ill App	Illinois Appellate Court Reports (US)
ILR	International Law Reports
IMF	International Monetary Fund
JAL	Journal of African Law
JALC	Journal of Air Law and Commerce
JBL	Journal of Business Law
JCP	Juris-Classeur Périodique, Paris
KB	Law Reports, Kings Bench Division, 1901–1952
Keb	Keble, Law Reports, 1661–1679

LEd	Lawyer's Edition, United States Supreme Court Reports, 1754–1956
LEd 2d	Lawyer's Edition, United States Supreme Court Reports, Second Series, 1956–(current)
Ld Raym	Lord Raymond, Law Reports, 1694–1732
LJ	Law Journal Newspaper, 1866–1965
Lloyd's Rep	Lloyd's List Law Reports, 1951–(current)
LMCLQ	Lloyd's Maritime & Commercial Law Quarterly
LQR	Law Quarterly Review
LR	Law Reports
LR HL	Law Reports, House of Lords, English and Irish Appeals 1866–1875
McGill LJ	McGill Law Journal
McNair	McNair *Law of the Air* (3rd edn, 1964)
Matte	Matte *Treatise on Air-Aeronautical Law* (1981)
Miller	Miller *Liability on international air transport* (1977)
Mod	Modern, Law Reports, 1669–1732
ND Cal	Northern District, California (US)
NE	North Eastern Reporter
NY	New York Reports
NY Ct of Apps	New York Court of Appeals
NYS	New York Supplement, 1888–1938
NYS 2d	New York Supplement, Second Series, 1938–(current)
NZLR	New Zealand Law Reports
OR	Ontario Reports
P	Pacific Reporter (US), 1883–1931
p/pp	page/pages
para	paragraph
PC	Privy Council
Pt	Part
QB	Law Reports, Queen's Bench Division 1891–1901 and since 1952
QBD	Law Reports, Queen's Bench Division, 1875–1890
RFDA	Revue Française de Droit Aérien
RGA(E)	Revue Générale de l'Air (et de l'Espace) (France)
RTR	Road Traffic Reports
s	Section (of an Act of Parliament)
S & B Av R	Shawcross & Beaumont Aviation Reports
Salmond & Heuston	Salmond & Heuston on the Law (21st edn)
S Ct	Supreme Court
SC	Session Cases
Sch	Schedule
SDC Kan	Southern District Court, Kansas (US)
SDNY	Southern District of New York (US)
SDR	Special Drawing Right
Shawcross	Shawcross & Beaumont *Air Law*
SLR	Scottish Law Reporter, 1865–1924
Sol J	Solictor's Journal, 1856–(current)
TAQ	The Aviation Quarterly
TR	Term Reports, 1785–1800

UCTA	Unfair Contract Terms Act
UK	United Kingdom
ULC	Uniform Law Cases (International Institute for the Unification of Private Law, Milan)
Uniform LR	Uniform Law Review (Unidroit)
US & C Av	United States and Canadian Aviation Reports
US Av	United States Aviation Reports, 1928–1978
US Ct of Apps	United States Court of Appeals
US	United States
USC	United States Code
vol	Volume
WWR	Western Weekly Reports (Canada)
ZLW	Zeitschrift fur Luft- und Weltraumrecht

Table of Statutes

Table of Statutory Instruments

Table of Cases

Chapter 1

Carriage by Air: Historical Background

International Carriage

1.1   International carriage by air is largely governed by international conventions given effect in the UK by legislation. The purpose of these conventions was essentially to deal with conflict of law problems which arose with the rapid growth of air transport from the beginning of the 1900s. Such conflicts had from the outset attracted considerable academic attention, both in England and abroad[1].

1.2   The Legal Commission of the International Air Traffic Association (IATA)[2] had in the 1920s produced standard conditions of carriage[3], but these were not comprehensively adopted and were subject to radically different interpretation in different jurisdictions. Clearly what was required was the implementation of a uniform set of rules governing international carriage. Greene LJ in *Grein v Imperial Airways Ltd*[4] emphasised the desirability of such a code thus:

> 'Without it questions of great difficulty as to the law applicable to a contract of international carriage by air would constantly arise. Our Courts are familiar with similar questions arising under contracts of through carriage otherwise than by air; and it is easy to imagine cases where questions of the greatest difficulty might arise as to which law or laws governed the contract and whether different laws might not apply to different stages of the journey . . . It is not too much to suppose that similar questions would arise in the Courts of foreign

---

[1]   See, for example, the works cited by McNair *Law of the Air* (3rd edn, 1964) p 4, particularly Hazeltine *Law of the Air* (1911).

[2]   The precursor to the modern International Air Transport Association, founded in 1919. This is a private organisation of (in practice scheduled) airlines, the aim of which is to promote safe, regular and economical air transportation. See J W S Brancker *IATA and What it Does* (1977).

[3]   These had been in use from about 1921. After the Warsaw Convention the IATA attempted to bring its standard conditions in line with the Convention for both international and non-international carriage: see D Goedhuis *National air legislation and the Warsaw convention* (1937) pp 7–8.

[4]   [1937] 1 KB 50 at 74–75.

countries; and it may well be that those Courts would follow principles different to our own in deciding the proper law applicable in the various cases which might arise. In the case of air carriage examples of the confusion which might arise in the absence of an international code readily suggest themselves. Thus different laws might be held to apply according as a ticket (to take a simple case) was taken in Paris for a flight to London or in London for a flight to Paris, according as the carrier was a French or an English Company, according as an accident took place in England or in France. Where the carriage is effected by stages covering several countries and involving aeroplanes belonging to companies incorporated in several countries, the difficulties increase as well as the unlikelihood of finding in the various countries in which actions might be brought any uniformity of legal principles for their decision . . .'[5].

1.3 The other major concern, particularly of airlines, was the implementation of internationally accepted limits on carriers' liability for death, injury or damage[6]. The reasons advanced for such special provisions for air carriers included: the protection of a fledgling and financially weak aviation industry[7]; the spreading of possibly catastrophic risks; the desirability of the carrier being able fully to insure its liabilities; the standardisation of damages awards; the ability of passengers to obtain insurance on their own behalf; and the reduction of litigation against airlines by facilitating settlement[8]. It is a matter of some controversy among commentators whether these reasons, either individually or cumulatively, justified the imposition of a limited liability regime; still more, whether they continue to do so[9].

1.4 In August 1923 the French premier, M Poincaré, wrote to the diplomatic representatives accredited in France stating that the French government had been led to studying the question of the liability of the carrier and was planning to convene an international conference in Paris to discuss the issue. The French government produced a draft international convention dealing with carriers' liability. A conference, the first session of the Conférence Internationale de Droit Privé Aérien (CIDPA), eventually took place in Paris in October 1926, attended by 76 delegates, representing 41 states. The view of the conference was that the issues were sufficiently complex to require the creation of a special committee of experts. The French government subsequently convened such a committee of experts nominated by different countries, the

---

[5] For a more convoluted example of the private law difficulties caused by international air travel, see *Goedhuis* pp 2–3.

[6] For a discussion of the various reasons advanced to justify the limitation of liability, see Drion *Limitation of liabilities in international air law* (1954) ch 1.

[7] This appears to have been the major factor in the early international conferences, see *Drion*, pp 14–15.

[8] It is only the ability of the passenger to obtain insurance and the reduction of litigation which Drion, in his comprehensive analysis, found to have a sound rationale and was sufficiently persuasive to justify the general structure of the Warsaw Convention (p 42).

[9] See para **1.38** below.

Comité International Technique d'Experts Juridiques Aériens (CITEJA)[10], in Paris in May 1926[11].

Warsaw Convention, 1929

1.5   The Warsaw conference, the second session of CIDPA, took place in October 1929 primarily to consider a draft convention prepared by CITEJA: the Convention[12] eventually agreed by the delegates was based largely on the CITEJA draft. The original text of the Convention is in French[13] and it dealt with the carriage of passengers, baggage and cargo.

1.6   The Warsaw Convention attempted to eliminate many of the conflicts problems which might arise in international air travel, to create a system of internationally recognised documentation[14], to prescribe a limitation period for claims[15], to resolve questions of jurisdiction[16] and, perhaps most importantly, to impose very strict limits on carriers' liability. The *quid pro quo* of the limitation of liability was the reversal of the burden of proof[17]. Fault on the part of the carrier would be assumed on proof of damage: the carrier could only escape liability by establishing that it (and its servants and agents) had taken all necessary measures to avoid the damage[18]. This has in practice proven a difficult hurdle for carriers to overcome. The limitations on liability have, however, proven to be a major benefit for carriers. Such limits on liability could only be avoided under the Warsaw Convention by proof of the

---

[10]   See *Fothergill v Monarch Airlines Ltd* [1981] AC 251 at 278. A useful summary of the work of CITEJA can be found in Ide 'The History and Accomplishments of the International Technical Committee of Aerial Legal Experts CITEJA' [1933] JAL 27; see also Plaisant 'Le CITEJA et son oeuvre' [1946/7] RFDA 153.

[11]   It should be noted that the US did not participate in the work of CITEJA, although it sent an observer to the Warsaw conference.

[12]   The full title of the Convention is the 'Convention for the Unification of Certain Rules relating to International Carriage by Air' Cmd 4284. The text of most of the international agreements referred to in this chapter can be found in *Shawcross & Beaumont: Air Law* Appendices A and AB. References to the 'unamended Convention' or 'the Warsaw Convention' relate to this original Convention of 1929.

[13]   For the French text of the proceedings see ICAO document 7838; for an English translation see that of Horner and Legrez, published by Rothman & Co, New Jersey in 1975. As to the Convention itself, no internationally recognised translation has ever been provided. Different translations can be found in the English Carriage by Air Act 1961, the Australian Civil Aviation (Carriers' Liability) Act 1959–73 and the Canadian Carriage by Air Act. Another translation is provided by the text ratified by the US Senate on 15 June 1934. For certain criticisms of the English translation, see N M Matte *Treatise on Air-Aeronautical Law* (1981) para 162; and Mankiewicz 'From Warsaw to Montreal with certain intermediate stops; marginal notes on the Warsaw system' [1989] 14 Air Law 239, p 241.

[14]   Articles 3–16. See Chapters 5 and 6 below.

[15]   Article 29. See para **11.42** below.

[16]   Article 28. See para **11.17** below.

[17]   The Presidential recommendation of the Warsaw Convention to the US Senate stated that '[t]he principle of placing the burden on the carrier to show lack of negligence in international air transportation in order to escape liability, seems to be reasonable in view of the difficulty which a passenger has in establishing the cause of an accident in air transportation.'

[18]   Article 20(1). See Chapter 9 below.

carrier's 'wilful misconduct'[19]. The Warsaw Convention fixed the maximum sum in the case of injury to a passenger at 125,000 Poincaré or Convention francs[20].

1.7   The UK was one of the original signatories to the Warsaw Convention, signing it on 12 October 1929 (along with twenty two other nations) and ratifying it on 14 February 1933[21].

1.8   The main issue which has bedevilled the history of the system initiated in Warsaw has been at what level limits on liability should be set, particularly in the case of injury to passengers[22]. Practical problems, such as converting any such limits into national currencies[23], have been no less difficult to resolve.

The Hague Protocol, 1955

1.9   The Warsaw Convention has attracted considerable criticism from an early stage in its history for the comparatively low limits on carriers' liability for death and injury to passengers and the different interpretations of 'wilful misconduct' adopted by the courts of contracting countries.

1.10   As far as the definition of wilful misconduct in art 25 was concerned, the language used in the French text and in the English translations was obscure[24] and has led to widely differing interpretations in different countries and courts[25]. There was doubt also whether art 25 covered wilful misconduct on the part of servants or agents of the carrier. This article, perhaps more than any other, has failed to achieve the objectives of international uniformity and of minimising litigation.

1.11   With regard to higher limits, it was apparent from the outset that in developed countries, such as France, the UK and the US, average awards in personal injury actions were considerably higher than the Warsaw limits. Further, as air travel became progressively safer, liability insurance could be obtained at a much lower cost per passenger mile than when the Warsaw Convention was first implemented. As airlines grew in size there also

---

[19]   Article 25. See Chapter 10 below.
[20]   Article 22(1). *Shawcross* estimates that this would have been worth some £1,000 or US$ 5,000 at the rates of exchange prevailing in 1929: Div VII, para [106].
[21]   It was implemented into English law by the now repealed Carriage by Air Act 1932. For certain flights the unamended Convention remains part of English law pursuant to the Carriage by Air Acts (Application of Provisions Order 1967). See **2.15** below. The text of most of the statutory material referred to in this book can be found in *Shawcross* Apps B and C.
[22]   An associated question being the circumstances in which the limits might be breached.
[23]   See *Shawcross* Div VII, paras [106] and [422]–[428].
[24]   See eg Beaumont 'Need for Revision and Amplification of the Warsaw Convention' [1949] 16 JALC 395, especially 408.
[25]   See *Drion*, pp 195–264; Mankiewicz 'The Judicial Diversification of Uniform Private Law Conventions' [1972] 21 ICLQ 718.

appeared to be less good reason to accord special protection to the aviation industry than may have been the case in 1929[26]. As the scale of international air travel expanded, any increased insurance costs appeared correspondingly smaller. On the other side of the equation, many countries considered the Warsaw limits, calculated by reference to the value of gold, satisfactory, particularly with general devaluation after the Second World War. Others considered the limits too high: certainly some Latin American countries had been discouraged from joining the Warsaw Convention on this ground. Raising limits might therefore jeopardise the objective of achieving universality. Some opposition was based on the perception that poorer countries would be forced to pay for insurance cover for large damages awards in the developed world by way of higher fares[27].

1.12 Moves in the 1930s to make amendments to the Warsaw Convention were interrupted by the Second World War. In 1951 the International Civil Aviation Association (ICAO)[28] authorised a legal sub-committee designated 'Warsaw' to prepare a new draft convention, drawing on a draft prepared by Major K M Beaumont of the UK[29]. In January 1952 this sub-committee met in Paris and it subsequently presented its conclusions at the tenth session of the ICAO Legal Committee in Rio de Janeiro in 1953: the text of the Warsaw Convention itself was discussed as well as the new draft proposed by the sub-committee. The delegates were in favour of elaborating the existing Convention, by way of a draft protocol, rather than proceeding with the new draft. This proved a much more practicable solution than wholesale change to the Warsaw Convention. The draft Protocol prepared by the delegates was submitted to the Council of the ICAO which collected comments from individual countries on the draft.

1.13 The Hague conference of 1955, convened by the ICAO primarily to address mounting concerns that liability limits, particularly for physical injury or death, had been set too low, debated the Rio de Janeiro draft protocol at length[30]. A new revised version of the Warsaw Convention, the Hague Protocol[31], was agreed upon at this conference. The main changes made related to limits of liability (doubling the limit contained in the unamended Convention[32]), the replacement of the concept of wilful misconduct with reference to intentional or reckless conduct[33], the extension of

---

[26] See eg Beaumont 'Liability of International Air Carriers' [1947] 97 LJ 643.
[27] See Clare 'Evaluation of Proposals to increase the "Warsaw Convention" Limit of Passenger Liability' [1949] 16 JALC 53.
[28] See generally FitzGerald 'The International Civil Aviation Organization and the Development of Conventions on International Air Law' [1978] 3 Annals ASL 51.
[29] One of the original authors of *Shawcross*. For his draft, see ICAO document 4498.
[30] For the minutes see ICAO document 7686–LC/140.
[31] The full title of the Protocol is 'Protocol to amend the Convention for the Unification of Certain Rules relating to International Carriage by Air' ICAO document 763, Cmd 9824. References to 'the amended Convention' or 'the Warsaw-Hague Convention' relate to the Warsaw Convention 1929 as amended by The Hague Protocol.
[32] Article 22.
[33] Article 25.

protection to the carrier's servants and agents[34] and the extension of notification times[35].

1.14   The Hague Protocol was signed by the UK on 23 March 1956 and was ratified on 3 March 1967[36]. The US signed the Protocol, but did not ratify, largely as a result of what it saw as excessive limitations of liability in the case of death or injury to passengers, notwithstanding the new increased limits[37]. US public opinion had become very antagonistic to the Warsaw liability limits, particularly following the serious injuries to the entertainer Jane Froman on a Pan American flight in Portugal[38]. Professor Bin Cheng has observed that there was an increasing tendency for US juries and judges to bypass or re-write the Warsaw Convention[39]. Other countries, such as Canada, did not ratify the Protocol despite (like the US) its significant involvement in the preliminary work at Rio and at The Hague: this was largely a result of the reservations expressed by the US[40].

The Guadalajara Convention, 1961

1.15   A particular weakness of the unamended and the amended Conventions was their failure adequately to address the liability of the actual carrier who undertook the carriage in particular circumstances. While both the amended and unamended Conventions addressed the liability of the carrier who made the contract of carriage and any successive carriers, namely carriers who by agreement with the customer or passenger took over from the contracting carrier and performed part of the carriage, neither addressed the situation where the whole of the carriage was sub-contracted to another carrier; nor where part of the carriage was sub-contracted without the agreement of the customer or passenger[41].

1.16   The problem was first highlighted during the tenth International Aerial Legislation Congress in 1948[42]. The ICAO's sub-committee drew up drafts to address this problem at the 11th session of the Legal Committee

---

[34]   Article 25A.

[35]   Article 26.

[36]   See s 1 of the Carriage by Air Act 1961 which implemented the amended Convention (and came into force in 1967).

[37]   It is to be noted that on 28 September 1998 the US ratified the Hague Protocol, which entered into force in the US on 4 March 1999.

[38]   See *Froman v Pan American Airways* 284 App Div 935, 135 NYS 2d 619 (1954). In 1952 H J Sherman's emotively titled and influential *The Social Impact of the Warsaw Convention* was published in the US.

[39]   'Centrifugal Tendencies in Air Law' [1957] 10 Current Legal Problems 200, p 225 ff; 'Wilful Misconduct: From Warsaw to The Hague and From Brussels to Paris' [1977] 2 Annals ASL 55, p 98.

[40]   See *Matte* para 166.

[41]   There appears to be a conflict of views between continental and common law jurists as to the effect of the Warsaw and Warsaw-Hague Conventions on this topic and whether the Guadalajara Convention was necessary at all: see Mankiewicz *The Liability Regime of the International Air Carrier* (1981) pp 6–7.

[42]   See *Matte* para 170.

held in Tokyo in 1957[43]. In 1959 the ICAO Council commissioned further work on this draft, which was completed in 1960 and discussed at the 13th session of the ICAO Legal Committee held in Montreal in that year[44].

1.17   The Guadalajara conference took place in the Autumn of 1961, principally to deal with this definitional problem and to discuss the draft produced by the ICAO[45]. The result of the conference, known as the Guadalajara Convention[46], in essence unequivocally extended the same rights and liabilities under the Warsaw system to the actual carrier which already applied to the contracting carrier (although the actual carrier is only liable in relation to the actual portion of the carriage performed by it)[47]. It was signed by the UK on 18 September 1961 and ratified by it on 4 September 1962[48]. The US has not ratified the Guadalajara Convention, the issue having become inexplicably linked with its refusal to ratify the Hague Protocol.

The Montreal Agreement, 1966

1.18   Not only has the US (until very recently) refused to ratify the Hague Protocol; it has from time to time threatened to withdraw from the unamended Convention over the issue of liability limits[49]. US public opinion has remained hostile to the perceived low liability limits and successive US administrations have lobbied the international community to reach agreement on higher limits. In 1961 the Kennedy administration, through the Interagency Group on International Aviation (IGIA), undertook a broad review of the Warsaw system[50]. In May 1965 the question of ratification came before the Senate Committee on Foreign Relations. The Committee considered representations from various interest groups, including leading academics, the American Trial Lawyers' Association and several airlines and eventually recommended that, unless legislation requiring carriers to carry additional insurance to compensate passengers above Warsaw limits[51] was

---

[43] ICAO documents 7931–LC/143–1 and 7921–LC/143–2.
[44] See ICAO document 8301, vol II.
[45] See ICAO document 8301–LC/149–1 and 8302–LC/149–2.
[46] The full title of the Convention is 'Convention, Supplementary to the Warsaw Convention, for the Unification of Certain Rules Relating to International Carriage by Air Performed by a Person Other than the Contracting Carrier, signed at Guadalajara on 18th September 1961' Cmd 1568, ICAO document 8181.
[47] See para **2.11** below.
[48] See art II of the Guadalajara Convention. This Convention was implemented in English law by the Carriage by Air (Supplementary Provisions) Act 1962, which came into force on 1 May 1964 by virtue of the Carriage by Air (Supplementary Provisions) Act 1962 (Commencement) Order 1964: see para **2.11** below.
[49] A good introductory survey of the US position can be found in Blackshaw *Aviation Law and Regulation* (1992) ch 34; for a more detailed, if partisan, survey see Lowenfeld and Mendelsohn 'The United States and the Warsaw Convention' [1967] 80 Harv LR 497. Both Lowenfeld and Mendelsohn were members of the US delegation to the Montreal conference of 1966.
[50] See Lacey 'Recent Developments in the Warsaw Convention' [1967] 33 JALC 385, p 386.
[51] The origin of this proposal appears to have been a paper by a graduate student at the University of California Law School: Sand 'Limitation of Liability and Passengers' Accident Compensation under the Warsaw Convention' [1962] 11 AJCL 21.

enacted swiftly, the US should denounce the Warsaw Convention[52]. Such legislation was not enacted — the reaction of airlines and claimants' attorneys being generally negative and the practical difficulties involved being perceived to be formidable[53]. In November 1965 the US gave Notice of Denunciation of the Warsaw Convention to the Polish government, which would take effect six months later[54]. *The New York Times* commented[55]:

> 'In announcing its intention to withdraw from the Warsaw Convention, the United States has moved to end an anachronistic and unfair scheme limiting airline liability to passengers on international flights.

> The Warsaw Convention was set up to protect airlines when flying was in its infancy. Its rigid and inadequate liability of $8,300 for death or injury of a traveller was designed to prevent airlines from being put out of business as a result of liability claims.

> In 1955 The Hague Protocol called for doubling the liability limit to $16,600, which was still grossly inadequate. The United States did not ratify The Hague Protocol; but earlier this year the Johnson administration requested Congressional approval of it as "the first step in recognition of the need for greater protection of passengers in international aviation."

> Now the administration has wisely decided to take a much bigger step to protect airline passengers. It plans to renounce the Warsaw Convention by May 15 and reject the Hague Protocol unless the airlines agree to raise the liability ceiling to $100,000 per passenger. It would be preferable to follow domestic airlines, but the Administration plan does at least scrap the wholly inadequate limits that the airlines have maintained.

> . . . we would prefer out-right renunciation of the Warsaw Convention and rejection of the protocol because they are no longer needed by the airlines and have never been in the interests of passengers. But the Administration's proposal is one that can reasonably be met by foreign airlines and will protect passengers instead of penalizing them.'

1.19   The US press release accompanying the Notice of Denunciation stated[56]:

---

[52]   See FitzGerald 'Liability Rules in International Carriage of Passengers by Air and the Notice of Denunciation of the Warsaw Convention by the United States of America' [1966] 4 Can YBIL 194, pp 197–198.

[53]   See Lowenfeld and Mendelsohn [1967] 80 Harv LR 497, p 535 ff.

[54]   Pursuant to art 39 of the Warsaw Convention. For the text of the denunciation see [1965] 31 JALC 303.

[55]   Editorial, 23 October 1965.

[56]   Lowenfeld and Mendelsohn [1967] 80 Harv LR 497, p 552.

'The United States would be prepared to withdraw the notice of denunciation deposited today if there is a reasonable prospect of an international agreement on limits of liability in international air transportation in the area of $100,000 per passenger or on uniform rules but without any limit of liability, and if, pending the effectiveness of such international agreement, there is a provisional arrangement among the principal international airlines waiving the limits of liability up to $75,000 per passenger.'

1.20   A conference inter alia on the topic of liability limits was due to take place in Montreal in February 1966 and the US's announcement was carefully timed as an exercise in brinkmanship[57]. At an IATA Legal Committee meeting in Paris in October 1965 airline representatives had rejected not just the US State Department's request for a limit of US $100,000, but apparently also TWA's suggested limit of US $66,000[58]. A proposal by IATA that its members would accept a limit of US $50,000 per passenger was apparently rejected by the US[59]. The international aviation community faced a genuine crisis, while the major airlines, even the five main US carriers, remained hopelessly divided[60]. Less than four months remained before the US Notice came into effect. One commentator observed at the time that because of its pre-eminent role in international civil aviation the US's rejection of the Warsaw liability limit would probably deal a fatal blow to four decades of halting efforts by international lawyers to develop a body of private international air law[61].

1.21   The importance of the meeting in Montreal is underlined by the fact that it was attended by 157 delegates from 59 contracting states of ICAO[62]. It was the best attended meeting to date on a legal subject in the history of the organisation[63]. The meeting resolved itself into a bargaining session during which states negotiated with the US as to what limit of liability would suffice to keep it in the Warsaw system. The small window of opportunity before the US Notice took effect lent a sense of urgency to the debate.

1.22   The US delegation proposed an increase of liability limits to US $100,000 per passenger. A number of points were made in support of the proposed increase, including: that the aviation industry had come of age and no longer required the special protection which it might have required in 1929[64];

---

[57]   The US's tactics were a matter for considerable complaint by some of the delegates at the conference. For the minutes of the conference see ICAO documents 8584–LC/154–1 and 8584–LC/154–2. For a detailed account of the main options discussed at the meeting see *Matte* paras 173–175.

[58]   Kreindler 'The Denunciation of the Warsaw Convention' [1965] 31 JALC 291, p 292.

[59]   FitzGerald [1966] 4 Can YBIL 194, p 200.

[60]   See Lowenfeld and Mendelsohn [1967] 80 Harv LR 497, pp 547–548.

[61]   Cabranes 'Limitations of Liability in International Air Law: the Warsaw and Rome Conventions Reconsidered' [1966] 15 ICLQ 660, p 663.

[62]   At the time the ICAO had 110 members.

[63]   FitzGerald [1966] 4 Can YBIL 194, p 200, footnote 24.

[64]   It was estimated that in 1964 some 38 million passengers were carried on scheduled international air services: see FitzGerald [1966] 4 Can YBIL 194, p 202.

the vastly improved safety records of international operators since 1929 meant that any increased insurance premiums would be modest[65]; the increased volume of traffic meant that risks could be spread far more evenly; and the limit in international flights was in many cases anomalous when no such limits applied in many states' domestic flights. Opponents of the US position pointed to the fact that in developing countries the aviation industry was, as in 1929, still in its infancy and needed the protection of low limits of liability; the reversed burden of proof remained an important provision operating to the advantage of passengers and resulting in less litigation; higher limits would mean higher insurance premiums and thus higher fares all round merely to compensate a few US citizens who might attract a high level of compensation; and it was suggested that many airlines had low, if any, profit margins and were subject to constraints, such as over the choice of routes, which other industries did not have[66].

1.23   The conference divided essentially into three groups: (i) the US; (ii) a group of countries led by the UK, West Germany, Sweden, Jamaica and New Zealand that searched for compromise; (iii) a group which was apparently not prepared to agree to any limit above US $50,000 and thought either that the US would back down or that they should not yield to American pressure. This last group included all the African countries at the conference, France, Poland, Czechoslovakia and some of the Latin American countries.

1.24   The conference ended with a decision not to express itself in favour of any of the proposals advanced. Intense lobbying followed the conference, since the withdrawal of the US would have had a catastrophic effect on the Warsaw system. IATA was eventually able to communicate to the US government the agreement of its leading members to a package of measures which would apply to all flights to or with an agreed stopping place in the US. On 13 May 1966 the US State Department indicated its agreement to the proposal, which has come to be known as the Montreal Agreement[67].

1.25   The Montreal Agreement, which has the force of law in the US[68], affects all flights to or with an agreed stopping place in the US. All carriers are required to contract with their passengers for a higher limit of liability in the case of death or personal injury (US $75,000, including legal costs) and to waive any reliance on art 20(1) of the Warsaw Convention, regardless of fault (ie the imposition of strict liability, subject only to any contributory

---

[65]   Figures compiled by the US working group preparing for the conference, which were eventually circulated by the ICAO, showed inter alia that the cost of a US $100,000 limit would be US $0.96 per thousand revenue passenger miles: see Lowenfeld and Mendelsohn [1967] 80 Harv LR 497, pp 552–556.

[66]   See FitzGerald [1966] 4 Can YBIL 194, pp 202–203.

[67]   The text of the State Department's press release can be found in [1966] 32 JALC 247.

[68]   By virtue of its approval by the Civil Aeronautics Board, acting under US Federal legislation: CAB No 18900 approved by CAB Order E23680 on 13 May 1966. The legal effect of the Montreal Agreement has been described as uncertain: see Mankiewicz [1989] 14 Air Law 239, pp 254–255.

negligence[69] of the passenger). The carrier is obliged to deliver to the passenger a ticket with a prescribed notice informing the passenger in clear terms inter alia that liability in most cases is limited to US $75,000. The Montreal Agreement does not operate as an amendment to the unamended or amended Conventions: it originated as an agreement with airlines and operates as a matter of contract between carriers and their passengers[70]. It does not apply to the carriage of cargo.

1.26   On 14 May 1966 the US informed the Polish Government of the withdrawal of its Notice of Denunciation of the Warsaw Convention.

The Guatemala Protocol, 1971

1.27   The ICAO had by the late 1960s taken the leading role in attempting to formulate consensual revisions to the Warsaw and Warsaw-Hague Conventions, primarily to deal with issues of liability, limits and documentation. The US has continued to lobby for higher limits, notwithstanding the Montreal Agreement—which the US regards as an interim measure[71]. Resolution A16–35 of the ICAO General Assembly charged the ICAO Legal Committee with preparing further draft reforms to the Warsaw Convention by 1970. A legal sub-committee held sessions considering draft proposals in 1965 and in 1969[72], following which the Legal Committee reported to the ICAO Council[73]. The ICAO Council convened a diplomatic conference in Guatemala in February 1971 to discuss the proposals[74].

1.28   The Guatemala conference of 1971[75] considered a revised text of the Warsaw-Hague Convention put forward by the ICAO, resulting in the Guatemala Protocol of 1971[76]. This dealt with certain provisions relating to passengers and their baggage, including a proposed strict liability regime, and introduced new higher limits of liability[77]. It was signed by very few countries and ratified by even fewer. The UK has signed but has not ratified the Guatemala Protocol and it has not been implemented in English law[78]. It is unlikely that it will be in the future[79].

---

[69]   See Caplan 'The Warsaw Convention Revitalised' [1966] JBL 335, p 336.
[70]   Permitted by art 22(1) of the Warsaw Convention.
[71]   See the US press release set out in para **1.19** above.
[72]   ICAO document 8839–LC/158.
[73]   ICAO document 8878–LC/162.
[74]   See FitzGerald 'The Revision of the Warsaw Convention' [1970] 8 Can YBIL 284 for a commentary on the proposals.
[75]   ICAO documents 9040–LC/167–1 and 9040–LC/167–2.
[76]   ICAO document 8932/2, Cmd 4691. For commentary see FitzGerald 'The Guatemala City Protocol to Amend the Warsaw Convention' [1971] 9 Can YBIL 217.
[77]   See *Shawcross*, Div VII, paras [141]–[167].
[78]   Although provision to do so, in respect of some of the amendments contained in the Protocol exists in the Carriage by Road and Air Act 1979.
[79]   See *Matte* para 177.

The Montreal Protocols, 1975

1.29 A further international conference, again under the auspices of ICAO, was held in Montreal in 1975 to deal inter alia with the continuing disputes as to liability limits and conversion into national currencies, as well as cargo and postal items[80]. The four Montreal Protocols eventually arrived at in 1975 attempted to amend earlier Conventions. The Carriage by Air and Road Act 1979 made provision for the second, third and fourth Montreal Protocols to be implemented in English law[81]. With the exception of the Third Protocol, this power has been exercised, since the Second and Fourth Montreal Protocols have recently been ratified by a sufficient number of countries[82].

1.30 The First Protocol[83] introduced the use of the Special Drawing Right (SDR)[84] instead of the Poincaré or Convention franc for member states which were members of the International Monetary Fund. Those member states who were not members of the International Monetary Fund, and whose law did not permit the use of the SDR could continue to use the Poincaré franc under the name 'monetary unit'[85]. The First Protocol amended the Warsaw Convention by substituting a new art 22, in which the limits were expressed in SDRs or monetary units[86]. The First Protocol came into force in the UK on 15 February 1996. It should be noted that the Warsaw Convention as amended by the First Protocol applied to international carriage as defined by art 1 of the Convention, provided that either the places of departure and destination are in two states who are parties to the First Protocol, or they are in the territory of a single party to the First Protocol with an agreed stopping place in the territory of another state[87].

1.31 The Second Protocol[88] contained similar provisions to the First Protocol, but applied in relation to the Hague Protocol[89]. The Second Protocol therefore amended the Amended Convention by substituting a new art 22 with limits being expressed in SDRs or monetary units. The Second Protocol

---

[80] ICAO documents 9154–LC/174–1 and 9154–LC/174–2.
[81] There was no such need in respect of the first, since there was already the power to implement it under the Carriage by Air Act 1961.
[82] Each additional Protocol comes into force on the ninetieth day after the deposit of the thirtieth instrument of ratification with the Polish Government: (see each respective additional protocol). The UK ratified the first Protocol in 1984. The Carriage by Air and Road Act 1979 enables the UK to ratify the Second, Third and Fourth Protocols.
[83] Additional Protocol No 1 to Amend the Convention for the Unification of Certain Rules Relating to International Carriage by Air: ICAO document 9145.
[84] For a detailed analysis of the SDR see Tobolewski 'The Special Drawing Right in liability conventions: An acceptable solution?' [1979] 2 LMCLQ 169. The SDR is defined by the IMF and is now valued by reference to a basket of currencies: Tobolewski [1979] 2 LMCLQ 169, p 172. For a criticism of the SDR solution, see Bin Cheng 'Fifty Years of the Warsaw Convention: Where Do We Go from Here?' [1979] ZLW 373, p 375.
[85] Article II.
[86] The actual limits introduced are dealt with below in Chapter 10.
[87] Article III.
[88] Additional Protocol No 2 to Amend the Convention for the Unification of Certain Rules Relating to International Carriage by Air: ICAO document 9146.
[89] Article II.

came into force in the UK on 15 February 1996. The Second Protocol applies in the same way as the First to international carriage as defined by art 1 of the Amended Convention either where the place of departure and destination are in two states who are parties to the Second Protocol, or they are in the territory of a single party to the Second Protocol.

1.32   The Third Protocol[90] provided for the same with respect to the Guatemala Protocol[91]. It has not come into force in the UK.

1.33   The Fourth Protocol[92] modernised the provisions of the Warsaw Convention as amended at the Hague which dealt with cargo. It modernised cargo provisions in the same way as the Guatemala Protocol modernised provisions of the Amended Convention which dealt with passengers and baggage[93].

1.34   The Fourth Protocol[94] imposes on a carrier a system of strict liability subject to a defence of contributory negligence[95], inherent defect, defective packing by persons other than the carrier, act of war, or act of public authority in connection with entry, exit or transit of the cargo[96]. The defence of all necessary measures provided by art 20(1) has been removed from claims in respect of cargo other than those for delay[97]. Importantly, in a cargo related claim, under the Fourth Protocol a claimant will not be able to exceed the limits imposed by art 22, either because the documentation was defective, or reckless misconduct can be established[98]. The limit of liability, where a special declaration of value has not been made is 17 SDRs per kilogramme or 250 monetary units[99]. The Fourth Protocol applies to international carriage as defined by art 1 of the Amended Convention either where the places of departure and destination are in two different states who are parties to the Fourth Protocol, or they are in the territory of a single party to the Fourth Protocol.

1.35   Until 28 September 1998 the US had refused to ratify the Fourth Protocol[100]. However, on 28 September 1998 the US ratified the Fourth Protocol[101].

---

[90] Additional Protocol No 3 to Amend the Convention for the Unification of Certain Rules Relating to International Carriage by Air: ICAO document 9147.

[91] Article II. For a commentary on the Third Protocol see Bin Cheng 'What is wrong with the 1975 Montreal Additional Protocol No. 3?' [1989] 14 Air Law 220.

[92] Additional Protocol No 4 to Amend the Convention for the Unification of Certain Rules Relating to International Carriage by Air: ICAO document 9148.

[93] Article IV.

[94] The scheme of liability introduced by the Fourth Protocol is dealt with more fully in Chapter 6 on air waybills.

[95] Article VI.

[96] Article IV.

[97] Article V.

[98] See arts III, IX and X.

[99] Article VII.

[100] For the reasons behind the US's failure to ratify the Third and Fourth Montreal Protocols see Tompkins 'The Montreal Protocols: What Happens Next?' [1983] 12 The Brief (No 4) 26.

[101] The instrument of ratification was signed and forwarded to the Polish Government on 5 November 1998.

The Fragmentation of the Warsaw System

1.36   The Montreal conference of 1975[102] was ultimately unproductive because of a failure by a sufficient number of countries to ratify the Third and Fourth Protocols. The Warsaw System has been fragmented as a result of the amendments and their piecemeal ratification by different countries. Several protocols have now been produced, some exclusive of others, some intertwined with the others[103]. Even passengers on the same aircraft, whose fares are calculated on the same basis, might be subject to different regimes or different permutations of the same regime or no regime at all[104].

1.37   The position of the US remained a major stumbling block to achieving global uniformity, premised on the Warsaw System of limiting liability. There were continuing efforts by ICAO to promote an acceptable compromise[105]. US policy however, has been and remains hostile to liability limits in principle. Whilst the Warsaw System remained unreformed, the denunciation of the Warsaw Convention remained a possibility[106], despite the fact that the Senate Foreign Relations Committee had voted to recommend ratification of the Montreal Protocols as long ago as 1989.

1.38   Airlines have come in for considerable criticism, one distinguished commentator describing the behaviour of some airlines in resisting any upward move in liability limits as 'disgraceful'[107]. It is certainly difficult to defend the adequacy of either the unamended or the amended Convention limits when compared to sums awarded in non-Convention cases and with capital sums needed to produce an adequate annual income[108]. While limits are perceived to be low the unjustified effect will be to deflect claims onto other parties, such as aircraft manufacturers, who do not enjoy the protection of limited liability[109]. The aviation industry is now well organised and technologically sophisticated. It is unlikely that public opinion would regard it as being in need of special protection. The ICAO's own statistics show that air travel now has a remarkably good safety record, making

---

[102] Described by the editor of *The Journal of Business Law* as 'Monty Python's Flying Circus': (1977) JBL 46.

[103] The Montreal conference of 1975 understandably adopted a resolution asking the Legal Committee of the ICAO to prepare a draft text consolidating the Warsaw Convention, its supplement and amendments. For analyses of the complexity of the resulting situation see the articles cited by Miller *Liability in international air transport* (1977) p 39, note 4a.

[104] Bin Cheng [1979] ZLW 373, p 377.

[105] For a discussion of the work of the ICAO's Legal Committee on draft consolidated conventions following the Montreal conference of 1975 see Sözer 'Consolidation of the Warsaw/Hague System' [1979] 25 McGill LJ 217.

[106] Milde 'Warsaw System and the Limits of Liability: Another Cross-roads?' [1993] 18 Annals ASL 201.

[107] Bin Cheng [1979] ZLW 373, p 374. See also Bin Cheng 'Sixty Years of the Warsaw Convention: Airline Liability at the Crossroads (Part 1)' [1989] 38 ZLW 319.

[108] See Martin 'Death and Injury in International Air Transport' [1975] 41 JALC 255.

[109] Powerful opposition from US aircraft and component manufacturers on this basis has contributed to opposition to the Guatemala Protocol in the US Senate.

appear less plausible suggestions that insurance cover for unlimited liability would be prohibitively expensive[110]. The arguments in favour of the Warsaw system found wanting by Drion forty years ago[111] appear even more so today.

Reform of the Warsaw System

1.39　After the stagnation in the 1970s and 1980s, the 1990s have seen a number of different attempts to reform the liability system which applied to international carriage by air. The inability of governments to produce reform of the Warsaw System resulted initially in action being taken by individual airlines. Subsequently IATA and the European Union introduced their own proposals. At the same time ICAO had produced a draft convention, which at a conference in Montreal in May 1999, resulted in the agreement to a new convention[112].

1.40　Faced with the lack of progress in bringing the Third and Fourth Montreal Protocols into force and the stagnation of attempts to agree a new amending Convention, certain airlines availed themselves of the power to make 'special contracts' with passengers contained in art 22(1) of the Warsaw Convention. This was either a voluntary response to public concern about the levels of compensation, or a requirement of national aviation authorities[113]. A concerted initiative was made in November 1992 by a group of Japanese airlines who agreed to adopt new conditions of carriage; these conditions disapplied the Convention limit on liability for death, wounding or other bodily injury of a passenger, and waived the art 20 defence (ie that all necessary measures have been taken to avoid the damage) on claims up to 100 000 SDRs. Despite the fact that this example was not followed by many other airlines, it was gesture which undoubtedly influenced the IATA conference of 1995[114].

1.41　That conference, which took place in Washington DC in June 1995, resulted in the Intercarrier Agreement on Passenger Liability, adopted at the IATA Annual General Meeting in October 1995. The signatories to the Agreement[115] undertook to 'take action to waive the limitation of liability on recoverable compensatory damages in Article 22 paragraph 1 of the Warsaw Convention as to claims for death, wounding or other bodily injury of a passenger, so that recoverable compensatory damages may be determined by reference to the law of the domicile of the passenger'[116]. Defences available

---

[110] See Martin '50 Years of the Warsaw Convention: A Practical Man's Guide' [1979] 4 Annals ASL 233, pp 247 and 250–251.

[111] See para **1.3** above, especially notes 6 to 8.

[112] See below at para **1.47**.

[113] Including the UK CAA; see condition H of the CAA's Standard Conditions for Air Transport Licences.

[114] See Bin Cheng 'Air Carrier's Liability for Passenger Injury or Death: The Japanese Initiative and Response to the recent EC Consultation paper' [1993] 18 A & SL 109.

[115] By July 1998 107 carriers had signed the agreement.

[116] Paragraph 1, IATA Intercarrier Agreement.

under the Convention were reserved; however, the Agreement provided that any carrier may waive any defence 'as circumstances may warrant'[117]. The signatories agreed to implement the Agreement by 1 November 1996, or upon receipt of the requisite Government approval, whichever was later[118]. The Agreement, while committing signatories to no more than taking action to reduce liability limits, was nevertheless a significant declaration of dissatisfaction with the current system and paved the way for more radical reforms.

1.42 In February 1996, the IATA adopted an instrument to give effect to the terms of the Intercarrier Agreement. The resulting IATA Implementation Agreement takes effect as a 'special contract' pursuant to art 22(1) of the Warsaw Convention. The signatories[119] agreed to incorporate certain conditions into their contracts of carriage. The condition in para I,I states that the carrier shall not invoke the limitation of liability in art 22(1) of the Warsaw Convention[120]. Defences under the Convention are reserved, with the exception of the art 20(1) defence which is waived in respect of that portion of the claim below 100,000 SDRs. Paragraph II lays out optional conditions of carriage, one of which provides that compensatory damages in respect of death or bodily injury may be determined by reference to the law of domicile or permanent residence of the passenger. In this respect, as in certain others, the Implementation Agreement differed from the Intercarrier Agreement, which had included this provision as an integral part of para 1.

1.43 The United States' Air Transport Association also adopted, in May 1996, a convention implementing the IATA Intercarrier Agreement, the Air Transport Implementing Agreement, which laid out conditions of carriage to be incorporated by the signatories. These largely mirrored those of the IATA Implementation Agreement; however, the provision allowing recovery under the law of the passenger's domicile or permanent residence was mandatory. Signatories were taken to have withdrawn from the 1966 Montreal Agreement.

1.44 The Warsaw-Hague regime had also been the subject of European Community scrutiny since the early 1990s[121]. An initial proposal made by the European Civil Aviation Conference for a new European inter-carrier

---

[117] Paragraph 2, IATA Intercarrier Agreement.

[118] Paragraph 5, IATA Intercarrier Agreement.

[119] According to the editors of *Shawcross* (see App AB) by 1 Novermber 1999 86 carriers which had signed the Intercarrier Agreement had also signed the Intercarrier implementation agreement. There were an additional 35 carriers which had signed the Intercarrier agreement but not the implementation agreement. *Shawcross* is critical of the fact that there is no central record of the carriers which sign the further implementation agreement. Their information has been obtained from 'unattributable sources'.

[120] Paragraph I, I IATA Implementation Agreement.

[121] In 1991 the European Commission received a report from ST Brise entitled 'Study on the Possibilities of Community Action to Harmonise Limits of Passenger Liability and Increase the Amounts of Compensation for International Accident Victims in Air Transport'. The Commission then issued a Consultation paper in October 1992 entitled 'Passenger Liability in Aircraft Accidents: Warsaw Convention and Internal Market Requirements'.

agreement was considered throughout 1993 and 1994 but was eventually rejected in favour of legislative reform. Legislation was felt to be a more consistent and comprehensive solution; although this would take longer to effect than a new treaty, it had the advantage of ensuring uniform levels of liability throughout the Community, which in turn would simplify insurance considerations. Furthermore, there were fears that a treaty might infringe EC competition rules.

1.45   A Regulation was eventually adopted by the Council on 9 October 1997[122], to come into force on 17 October 1998; it was implemented in the UK by the Air Carrier Liability Order 1998[123]. It provides that Community air carriers' liability for damages in respect of death wounding or other bodily injury of a passenger in the event of an accident is not to be subject to any financial limit, be it defined by law, conventions or contract. In respect of damages above the equivalent in ecus of 100,000 SDRs the carrier may avail itself of the defence that it has taken all necessary measures to avoid the damage or that such measures were impossible[124]. The defence of contributory negligence of the passenger is available in respect of all levels of damages. The Regulation also requires carriers to make interim payments to passengers to meet immediate economic needs.

1.46   The status of the Regulation is currently unclear following a recent High Court decision that it conflicts with the treaty obligations owed by Member States to non-Member States under the Warsaw Convention[125].

The Montreal Convention, 1999

1.47   To some extent the above initiatives had the effect of fragmenting the system still further. Nevertheless, the aim of drawing up a single unifying instrument which would update the Warsaw-Hague regime continued to be pursued by the ICAO, and as a result the Montreal Convention 1999[126] was signed by 52 nations (including the US) on 28 May 1999. It will enter into force after ratification by 30 States[127].

1.48   The Convention supercedes the main Warsaw Instruments, namely the Warsaw Convention, the Hague Protocol, the Guadalajara Convention, the Guatemala City Protocol and the four Montreal Additional Protocols[128]. However, since much of the text and the structure of the Convention is drawn from those instruments, many concepts and principles remain unchanged.

---

[122] Regulation 2027/97, OJ L 285/1, 17.10.97.
[123] SI 1998/1751.
[124] Ie the Warsaw Convention art 20 defence.
[125] *R v Secretary of State for the Environment, Transport and the Regions, ex p International Air Transport Association (No 2)* [1999] 2 CMLR 1385. See further Chapter 12.
[126] Officially, the Convention for the Unification of Certain Rules for International Carriage by Air.
[127] It was hoped at the time the Convention was concluded that this may happen as early as 2001.
[128] Article 55 Montreal Convention 1999.

Thus, for example, the carrier's liability under the Montreal Convention 1999, as under the Warsaw Convention, arises for bodily injury and death caused by an accident on board the aircraft in the course of embarking or disembarking[129].

1.49   The main changes relate to liability limits and jurisdiction. Essentially the precepts of the IATA Intercarrier Agreement have been adopted, in that there is now no monetary limit on the amount of compensation recoverable for bodily injury and death. Up to 100,000 SDRs of a claim the carrier faces strict liability, subject to any defence of contributory negligence on the part of the passenger[130]. Above 100,000 SDRs the carrier is liable unless it proves that the damage was not caused by the negligence or other wrongful act or omission of the carrier its servants or agents, or was solely due to the negligence or other wrongful act or omission of a third party[131].

1.50   The Montreal Convention has also added a 'fifth jurisdiction' to the four long established jurisdictions available to a claimant under the Warsaw Convention[132]; an action for damages for bodily injury or death can now be brought where the passenger has his principal or permanent residence, provided that the carrier operates services to or from there and conducts its air carriage business there[133].

1.51   The Convention also aims to simplify and modernise documentation relating to passengers' baggage and cargo, which should facilitate more electronic ticketing and cargo handling[134]. The 100,000 SDR threshold, as well as the remaining liability limits in relation to baggage, cargo and delay, are subject to periodic review and may be revised once every five years[135]. This should avoid the stagnation which plagued the Warsaw-Hague system.

1.52   In 1954 Drion described limitation of liability in the field of aviation as the *leitmotiv* of an unfinished symphony[136]. He would perhaps have been surprised to find that the symphony is still partially unfinished today. The failure—until now—to achieve agreement on this topic is largely responsible for the absence of a uniform regime applying to international and domestic aviation and the overlapping and often confusing regimes applying to international and domestic carriage by air.

1.53   However, the Montreal Convention of 1999 represents a major breakthrough. Although much depends on its future ratification and implementation by states, the fact that it has been signed by the US is particularly significant and gives weight to its authors' claims that '[we] have

---

[129] Article 17 Warsaw Convention, art 17 Montreal Convention 1999.
[130] Articles 20 and 21(1) Montreal Convention 1999.
[131] Article 21(2) Montreal Convention 1999.
[132] Article 28 Warsaw Convention.
[133] Article 33 Montreal Convention 1999.
[134] See Montreal Convention 1999, ch II.
[135] Montreal Convention 1999, art 24.
[136] *Drion* p 1.

succeeded in modernizing and consolidating a 70-year old system of inter-national instruments of private international law into one legal instrument that will provide, for years to come, an adequate level of compensation for those involved in international air accidents.'[137]

Non-International Carriage

1.54   Flights to the UK from countries which have ratified neither the una-mended nor the amended Convention are not subject to either Convention. Nor are flights which take place within the UK. Neither the unamended or amended Conventions apply to the carriage by air of mail and postal pack-ets[138]. It was therefore thought expedient to bring a measure of harmony by subjecting such flights to some of the rules applying to international carriage between contracting parties to the amended and unamended Conventions. Such flights[139] are catered for under domestic legislation by the Carriage by Air Acts (Application of Provisions) Order 1967, Sch 1[140]. The Order essen-tially applies many of the rules of the amended Convention to such flights[141]. There is a presumption that the Order is not intended to be extra-territorial in its effect. Thus parliament did not intend the Order to regulate carriage by air in which the place of departure, destination and any agreed stopping place were within the territory of a foreign state[142]. Flights or claims not governed by any of the statutory frameworks continue to be subject to the common law[143].

---

[137] Comments of Dr Assad Kotaite, President of the ICAO Council, at the conclusion of the Montreal Conference.
[138] See art 2(2) of the amended Convention, and art 2(2) of the Unamended Convention.
[139] Ie carriage which is international, but outside the amended or unamended Conventions, domestic carriage in the UK and carriage of mail and postal packets.
[140] Issued pursuant to powers granted by s 10 of the Carriage by Air Act 1961.
[141] The notable exception being the absence of the documentation provisions in arts 3 to 16 of the Hague Protocol. See Chapters 5 and 6 below.
[142] See *Holmes v Bangladesh Biman Corpn* [1989] AC 1112, pp 1137–1138.
[143] See Chapter 13 below.

Chapter 2

The Regimes Governing Carriage by Air

2.1

RULE 1—Carriage by air in the United Kingdom is governed by one of the following sets of rules:

(1) By the rules set out in the Warsaw-Hague Convention, as set out in Schedule 1 of the Carriage by Air Act 1961 (hereinafter referred to as 'the Warsaw-Hague Rules');

(2) Provided the Warsaw-Hague Rules do not apply, by the rules set out in Schedule 2 of the Carriage by Air Acts (Application of Provisions) Order 1967 (hereinafter referred to as 'the Warsaw Rules');

(3) Provided neither the Warsaw-Hague Rules, nor the Warsaw Rules apply, the rules set out in Schedule 1 of the Carriage by Air Acts (Application of Provisions) Order 1967 (hereinafter referred to as 'the Rules of Non-International Carriage');

(4) In any event, where a carrier is one which has a valid operating licence granted a European Community State, then Council Regulation (EC) No 2027/97 on Air Carrier Liability will apply in respect of claims for personal injury;

(5) Where none of the above rules govern, the common law rules of carriage apply.

2.2   The respective roles of the common law and statute. Absent statutory intervention, the legal position of an aircraft operator in relation to passengers and goods carried by him is governed by the common law, and generally by the law of contract[1]. However, although the common law retains a role in the regulation of carriage by air, the intervention of statute has ensured that in the

---

[1]   The cases where persons or goods are carried without a contract of carriage coming into being may be regarded as rare. Examples are where a person is a stowaway; or where goods are loaded onto an aircraft by mistake; or where the 'contract' in question was not perfected by reason of illegality (cf *Gurtner v Beaton* [1993] 2 Lloyd's Rep 369, CA).

vast majority of cases, the remedy of a passenger or a consignor of goods will arise out of statute or statutory instrument, and not by reason of the terms of any contract or other common law cause of action[2]. This statutory intervention is largely as a result of the UK's accession to various international agreements, notably the Warsaw Convention of 1929, the Hague Protocol of 1955 and the Guadalajara Convention of 1961. The manner in which the UK came to be a party to these treaties has already been described[3]; however, it is clear law that even if an international agreement has been signed and ratified by the UK, it has no effect as a matter of *municipal* law until incorporated into that law by Act of Parliament or secondary legislation[4, 5].

2.3   The rationale for this rule is that the conclusion and ratification of treaties lies within the prerogative of the Crown: were it possible for an unincorporated treaty to affect municipal law, then the Crown would be able to legislate for the subject without Parliamentary consent and in breach of the doctrine of Parliamentary sovereignty. These points were made very clearly by Lord Oliver in *JH Rayner (Mincing Lane) Ltd v Department of Trade and Industry*[6]:

> 'It is axiomatic that municipal courts have not and cannot have the competence to adjudicate upon or to enforce the rights arising out of transactions entered into by independent sovereign states between themselves on the plane of international law[7]... [A]s a matter of the constitutional law of the United Kingdom, the Royal Prerogative, whilst it embraces the making of treaties, does not extend to altering the law conferring rights on individuals or depriving individuals of rights which they enjoy in domestic law without the intervention of Parliament.[8']

2.4   By contrast as regards European Community law, which is derived from international treaties, English courts can by way of interim relief,

---

[2]   It must be stressed that this statutory regulation seeks to govern the liability of *carriers* and not, in general, the liability of third parties who may cause injury to passengers or goods (eg operators of other aircraft colliding with the aircraft carrying the passenger or goods in question; or a manufacturer of an aircraft failing to construct the aircraft to the requisite standards).

[3]   See para **1.17** as regards the Warsaw Convention; para **1.14** as regards the Hague Protocol; and para **1.17** as regards the Guadalajara Convention.

[4]   Ie statutory instrument or order in council.

[5]   The clearest statement of this is Lord Atkin's in *A-G for Canada v A-G for Ontario* [1937] AC 326, PC at 347: 'Within the British Empire there is a well-established rule that the making of a treaty is an executive act, while the performance of its obligations, if they entail alteration of the existing domestic law, requires legislative action. Unlike some other countries, the stipulations of a treaty duly ratified do not, within the Empire, by virtue of the treaty alone, have the force of law.' See also Brownlie *Principles of Public International Law* (5th edn, 1998), pp 47–48; *Shawcross* Div I, para [114].

[6]   [1990] 2 AC 418, HL.

[7]   [1990] 2 AC 418 at 499E.

[8]   [1990] 2 AC 418 at 500B.

suspend an Act of Parliament pending the result of a challenge of that Act on the grounds that it is inconsistent with European Community law[9].

2.5   Incorporation of treaties into municipal law.   In essence, there are two ways in which a treaty can be incorporated into municipal law[10]. The first method — called 'direct' enactment — involves passing an Act which embodies, whether or not in the same words, provisions having the effect of the treaty. This approach has the advantage of allowing the Act to be couched in the manner and form to which a lawyer practising in the UK will be accustomed. The concomitant disadvantage is the risk of a divergence occurring between the stipulations of the treaty and the terms of the Act seeking to incorporate that treaty, a disadvantage that is particularly acute where — as here — a premium is placed on the uniformity of application of the treaty in different jurisdictions[11]. The second method of incorporation simply involves passing an Act that states that the treaty in question shall have the force of law, leaving the treaty's provisions to apply, whether with or without modification. This is known as 'indirect' enactment, and its effect is to imbue the stipulations of a treaty with the character of a statutory enactment[12]. As is more specifically described below, the general approach of the United Kingdom has been to incorporate its international treaty obligations under the Warsaw Convention, the Hague Protocol and the Guadalajara Convention indirectly.

2.6   Incorporation of the Warsaw Convention: the Carriage by Air Act 1932. The Warsaw Convention was given effect in English municipal law by the Carriage by Air Act 1932. An English translation of the French text of the Warsaw Convention was appended to the Carriage by Air Act 1932 as its First Schedule. In s 1(1), the 1932 Act provided that the provisions of the Warsaw Convention, as set out in the First Schedule, should have the force of law in the UK from such day as might be certified by Order in Council. The Carriage by Air Act 1932 came into force on 13 May 1933 and (as is described in para **2.8**) was repealed by the Carriage by Air Act 1961, which incorporated the provisions of the Warsaw-Hague Convention into English law.

---

[9]   See *R v Secretary of State for Transport, ex p Factortame Ltd* (C-213/89) [1991] 1 AC 603, EC; and see *Shawcross*, Div I, para [114].

[10]   As to this, see Bennion *Statutory Interpretation* (3rd edn) s 221. The terms 'direct' and 'indirect' enactment used in this paragraph are *Bennion's*.

[11]   A point made by Lord Diplock in relation to the Warsaw Convention in *Fothergill v Monarch Airlines Ltd* [1981] AC 251, HL at 281G-282A: 'The language of that Convention that has been adopted at the international conference to express the common intention of the majority of the states represented there is meant to be understood in the same sense by the courts of all those states which ratify or accede to the Convention. Their national styles of legislative draftsmanship will vary considerably as between one another . . . The language of an international convention has not been chosen by an English parliamentary draftsman. It is neither couched in the conventional English legislative idiom nor designed to be construed exclusively by English judges. It is addressed to a much wider and more varied judicial audience than is an Act of Parliament that deals with purely domestic law.'

[12]   To adopt the words of Sir Sebag Shaw in *The Hollandia* [1982] QB 872, CA at 885E.

2.7   'Non-international' carriage under the Carriage by Air Act 1932.   As will be seen, the Warsaw Convention applies only to 'international carriage' as defined in art 1 of that Convention[13]. Thus the Convention does not, for instance, apply to purely domestic flights and s 1(1) of the 1932 Act, referring as it did to the terms of the Convention, was similarly limited. However, s 4 of the Carriage by Air Act 1932 allowed for the application of the provisions of the First Schedule of the Act by Order in Council 'to such carriage by air, not being international carriage by air as defined in the First Schedule, as may be specified in the Order, subject however to such exceptions, adaptations and modifications, if any, as may be so specified.' This provision was used to apply the First Schedule of the Act to non-international carriage in, inter alia, the Carriage by Air (Non-International Carriage)(United Kingdom) Order.

2.8   Incorporation of the Hague Protocol: the Carriage by Air Act 1961.
The Hague Protocol effected various changes to the Warsaw Convention. The resultant Warsaw-Hague Convention was given force of law in the UK by the Carriage by Air Act 1961. Like the Carriage by Air Act 1932, which the 1961 Act repealed in its entirety[14], the Carriage by Air Act 1961 annexed as its First Schedule a copy of the Warsaw Convention as amended by the Hague Protocol. On this occasion, however, both the French *and* English versions of the Convention were appended[15]. As with the Carriage by Air Act 1932 the provisions of the Warsaw-Hague Convention, as set out in the First Schedule to the Act, were given the force of law in the UK by s 1(1) of the 1961 Act[16]. Section 1(1) thus gives legal effect to the Warsaw-Hague Convention in all cases of 'international carriage' as defined by art 1 of that Convention. The Carriage by Air Act 1961 came into force on 1 June 1967[17].

2.9   'Non-international' carriage under the Carriage by Air Act 1961.   As far as carriage falling outside the scope of the Warsaw-Hague Convention was concerned, the 1961 Act again followed the model of the 1932 Act, providing in s 10(1) that 'Her Majesty may by Order in Council apply the First

---

[13]   See paras **4.9–4.11** as to the meaning of 'international carriage'.

[14]   Sections 1(1) and 14(3) of the Carriage by Air Act 1961 and Sch 2 thereto.

[15]   The English version is at Pt I of the First Schedule and the French version at Pt II.

[16]   Section 1(1) only gives the Convention the force of law as far as the UK is concerned. Section 9 of the 1961 Act provides that the Act may be extended (subject to such exceptions, adaptations and modifications as may be specified) to the Isle of Man, the Channel Islands and any colony or protectorate, protected State or UK trust territory by Order in Council. The Carriage by Air Act 1961 was extended to Jersey by the Carriage by Air (Jersey) Order 1967, SI 1967/803; to Guernsey by the Carriage by Air (Guernsey) Order 1967, SI 1967/804; to the Isle of Man by the Carriage by Air (Isle of Man) Order 1967, SI 1967/805; to the overseas territories identified in Sch 3 of the Carriage by Air (Overseas Territories) Order 1967, SI 1967/809 according to the terms of that Order; and to the overseas territories identified in Sch 5 of the Carriage by Air (Application of Provisions)(Overseas Territories) Order 1967, SI 1967/810 (as amended by SI 1984/701) according to the terms of that Order. All of these Orders came into force on 1 June 1967.

[17]   Pursuant to s 1(3) of the Act and the Carriage by Air (Convention) Order 1967, SI 1967/479.

Schedule to this Act, together with any other provisions of the Act, to carriage by air, not being carriage by air to which the Convention applies, of such descriptions as may be specified in the Order, subject to such exceptions, adaptations and modifications, if any, as may be so specified.' For these purposes, carriage by air 'not being carriage by air to which the Convention applies' includes carriage under the *unamended* Warsaw Convention. The reason for this is that not all those states which signed and ratified the Warsaw Convention, signed or ratified the Hague Protocol[18]. Thus, for example, flights from London to Paris will be governed by the Warsaw-Hague Convention, because the UK and France are parties both to the Warsaw Convention *and* the Hague Protocol. However, flights from London to New York undertaken prior to 4 March 1999 were still governed by the Warsaw Convention, because the United States had until September 1998 declined to ratify the Hague Protocol[19]. In these circumstances, the Warsaw Convention cannot simply be consigned to history and still needs to be incorporated into municipal law if the UK's international treaty obligations are to be met. Thus, although the 1932 Act was repealed by the Carriage by Air Act 1961, the unamended Warsaw Convention remains part of the law of the UK by virtue of art 5 of the Carriage by Air Acts (Application of Provisions) Order 1967 and Pt A of Sch 2 of that Order[20].

2.10   In addition to incorporating the unamended Warsaw Convention into English law, the Carriage by Air Acts (Application of Provisions) Order 1967 also applies a variation of the Warsaw-Hague Convention to:
(1)   Carriage falling outside the scope of the Warsaw Convention[21]; and
(2)   To carriage of mail or postal packages[22]. Carriage of mail and postal packages falls outside both the Warsaw and the Warsaw-Hague Conventions[23].

---

[18]   The most important example was until 4 March 1999 the US.
[19]   American public opinion has been antagonistic to the Warsaw liability limits. See paras **1.18** and **1.26**, above.
[20]   SI 1967/480 (as amended by SI 1969/1083, SI 1979/931 and SI 1981/440). The full wording of the unamended Warsaw Convention as it applies in the UK is set out in Pt B of Sch 2 of the Carriage by Air Acts (Application of Provisions) Order 1967. The Carriage by Air (Application of Provisions) Order was extended under s 10 of the 1961 Act to Jersey by the Carriage by Air Acts (Application of Provisions)(Jersey) Order 1967, SI 1967/806; to Guernsey by the Carriage by Air Acts (Application of Provisions)(Guernsey) Order 1967, SI 1967/807; to the Isle of Man by the Carriage by Air Acts (Application of Provisions)(Isle of Man) Order 1967, SI 1967/808 and to the overseas territories identified in Sch 5 of the Carriage by Air (Application of Provisions)(Overseas Territories) Order 1967, SI 1967/810 (as amended by SI 1984/701) according to the terms of that Order.
[21]   See art 4(a). Carriage falling outside the scope of the Warsaw Convention as set out in Pt B of Sch 2 of the 1967 Order *necessarily* falls outside the Warsaw-Hague Convention also. This is because s 10(1) of the 1961 Act only applies in relation to carriage by air 'not being carriage by air to which this convention applies.' It is clear law that the 1967 Order can have no wider scope and effect than is duly authorised by the power conferred by s 10 of the 1961 Act: *Holmes v Bangladesh Biman Corpn* [1989] AC 1112 at 1126D-E (per Lord Bridge).
[22]   Article 4(b) of the 1969 Order.
[23]   See arts 2(2) of the Warsaw and the Warsaw-Hague Conventions.

2.11   The Guadalajara Convention 1961.   The Guadalajara Convention was given force of law in the UK by the Carriage by Air (Supplementary Provisions) Act 1962. The Guadalajara Convention is appended — in both its English and French versions — as a Schedule to the Act[24]. Section 1 of the Act provides that the provisions of the Convention shall 'have the force of law in the UK in relation to any carriage by air to which the Convention applies'. The Guadalajara Convention is expressed to supplement both the Warsaw Convention as originally enacted under the Carriage by Air Act 1932, *and* the Warsaw-Hague Convention as enacted under the Carriage by Air Act 1961. Section 2(1) of the Act provides:

'In the Schedule to this Act 'the Warsaw Convention' means —
(a) before the day on which section one of the Carriage by Air Act 1961 comes into force, the Convention set out in the First Schedule of the Carriage by Air Act 1932, and
(b) on or after that day, the Convention set out in the First Schedule to the said Act of 1961,

but, in relation to rights or liabilities arising out of an occurrence before that day, 'the Warsaw Convention' shall continue to have the same meaning as before that day.'

Because of its repeal, it is inconceivable that a case under the 1932 Act could arise today: the reference to 'the Warsaw Convention' is, for all practical purposes, a reference to the Warsaw-Hague Convention[25].

2.12   The Guadalajara Convention also applies to 'non-international' carriage under the Carriage by Air Act 1961. As regards the unamended Warsaw Convention[26], the Guadalajara Convention is given the force of law by virtue of art 5 of the Carriage by Air Acts (Application of Provisions) Order 1967 and para 4 in Pt A of Sch 2 of that Order[27]. As regards non-international carriage falling outside the unamended Warsaw Convention[28], the Guadalajara Convention is given force of law by virtue of art 4 of the Carriage by Air Acts (Application of Provisions) Order 1967 and Sch 1 of that Order[29].

2.13   European Community Law.   The laws of the European Communities have effect directly of indirectly in the UK as a result of its membership of the European Communities[30]. Three sources of European law are outlined

---

[24] The English text is at Pt I of the Schedule and the French text at Pt II.
[25] The historical reason for this provision is that at the time the Carriage by Air (Supplementary Provisions) Act 1962 was passed, the Carriage by Air Act 1961 was not yet in force. The 1961 was only brought into force by SI 1967/479 on 1 June 1967.
[26] As to which see para **2.9**.
[27] The wording is set out in full in Pt B of Sch 2 of the Order.
[28] As to which see para **2.10**.
[29] The wording is set out in full in Pt III of Sch 1 of the Order.
[30] Section 2 of the European Communities Act 1972.

here[31]. First, provisions of European Communities Treaties will need to be implemented into national law[32]. It should be noted however, that certain European treaty provisions are directly applicable and confer rights on individuals without any further implementation[33]. Second, Regulations are directly applicable in member states without the need for implementation by national legislation. Third, Directives are binding on member states, but must be implemented by legislation into national law.

2.14   The European Regulation. The European Council adopted Regulation 2027/97 of October 9 1997 on air carrier liability in the event of accidents[34]. Regulation 2027/97 came into force one year after its publication in the *Official Journal of the European Communities*. It actually came into force on 17 October 1998. The regulation was expressed to be binding in its entirety and directly applicable in all Member States. A European Council Regulation is directly applicable in member state without the need for further legislation by the member state. The British government also introduced the Air Carrier Liability Order 1998[35] to implement the regulation[36]. The Air Carrier Liability Order 1998 amended the Carriage by Air Act 1961 and also the Carriage by Air Acts (Application of Provisions) Order 1967 to incorporate the provisions of Council Regulation 2027/97.

2.15   The discrete statutory regimes in force. From the foregoing, it is clear that there exist within the municipal law of the UK numerous variants on the basic scheme of liability originally outlined in the Warsaw Convention. This is in the first instance because not all states party to the Warsaw Convention are party to the Hague Protocol (and, indeed, vice versa), and because some states party to either or both of the Warsaw and Warsaw-Hague Conventions are *not* party to the Guadalajara Convention; moreover, the UK has applied the 'Warsaw Scheme' to cases falling outside the scope of either the Warsaw-Hague Convention or the unamended Warsaw Convention. In addition European Community Carriers are subject to Regulation (EC)

---

[31] A more full exposition of European Community law is beyond the scope of this book and reference should be made to specialist texts.
[32] In accordance with para **2.4**, above.
[33] See for example arts 85 and 86 of the Treaty of Rome.
[34] This topic is dealt with fully in Chapter 12. In essence the Regulation requires Community Carriers, who are defined by art 2(1)(b) as an air carrier with a valid operating licence granted by a member state in accordance with the provisions of Regulation 2407/92, to act as follows: (1) not to limit liability for damages for death, wounding or bodily injury; (2) not to rely on a defence of 'all necessary measures' (ie art 20 of the Warsaw Convention) for sums below 100,000 SDRs; and (3) to make interim payments to passengers to meet their immediate economic needs. Non community carriers are required to give notice of the fact that they do not comply with these steps.
[35] SI 1998/1751.
[36] As a matter of applicability of EU law, it was unnecessary to implement the Regulation into British law by passing an Order.

2027/97. The following forms of statutory regime, set out in their order of applicability, may be distinguished[37]:

(1)   Carriage governed by the Warsaw-Hague Convention, as supplemented by the Guadalajara Convention. This regime is implemented into the municipal law of the UK by the Carriage by Air Act 1961 and the Carriage by Air (Supplementary Provisions) Act 1962.

(2)   Carriage governed by the Warsaw-Hague Convention, unsupplemented by the Guadalajara Convention. This is governed by the Carriage by Air Act 1961 alone.

(3)   Carriage governed by the unamended Warsaw Convention, but supplemented by the Guadalajara Convention.

(4)   Carriage governed by the unamended Warsaw Convention, unsupplemented by the Guadalajara Convention.

(5)   Carriage of passengers by a Community Carrier which will be subject to the provisions of Regulation (EC) 2027/97, and which is subject to the unamended or amended Warsaw Conventions.

(6)   Carriage falling outside the scope of the Warsaw Convention and carriage of mail or postal packages.

The regimes described in (3), (4) and (6) above have all been implemented into the law of the UK by the Carriage by Air Acts (Application of Provisions) Order 1967.

2.16   Common law.   There remains the common law. The common law continues to be of importance for two reasons. First, and as indicated above, the common law provides the context or background within which the various statutory regimes operate. Secondly, in those cases where there is *no* applicable statutory regime — in other words, where even the sixth regime described above does not apply — the common law will govern exclusively. This will be rare insofar as a claim by a passenger or consignor of goods against the carrier is concerned. In such cases, one of the above statutory regimes will almost certainly be applicable.

---

[37]   See also the analysis of Lord Bridge in *Holmes v Bangladesh Biman Corpn* [1989] AC 1112 at 1126B-C: 'Thus there are now three sets of rules in the law of the UK and other British territory which govern different categories of carriage by air to which I shall refer for convenience as 'the Hague rules' (Schedule 1 to the Act of 1961), 'the Warsaw rules' (Schedule 2 to the Order of 1967) and 'the UK rules' (Schedule 1 to the Order of 1967).'

Chapter 3

The Construction of Treaties

3.1

RULE 2—Where there exist several versions in different languages of the same convention, then:

(1) Where there is express statutory provision as to which version shall prevail, effect shall be given to that provision;

(2) Where there is no express statement as to which version shall prevail, then the statute or statutory instrument in question must be construed and effect given to the version that has implicitly been selected.

3.2 **Choice of the prevailing language: express statutory provision.** The Carriage by Air Act 1961 sets out both the English and the French versions of the Warsaw-Hague Convention in its First Schedule. Similarly, the Carriage by Air (Supplementary Provisions) Act 1962 sets out in its Schedule the English and French texts of the Guadalajara Convention. Both Acts provide that if there is any inconsistency between the English text and the French text, then the text in French shall prevail[1]. Lord Wilberforce considered the effect of such a provision in *Fothergill v Monarch Airlines Ltd*[2]. He held that the correct approach was as follows:

'. . . it cannot be judged whether there is an inconsistency between two texts unless one looks at both. So, in the present case the process of interpretation seems to involve:
1. Interpretation of the English text, according to the principles upon which international conventions are to be interpreted (see *Buchanan's* case and *Stag Line Ltd v. Foscolo, Mango & Co. Ltd*, [1932] A.C. 328, 350).

---

[1] Section 1(2) of the Carriage by Air Act 1961 and s 1(2) of the Carriage by Air (Supplementary Provisions) Act 1962.

[2] [1981] AC 251, HL.

2.   Interpretation of the French text according to the same principles but with additional linguistic problems.
3.   Comparison of these meanings.[3']

3.3   No statutory provision as to construction.   By contrast, the Carriage by Air Acts (Application of Provisions) Order 1967 contains no express statement that the French text should prevail in the event of inconsistency between it and texts in other languages. Indeed, as the wording of the Order[4] and the text of the conventions set out in the Order makes clear, *English* is the language referred to. It is therefore difficult to resist the conclusion reached by *Shawcross* that it is the English texts, as set out in the Schedules to the Order, that are to be construed and given effect[5] and that the decision of the Court of Appeal in *Corocraft Ltd v Pan American Airways Inc*[6] must be distinguished.

3.4   In *Corocraft*, the Court of Appeal was construing the Carriage by Air Act 1932 which sets out in its First Schedule the *English* text of the Warsaw Convention. Lord Denning MR held as follows:

'Then, if you turn to Schedule 1, you find the English text of the Convention: but it includes in article 36 the words: '*The Convention is drawn up in French in a single copy* which shall remain deposited in the archives of the Ministry for Foreign Affairs of Poland . . .'

It was plainly the intention of all the parties to the Convention that the French text should be one official and authorised text; and it was plainly the intention of the English Parliament to give effect to that French text by making an exact translation of it into English. The English Parliament failed in their object. The translator whom they employed, by introducing the word 'and', put his own gloss on the French text. He produced certainty where there was ambiguity: and clarity where there was obscurity. But this was a translator's gloss which he should not have inserted. In order to produce an exact translation, the translator should reproduce the French text faithfully, with all its defects, deficiencies, ambiguities and uncertainties. He should reproduce it, as Oliver Cromwell desired Mr Lely to do:

'Use all your skill to paint my picture truly like me, and not flatter me at all; but remark all these roughnesses, pimples, warts and everything as you see me, otherwise I will never pay a farthing for it.'

---

3   At 272E-F.
4   Article 2 of the Order defines 'the amended Convention' as 'the *English* text of the Warsaw Convention with the amendments made in it by the Hague Protocol as set out in Sch 1 to the Act of 1961 . . .', and defines 'the Guadalajara Convention' as 'the *English* text of the Convention . . .' (emphasis added).
5   Division VII, para [648].
6   [1969] 1 QB 616, CA.

Such being the clear intention of Parliament, I think we should follow it. If there is any inconsistency between the English text and the French text, the text in French should prevail.[7]'

Although the above reasoning may be persuasive in the context of the 1932 Act[8], it cannot apply in relation to the Carriage by Air Acts (Application of Provisions) Order 1967. The texts set out in the schedules to the Order are *not* intended to effect a precise translation of the original stipulations of the Warsaw and Guadalajara Conventions. The Order was made under s 10(1) of the Carriage by Air Act 1961, which provides that 'Her Majesty may by Order in Council apply the First Schedule to this Act, together with any other provisions of this Act, to carriage by air, not being carriage by air to which the Convention applies, of such descriptions as may be specified in the Order, *subject to such exceptions, adaptations and modifications, if any, as may be so specified[9]'*.

3.5

RULE 3—**Treaties that have been incorporated into the law of the UK are to be construed on broad principles of general acceptation, rather than in the strict manner according to which statues are generally construed. In construing the stipulations of treaties so incorporated, regard may be had to:**

(1) Foreign case law;
(2) Text books and articles;
(3) Provided the material is public and accessible, and provided it clearly points to a definite legislative intention, the travaux préparatoires of the convention in question.

3.6   Approach to construction.   There exists therefore the possibility that the provisions of the conventions implemented by way of the Carriage by Air Acts (Application of Provisions) Order 1967 will be construed differently from the provisions of the Warsaw-Hague Convention (as implemented by the Carriage by Air Act 1961) and the Guadalajara Convention (as implemented by the Carriage by Air (Supplementary Provisions) Act 1962), because the prevailing language differs. It is submitted that, in practice, such

---

[7]   At 652C-G.
[8]   However, in *James Buchanan & Co Ltd v Babco Forwarding and Shipping (UK) Ltd* [1978] AC 141, HL, Lord Wilberforce (considering the Carriage of Goods by Road Act 1965, which adopts the same approach as the 1932 Act, in relation to the Convention on the Contract for the International Carriage of Goods by Road Act 1956) did not go so far as to hold that the French text of the Convention actually prevailed over the English text, although he did hold that it was perfectly legitimate to look for assistance to the French text in interpreting the English text of the Convention. See further, para **3.7**, below.
[9]   Emphasis added.

divergence is unlikely. This is because English Courts adopt a reasonably flexible approach in construing provisions that seek to implement international conventions. Thus, in construing provisions scheduled to an Act of Parliament that have an 'international currency' and 'must come under the consideration of foreign Courts' it is, in the words of Lord MacMillan, 'desirable that in the interests of uniformity that their interpretation should not be rigidly controlled by domestic precedents of antecedent date, but rather that the language of the rules should be construed on broad principles of general acceptation.[10'] Equally, regard should be had to the fact that conventions 'are apt to be more loosely worded' than Acts of Parliament. In *Fothergill v Monarch Airlines Ltd*, Lord Diplock stated that the approach an English court should take was accurately stated in the Vienna Convention on the Law of Treaties:

> 'Article 31
> 1. A treaty shall be interpreted in good faith in accordance with the ordinary meaning to be given to the terms of the treaty in their context and in the light of its object and purpose.'

3.7   Finally, in *James Buchanan & Co Ltd v Babco Forwarding and Shipping (UK) Ltd*[11], the House of Lords was faced with an issue concerning the construction of the Carriage of Goods by Road Act 1965, which gave the force of law in the UK to the Convention on the Contract for the International Carriage of Goods by Road 1956. The convention itself was expressed in two languages — English and French — each text being equally authentic. The English text alone was scheduled to the Act of 1965 and was given the force of law. Lord Wilberforce set out the correct approach as follows:

> 'The Convention of 1956 is in two languages, English and French, each text being equally authentic. The English text alone appears in the Schedule to the Act and is by that Act (section 1) given the force of law. Moreover, the contract of carriage seems to have incorporated contractually this English text. It might therefore be arguable (though this was not in fact argued) — by distinction from a case where the authentic text is (for example) French and the enacted text an English translation — that only the English text ought to be looked at. In my opinion this would be too narrow a view to take, given the expressed objective of the Convention to produce uniformity in all contracting states. I think that the correct approach is to interpret the English text, which after all is likely to be used by many others than British businessmen, in a normal manner, appropriate for the interpretation of an international convention, unconstrained by technical rules of English law, or

---

[10]   In *Stag Line Ltd v Foscolo, Mango & Co Ltd* [1932] AC 328, HL at 350. Lord MacMillan was referring to the rules in the Schedule to the Carriage of Goods by Sea Act 1924. The Act was the outcome of an International Conference.

[11]   [1978] AC 141, HL.

by English legal precedent, but on broad principles of general acceptation: *Stag Line Ltd v. Foscolo, Mango & Co. Ltd* [1932] A.C. 328, *per* Lord
MacMillan, at p.350. Moreover, it is perfectly legitimate in my opinion
to look for assistance, if assistance be needed, to the French text. This is
often put in the form that resort may be had if (and only if) the English
text is ambiguous, but I think this states the rule too technically. As
Lord Diplock recently said in this House the inherent flexibility of the
English (and, one may add, any) language may make it necessary for
the interpreter to have recourse to a variety of aids: *Carter v. Bradbeer*
[1975] 1 W.L.R. 1204, 1206. There is no need to impose a preliminary
test of ambiguity.

My Lords, I would not lay down rules as to the manner in which reference to the French text is to be made.[12']

It is submitted that this approach, involving as it does the construction of the
English text by reference to the original French, if such assistance be needed,
is a perfectly proper approach in construing the provisions of the Carriage by
Air Acts (Application of Provisions) Order 1967.

**3.8   Materials open to English Courts to consider when construing interna-
tional conventions.**   In addition to having regard to the different languages
in which a convention has been expressed, English Courts may properly have
regard to the following sources and materials when considering the construction of an international convention:
(1)   Foreign case law[13], although regard must be had to the level of the court
     deciding the case in question and the process of law reporting[14];
(2)   Text books and articles[15].
(3)   The *travaux préparatoires* of the convention in question. However, such
     references should be 'rare' and should only be made where the material
     involved is 'public and accessible' and 'clearly and indisputably points
     to a definite legislative intention'[16].

---

[12] At 152C-G. But cf Viscount Dilhorne at 158F, who expressed 'some doubt as to the propriety
    of' Lord Wilberforce's approach; Lord Salmon at 161B-C, who appeared to place more weight
    on the 'ambiguity' test; and Lord Edmund-Davies at 167C, who expressly endorsed it. Lord
    Fraser at 170C, agreed with the speech of Lord Edmund-Davies. However, later case law
    appears to support the wider view of Lord Wilberforce. See in particular *Fothergill v Monarch
    Airlines Ltd* [1981] AC 251, HL at 286D-E (per Lord Fraser).
[13] See *James Buchanan & Co Ltd v Babco Forwarding and Shipping (UK) Ltd* [1978] AC 141, HL at
    161E-H (per Lord Salmon).
[14] See *Fothergill v Monarch Airlines Ltd* [1981] AC 251, HL at 275G-276B (per Lord Wilberforce)
    and 284C-E (per Lord Diplock).
[15] See *Fothergill v Monarch Airlines Ltd* [1981] AC 251, HL at 274G-H (per Lord Wilberforce),
    283H-284B (per Lord Diplock) and 287D-E (per Lord Fraser).
[16] See *Fothergill v Monarch Airlines Ltd*, [1981] AC 251, HL at 278A-E (per Lord Wilberforce),
    283A-D (per Lord Diplock). Lord Wilberforce expressly sanctioned reference to the work
    leading up to the Warsaw Convention and the Hague Protocol. However, Lord Fraser took a
    much narrower view (at 287E-G).

Chapter 4

Scope of the Conventions

The Warsaw-Hague Rules

4.1

RULE 4

(1) Carriage falls within the scope of the Warsaw-Hague Rules where the carriage in question is either:
   (i) International carriage of persons, baggage or cargo performed by aircraft for reward; or
   (ii) International carriage of persons, baggage or cargo by aircraft performed gratuitously by an air transport undertaking.
(2) Whether carriage amounts to 'international carriage' in the sense understood in paragraph (1) above depends upon the carriage that is anticipated according to the agreement or agreements that have been reached between the parties to that carriage.
(3) Carriage will be international:
   (i) Where, according to the agreement between the parties, the place of departure and the place of destination are situated within the territories of two states that are party to the Warsaw-Hague Convention. Where this condition is met, the carriage will remain international even if there is a break in the carriage or a transshipment; or
   (ii) Where, according to the agreement between the parties, the place of departure and the place of destination are situated within the territory of a single state party to the Warsaw-Hague Convention, provided there is an agreed stopping place within the territory of any other state, irrespective of whether that state is party to the Warsaw-Hague Convention.
(4) Where carriage falls within the scope of paragraph (3) above, then such carriage does not lose its international character where it is performed by several successive air carriers provided:
   (i) The carriage is regarded by the parties as a single operation;
   (ii) The carriage has been divided up into separate and successive stages, in terms of both time and place;

(iii) **The parties have agreed that the carriage be performed by several successive carriers.**

4.2   Scope of the Convention. The scope of the Warsaw-Hague Convention is set out in art 1(1), which states:

'This Convention applies to all international carriage of persons, baggage or cargo performed by aircraft for reward. It applies equally to gratuitous carriage by aircraft performed by an air transport undertaking.'

With the notable exception of the term '*international carriage*', which is defined in art 1(2), very few of the terms used in art 1(1) are further defined in the Warsaw-Hague Convention. Their meaning is considered further below.

4.3   Aircraft. Precisely what constitutes an aircraft is not defined in the Convention[1]. In seeking a definition, a number of commentators[2] have referred to ICAO's definition[3] of an aircraft:

'Aircraft is any machine that can derive support in the atmosphere from the reactions of the air other than the reactions of the air against the earth's surface.'

The words '. . . other than the reactions of the air against the earth's surface' were included to ensure that hovercraft did not fall within the definition of aircraft. This definition is a wide one that certainly embraces those aircraft described in the General Classification of Aircraft scheduled to the Air Navigation (No 2) Order 1995[4], which also does not include hovercraft.

**4.4   ** The legal position of hovercraft in the UK is specifically regulated by the Hovercraft Act 1968[5], which provides[6] that the Carriage by Air Act 1961

---

[1]   In *Cie la Minerve v Société Pugnat* (1970) 24 RFDA 445 (Tribunal de Grande Instance de Grenoble), it was held without difficulty that the Warsaw-Hague Convention applied to helicopters.

[2]   Notably Diederiks-Verschoor *An Introduction to Air Law* (5th edn, 1993) p 5; Giemulla/Schmid/Ehlers *Warsaw Convention* (1992) ch 1, para 27; *Miller* pp 15–17; Guldimann 'Rebuilding the airline liability system' 1989 IATA Review 11, art 1, paras 23–24.

[3]   Revised and amended text of Annex 7 to the Chicago Convention. It must, of course, be noted that the Chicago Convention is unrelated to the Warsaw-Hague Convention, and that this definition must be considered with this reservation in mind.

[4]   Ie Pt A of Sch 1 of the Air Navigation (No 2) Order 1995, SI 1995/1970. The definition of '*aircraft*' includes: free balloons; captive balloons; airships; gliders; kites; land aeroplanes; seaplanes; amphibian aeroplanes; self launching motor gliders; powered lift (tilt rotor) craft; rotorcraft (helicopter/gyroplane). *Shawcross* Div VII, para [364] states that the aircraft listed in Pt A of Sch 1 'should be regarded as an aircraft for present purposes'.

[5]   The Act defines '*hovercraft*' in s 4(1) as 'a vehicle which is designed to be supported when in motion wholly or partly by air expelled from the vehicle to form a cushion of which the boundaries include the ground, water or other surface beneath the vehicle.'

[6]   In s 1(1)(*i*) of the Hovercraft Act 1968.

and the Carriage by Air (Supplementary Provisions) Act 1962 may, where an Order in Council so specifies, apply to the carriage of persons and their baggage by hovercraft[7]. The Hovercraft (Civil Liability) Order 1986[8] provides in art 3 that '[t]he Carriage by Air Act 1961 and the Carriage by Air (Supplementary Provisions) Act 1962 shall apply subject to the modifications set out in Schedule 1 to this Order in relation to the carriage of passengers and their baggage by hovercraft as they apply in relation to the carriage of passengers and their baggage by air.'

4.5   Persons, baggage or cargo.   The carriage in question must be one of persons, baggage or cargo, *excluding* carriage performed pursuant to international postal conventions[9]. It is difficult to see how the inclusionary words 'persons, baggage or cargo' import any real limitation to the operation of the Warsaw-Hague Convention[10], However, there are indications that French Courts might hold that a cadaver could not be regarded as 'goods' or 'merchandises' within the terms of the Convention. Certainly, this was the conclusion reached in a case dealing with carriage governed by French municipal law, *Djedraoui v Tamisier*[11]. This conclusion is contradicted by case law in the US, where it has been expressly held that human remains qualified as 'goods' subject to the Convention[12].

4.6   Exclusion of carriage performed pursuant to international postal conventions.   This exclusion is not further defined in the Convention, and reference must be had to such specific postal conventions as are in force in order to determine the ambit of the exception. This has the benefit of avoiding the need of setting out the ambit of the postal conventions, and means that the Convention does not get out of date if the postal conventions change.

4.7   For reward.   Unless performed by an air transport undertaking, the carriage must be 'for reward'. There are two different views as to what is

---

[7]   But *not* to the carriage of property by hovercraft *other* than baggage. Carriage of property other than baggage is governed by the Carriage of Goods by Sea Act 1924 and ss 17 and 18 of the Merchant Shipping Act 1979 so far as those sections relate to property on board a ship: s 1(1)(*i*) of the Hovercraft Act 1968.

[8]   SI 1986/1305. This Order revoked and re-enacted the provisions of the Hovercraft (Civil Liability) Order 1979 with amendments.

[9]   See art 2(2).

[10]   A conclusion shared by *Drion* at para 55. *Miller* (at pp 10–11) argues that the use of the term 'goods' instead of 'cargo' in the Carriage by Air Act 1932 might have given rise to difficulties in that '[g]oods' in a contractual common law context, refers to inanimate objects only, thus excluding live animals.' In *Miller*'s view, the use of the term 'cargo' avoids such difficulties. *Shawcross* Div VII, para [100] discusses the breath of the category of 'persons' at some length, in the context of whether persons such as employees fall within the scope of the Convention. It is submitted that such issues are not so much to do with the concept of what is, and what is not, a 'person' but rather relate to the meaning of 'international carriage'. See below, paras **4.9–4.11**.

[11]   (1953) 7 RFDA 494. See also *Miller* at p 11.

[12]   *Onyeanusi v Pan Am* 952 F 2d 788, (US Ct of Apps, 3rd circuit, 1992).

necessary to constitute carriage for reward, effectively representing the different views of continental and common law jurists. The continental view is that the Convention is only intended to deal with commercial transportation[13]; that the interest of the carrier must be a commercial one[14]; and even that the remuneration must be of material significance[15]. *Shawcross* takes a wider view that 'any kind of remuneration, whether monetary or other, which the operator receives from someone else for the carriage' should suffice[16], a view that clearly draws support from the common law tradition of not looking to the adequacy of the consideration furnished.

4.8   Gratuitously by an air transport undertaking.   Gratuitous carriage only falls within the Convention when performed by an air transport undertaking. The term 'air transport undertaking' is not defined. In *Gurtner v Beaton*[17], Owen J was referred to the definition of 'air transport undertaking' in art 93 of the Air Navigation Order 1980, namely 'an undertaking whose business includes the carriage by air of passengers or cargo for hire or reward'[18] and stated:

> 'I am satisfied that the business of which Mr Beaton was manager did include such carriage for reward. It is true that the definition used the present tense 'includes', which must mean that past carriage for reward will not necessarily lead to a finding that a business is an air transport undertaking but when there has been even one flight for reward in the past and such flights are available for the future a finding that the business of the undertaking includes the carriage by air of passengers for reward is, in my judgment, irresistible.[19]'

The court in *Sulewski v Federal Express Corpn*[20] also took a wide view of the meaning of an 'air transportation enterprise' (the American translation of air transport undertaking):

> 'The reference to 'gratuitous transportation' also indicates that, as long as the carrier is commercial ('an air transportation enterprise'), the nature of the carrier's business should not be dispositive. As a result,

---

[13]   *Drion* at para 56.
[14]   *Giemulla/Schmid/Ehlers* at art 1, paras 31–32.
[15]   *Guldimann* at paras 11–13.
[16]   At Div VII, para [101]. This view derives some support from the French decision in *Companie la Minerve v Société Pugnat*, [1970] 24 RFDA 445, Tribunal de Grande Instance de Grenoble. This case concerned the carriage of equipment by helicopter. The equipment was accompanied by an employee of the consignor to guide the pilot to the place of delivery. It was held that the transport was for reward, even though no identifiable part of the total payment could be earmarked as the fare.
[17]   1990 1 S & B Av R VII/499, QBD.
[18]   SI 1980/1965. The definition in art 118(1) of the Air Navigation Order 1995, SI 1999/1970 is similar but not identical: '. . . an undertaking whose business includes the carriage by air of passengers or cargo for valuable consideration.'
[19]   At VII/517.
[20]   933 F 2d 180 (US Ct of Apps, 2nd circuit, 1991).

Flying Tiger [the carrier], although in the business of carrying cargo, may be held liable not only for accident-related damages to transported 'goods' but also for injuries to 'persons' to whom it provides 'gratuitous transportation'[21].

4.9   International carriage.   As appears from art 1(2), the term 'international carriage' is a complex one. It is defined as:

'. . . any carriage in which, according to the agreement between the parties, the place of departure and the place of destination, whether or not there be a break in the carriage or a transhipment, are situated either within the territories of two High Contracting Parties or within the territory of a single High Contracting Party if there is an agreed stopping place within the territory of another State, even if that State is not a High Contracting Party. Carriage between two points within the territory of a single High Contracting Party without an agreed stopping place within the territory of another State is not international carriage for the purposes of this Convention.'

4.10   The emphasis of the definition is clearly on 'international' rather than 'carriage'. Whether or not carriage is regarded as international depends upon the carriage that is *anticipated* by the parties to that carriage *according to* their agreement: it does not depend upon the nationality or place of residence of either party to the carriage; nor does it depend upon the carriage that actually takes place. Thus, for instance, provided the anticipated carriage is from State A to State B, both States being party to the Warsaw-Hague Convention, then that carriage is international, even if the flight for some reason never leaves State A. The point was clearly put by Greene LJ in *Grein v Imperial Airways Ltd*[22]:

'The rules are rules relating not to journeys, not to flights, not to parts of journeys, but to carriage performed under one (or in some cases falling under para. 3 more than one) contract of carriage. The contract (or under para. 3 the series of contracts) is, so to speak, the unit to which attention is to be paid in considering whether the carriage to be performed under it is international or not[23].'

4.11   The rationale behind this approach was clearly put in *Egan v Kollsman Instrument Corpn*[24]:

'The Convention's emphasis on the contract actually 'made' appears to have been specifically designed to prevent any subsequent intervening

---

[21] At 183.
[22] [1937] 1 KB 50, CA.
[23] At 77.
[24] 234 NE 2d 199 (NY Ct of Apps, 1967).

circumstances from affecting the result. The reason is manifest; as one commentator put it, '[t]his prescription possesses, for the parties involved, the appreciable advantage of settling in advance the application of the Warsaw Convention thus becoming independent of fortuitous events'[25].'

4.12   The agreement between the parties.   The touchstone, then, for international carriage, is therefore the agreement between the parties. Precisely what this entails is more difficult to state. In the first place, there is some difficulty in the translation of the French text which, by virtue of s 1(2) of the Carriage by Air Act 1961, is to prevail. The English version of the Warsaw-Hague Convention refers to 'the agreement between the parties'. The French version of the text refers to 'les stipulations des parties'. The poor translation of 'les stipulations' in the English versions of the Conventions, which is respectively translated as 'the contract' in the Schedule to the Carriage by Air Act 1932 and 'the agreement' in the First Schedule to the Carriage by Air Act 1961, has been commented upon. Thus, in *Block v Cie Nationale Air France*[26], Wisdom J stated (referring to the American translation of the Warsaw Convention):

> 'This is a poor translation of the original and official French version, which also states that both parties need to agree to the stopping places but which does not assert or imply that this agreement need be made as part of a single and direct contract. Instead of the language 'according to the contract made by the parties', the French version reads 'd'après les stipulations des parties'. Thus, the French version refers to the *stipulations* (conditions) agreed to by the parties rather than to '*the contract made by the parties*'. The French version would therefore include the situation where both main parties agree to the same route but do so through a third party . . .[27]'.

4.13   The reference to 'stipulations' in art 1(2) of the French text would appear to be explicable on the basis that the reference is to *specific terms* of the agreement between the parties, namely the place of departure and the place of destination. Elsewhere in the Convention, the French text refers not to 'les stipulations' but to 'le contrat'[28], when the entirety of the arrangement between the parties is intended to be referred to. Thus, it would appear that although the English translations of the French text might have been clearer, there is no real divergence in meaning between the French and the English texts: there must be an agreement between the parties. It follows that a

---

[25] At 201, citing Coquoz *Le Droit Privé Internationale Aérien* at p 95. See also *Wyman and Bartlett v Pan American Airways* (1943) US Av 1 at 3; *Grey v American Airlines Inc* (1950) US & C Av 507; *Surprenant v Air Canada* [1973] Que CA 107.
[26] 386 F 2d 323 (US CA, 5th Cir, 1967).
[27] At 333.
[28] Notably in arts 3(2), 3(4) and 5(2), as *Drion* points out in para 50.

stowaway will not enjoy the benefits of — and will not be subject to the restrictions of — the Convention[29].

4.14   It would be a both undesirable and curious state of affairs were the Convention to require or even allow a court to apply with rigour its own municipal provisions as to precisely what constitutes an agreement, and what does not. The very aim of the Convention is to promote uniformity in the context of carriage by air, an objective that would be undermined were the scope of the Convention to depend upon widely varying understandings of what an agreement is. There is a good deal of case law that indicates that the concept of an agreement is much wider than municipal law definitions. In *Gurtner v Beaton*[30], which concerned a contract unenforceable by reason of illegality, Owen J held that:

> '. . . I also find that the carriage was meant to be and was for hire or reward within the meaning of the Warsaw Convention, there being no requirement for a perfected contract, an agreement for carriage being sufficient to bring the carriage within the provisions of the convention.[31]'

4.15   A similar approach has been taken in cases where the arrangements for the carriage, and the payments therefor, have been made by a third party other than the passenger[32]. *Block v Cie Nationale Air France*[33] concerned an agreement between Air France and the Altanta Art Association, which obliged Air France to furnish a Boeing 707 in return for payment. Air France was to be in control of the physical conduct of the flight; the Art Association had complete control over the choice of passengers. The Art Association then entered into a 'more informal' arrangement with its members regarding the flight, and notified Air France of the member's name. Air France then issued a ticket in that member's name. The Court held that '[t]he existence of the airline-passenger relationship is not destroyed by the fact that a third party negotiated the agreement and signed the charter'[34]. Wisdom J's reasoning on this point is of interest:

---

[29] See *Drion* para 51.

[30] (1990) 1 S & B Av R VII/499.

[31] On appeal to the Court of Appeal, this approach was confirmed. See [1993] 2 Lloyd's Rep 369 at 385: 'It is right to note at this stage that during the course of argument the Court drew attention to the fact that, as the Judge held, the contract made by Mr Beaton for the carriage of the Swiss passengers was unlawful. It has not been suggested, however, that that illegality is relevant in any way to the application of the provisions of the Convention.'

[32] See *Drion* para 52: 'It is not essential that the contract of carriage be concluded with the passenger or the owner of the goods. The contract may be with any person, employer, husband, father of friend of the passenger, and with the forwarding agent or owner of the goods, provided the contract includes the points of departure and destination of the passenger or goods concerned.'

[33] 386 F 2d 323 (US CA, 5th Cir, 1967).

[34] At 334.

'The applicability of the Convention undeniably is premised upon a contract of a particular kind. It is based on a contract of carriage that arises from the relationship between a 'carrier' and the passengers. This contractual relationship requires only that the carrier consent to undertake the international transportation of the passenger from one designated spot to another, and that the passenger in turn consent to the undertaking.

. . .

Since the Convention does not anticipate bargaining between two primary parties, it does not limit participation in the negotiation of the contract to these two parties. Thus, the Convention refers to the existence of a contract in many places, but it never once describes this contract in terms of the passenger and the carrier. There is no Warsaw objection therefore to a third person acting as agent of passengers or entering into a contract with the carrier for the benefit of passengers ('stipulation pour autrui')[35]'.

4.16   A similar question arose on the facts of *Ross v Pan American Airways Inc*[36]. In this case, the claimant passenger was a theatrical performer who had made an arrangement with U.S.O. Camp Shows Inc. to entertain soldiers in war areas. All flight arrangements were made by officers or employees of U.S.O. Camp Shows Inc. The passenger knew nothing of how the flights were arranged on her behalf, nor did she know precisely what those arrangements were. Indeed, she never even received an airline ticket, receiving instead a slip of paper from the U.S.O. Camp Shows Inc. representative. Although the case centred on whether a passenger ticket had been 'delivered' to the claimant[37], it was necessarily implicit in the decision of the Court that there was an 'agreement' within the meaning of the Convention.

4.17   In *Herd v Clyde Helicopters Ltd*[38] the House of Lords adopted a similar approach to that in the *Block* and *Rose* cases. In the Herd case, the claimant, Sergeant Herd was a member of the police helicopter unit of the Strathclyde police force. His duties were to carry out aerial surveillance. The helicopters used by the police helicopter unit were supplied by Clyde Helicopters Ltd. The contract between Strathclyde police force and Clyde Helicopters Ltd was a wet lease, by which Clyde Helicopters Ltd supplied the helicopters, the flying crew and carried out all maintenance. Although this case concerned whether Sergeant Herd was a passenger in non-international carriage[39], it

---

[35] At 330–332.
[36] 85 NE 2d 880 (1949).
[37] In accordance with art 3 of the Convention.
[38] [1997] AC 534 (HL: Scottish case).
[39] For the purposes of whether or not the agreement was a contract of carriage, it is not relevant that this was not international carriage, and that it would therefore have been subject to the provisions of Pt IIIA of Sch 1 of the Carriage by Air Acts (Application of Provisions) Order 1967.

was decided by Lord Mackay that Clyde Helicopters Ltd were carriers[40]. Implicit in that decision was that there was an agreement of carriage between Clyde Helicopters and Strathclyde Police force.

4.18   An agreement 'for carriage'.   It is not sufficient to satisfy art 1(2) for there merely to be an 'agreement', in the loose sense considered above. Rather, there must be an agreement *for carriage*. In other words, something over and above mere physical presence on board an aircraft is required in order to amount to carriage. This distinction between types of contract is one not generally very clearly drawn by common law jurisdictions. It is, however, one rooted in continental jurisprudence[41]. Thus, the French case law is replete with instances where the courts consider the essential purpose of the contract before them, namely whether this purpose is one of carriage, or whether the purpose is something else, such as a flying lesson or a test flight, where the carriage is a mere incident — albeit a necessary one — of the main object of the contract[42]. There are two areas where this distinction is of practical importance, namely contracts of hire or charter and contracts of employment.

4.19   Contracts of hire or charter.   Whether an agreement for the hire of an aircraft constitutes an agreement for carriage depends upon the terms of the charter[43]. Clearly, a voyage charter[44] *will* constitute an agreement for carriage. Equally clearly, a time charter or 'bare-boat' charter, where the entire aircraft is put at the disposal by the owner to the charterer for a given period of time is unlikely to amount to an agreement for carriage[45]. Of course, there is no reason why although the owner of the aircraft has not entered into an agreement for carriage with the charterer, the charterer nevertheless enters into agreements for carriage with third persons.

4.20   Contracts of employment.   It is clear law that there can be no contract of carriage as regards employees of the carrier actually carrying on work while the carriage is being effected — ie pilots, flight attendants, etc[46] . Thus,

---

[40] See p 542 D of Lord Mackay's speech.

[41] See *Nicholas* p 49; *Miller* p 8.

[42] See *Sté Mutuelle d'Assurances v Aéro-Club d'Angoulême* (1967) 21 RFDA 436, Cour de Cassation, where the court distinguished between a flying lesson and a contract of carriage by air. Similarly, in *Aéro-Club de l'Aisne, Mutuelle d'assurances aériennes v Klopotowska, Pekacz et Agent judiciare du Trésor public* (1970) 24 RFDA 195 Cour de Cassation, the court distinguished between a test flight that did not have as its aim the movement of persons or goods from a true contract of carriage. See also: *Lefebvre v Sté Aéro-Club, 'Les Ailes Diesppoises'* (1974) 28 RFDA 202 (Cour d'Appel de Rouen); *Valade v Association Aéro-Club de Brive* (1975) 29 RFDA 202 (Cour d'Appel de Riom); *Korper v Aéro-Club Sarre Union, Mutuelle d'Assurances Aériennes, M. Hewer* (1992) 45 RFDA 323 (Cour d'Appel de Colmar).

[43] As to this generally, see *Drion* at para 53.

[44] Such as that in *Block v Cie Nationale Air France* 386 F 2d 323 (1967); and *Herd v Clyde Helicopters Ltd* [1997] 1 AC 534.

[45] An additional reason for this is that a charter of this sort would not generally specify a place of departure and a place of destination.

[46] As to this generally, see *Drion* para 54.

in *Re Mexico City Aircrash of October 31 1978*[47], the claimants were three employees of the carrier, two of whom were acting as flight attendants on board the aircraft. The third was on-board the aircraft by virtue of her employment, but had no function assigned to her on that flight — she was present in what was referred to as a 'dead-heading' capacity. The court held that the two working flight attendants did not fall within the scope of the Convention. As regards the third, it was held not possible to reach a conclusion on *summary* judgment that she did *not* fall within the Convention. The court reached this conclusion by reference to both art 1 of the Convention, and art 17, which provides for the liability of a carrier to a 'passenger'. The court held that for purposes of logical consistency the term 'passenger' comprised all persons receiving 'transportation'[48] within the meaning of art 1[49]. The court defined 'transportation' in the following way:

> 'The term 'transportation' seems to us to require as a minimum that the voyage be undertaken for the principal purpose of moving the individual from point A to point B.'

Thus, the position is clear as regards employees who, according to the agreement, are intended to work on the flight in question. However, it is submitted that the court in *Re Mexico City* was correct in regarding an employee having *no* duties on the flight as being in a different category. There seems no good reason for holding that an employee is for that reason alone not within the Convention.

4.21   Where a person is carried on an aircraft as a result of an agreement between a third party and the carrier, then that person is likely to be a passenger provided that he is not engaged in any flying responsibility. In *Herd v Clyde Helicopters Ltd*[50] a police sergeant who was employed by Strathclyde Police force as a surveillance officer on its helicopter unit was found to be a passenger on board a helicopter which had been leased by the police force from Clyde Helicopters Ltd. Strathclyde had leased the helicopter and the flying crew. Sergeant Herd was not responsible for any flying duties. Lord Mackay analysed Sergeant Herd's role in the following way[51]:

> 'In my view it is clear that the respondents (Clyde Helicopters Ltd) were the carrier in respect of Sergeant Herd. It is true that Sergeant Herd was on the aircraft for the purpose of carrying out his duties as a member of the Police Helicopter Unit, but from the facts as alleged, which I have quoted above, it is clear that he had no responsibility whatever in respect of the operation of the aircraft, which was solely

---

[47]   708 F 2d 400 (US CA, 9th Cir, 1982).
[48]   To use the American translation of 'transport'. The English version of course refers to carriage.
[49]   See footnote 31 of the judgment.
[50]   [1997] AC 534 (HL: Scottish case).
[51]   See page 542D-E.

under the control of the pilot, and therefore in my opinion the activities which Sergeant Herd was carrying on while on the aircraft are not to be regarded as contributing in any way to the carriage of himself or the other persons on board. He therefore is properly regarded as a passenger.'

4.22   In other words, such a person will be a passenger because he is not in any way contributing in any way to the act of carriage. In the first instance decision in *Herd v Clyde Helicopters Ltd* (unreported), Lord Milligan analysed the following examples: a sightseer using a helicopter would be a passenger; a businessman who used a helicopter to view a business opportunity would be a passenger; a helicopter winchman employed to winch people from the sea would be a member of crew and not a passenger; and where there were two persons carrying out surveillance on a flight, one of them employed by the carrier to examine the attitudes of passengers, the other not employed by the airline but surveying the performance of the airline crew, then the first would not be a passenger, but the second would[52].

4.23   **The transport anticipated by the agreement between the parties.** Only if the agreement between the parties anticipates carriage of a certain type, can the carriage be termed 'international'. Thus, as is clear from the last sentence of art 1(2), if the carriage envisaged is simply between two points within the territory of a single High Contracting Party (with no agreed stopping place within the territory of another State) then the carriage cannot fall within the scope of the Warsaw-Hague Convention. Essentially, in order for carriage to be 'international', it must fall within one of the following categories:
(1)   The agreed place of departure must be situate within the territory of one High Contracting Party and the agreed place of destination must be situate within the territory of another, *different*, High Contracting Party; *or*
(2)   The agreed place of departure and the agreed place of destination may be situate within the *same* High Contracting Party, *provided* there is an agreed stopping place within *another* State, irrespective of whether that State is itself a High Contracting Party.

4.24   **High Contracting Parties.**   As a matter of English law, the identification of the parties participating in the Warsaw-Hague Convention — so-called 'High Contracting Parties' — is straightforward. Section 2(1) of the Carriage by Air Act 1961 provides that 'Her Majesty may by Order in Council from time to time certify who are the High Contracting Parties to the Convention, in respect of what territories they are respectively parties and to what extent they have availed themselves of the provisions of the Additional Protocol at the end of the Convention as set out in the First Schedule to this Act.' The current Order in Council specifying the present High Contracting Parties to the

---

[52]   See *Shawcross* Div VII, para [361].

Warsaw-Hague Convention is the Carriage by Air (Parties to Convention) Order 1988[53]. By virtue of s 2(3) of the 1961 Act, an Order in Council made under s 2 of the Act 'shall, except so far as it has been superceded by a subsequent Order, be conclusive of the matters so certified.'

4.25   **The place of departure and the place of destination.**   This phrase was considered in *Grein v International Airways Ltd*[54] by Greene LJ:

> 'The use of the singular in this expression indicates that in the minds of the parties to the Convention every contract of carriage has one place of departure and one place of destination. An intermediate place at which the carriage may be broken is not regards as a 'place of destination'. Having regard to its context, and particularly to the fact that it is in the contract that the place of departure and the place of destination are to be looked for, the meaning of the expression appears to me to be 'the place at which the contractual carriage begins and the place at which the contractual carriage ends.'[55]'

4.26   **An agreed stopping place**.   In *Grein v Imperial Airways Ltd*[56], Greene LJ defined an agreed stopping place as follows:

> 'The expression 'stopping place' cannot in my judgment be confined to cases where the aeroplane descends without any right in the passenger to break his journey. . . If I am right in thinking that the expression 'place of departure and place of destination' means the place at which the contractual carriage begins and the place at which it ends, 'agreed stopping place' means a place where according to the contract the machine by which the contract is to be performed will stop in the course of performing the contractual carriage, whatever the purpose of the descent may be and whatever rights the passenger may have to break his journey at that place.[57]'

4.27   **Break in the carriage or a transhipment.**   Provided that the agreement between the parties specifies only one place of departure and one place of destination, then it is irrelevant for the purpose of determining whether the carriage is international or not whether there is a break in the carriage or a transhipment.

4.28   **Successive carriage.**   Article 1(3) of the Convention reflects the fact that in practice destinations may be reached using more than one carrier, whether because of the limited number of carriers flying a particular route, or whether simply as a matter of convenience. This provision avoids the

---

53   SI 1988/243.
54   [1937] 1 KB 50, CA.
55   At 78–79.
56   [1937] 1 KB 50, CA.
57   At 80.

need, provided its conditions are met, of looking at particular limbs of a journey, and allows the entirety of the journey to be considered: single legs of a journey are added up and considered collectively. The effect of the provision is that provided the journey considered as a *whole* falls within the meaning of international carriage as defined by the Convention, the journey does not cease to be international carriage simply because one contract (or a series of contracts) is to be performed entirely within the territory of the same State.

4.29   Article 1(3) reads as follows:

> 'Carriage to be performed by several successive air carriers is deemed, for the purposes of this Convention, to be one undivided carriage if it has been regarded by the parties as a single operation, whether it has been agreed upon under the form of a single contract or a series of contracts, and it does not lose its international character merely because one contract or a series of contracts is to be performed entirely within the territory of the same State.'

4.30   To amount to successive carriage, the carriage must possess the following characteristics at the time the contract or contracts are made: first, the carriage must be regarded by the parties as a single operation; secondly, it must have been divided up into separate and successive stages, both in terms of time and place; thirdly, the parties must have agreed that that carriage was to be performed by several successive carriers.

4.31   Where carriage amounts to successive carriage within the sense of art 1(3), each carrier who accepts passengers, baggage or cargo is subjected to the rules of the Convention, and is deemed to be one of the contracting parties to the contract of carriage in so far as the contract deals with that part of the carriage which is performed under his supervision[58].

4.32   Multimodal transport.   Article 31(1) of the Convention provides as follows:

> 'In the case of combined carriage performed partly by air and partly by any other mode of carriage, the provisions of this Convention apply only to the carriage by air, provided that the carriage by air falls within the terms of Article 1.'

Article 31(2) goes on to provide that nothing in the Convention shall prevent the parties in the case of combined carriage from inserting in the document of air carriage conditions relating to other modes of carriage, provided

---

[58] Article 30(1) of the Warsaw-Hague Convention. The effect of art 30(1) is thus to extend the number of carriers who are party to the contract of carriage. This may, but will not always, extend the number of potential defendants a passenger or consigor may sue. Precisely who the appropriate defendant is in a given case is determined by art 30(2) and 30(3).

always the provisions of the Convention are observed as regards the carriage by air.

4.33

RULE 5—**The test for whether the carriage will fall within the scope of the Montreal Convention 1999 is broadly similar to that for the Warsaw-Hague Rules, except that in the case of multimodal transport the scope of what is presumed to be carriage by air is broadened to cover certain ancillary non-carriage.**

4.34   The Montreal Convention, 1999.   The Montreal Convention[59] makes very few changes to the equivalent provisions in the amended Warsaw Convention in this context. The provisions of arts 1(1), 1(2), and 1(3) of the amended Warsaw Convention have identically worded equivalents[60] in the Montreal Convention (save that 'High Contracting Parties' are referred to as 'State Parties' in the latter Convention).

4.35   The only significant change is in art 31(1) which deals in the amended Warsaw Convention with 'multimodal' transport[61]. This article has an almost equivalent provision in art 38 of the Montreal Convention. Unlike art 31(1), however, art 38 makes an express reservation by reference to para 4 of art 18 of the Montreal Convention, which provides as follows:

> 'The period of carriage by air does not extend to any carriage by land, by sea or by inland waterway performed outside an airport. If, however, such carriage takes place in the performance of a contract for carriage by air, for the purpose of loading, delivery or transhipment, any damage is presumed, subject to proof to the contrary, to have been the result of an event which took place during the carriage by air. If a carrier, without the consent of the consignor, substitutes carriage by another mode of transport for the whole or part of a carriage intended by the agreement between the parties to be carriage by air, such carriage to be carriage by air, such carriage by another mode of transport is deemed to be within the period of carriage by air.'

The effect of this provision is to broaden the scope of what should be presumed to be carriage by air to cover certain ancillary non-air carriage such as loading, delivery and trans-shipment[62]. It also extends to non-consensual substitution of an alternative mode of Carriage.

---

[59] See paras **1.47–1.53** above.
[60] Articles 1(1), 1(2) and 1(3) respectively.
[61] See para **4.32**.
[62] It is to be noted that a similar presumption existed as a result of art 18(2) of the amended Warsaw Convention in respect of registered baggage and cargo.

The Warsaw Rules

4.36

Rule 6—

(1) Carriage falls within the scope of the Warsaw Rules where the carriage in question is either:
  - (i) International carriage of persons, baggage or cargo performed by aircraft for reward; or
  - (ii) International carriage of persons, baggage or cargo by aircraft performed gratuitously by an air transport undertaking.

(2) Whether carriage amounts to 'international carriage' in the sense understood in paragraph (1) above depends upon the carriage that is anticipated according to the agreement or agreements that have been reached between the parties to that carriage.

(3) Carriage will be international:
  - (i) Where, according to the contract between the parties, the place of departure and the place of destination are situated within the territories of two states that are party to the Warsaw-Hague Convention. Where this condition is met, the carriage will remain international even if there is a break in the carriage or a transshipment; or
  - (ii) Where, according to the contract between the parties, the place of departure and the place of destination are situated within the territory of a single state party to the Warsaw-Hague Convention, provided there is an agreed stopping place within the territory of within the territory of any other state, irrespective of whether that state is party to the Warsaw-Hague Convention.

(4) Where carriage falls within the scope of paragraph (2) above, then such carriage does not lose its international character where it is performed by several successive air carriers provided:
  - (i) The carriage is regarded by the parties as a single operation;
  - (ii) The carriage has been divided up into separate and successive stages, in terms of both time and place;
  - (iii) The parties have agreed that the carriage be performed by several successive carriers.

4.37   **Scope of 'international carriage'.**   In *Holmes v Bangladesh Biman Corpn*[63], Lord Bridge commented that[64]:

---

[63] [1989] AC 1112, HL.
[64] At 1125C-D.

'Article 1(1) of the Hague Convention repeats article 1(1) of the Warsaw-Convention and the definition of 'international carriage' in article 1(2) repeats with immaterial drafting amendments that contained in article 1(2) of the Warsaw-Convention. But a number of countries, notably the United States of America, which are party to the Warsaw Convention have never adopted the Hague Convention. Hence the scope of the 'international carriage' to which each Convention applies is quite different.'

The differences between the wording of the Warsaw Convention and that of the Warsaw-Hague Convention make this clear by substituting the cumbersome 'States Parties to the Convention for the Unification of Certain Rules relating to International Carriage by Air signed at Warsaw on behalf of His Majesty on 12th October 1929' for 'High Contracting Parties'. This makes it clear that the Schedule applies only to those States who are party only to the Warsaw Convention and not also to the Hague Protocol[65].

4.38   Substitution of 'contract' for 'agreement'.   Article 1(2) of the Warsaw-Hague Convention refers to the 'agreement' between the parties. The wording of the Warsaw Convention refers to 'contract' made by the parties.

4.39   No last sentence.   For sake of clarity, the Hague Protocol added the last sentence to art 1(2), which does not appear in the Warsaw Convention.

Rules of Non-International Carriage

4.40

R<small>ULE</small> 7—**The Rules of Non-International Carriage apply to all cases of carriage of persons, baggage or cargo performed by aircraft for reward where either the place or departure, the place of destination or an agreed stopping place is located in the UK.**

4.41   The scope of non-international carriage as set out in Pt III A of Sch 1 of the Carriage by Air Acts (Application of Provisions) Order 1967 appears to be wide indeed. Article 1 provides that '[t]his Schedule applies to all carriage of persons, baggage or cargo performed by aircraft for reward.' Indeed, in *Holmes v Bangladesh Biman Corpn*[66], the Court of Appeal did hold that the

---

[65]   This is because if a state is party to the Warsaw-Hague Convention the carriage cannot be described as 'not being carriage by air to which this convention applies' and therefore cannot even fall within the scope of s 10(1) of the 1961 Act. See para **4.36**.

[66]   [1988] 2 Lloyd's Rep 120, CA.

schedule applied to an accident occurring on an *internal* domestic flight in *Bangladesh*[67]. Bingham LJ held[68]:

> 'The question whether a statutory enactment is intended to have extra-territorial effect is, however, one to be decided on the language of the enactment in question having regard to the subject-matter and other relevant circumstances. Here, it is accepted that the amended Convention scheduled to the 1961 Act and the unamended Convention in schedule 2 to the 1967 Order have the force of law and have extra-territorial effect. Schedule 1, as I have suggested, plainly has the force of law. The language used in the order and in schedule 1 could not have been more comprehensive. The draftsman could not have failed to appreciate that this language was broad enough to embrace international travel not covered by the amended or unamended Conventions and not touching the UK, domestic flights abroad and domestic flights at home. If he intended to differentiate, it seems to me inconceivable that he would not have done so, or that he would have relied on a presumption which in the context of this legislation read as a whole would have been quite inappropriate. No presumption against extra-territoriality can in my view survive a straightforward reading of these provisions.'

4.42   On appeal, the House of Lords reached a different conclusion[69]. Their Lordships held that because of the Order of 1967 could have no wider scope and effect than what was duly authorised by the power conferred by s 10 of the Carriage by Air Act 1961, the essential question to be answered, before attempting to construe the Order, was whether the words in s 10, 'carriage by air . . . of such descriptions as may be satisfied', ought to be read as subject to any limitation[70]. Construing the Order on this basis, their Lordships unanimously held that s 10 had to be construed subject to the presumption that Parliament was not to be taken, by the use of general words, to legislate in the affairs of foreign nationals who did nothing to bring themselves within its jurisdiction. The Order did not, therefore, apply to carriage in which the places of departure and destination and any agreed stopping places were all within the territory of a single foreign state.

4.43   As to the true scope of the Order, Lord Bridge held that the Order applied in the following two cases: first, carriage in which the places of departure and destination and any other agreed stopping places are all within the UK; and secondly, carriage involving a place of departure or destination or an agreed stopping place in a foreign state and a place of departure or destination or an agreed stopping place in the UK[71].

---

[67]   The flight did not provide for a stopping place outside Bangladesh.
[68]   At 123. Dillon LJ in a separate judgment agreed. Lord Donaldson MR agreed with both judgments.
[69]   [1989] AC 1112, HL.
[70]   At 1126E-F (per Lord Bridge); 1139B-D (per Lord Griffiths); 1139D-E (per Lord Ackner); 1150B-D (per Lord Jauncey); 1154D-E (per Lord Lowry).
[71]   At 1131F-G and 1133E. In his speech Lord Jauncey expressly agreed (at 1154A-C). Lords Griffiths, Ackner and Lowry agreed.

Chapter 5

The Passenger Ticket and Baggage Check

Introduction

5.1   The passenger ticket and baggage check are documents of carriage familiar to anyone who travels by air. Between them they perform a large number of functions: inter alia they can be a receipt, an indication of a passenger's right to travel, evidence of contractual terms and a means of registering a passenger and his baggage. Nevertheless, the requirements of the Warsaw-Hague Convention in relation to these documents are relatively few. If and when the 1971 Guatemala Protocol comes into force[1], these requirements will be dramatically reduced still further.

5.2   Under the Warsaw-Hague Convention, the primary function of the passenger ticket and baggage check is to regulate the carrier's ability to rely on the Convention provisions limiting liability for injury to passengers and loss or damage to their baggage (see art 22). The underlying policy is that the carrier will only be entitled to rely on the limitation of liability when the carrier has taken the specified steps to give the passenger notice of these limits. Such notice should enable the passenger to make alternative provision, generally by way of insurance, to ensure that he receives compensation for any loss that he suffers.

5.3   Although it is perhaps generally known that it is wise to arrange insurance before embarking on any flight, there must be doubt as to whether the requirements of the Warsaw-Hague Convention do much to add to this awareness. As will be seen, the elements of the passenger ticket and baggage check that are required to enable the carrier to limit its liability are parts of the travel documents to which the average traveller will pay little attention.

5.4   The relevant articles of the Warsaw-Hague Convention that govern these documents of carriage are arts 3 and 4. Article 3 governs passenger tickets and art 4 governs baggage checks. Their provisions are very similar but, nevertheless, the two articles do raise a number of separate issues and so will be considered separately. Articles 3 and 4 of the Warsaw-Hague Convention differ from the unamended Warsaw Convention in a number of

---

[1]   30 states must ratify the Protocol for it to enter into force but currently only 11 have done so.

respects, which will be commented on where they are of significance. However, the amendments to the Convention made by the Montreal Protocol had no impact on the provisions relating to passenger tickets and baggage checks.

Article 3 — Passenger Tickets

5.5

Rule 8—**Article 3 of the Warsaw-Hague Convention requires that in respect of the carriage of passengers by air, a ticket shall be delivered containing the following information:**

(1)   **An indication of the places of departure and destination[2];**
(2)   **If the places of departure and destination are within the territory of a single High Contracting Party, and one or more agreed stopping places are within the territory of any other State, an indication of at least one such stopping place[3];**
(3)   **A notice to the effect that, if the passenger's journey involves an ultimate destination or stop in a country other than the country of departure, the Warsaw Convention may be applicable and that the Convention governs and in most cases limits the liability of carriers for death or personal injury and in respect of loss of or damage to baggage[4].**

Such a ticket should be delivered in relation to every carriage of passengers governed by the Warsaw-Hague Convention.

Who is a passenger?

5.6   The three requirements of art 3(1) will be considered in detail below. However, art 3 as a whole applies only to the carriage of passengers. Accordingly, the question arises as to who is and is not a passenger. In most instances, the answer to this question is clear. However, where the 'passenger' is connected to the carrier or is otherwise involved in the flight it can be less easy to determine his status.

5.7   An employee of a carrier who is working on the flight (for example, an air steward) is an example of someone who will not be a passenger. However, an air steward who is travelling in a personal capacity rather than as an employee will be a passenger. In those circumstances, his employment is purely incidental to the travel and not the reason for it. Other situations are

---

[2]   Article 3(1)(a).
[3]   Article 3(1)(b).
[4]   Article 3(1)(c).

less clear cut. In *Herd v Clyde Helicopters Ltd*[5], the House of Lords considered the position of a policeman in the Strathclyde police force who was on board a police helicopter that crashed, killing him. Although the helicopter was marked in police colours and was entirely at the disposal of the Strathclyde police, it remained the responsibility of the Defendants and under the control of a pilot employed by them (albeit that the pilot flew as directed by the police on board).

5.8   The view of the House of Lords, as expressed by Lords Mackay and Hope, was that the claimant was a passenger since, despite being on board in the course of his employment, he had no responsibility for the operation of the helicopter. The determinative factor was that he was not 'contributing to the carriage' of himself or others.

5.9   However, it must be recognised that not every 'passenger' under this definition falls within the scope of the Warsaw Conventions[6]. The passenger must also be travelling under an agreement for international carriage that satisfies the requirements of art 1(2) of the Warsaw-Hague Convention. Such an agreement should, at least, specify the places of departure and destination for the flight[7]. It is for this reason that a passenger on a plane leased under a time charter will not fall within the scope of the Warsaw-Hague Convention unless the passenger has a separate contract for a particular voyage on the chartered aircraft[8].

Delivery of the ticket

5.10   Article 3(1) of the Warsaw-Hague Convention requires only that a ticket containing the stated information 'shall be delivered'. In contrast to the unamended Warsaw Convention, which expressly imposed the obligation of delivery on the carrier, the Warsaw-Hague Convention does not specify who must deliver the ticket. The removal of the obligation to deliver from the carrier reflects modern practice in which airline tickets are in most cases issued and supplied by a travel agent rather than the carrier.

---

[5]   [1997] AC 534. This decision concerned an internal flight and was governed not by the Warsaw-Hague Convention but by the rules in Sch 1 to the Carriage by Air Act (Application of Provisions) Order 1967. Nevertheless, the determinative issue was whether the claimant was a passenger and the reasoning of the Court is equally applicable to the meaning of 'passenger' under the Warsaw-Hague Convention: Lord Hope expressly stated that interpretation of the 1967 Order should be guided by the Warsaw-Hague Convention.

[6]   In his judgment, Lord Hope seemed to suggest that the Warsaw-Hague Convention could be applicable to international carriage by air under an arrangement similar to that considered in *Herd*. However, this suggestion was not adopted by the other members of the House of Lords and is probably stating the application of the Convention too broadly.

[7]   Sergeant Herd was not, of course, travelling under such a contract of carriage but the 1967 Order which applied to the case differs from the Warsaw-Hague Convention in encompassing passengers in Sergeant Herd's situation.

[8]   The application of the Warsaw-Hague Convention to charter flights was considered by the US Court of Appeal in some detail in *Block v Compagnie Nationale Air France* (1967) 386 F 2d 323.

5.11   In practice, the failure to deliver a passenger ticket is of itself of little consequence. It is hard to envisage a scenario in which a passenger would suffer loss purely by virtue of not having a ticket. The significance of failure to deliver a passenger ticket arises instead from art 3(2), which deprives the carrier of the limitation of liability provisions in art 22 if, with the consent of the carrier, the passenger embarks without a passenger ticket having been delivered. As a result, it makes little difference by (and to) whom the ticket is initially delivered. What is of importance is that the passenger has a ticket by the time of embarkation and that the carrier does not consent to embarkation without a ticket.

5.12   The Hague amendments to art 3(1) are reflected in art 3(2). The unamended Warsaw Convention removed the Convention limitations on the carrier's liability wherever the carrier accepted a passenger without a passenger ticket having been delivered. However, under the Warsaw-Hague Convention, art 3(2) has this effect only if the carrier consents to the passenger embarking without a passenger ticket having been delivered. This alters the fault required for the removal of the limitations on the carrier's liability: previously the fault was failure of the carrier to deliver the ticket; under the Warsaw-Hague Convention the fault is consenting to carry the passenger without the ticket being delivered.

5.13   Although the Warsaw-Hague Convention also does not specify to whom delivery should be made, the policy underlying the Convention is that the limitations on the carrier's liability should be brought to the attention of passengers prior to boarding. This policy can only be fulfilled if the ticket is delivered to the passenger himself. However, in practice it is often likely that the initial delivery will not be made to the passenger. For example, where a company purchases a ticket for an employee's business trip, where tickets are bought for other family members and where a group booking is made, it is likely that the tickets will be delivered to the individual co-ordinating the purchase and not to the individual passengers[9]. Again, the provisions of art 3(2) resolve this apparent difficulty. Delivery of the ticket can not only be carried out by anyone but it can be made to anyone: the only requirement on the carrier that has an impact on liability is the obligation not to consent to the embarkation of a passenger without a ticket having been delivered to the passenger.

The contents of the ticket

5.14   Under art 3(1) of the Warsaw-Hague Convention, a passenger ticket is required to contain three pieces of information. The first requirement, under art 3(1)(a), is for 'an indication of the places of departure and destination'.

---

[9]   It would appear that the Warsaw-Hague Convention does not allow for one ticket covering a single block booking; there must instead be a ticket for every passenger. However, the Guatemala Protocol will allow for the issue of collective passenger tickets.

Article 3(1)(b) of the unamended Warsaw Convention contained the equivalent but differently worded requirement of a statement of 'the place of departure and of destination'. The introduction of the words 'an indication of' appears to do little more than add unnecessary verbiage since it would be surprising if anything less than a precise statement of the places of departure and destination were sufficient.

5.15   Article 3(1)(b) of the Warsaw-Hague Convention also represents a relaxation from the equivalent provision of the unamended Convention. Article 3(1)(c) of the Warsaw Convention required the ticket to particularise 'the agreed stopping places' between departure and destination[10]. Under the Warsaw-Hague Convention, this requirement is limited in two ways. Firstly, it only applies where the places of departure and destination are within the territory of the same state and the stopping places are within the territory of another state[11]. Secondly, only one stopping place need be indicated.

5.16   Article 3(1)(b) should be viewed in the light of the decision of the Court of Appeal in *Grein v Imperial Airways Ltd*[12]. Greene LJ and Talbot J held that a return trip amounts to only one carriage for the purposes of the Warsaw Convention. What would usually be thought of as the destination on the outward bound leg of the trip is, according to the Court of Appeal, merely a stopping place on a single journey that has as its destination its original point of departure. The result of this is that the ticket for a return trip from London to Sydney that stops at Singapore en route can quite properly omit any reference at all to Sydney: the places of departure and destination would both be London and a reference to Singapore would satisfy the obligation to indicate one of the 'agreed stopping places'.

5.17   This analysis makes clear that art 3(1) is not designed to ensure that the passenger ticket contains information that the passenger will find useful. Its only purpose is to ensure that the passenger has sufficient information to be aware that the Warsaw-Hague Convention applies to carriage to which the ticket relates.

5.18   It is art 3(1)(c) of the Warsaw-Hague Convention that imposes the obligation for passenger tickets to contain what is commonly known as a Hague Notice. The standard wording of a Hague Notice mirrors the wording of art 3(1)(c):

> 'NOTICE — If the passenger's journey involves an ultimate destination or stop in a country other than the country of departure, the Warsaw

---

[10] There was a specific proviso allowing the carrier to reserve the right to alter the stopping places in case of necessity; such an alteration could not have the effect of depriving the carriage of its international character.

[11] The wording mirrors the provisions of art 1(2) that define the scope of international carriage.

[12] [1937] 1 KB 50. This decision was referred to with approval by Kerr LJ in his dissenting judgment in *Collins v British Airways Board* [1982] QB 734.

Convention may be applicable and the Convention governs and in most cases limits the liability of carriers for death or personal injury and in respect of loss of or damage to baggage. See also notice headed "Advice to International Passengers on Limitation of Liability".[13']

5.19   The policy behind the inclusion of this notice is to ensure that passengers are aware of the limits on the carrier's liability contained in the Warsaw-Hague Convention. Whilst that objective is a laudable one, the way in which the Hague Notice carries it out is remarkably unhelpful to most passengers.

5.20   Firstly, the wording is not only inaccurate in referring to the Warsaw Convention rather than the Warsaw-Hague Convention but also employs language that is wholly unsuited to modern mass transit. It would be straight-forward to explain the existence and effect of the limits to a carrier's liability without using the legalistic language of the Hague Notice and there is no reason why this could not be done. Equally, there is no reason why the Notice should not explain what the limits to the carrier's liability are. Furthermore, the requirements of art 3(1)(c) are very tentative as regards the extent to which the Warsaw-Hague Convention is applicable. The Hague Notice need only state that the 'Warsaw Convention *may* be applicable' (emphasis added). Yet, whenever there is an obligation to include a Hague Notice the Convention must, by definition, apply since it is the Convention that is the very source of that obligation. The language of the Hague Notice can only serve further to confuse passengers in this regard.

5.21   It should also be noted that the French wording of art 3(1)(c) is subtly different from the English translation[14]. The relevant part of the French text states: '. . . leur transport peut être régi par la Convention de Varsovie qui, en général, limite la responsabilité du transporteur en cas de mort ou de lésion corporelle . . .'. Lord Hope commented in *Abnett v British Airways plc*[15] that 'the English version does not follow the French wording precisely — the phrase "peut être régi" is not, as such, reproduced'[16]. This difference, in part, lead to Lord Hope rejecting the significance of art 3(1)(c) in determining whether the Warsaw-Hague Convention should be regarded as the exclusive basis of carriers' liability arising out of international carriage by air.

5.22   The unamended Warsaw Convention required the passenger ticket to contain two further particulars beyond those retained in the Warsaw-Hague Convention. Article 3(1)(a) required that the ticket should state the place and date of its issue and art 3(1)(d) required a statement of the name and address of the carrier or carriers.

---

[13]   This is the standard wording for the Hague Notice as specified by IATA Resolution No 724.
[14]   This is significant because under s 1(2) of the Carriage by Air Act 1961 the French text prevails in the event of any inconsistency between the French and English texts.
[15]   [1997] AC 430.
[16]   At p 445.

The evidential value of the passenger ticket

5.23

Rule 9—The passenger ticket constitutes prima facie evidence of the conclusion and conditions of the contract of carriage under which the passenger travels.

5.24   Article 3(2) of the Warsaw-Hague Convention[17] states that 'The passenger ticket shall constitute prima facie evidence of the conclusion and conditions of the contract of carriage.' This seemingly straightforward provision creates a number of difficulties.

5.25   It is unclear whether the words 'shall constitute prima facie evidence' can be read as requiring the ticket to contain the conditions of the contract of carriage. It makes little sense to regard a ticket that does not contain any reference to the conditions of carriage as being prima facie evidence of those conditions. Nevertheless, interpreting 'shall constitute' as meaning 'shall contain' considerably manipulates the language of the article and would introduce further information that the ticket must contain even though such requirements are wholly absent from art 3(1), which expressly sets out what information the ticket must contain[18].

5.26   Whilst art 3(2) may not extend the range of information that a passenger ticket must contain, it does constitute the information that is contained in the ticket as prima facie evidence of the terms of the contract of carriage. Since it is obligatory to include the information required by art 3(1), it follows that the information listed in art 3(1) prima facie becomes part of the terms of the contract between the carrier and the passenger[19].

5.27   However, it should be stressed that the passenger ticket is only prima facie evidence and there is nothing in the Warsaw-Hague Convention to prevent argument that the passenger ticket does not accurately or fully state the terms of the carrier-passenger contract. Of particular importance in this regard is the well-established rule of English law, applicable to terms and conditions printed on tickets, that a ticket issued after the formation of a contract cannot incorporate into the contract further terms beyond those agreed at the time the contract was made[20]. There does not appear to be any basis for arguing that art 3(2) alters this common law rule. Its effect seems to be limited to

---

[17] The unamended Warsaw Convention does not contain any equivalent provision.
[18] The Court of Appeal in *Collins v British Airways Board* [1982] QB 734 were divided as to the correct interpretation of the equivalent provision in art 4(2) that relates to the baggage check. See below for further consideration of this decision.
[19] Provided, of course, that the obligations imposed by art 3(1) are in fact complied with.
[20] See, by way of example, *Fosbroke-Hobbes v Airwork Ltd* [1937] 1 All ER 108; *McCutcheon v David MacBrayne Ltd.* [1964] 1 WLR 125; *Thornton v Shoe Lane Parking* [1971] 2 QB 163; *The Dragon* [1979] 1 Lloyd's Rep 257.

altering the burden of proof. The burden of proving that a particular term has been incorporated into a contract generally falls on the party seeking to rely on it. Although art 3(2) may not alter the formal incidence of the burden of proof, it certainly does alter the evidential burden so as to require the party arguing that the ticket does not correctly reflect the terms of the contract to produce some evidence rebutting the prima facie presumption created by this rule.

The absence, irregularity or loss of the passenger ticket

5.28

Rule **10**—**The failure of a carrier to comply with the requirements of art 3 does not affect either the existence or validity of the contract of carriage or applicability of the Convention. However, in two situations failure to comply with those requirements will prevent the carrier from limiting its liability to the passenger under art 22 of the Convention:**

(a)   **If, with the consent of the carrier, the passenger embarks without a passenger ticket having been delivered;**

(b)   **If, with the consent of the carrier, the passenger embarks with a ticket having been delivered which does not contain the notice required by art 3(1)(c) of the Convention.**

5.29   Article 3(2) is clear in stating that 'the absence, irregularity or loss of the passenger ticket does not affect the existence or the validity of the contract of carriage which shall, none the less, be subject to the rules of this Convention.' However, there are two circumstances in which a failure to comply with art 3 will affect the carrier's liability: if, with the consent of the carrier, the passenger embarks without a ticket having been delivered or if the ticket does not contain the Hague Notice required by art 3(1)(c) then the carrier will not be entitled to avail itself of the provisions of art 22.

5.30   In *Preston v Hunting Air Transport*[21] it was argued that the delivery of a ticket that did not satisfy the requirements of art 3(1) did not amount to the delivery of a 'ticket' at all, so preventing the carrier from relying on art 22 of the Convention. Ormerod J rejected this argument and held that the fact that the ticket was deficient did not mean that no ticket had been delivered. A mere irregularity is insufficient: the application of art 22 will only be excluded if no ticket at all has been delivered.

5.31   However, failure to deliver a ticket does not in itself expose the carrier to unlimited liability. This consequence will only follow if the passenger embarks without a ticket having been delivered and if the carrier consents to

---

[21]   [1956] 1 QB 454.

this. The Warsaw-Hague Convention does not specify either who may consent on behalf of carrier or what amounts to consent.

Who may consent?

5.32   The usual principles of agency will govern consent given by employees and sub-contractors of a carrier, but the question of who may give the relevant consent will also arise whenever a passenger is carried by a carrier other than the one with which he contracted. This may occur either as a result of code-sharing or during carriage by successive air carriers[22].

5.33   In a code-sharing situation, the actual carrier will be distinct from the contractual carrier and the 1961 Guadalajara Convention[23] will apply to provide a relatively straightforward answer to the problem. Article III(1) of the Guadalajara Convention provides that the acts and omissions of the actual carrier are deemed to be also those of the contracting carrier. Article III(2) provides that the reverse is also generally true save that no act or omission of the contracting carrier can subject the actual carrier to liability exceeding the limits specified in art 22 of the Warsaw-Hague Convention. Accordingly, the contractual carrier cannot provide the consent required so as to cause the actual carrier to be exposed to unlimited liability by virtue of art 3(2).

5.34   The Warsaw-Hague Convention is silent as to the position of successive carriers in this regard, save only that art 30(2) provides that an action can only be brought against the carrier who performed the carriage during which the event giving rise to liability occurred. However, the correct interpretation of art 3(2) must be that the carrier which is prohibited from relying on art 22 can only be the carrier which consents to the passenger embarking without a passenger ticket having been delivered.

5.35   Consideration of the treatment of successive carriage suggests that the relevant embarkation for the purposes of art 3(2) must be the embarkation with a particular carrier[24]. However, if this is correct, it would follow that the embarkation on the second leg of a two legged flight with a single carrier would also be a relevant embarkation (otherwise the definition of 'embarks'

---

[22]   Code-sharing occurs when one carrier sells tickets for a flight in its own name but another carrier in fact undertakes the carriage. Successive carriage arises where a flight has more than one leg with different carriers being responsible for different legs. Article 30 of the Warsaw-Hague Convention makes provision for successive carriage.

[23]   The Guadalajara Convention was given force of law in the UK by the Carriage by Air (Supplementary Provisions) Act 1961.

[24]   If the only relevant embarkation were the very first, it would be extremely rare for any other than the first of several carriers to be exposed to unlimited liability since it is unlikely that the second carrier would be found to have consented to the passenger embarking with the first carrier without a ticket having been delivered. Moreover, if this interpretation were correct the effect of *Grein v Imperial Airways* [1937] 1 KB 50 would be that, if a ticket were provided for the outbound leg of a return journey, there would be no obligation to deliver a ticket for the return leg.

would have to vary according to whether there was one or more than one carrier). If this were so, then a carrier could deliver a ticket to a passenger before the passenger embarked for the second leg of a two-legged flight with the carrier. This would allow the carrier to limit its liability in respect of any loss occurring in the second leg even where there would have been unlimited liability for the same loss on the first leg of the flight.

5.36   Such an interpretation would defeat the policy objective of the Warsaw-Hague Convention by allowing the carrier to limit its liability without providing due notice of those limitations to the passenger so as to allow him to arrange insurance or otherwise take the limits on his recovery into account before the commencement of the carriage. Once a passenger has embarked on the first leg of his flight, there is little option but to continue with the second leg even where doing so would expose the passenger to a potentially irrecoverable loss[25].

5.37   A contrast should be drawn with the wording of the unamended Warsaw Convention. Article 3(2) of that Convention stated that there could be no limitation of liability 'if the carrier accepts a passenger without a passenger ticket having been delivered'. The concept of acceptance of a passenger is perhaps even harder to interpret than the wording of the Warsaw-Hague Convention[26].

What amounts to consent?

5.38   The Warsaw-Hague Convention does not specify what amounts to consent for the purposes of art 3(2)[27]. Express consent is undoubtedly sufficient, but will also be rare. Consideration must, therefore, be centred on implied consent by reason of the carrier's actual or constructive knowledge of the absence of a ticket and on situations where the carrier was negligent in not knowing either that no ticket had been delivered or that the ticket did not contain a Hague Notice.

5.39   Unfortunately, there is no authority that decides the exact meaning of 'consent' in this context. It would be surprising if negligence alone on the part of the carrier were sufficient: not only would the limitations on liability serve little purpose if they did not apply where the carrier was negligent but it

---

[25] Assuming that there is no significant period of time between the various legs; if there is then the opportunity to obtain insurance is somewhat greater although it may still be thought that the passenger is left with little option but to continue with his travel.

[26] In *Manion v Pan American World Airways Inc* 55 NY 2d 398 (Ct of Apps NY) dealing with the unamended Convention, considered the problem of a ticket not being delivered until the second leg of a flight. It held that the ticket should have been delivered before the passenger was accepted for the first leg of the flight and so, even though the omission was rectified, the liability of the carrier was unlimited in relation to a loss occurring on the second leg.

[27] The requirement of consent appears to govern not merely the embarkation of the passenger but also the embarkation without a ticket having been delivered.

would also stretch the concept of 'consent'. Similar arguments apply where the carrier is reckless in allowing the passenger to embark without a ticket, although the arguments are somewhat weaker given the provisions of art 25 that disapply art 22 when the damage was caused by the recklessness of the carrier.

5.40   Where the carrier has actual knowledge that no ticket has been delivered to the passenger, it is easy to imply the relevant consent. However, more difficult again is the situation where the carrier could be said to have constructive knowledge that no ticket has been delivered. It is likely that a Court's view of this situation will depend on the precise facts of the case before it.

Omission of the Hague Notice

5.41   Much of the above consideration of questions relating to the consent of the carrier applies with equal force to the failure to include in the ticket the notice required by art 3(1)(c). However, whilst it is reasonably clear whether a ticket has or has not been delivered to the passenger, further issues can arise as to whether the ticket includes the required notice under art 3(1)(c).

5.42   Whilst the wording for the notice set out above is the wording approved by IATA Resolution, it is not compulsory to adopt that wording in order to comply with the article. The US Court of Appeals in *Seth v BOAC*[28] considered a statement that carriage was 'subject to the rules and limitations relating to liability established by the Convention unless such carriage is not "international carriage" as defined by the Convention'. Whilst this wording is as unfathomable as the IATA approved text, the Court held that it was sufficient to comply with the Convention.

5.43   A second and controversial US decision of relevance on this point is *Lisi v Al italia*[29]. The passenger tickets considered in this case contained the full text of the Hague notice. However, the information was printed in very small type. The majority of the Court of Appeals described the notice as being camouflaged and in 'Lilliputian' print and so failed to give the passenger proper notice of the limitations on the carrier's liability. They reasoned that the passenger had to have sufficient notice of the limits of liability to enable him to take appropriate self-protection measures: if the ticket did not give the required notice then art 3(1)(c) was not satisfied. In a powerful dissenting judgment, Circuit Judge Moore pointed out that the Warsaw-Hague Convention contained no requirement that the passenger be given actual notice of the limitations. It was enough merely that the tickets

---

[28]   [1964] 1 Lloyd's Rep 268.
[29]   [1967] 1 Lloyd's Rep 140; US 2nd Circuit Court of Appeals, affirmed by the Supreme Court at [1968] 1 Lloyd's Rep 505.

contained the prescribed information, which, in this case, they did. He criticised the majority for what he termed 'judicial rewriting of the treaty'. Even within the US, this has proved to be a controversial decision that has not been followed in all jurisdictions. It would be surprising if the English courts were to adopt it.

Article 4 — Baggage Check

5.44

Rule 11—Article 4 of the Warsaw-Hague Convention requires that in respect of the carriage of registered baggage by air, a baggage check shall be delivered containing the following information:

(1) An indication of the places of departure and destination[30];

(2) If the places of departure and destination are within the territory of a single High Contracting Party, and one or more agreed stopping places are within the territory of any other State, an indication of at least one such stopping place[31];

(3) A notice to the effect that, if the passenger's journey involves an ultimate destination or stop in a country other than the country of departure, the Warsaw Convention may be applicable and that the Convention governs and in most cases limits the liability of carriers for death or personal injury and in respect of loss of or damage to baggage[32].

5.45   Article 4 of the Warsaw-Hague Convention, which applies to the carriage of 'registered baggage' is very similar to art 3 and so many of the matters considered in relation to art 3 apply equally to art 4. Since the Warsaw-Hague Convention (unlike the unamended Warsaw Convention) expressly permits the combination of the passenger ticket and baggage check into a single document[33], this similarity between the two articles is unsurprising. However, there are also a number of issues that are relevant only to baggage and which do not apply to passengers. In particular, art 4 was amended to a much greater degree by the introduction of the Warsaw-Hague Convention, especially as regards the terminology used. Even the title of the document has been altered: whereas under the unamended Warsaw Convention the document was called a 'luggage ticket', the Warsaw-Hague Convention employs the title 'baggage check'[34] — a change that has been

---

[30] Article 4(1)(a).
[31] Article 4(1)(b).
[32] Article 4(1)(c).
[33] This is near universal practice.
[34] The French text does not contain any equivalent change: 'Bulletin de baggage' is used in both the unamended Warsaw Convention and the Warsaw-Hague Convention.

attributed to the American influence on the drafting of the Warsaw-Hague Convention[35].

What is baggage?

5.46   Baggage should be contrasted with cargo, for which an air waybill and not a baggage check should be issued. The distinction should in most cases be clear and can often be determined by reference to the intentions of the parties. Baggage is always connected to a particular passenger and will be both delivered to the carrier and collected by that passenger. Cargo need not be the responsibility of any particular passenger and the consignor and consignee of the cargo need not be the same party.

What is 'registered baggage'?

5.47   Registered baggage is not defined anywhere in the Warsaw-Hague Convention. There is no reference to unregistered baggage; instead, the contrast is drawn with 'objects of which the passenger takes charge himself' which is referred to in art 22(3) (although not mentioned elsewhere). Article 4(2) describes the consequences of the carrier taking charge of the baggage without a baggage check having been completed. It seems, therefore, that the relevant distinction is between baggage of which the carrier takes charge (which should therefore be registered) and baggage for which the passenger retains responsibility[36].

5.48   The terms of the unamended Warsaw Convention support this interpretation of the Warsaw-Hague Convention. Article 4 of the unamended Convention does not refer to registered baggage but instead art 4(1) stated:

> 'For the carriage of luggage, other than small personal objects of which the passenger takes charge himself, the carrier must deliver a luggage ticket.'

Article 22(2), however, does refer to registered luggage in equivalent terms to the reference to registered baggage in the Warsaw-Hague Convention. Article 22(3) of the unamended Convention again refers to 'objects of which the passenger takes charge himself'.

5.49   Lord Denning MR considered the meaning of 'registered baggage' in *Collins v British Airways Board*[37] and described the absence of any definition as

---

[35]   See, for example, *Collins v British Airways Board* [1982] QB 734, 749 per Eveleigh LJ.
[36]   Baggage which should be registered but which is not must be 'unregistered baggage'; baggage for which the passenger retains responsibility need not be registered and so is also 'unregistered baggage'. This ambiguity probably explains why the Warsaw-Hague Convention does not use this terminology.
[37]   [1982] QB 734.

an 'amazing omission'. He explained the omission by presuming that the Convention draftsmen must have expected airlines to keep a register (by an entry in a book) of every piece of baggage accepted for carriage. Since this is not done by any airline, Lord Denning concluded that no baggage is ever registered and so the only solution to make sense of the Convention was to strike out the words 'registered' and 'registration' wherever they occur. Kerr LJ, by contrast had rather less difficulty with the concept of registered baggage:

> 'However, I see no difficulty about the meaning of "registered baggage" in the Convention. I think that it has exactly the same meaning as in the ordinary context of registering a letter or parcel for carriage by post or registering articles for carriage by rail, etc. Registration in all these contexts means the delivery of the articles to the carrier for carriage, and his acknowledgement of their acceptance by keeping some written record for himself and the delivery of a corresponding receipt to the consignor, who, in the context of the carriage of passengers, is likely to be the passenger himself.'

5.50   This definition is consistent with usual airline practice as regards registered baggage: an entry is made on the combined passenger ticket and baggage check, the carrier detaches and retains one portion of this and the passenger retains either a ticket stub or a carbon copy of the detached ticket.

Delivery and terms of the baggage check

5.51   As with the passenger ticket, there is a requirement that the baggage check be delivered. The information that the baggage check must contain is set out in art 4(1) and is identical to the information required for a passenger ticket by art 3(1). Article 4(1) provides that, where the baggage check is combined with or incorporated in a passenger ticket which complies with art 3(1), the baggage check need not contain that same information separately from the passenger ticket. The similarity of the terms of arts 3(1) and 4(1) means that the matters considered above in relation to passenger tickets are of equal relevance to baggage checks.

5.52   However, attention should also be drawn to more onerous requirements that were contained in the unamended Warsaw Convention. Article 4(2) of that Convention required that the luggage ticket be made out in duplicate, with one part for the passenger and the other part for the carrier. This requirement of duplication is omitted from the Warsaw-Hague Convention, but it is noteworthy that Kerr LJ's definition of registered baggage quoted above continues to incorporate the idea that the carrier and the passenger should each have their own copy of the carrier's acknowledgement of acceptance of the baggage.

5.53   Article 4(3) of the unamended Warsaw Convention contained a longer list of particulars required in the luggage ticket than is to be found in the

Warsaw-Hague Convention:
(a)   The place and date of issue;
(b)   The place of departure and of destination;
(c)   The name and address of the carrier or carriers;
(d)   The number of the passenger ticket;
(e)   A statement that delivery of the luggage will be made to the bearer of
      the luggage ticket;
(f)   The number and weight of the packages;
(g)   The amount of the value declared in accordance with art 22(2);
(h)   A statement that the carriage is subject to the rules relating to liability
      established by this Convention.

5.54   Article 4(4) provided that the carrier could not rely on the provisions
of the Convention excluding or limiting its liability if the luggage ticket did
not contain the particulars set out at (d), (f)[38] and (h) above. It is slightly surprising that one of the particulars required in order to be able to limit liability
is the requirement that the luggage ticket contain the number of the passenger ticket: art 3 of the unamended Warsaw Convention does not contain any
requirement that the passenger ticket be given a number.

The evidential value of the baggage check

5.55

RULE 12—**The baggage check constitutes prima facie evidence of the
registration of baggage and of the conclusion and conditions of the contract of carriage under which the baggage is carried.**

5.56   Article 4(2) of the Warsaw-Hague Convention contains a provision
very similar to that found in art 3(2) that the baggage check shall constitute
prima facie evidence of the registration of the baggage and of the conditions
of the contract of carriage.

5.57   This provision, in relation to the registration of baggage, was considered by two members of the Court of Appeal in *Collins v British Airways
Board*[39], who came to different conclusions as to its effect. The issue arose in
the context of an argument that a document could not constitute a baggage
check without the number of pieces of baggage and their weight being
marked on it. In support of this argument, reliance was placed on the sentence in art 4(2) under consideration. Eveleigh LJ (who was in the majority
with Lord Denning, although Lord Denning did not consider this point) said

---

[38]   It is not clear whether the omission of only one of the number and weight of the packages was
       sufficient to prevent the carrier from limiting its liability.
[39]   [1982] QB 734.

that he could not regard the words 'shall constitute' as equivalent to 'shall contain'. Kerr LJ, delivering a dissenting judgment, adopted a different analysis. He regarded the provisions of art 4(2) in the Warsaw-Hague Convention concerning the evidential value of the baggage check as replacing the fuller list of particulars found in art 4(3) of the unamended Convention. The result of this is that the baggage check must, according to Kerr LJ, contain something which is capable of providing prima facie evidence of the receipt by the carrier of the registered baggage. Without any entry, there would be no evidence of the receipt of the baggage and Kerr LJ did not think that this was the intention behind this article.

5.58   The difficulty with Kerr LJ's argument is that, whilst there may be some justification for interpreting this sentence in art 4(2) as requiring the baggage check to contain evidence of receipt of the baggage, such an interpretation would logically also require the baggage check and passenger ticket to contain a statement of the conditions of the contract of carriage. As considered above in relation to art 3(2), it is thought that such a reading of art 4(2) stretches its meaning too far.

The absence, irregularity or loss of the baggage check

5.59

RULE 13—The failure of a carrier to comply with the requirements of article 4 does not affect either the existence or validity of the contract of carriage or applicability of the Convention. However, in two situations failure to comply with those requirements will prevent the carrier from limiting its liability in respect of the baggage under article 22 of the Convention:

(a)   If, with the consent of the carrier, the carrier takes charge of the baggage without a baggage check having been delivered;

(b)   If, with the consent of the carrier, the carrier takes charge of the baggage with a ticket having been delivered which does not contain the notice required by article 4(1)(c) of the Convention.

5.60   As with the equivalent provisions relating to passenger tickets, art 4(2) states that the absence, irregularity or loss of the baggage check does not affect the existence or the validity of the contract of carriage which remains subject to the rules of the Warsaw-Hague Convention. The argument was raised in *Collins v British Airways Board* (above) that a failure by the carrier to enter the number of pieces of baggage and their weight in the appropriate boxes on the baggage check meant that no 'baggage check' had been delivered at all. However, both Lord Denning MR and Eveleigh LJ held that such an omission amounted only to an 'irregularity' in the baggage check and so no consequences flowed from the omission. Eveleigh LJ pointed out that the baggage check and passenger ticket were generally incorporated into a single document: yet if the baggage check were not delivered until the number of pieces of baggage were entered on to it, the result would be the same document being delivered at two different times according to its different functions[40]. Such a result would defy common sense.

5.61   Eveleigh LJ's conclusion is also consistent with the policy underlying the requirement for the delivery of both passenger tickets and baggage checks. Their purpose is not to provide the passenger with any particular information or evidence of the receipt of baggage but, instead, to give the passenger notice of the limitations on the carrier's liability imposed by the Warsaw-Hague Convention. This objective is satisfied whether or not the baggage check has an entry on it stating the number of pieces of baggage received. Had such an entry been deemed important the provisions of the unamended Warsaw Convention would surely have been retained following the Hague amendments.

5.62   It should be noted that the time by which a baggage check must be delivered is the time at which the carrier takes charge of the baggage. Failure to deliver a baggage check or the omission of the Hague Notice from that document deprives the carrier of the protection of art 22(2), which limits its liability in relation to loss or damage caused to registered baggage.

Objects of which the passenger takes charge himself

5.63   The Warsaw-Hague Convention does not impose any requirements in respect of baggage for which the passenger retains control. However, art 22(3) does limit the carrier's liability for loss of or damage to such baggage.

The Guatemala Protocol 1971

5.64   The Guatemala Protocol is not yet in force but if and when it does take effect it will radically alter the requirements for passenger tickets and baggage checks as currently contained in the Warsaw-Hague Convention. The Guatemala Protocol will take effect when 30 states have ratified it[41], provided that the airlines of five of those states represent at least 40% of the scheduled international air traffic for the relevant year. The Carriage by Air and Road Act 1979 allows the UK to give effect to the Guatemala Protocol, although the Act is not yet in force.

5.65   The changes that the Guatemala Protocol will bring about to the rules on passenger tickets can be summarised as follows:
(1)   A passenger ticket may be 'an individual or collective document of carriage' so allowing for groups to be accommodated on one joint ticket.
(2)   The requirement for the ticket to contain a Hague Notice as provided by art 3(1)(c) of the Warsaw-Hague Convention is removed entirely.

---

[40] Since there is no reason to regard the passenger ticket as being 'delivered' any later than the time at which it is in fact received.
[41] Currently, only 11 states have ratified the Protocol.

(3)   The delivery of a passenger ticket may be replaced with 'any other means which would preserve a record of the information' now required under arts 3(1)(a) and (b) of the Warsaw-Hague Convention.

(4)   The provision constituting the passenger ticket as prima facie evidence of the conclusion and conditions of the contract of carriage is removed.

(5)   Failure to comply with the requirements for a passenger ticket does not have any impact on the right of the carrier to limit its liability according to the Convention rules.

5.66   There are equivalent changes to the provisions of article 4 relating to baggage checks.

5.67   These amendments represent a radical departure from the previous policy objective of ensuring that the Convention limitations on the carrier's liability were brought to the attention of the passenger. Under the Guatemala Protocol, there is no attempt to ensure that the passenger is aware of the limits imposed on his recovery and there are no circumstances in which those limits can cease to apply because of the carrier's failure to issue the correct passenger documentation. Instead, the principle of the absolute liability of the carrier is adopted, subject only to a defence of contributory negligence. The Guatemala Protocol also increases the limits on the carrier's liability. Since notice given to the passenger under the Warsaw-Hague Convention is not particularly effective in ensuring that the passenger is aware of the full impact of the Convention, the amendments of the Guatemala Protocol seem likely to place the passenger in a more favourable position than applies under the Warsaw-Hague Convention.

Chapter 6

The Air Waybill

6.1

RULE 14—The air waybill identifies the cargo to be carried and the terms of the contract of carriage between the carrier and consignor. The formal requirements of the air waybill, and penalties for failure to comply with these requirements, differ according to the Warsaw Regime in place. In particular:

(a) Under the unamended Warsaw Convention, there are a considerable number of formal requirements. Failure to comply with these denies the carrier the opportunity to rely on any defences or limitations of liability otherwise available under the Convention;

(b) Under the Warsaw Convention as amended at the Hague 1995, the formal requirements are less and the penalty for failure to comply is restricted to denial to the carrier of the limitation of liability;

(c) Under the Montreal Protocol (No 4) 1975 and the 1999 Montreal Convention, failure to comply with any formal requirements does not restrict the defences of limitation on liability otherwise available.

Introduction

6.2   The air waybill, as its name applies, is a document which is used in connection with carriage by air, and it is concerned with cargo. Its essential function is to identify the cargo to be carried and to evidence the terms of carriage. Responsibility for its preparation and, subject to the qualifications considered below, responsibility for the accuracy of the statements made in it concerning the cargo rest with the consignor, and not the carrier. In the unamended Warsaw Convention[1] it was referred to simply as an 'air consignment

---

[1]   Although often referred to as 'the Un-amended Warsaw Convention', the version of the treaty to which English law now gives effect is that contained in Sch 2 to the Carriage by Air Act (Application of Provisions) Order 1964, SI 1967/480; this is an amended version of Sch 1 to the Carriage by Air Act 1961, which in turn sets out the English text of the Warsaw Convention as amended at the Hague; the version in Sch 2 refers to 'Airway Bills', but the original Warsaw Convention referred to 'air consignment notes'.

note'. It may be contrasted with a cargo receipt[2], which evidences the receipt of cargo by the carrier and it is the carrier who is responsible for its preparation and contents. The air waybill is not infrequently compared to the maritime cargo carriage document, the Bill of Lading, but the latter is materially different and analogies with it are liable to be misleading.

6.3   The air waybill typically is in printed form, consisting of three top copies (and perhaps a dozen others). It is usually provided by the carrier, who incorporates into the form its standard contract terms and conditions. It is often filled in by the carrier. In doing this, the carrier is to be assumed to be acting as the consignor's agent, and so the carrier's activity does not alter the basic scheme of responsibility for the preparation and contents of the air waybill, which remains with the consignor. The carrier provides the consignor with an original copy of the air waybill signed by the carrier. A top copy signed by both of them accompanies the cargo, and the carrier retains a third top copy signed by the consignor.

6.4   There is no established custom and practice that has been recognised in any English Court by which the transfer of an air waybill is treated as passing to its new holder constructive possession of the cargo to which it relates. It is probably not negotiable, though the Warsaw Convention as amended at the Hague makes it clear that, should it otherwise arise, the provisions of that Convention do not prevent negotiability. In practice air waybills simply name consignees, and do not refer to 'assigns' nor are they made out 'to order' or 'to bearer'. Indeed they may even be marked 'non negotiable'. Nevertheless an air waybill may constitute a 'document of title' for the purposes of the Sale of Goods Act 1979.

6.5   The air waybill (or air consignment note) has a defined role within the Warsaw regime, though successive amendments to that regime have reduced its importance progressively to the point where now, provided the consignor agrees, an air waybill may be dispensed with altogether in favour of an alternative record of the consignment made by the carrier. The position of the air waybill needs to be considered under four versions of the Warsaw Regime:
(1)   the unamended Warsaw Convention 1929 ('Warsaw Convention')[3];
(2)   the Warsaw Convention as amended at the Hague 1955 ('Warsaw-Hague Amendment'); and
(3)   the Montreal Protocol (No 4) 1975 ('Montreal Protocol (No 4)')[4];
(4)   the 1999 Montreal Convention[5];

---

[2]   MP art 10(3); the consignor is however obliged to indemnify the carrier in respect of its liability to any other person as a result of the irregularity or incorrectness in the information concerning the cargo which the consignor supplied to the carrier for insertion into the cargo receipt, see art 10.

[3]   The contracting parties to the Warsaw Convention and to the Warsaw-Hague Amendment are usefully listed in a table in *Shawcross* (4th edn) at A16.

[4]   This is contained in Sch 1 to the Carriage by Air and Road Act 1979. It came into effect as of 14 June 1998. The contracting parties to the Montreal Protocol (No 4) are listed in *Shawcross* at A29.

[5]   Which was enacted into English law with effect of 21 May 1999, art 1(2) Carriage by Air Acts (Implementation of Protocol No 4 of Montreal, 1975) Order 1999.

6.6   Both the Warsaw Convention and the Warsaw-Hague Amendment require the issue and use of an air waybill, which has to carry a Notice concerning the applicability of the Warsaw regime ('Warsaw regime notice'). The Warsaw Convention contains many detailed stipulations as to the information to be given in the air waybill, and failure to provide that information or to set out the Warsaw regime notice, or failure, with the carrier's consent, to make out an air waybill has the draconian and surprising consequence that the carrier is deprived of the defences and limitations of liability otherwise available to it under the Warsaw Convention. The Warsaw Hague Amendment simplifies the amount of information to be given in the air waybill. The carrier is deprived of its right to limit liability if no air waybill is made out or if the notice is not given, but its defences are unaffected by these matters. The Montreal Protocol provides that the consignor and carrier may agree to dispense with an air waybill provided the carrier maintains an adequate record of the consignment and allows the consignor access to it. In these circumstances the consignor can require the carrier to produce a cargo receipt. Even if such alternative means do not exist or are not provided the failure to make out or use an air waybill or to put on it a Warsaw regime notice no longer deprives the carrier of its right to limit liability. The same is true under the 1999 Montreal Convention.

Creation and Form

6.7   The air waybill is a document. This is its customary form, and it would appear to be required both by its function as a permanent record of the cargo consigned for carriage and of the terms of carriage and also by the stipulation under the Warsaw regimes that it be signed[6]. Those Conventions require that the air waybill be made out in three original parts[7], the first part is to be marked 'for the carrier' and be signed by the consignor (and handed to the carrier who retains it), the second part (which is to accompany the cargo) should be marked 'for the consignee' and signed by the consignor and the carrier, and third part (which is to be handed to the consignor after acceptance of the cargo) is to be signed by the carrier[8]. The signature of the consignor may be printed or stamped, but both the Warsaw Convention and Warsaw Hague Amendment require the signature of the carrier to be stamped, whereas under the Montreal Protocol and the Montreal Convention it may be printed or stamped[9] like that of the consignor.

6.8   If an air waybill has not been 'made out' before the time the carrier accepts the cargo, then under the Warsaw Convention the carrier loses its

---

6   Article 5(2).
7   Article 6(1) of each of Warsaw Convention, Warsaw Hague Amendment and Montreal Protocol No 4 and art 7(1) of Montreal Convention 1999.
8   Article 6(2) of each of Warsaw Convention, Warsaw Hague Amendment and Montreal Protocol No 4 and art 7(2) of Montreal Convention 1999.
9   Warsaw Convention art 6(4): Warsaw Hague Amendment art 6(4): Montreal Protocol No 4 art 6(3); Montreal Convention 1999 art 7(3).

ability to rely on the defences and limitation of liability provided by that Convention[10]. On acceptance of the cargo the carrier is also required to sign the air waybill[11]. It follows that an air waybill can be 'made out' without it being signed by the carrier. The requirement for such early completion and signature of the air waybill could in practice create difficulties, eg suppose a package is delivered to the carrier out of office hours one evening for carriage the following afternoon. Does the carrier, who is to make out the air waybill on the consignor's behalf, lose its protection under the Convention by arranging to receive such cargo? The outcome should not depend on judicial interpretation from case to case of what constitutes 'acceptance' of cargo. The position was improved by the Warsaw Hague Amendment so that the moment by which the air waybill had to be made out[12] and the carrier's signature stamped on it[13] was deferred to immediately before loading the cargo on board the aircraft. The Montreal Protocol and the Montreal Convention do not stipulate any time by which the air waybill is to be delivered[14] or to be made out[15], and failure to make out an air waybill does not affect the application of the rules of the Convention including those as to limitation of liability.

6.9   In practice air waybills are prepared in sets of standard form preprinted copy documents. Each set of documents consists of a series of original or top copies, and various further copies. Each copy document is a single page. Its front consists of various boxes to be completed by inserting information about the consignment to which the air waybill relates, and on its reverse side are printed conditions of carriage.

6.10   Generally forms are provided by the carrier and so include its standard contract conditions of carriage. The forms are provided usually either to shipping agents or freight forwarders or are filled out by the carrier itself. Although art 6(1) of all four[16] versions of the Warsaw regime require the consignor to make out the air waybill, and in the case of Warsaw Convention and Warsaw Hague Amendment, they also require the air waybill to be handed over with the cargo, art 6(5) of Warsaw Convention and Warsaw Hague Amendment, art 6(4) of Montreal Protocol No 4 and art 7(4) of the Montreal Convention 1999 permit the carrier, at the consignor's request, to make out the air waybill. If this is done the consequence under all four versions of the Conventions is that, subject to proof to the contrary, the carrier is deemed to be acting on behalf of the consignor.

---

[10]   Article 9.
[11]   Article 6(3).
[12]   Article 9.
[13]   Article 6(3).
[14]   Article 5(1) is silent on this point. The reference to the air waybill being handed over with the goods which is set out in the corresponding article in the two earlier versions of the Convention has been omitted.
[15]   The provision in art 6(3) of the two earlier versions of the Convention has been omitted.
[16]   Article 7(1) of the Montreal Convention 1999.

6.11   The carrier is entitled to require the consignor to make out and hand over to it a separate Airway Bill for each package[17]. The Montreal Protocol No 4 and Montreal Convention 1999 provide the consignor with an equivalent right to separate cargo receipts when other means than air waybills are being used[18]. Separate air waybills are likely to be required when the packages contain different types of goods, or separate values are being declared for individual packages or the packages are to be taken to different destinations. The consignor has the right to require the carrier to accept each air waybill which the consignor is obliged to provide[19]. The carrier presumably signifies his acceptance of the document by signing it. In principle it would seem right that the carrier may both accept and amend the air waybill, otherwise it would be unable to correct manifest errors in the air waybill concerning the cargo and it could not set out any variations it may require to the terms of carriage.

Nature

6.12   Although an air waybill may frequently constitute or incorporate the contract made between the consignor and carrier, it need not necessarily do so; it will however constitute evidence as to the terms of that contract. By contrast the issue and signing of an air waybill will not by itself ordinarily constitute or evidence any contract between the carrier and the consignee. The terms of an air waybill are unlikely to be apt to achieve that result. However on arrival of the cargo at its destination, and unless the consignor has exercise his right of stoppage, all variants of the Warsaw regime give the consignee the right to require the carrier to deliver the cargo to him on payment of the charges due and on the consignee complying with the conditions of carriage[20]. In the latter circumstances, under the Warsaw Convention and Warsaw Hague Amendment but not the Montreal Protocol or Montreal Convention 1999, the consignee has the additional right that it may require the carrier to hand over to it the copy of the air waybill accompanying the cargo. Furthermore[21] if the carrier admits the loss of the cargo, or if the cargo has not arrived on the expiration of seven days after the date on which it ought to have arrived, the consignee is entitled to enforce against the carrier the rights which flow from the contract of carriage[22].

6.13   Quite apart from the consignee's Convention rights against the carrier, it may be that by its acts of discharging any sums due in respect of the cargo or by carrying out other acts specified in the terms of carriage contained

---

[17]   Article 13(1).
[18]   Article 13(1) of the MP and art 8 of the MC.
[19]   Article 13(3).
[20]   Article 13(1).
[21]   Article 13(1).
[22]   Article 13(3).

in the air waybill a contract comes into existence between the carrier and the consignee on the terms of the air waybill[23].

Contents

6.14   The Montreal Convention 1999 and the Montreal Protocol 1975 both make sweeping changes to the formal rules for the contents of an air waybill by considerably simplifying the requirements. The Convention also does away with the draconian penalties for breach of these formal rules. The details of these changes are set out below (para **000**) after an examination of the rules as they stand under the unamended Convention.

6.15   Article 8 of the Warsaw Convention provides a lengthy list of particulars to be contained in an Airway Bill:
(a)   the place and date of its execution;
(b)   the place of departure and of destination;
(c)   the agreed stopping places, provided that the carrier may reserve the right to alter the stopping places in case of necessity, and that if he exercises that right the alteration shall not have the effect of depriving the carriage of its international character;
(d)   the name and address of the consignor;
(e)   the name and address of the first carrier;
(f)   the name and address of the consignee, if the case so requires;
(g)   the nature of the cargo;
(h)   the number of the packages, the method of packing and the particular marks or numbers upon them;
(i)   the weight, the quantity and the volume or dimensions of the cargo;
(j)   the apparent condition of the cargo and of the packing;
(k)   the freight, if it has been agreed upon, the date and place of payment, and the person who is to pay it;
(l)   if the cargo is sent for payment on delivery, the price of the cargo, and, if the case so requires, the amount of the expenses incurred;
(m)   the amount of the value declared in accordance with art 22(2);
(n)   the number of parts of the air waybill;
(o)   the documents handed to the carrier to accompany the air waybill;
(p)   the time fixed for the completion of the carriage and a brief note of the route to be followed, if these matters have been agreed upon;
(q)   a statement that the carriage is subject to the rules relating to liability established by the Warsaw Convention.

6.16   Article 9 goes on to provide that if the Airway Bill does not contain all the particulars set out in subparas (a)–(i), inclusive, and (j) then the carrier is

---

[23] See *Brandt v Liverpool*, where payment of freight due under a Bill of Lading was made by the receiver of the cargo, as it was held that such payment was sufficient to give rise to a contract between the carrier and the receiver which incorporated the terms of the Bill of Lading contract.

not entitled to avail itself of the defences and limitations of liability that the Convention provides. This has been described as a 'remarkable provision'[24]. Not only is there little rational justification for attaching the art 9 sanction to omissions from the air waybill of many of the required particulars, but given the scheme of the Convention, to place responsibility for preparation of the air waybill on the consignor, rather than the carrier, it is an illogical provision. In the main these provisions have received hostile judicial interpretation. In *Corocraft Ltd v Pan American Airways Inc* the Court of Appeal found the requirements of art 8(i) (namely, 'the weight, the quality and the volume or dimensions of the cargo') to be satisfied by an air waybill which gave only the weight of the cargo. The Court reached this conclusion by basing itself in part on the French text of the Convention in preference to the English text, and in part by construing the text 'to make good commercial sense', which the Court found obviated the need to give details in the air waybill of volume or dimensions of the cargo when its weight had been given, unless it was useful or necessary to do so[25].

6.17   It may well be that this purposive approach is to be limited to the construction of art 8(h) and (i), where there is some (albeit limited) scope for questioning the full extent of those requirements. When there can be no such doubt the Convention must be applied strictly according to its plain terms. Article 8(q), which requires the air waybill to contain a statement that the carriage is subject to the Convention, has been held not to be satisfied by an air waybill, which when applying the carrier's conditions of carriage explained that they 'were based upon' the Warsaw Convention[26]. However subsequent authority in the US Court of Appeals has taken a more liberal approach by holding that a statement on a baggage ticket did provide sufficient notice when it said: 'Carriage hereunder is subject to [the Convention] unless such carriage is not international carriage as defined by the Convention.' The latter approach is to be preferred, and it should be sufficient to comply with art 8(q) that the air waybill states that if the carriage to which it relates is international carriage then the rules applicable are those contained in the Convention.

---

[24] *Corocraft Ltd v Pan American Airways Inc* [1969] 1 QB 616, per Lord Dening MR at p 649 D-E. After reciting art 9 he said: 'That is a remarkable provision. I cannot understand how it got into the Convention. It appears to mean this: suppose the sender, when he makes out the consignment note, omits some particular or other: and the carrier does not notice the omission or does not insist on it being filled in. That omission means that the carrier is under an unlimited liability — the liability of an insurer of goods — without receiving any premium for it.'

[25] A similar approach was adopted in the US in relation to requirement (h) (namely, number of packages, method of packaging, and the particular marks or numbers); there the requirement has been held to be satisfied by a statement only of the number of packages, and the omission of all the other information was regarded as merely 'technical and insubstantial' and that it 'did not prejudice the shipper and was of little commercial significance' with the result that the Court disregarded it, see *Exim Industries Inc v Pan American World Airways Inc* 754 F 2d 106 (1985).

[26] *Westminster Bank v Imperial Airways Ltd* [1936] 2 All ER 890; at p 896 Lucas J said 'In my opinion a statement that the carriage is subject to certain general conditions of carriage of goods, which general conditions are based on the Convention is not a statement that the carriage is subject to the rules relating to liability established by the Convention.', and see *Seth v B.O.A.C.* [1964] 1 Lloyd's Rep 268.

6.18   Some ways of note in which the US Courts have sought to minimise the effect of arts 8 and 9 of the Warsaw Convention have been:

(1)   to find the required particulars to be supplied by information wherever or however it is set out in the air waybill[27] this approach is justifiable in principle, though its application on occasions can be contrived;

(2)   to apply art 9 only to failures to provide particulars when the failure could be regarded as causative of the loss claimed[28] this approach appears unfounded as it involves placing an unjustified gloss on the wording of the Convention;

(3)   holding that a material distinction exists between the failure to provide the required particulars and the provision of incorrect information; while the distinction may appear somewhat artificial, it is justifiable on the basis of a literal interpretation of the language of the Convention; and as a matter of practicality, an immaterial misstatement of the weight of a package should not bring art 9 into operation.

6.19   The position is much simpler under the Warsaw Hague Amendment, Montreal Protocol No 4 and Montreal Convention 1999. The only required particulars under Warsaw Hague Amendment are:

(a)   the places of departure and destination;

(b)   if the places of departure and destination are within the territory of a single High Contracting Party one or more agreed stopping plans being within the territory of another state, an indication of at least one such stopping place;

(c)   a notice to the consignor to the effect that, if the carriage involves an ultimate destination or stop in a country other than the country of departure, the Warsaw Convention may be applicable and that the Convention governs and in most cases limits the liability of the carrier in respect of loss of or damage to the cargo[29].

The omission from the air waybill of particulars (a) and (b) does not affect in

---

[27]   Eg identifying letters used on an air waybill (RDU) have been had to be sufficient to satisfy requirement (b) as to the place of departure (Raleigh Durham International Airport), see *Royal Insurance Co of America v Air Express International* 906 F Supp 218 (1995); more remarkably requirement (a) (place of execution) of the AWB has been held satisfied by a statement of the name and address of the carrier when this happened to coincide with the place of execution of the air waybill, see *Martin Marietta Corp v Harpers Group* 950 F Supp 1250 (1997); requirement (c) (agreed stopping places) has been held satisfied by a statement in the box for agreed stopping places: 'see lists of scheduled stopping places in the timetable of the carriers concerned, which lists . . . are parts hereof' see *Kraus v KLM* 92 NYS 2nd 315 (NYS 1949), approved in *Brink's v South African Airways* 93 F 3rd 1022 (1996).

[28]   *American Smelting and Refining Co v Philippine Airlines Inc of Manifa* 1 2nd 866 (NY 1956) (omission of stopping places did not matter since it was already clear from the statement of the departure and destination airports that the carriage was international); *Flying Tiger Line Inc v US* 170 F Supp 422 (1959).

[29]   Article 8.

any way the application of the Convention. However under Warsaw Hague Amendment if particular (c) is omitted, the carrier loses its right to limit liability[30].

6.20   In the case of the Montreal Protocol No 4 and Montreal Convention 1999, required particulars (a) and (b) remain, however particular (c) need no longer be given. There remains a requirement to indicate the weight of the cargo[31]. Omission of these particulars from the air waybill does not affect the application of the Convention or the carrier's right under it to limit liability[32].

Responsibility for the accuracy of the contents; evidential status of the contents

6.21

RULE 15—The consignor is responsible for the accuracy of the contents of the Air Waybill and is liable to any person for any loss or damage caused by its irregularity, incorrectness or incompleteness. This usually remains so even if the Air Waybill is prepared by the carrier.

6.22   The consignor is responsible for the correctness of the particulars and statements relating to the cargo which it inserts in the air waybill, and the consignor is liable for all damage suffered by the carrier or any other person by reason of the irregularity, incorrectness or incompleteness of the particulars and statements so made. Ordinarily the consignor will continue to be responsible for this information, even though the carrier prepares the air waybill, since he will be deemed, subject to proof to the contrary, to have acted at the latter's request[33]. The Conventions are silent as responsibility in the case where the carrier misstates in the air waybill information which has been given to him correctly by the consignor. Although in general this should not affect the position of the consignor vis-á-vis third parties, it ought to affect that between the carrier and the consignor. These circumstances would place the carrier in breach of his implied obligation to the consignor to carry out the latter's instructions and/or to act diligently and competently. Accordingly, the carrier should indemnify the consignor. This is

---

[30] Article 9.
[31] Article 8 of the Montreal Protocol No 4 and art 5 of the Montreal Convention 1999.
[32] Article 9.
[33] Article 6, and see also art 10; under Montreal Protocol No 4 and Montreal Convention 1999 where other means than an air waybill are used to identify the consignment and the terms of carriage, the consignor remains responsible for the information concerning the cargo which it gives to the carrier to use in the alternative record or in the cargo receipt, see Montreal Protocol No 4 and Montreal Convention 1999 art 10(1).

consistent with the position adopted in the MP, which holds the carrier responsible to indemnify the consignor, if, after being given accurate details by the consignor[34], the carrier incorrectly fills out the cargo receipt or the other means of recording the consignment.

6.23   The Airway Bill, or where it is used a receipt for the cargo, is prima facie evidence of the conclusion (ie making) of the contract of carriage, of the acceptance of the cargo by the carrier and of the conditions of carriage set out in that document[35].

6.24   Any statements in the Airway Bill, or cargo receipt, relating to the weight, dimensions and packaging of the cargo and to the number of packages are prima facie evidence of the facts stated. Statements relating to the quantity[36], volume or condition of the cargo do not constitute evidence against the carrier except so far as they have been, and are stated in the Airway Bill to have been, checked by the carrier in the presence of the consignor, or are statements which relate to the apparent condition of the cargo[37].

6.25   These provisions as to the evidential standing of the statements made in the Airway Bill have remained unchanged through the different versions of the Convention. Broadly, the statements that may be relied upon against the carrier are those which the carrier is likely to have checked (eg the weight and packing) or which will be apparent to it as being matters which concern the apparent condition of the cargo or they are matters which the carrier has made clear on the air waybill it has checked. The requirement in the latter instance that such checking needed to have been carried out in the consignor's presence is not obviously justifiable, unless those statements are to constitute evidence against the consignor as well as the carrier this however is not what the Article says and does not appear to be its effect.

Irregularity, inaccuracy or incompleteness of contents

6.26   Irregularity in or the inaccuracy or incompleteness of any statements made in an air waybill do not render the contract of carriage null and void, nor do they affect the application of any of the provisions of the Convention except in the case of the omission of any of the prescribed information or notices, as discussed above in paras **6.14–6.20**, inclusive[38].

---

[34]   Article 10(3).
[35]   Article 11(1).
[36]   As volume is purely a function of dimensions the reconciliation between statements as to dimensions, which are pf evidence, and those as to the volume of the cargo, which are not, is presumably that dimensions refers to the packaging and not to the cargo which it contains.
[37]   Article 11(2).
[38]   Article 9.

Negotiability; Document of Title

6.27

RULE 16—**As a matter of English law, air waybills are not negotiable, in the absence of a clear and well-defined custom to the contrary. However, the better view is that they are to be regarded as 'documents of title' within the meaning of the Sale of Goods Act 1979.**

6.28   In this context[39] negotiability means the ability to transfer constructive possession of the cargo by transferring the air waybill by well-established custom over centuries subsequently embodied in legislation[40]. Bills of Lading[41] possess this characteristic, which enables the owner of goods to deal with them and pass title to others during what may be lengthy marine voyages. Indorsement of a Bill of Lading and its delivery to the person named on it as the indorsee passes to that person the right to possession of goods, and title to them, if that is the parties' intention. No such custom appears to exist in the case of air waybills, and certainly none has been established in any case before the Courts. In the absence of an established, clear and well-defined custom treating air waybills as negotiable, in the sense discussed above, it is clear that under English law air waybills are not negotiable.

6.29   The provisions of art 15(3) in Warsaw Hague Amendment do not alter this position. This Article provides 'Nothing in this Convention prevents the issue of a negotiable air waybill'. The purpose of this Article, which does appear in either the Warsaw Convention or Montreal Protocol No 4 or Montreal Convention 1999, appears to be to counter any suggestion that the extensive rights of stoppage granted to the consignor by art 12 involve a reservation of interest in the cargo by the consignor which is necessarily inconsistent with an intention that the air waybill be negotiable. It is doubtful

---

[39]   A negotiable instrument in the true sense is one that is transferable by delivery and confers on its holder the right of action it comprises. Typically (perhaps necessarily) such instruments involve contracts to pay money or transfer other security. The consequence of negotiability in this sense is that the instrument can 'pass property' by mere delivery to a bona fide transferee for valuable consideration, without regard to the title of the parties who made the 'transfer' see Lord Campbell CJ in *Gurney v Behrend* (1854) 3 E & B at 633. Whatever else it is an air waybill is not an instrument of this type.

[40]   Bills of Lading Act 1855, s 1, and now Carriage of Goods by Sea Act 1992.

[41]   A Bill of Lading is a document issued by the Master of the vessel onto which goods have been loaded, which evidences their shipment, and it sets out the terms of carriage. A Bill of Lading is typically made out 'to x or assigns' or 'to order'. The Master acts on behalf of the carrier who is responsible for the accuracy of the information which is given in the Bill of Lading concerning the goods and their apparent condition. This latter feature is shared by cargo receipts, but not by air waybill. Furthermore endorsement of a Bill of Lading has the effect of making the endorser a party to the contract with the carrier on the terms of carriage set out in the Bill of Lading. For a full treatment of the subject of Bills of Lading see Carrier Carriage of Goods by Sea.

whether there is such an inconsistency[42]. Even if this were to be the case, art 15(2) acknowledges in terms that art 12 may be varied by the express provisions of the air waybill. It should be noted that art 15(3) is deliberately framed in terms which do not confer negotiability on air waybills which otherwise would not be negotiable. Accordingly, whether or not an air waybill has that characteristic is a matter for the general law, and it is not determined by the provisions of the Convention.

6.30   As a matter of practice air waybills are made out simply in favour of a named consignee, and not 'to x and assigns' or 'to order'. Nor is it necessary for the consignee to produce the air waybill in order to obtain delivery of the cargo. The consignee's original part of the air waybill has travelled with the cargo, and so it is not a document which is available to the consignee during the course of carriage for the purposes of negotiation or dealing with the cargo.

6.31   Nevertheless air waybills are probably documents of title for the purposes of the Sale of Goods Act 1979. The question is whether they satisfy the test provided by s 1(4) of the Factors Act 1889, namely whether they fall within the category of 'any other document used in the ordinary course of business as proof of the possession or control of goods, or authorising or purporting to authorise, either by indorsement or by delivery, the possessor of the document to receive the goods thereby represented.'

6.32   As already stated the consignee does not need to produce the air waybill to obtain delivery of the cargo, nor does there appear to be any established custom or practice of endorsing air waybills. Accordingly an air waybill does not fall within the second part of the definition given in the preceding paragraph, namely a document which by indorsement or delivery authorises its possessor to receive goods. However it is likely that it is a document which is used in the ordinary course of business as proof of the possession or control of the goods. Perhaps the main example of such use is indicated by art 12(3), which renders the carrier liable to a third party who is lawfully in possession of the consignor's original part of the air waybill for any damage caused to that party through the carrier complying with the consignor's instructions as to disposition of the cargo without having required production of the consignor's part of the air waybill. This article acknowledges both that during the course of the carriage of the cargo the consignor may have passed the right of property in or of possession of the cargo to a third party by using the air waybill, and also it effectively forces the carrier, before it acts on the consignor's instructions concerning disposal of the cargo,

---

[42] Reservation by the consignor of rights of stoppage are not necessarily inconsistent with the passing of property or even the right to possession of goods, provided that the right of stoppage may only be exercised in restricted circumstances. In any event art 15(1) states that arts 12, 13 and 14 do not effect relations between the consignor and consignee or parties deriving their title through them. Those articles concern their relations with the carrier, and the extent to which the carrier is bound by their instructions.

to insist on the consignor producing the air waybill as proof of its continuing interest in the cargo. In each of these respects the air waybill is used as proof of the right to possess or control goods, so bringing it within the statutory definition of a 'document of title'.

6.33   The principal consequences of an air waybill becoming a document of title within the meaning of the Sale of Goods Act 1979 are that ss 23 and 24 of that Act may apply to override the general principle of English law *nemo dat quod habet* with the consequence that good title to the cargo may pass to a third party who purchases it from a seller or buyer in possession of the air waybill notwithstanding that they may not good title to the cargo.

The conditions of carriage contained in the air waybill

6.34

RULE 17—**The restrictions on the terms of an air waybill are relatively minor. It cannot contain any terms which seek to relieve the carrier of liability or to fix a lower limit than otherwise provided for under the Convention. The Unfair Contract Terms Act 1977 probably does not apply, but the Unfair Terms in Consumer Contract Regulations 1994 probably do.**

6.35   The Warsaw regime does not provide any code for standard terms for air waybills, though it does stipulate the nature and extent of liability on the carrier's part for loss of or damage to the cargo or for delay during carriage, and the Warsaw Convention and Warsaw Hague Amendment do provide minimum information requirements for the air waybill. Moreover any term in an air waybill which purports to relieve the carrier of liability or to fix a lower limit than that laid down by the relevant version of the Warsaw regime is null and void, but this does not invalid the whole contract, which remains subject to the Warsaw regime[43]. The air waybill may however contain terms defining the nature, extent and limit of the carrier's liability, if it has any, for loss of or damage to the cargo which result from inherent defect, quality or vice of the cargo[44].

6.36   There are therefore many different terms in the contract of carriages to be set out in the air waybill, which are terms left by the Warsaw regime for the consignor and carrier to settle between themselves. As already noted usually the air waybill is issued using a pre-printed form provided by the carrier, which therefore is likely to embody the carrier's standard terms and

---

[43]   Article 23(1).
[44]   A detailed consideration of these model terms is outside the scope of this work; the most recent version of the terms is set out in *Shawcross* at Section AB 33b, and there is a commentary on these terms at Div VII para [287].

conditions of carriage. Indeed IATA has produced a model set of contract terms for air waybills, which its members are required to use: see IATA Resolution 660 (air waybills).

6.37   The Unfair Contract Terms Act 1977 ('UCTA') is unlikely to have any substantial impact on these terms and conditions as in general the Warsaw regime provides for a standard of liability on the carrier's part which is higher than that of negligence, which is the standard of contractual duty that the UCTA seeks to preserve. The EC Directive on Unfair Terms in Consumer Contracts may be applicable. There is however an argument that the provisions of that Directive may not apply to the conditions of carriage in IATA Resolution 660(b) (air waybills) on the grounds that the resolution requires government approval, or they may be said to be contractual terms which reflect regulatory or Convention provisions. The argument is not altogether an easy one. In particular the provisions of IATA Resolution 600(b) are intended to cover ground not dealt with by the regulatory regime, namely the relevant version of the Warsaw Convention. As yet the point does not appear to have been tested in the Courts.

Chapter 7

The Liability Provisions of the Warsaw Convention (Article 17)

Overview of the liability provisions of the Warsaw Convention

7.1

RULE 18—The Warsaw Convention creates a code which supersedes national law relating to the liability of the carrier during carriage by air. The main elements of the code which concern liability are:

(1) The carrier is liable, without proof of fault, for death/bodily injury, loss or damage to baggage or cargo and delay.
(2) Limited defences are available to the carrier.
(3) The liability of the carrier is limited to defined financial limits, save in certain defined circumstances.
(4) The carrier is unable to exclude or limit liability by its contractual terms, but it may agree to pay higher limits by agreeing a special contract.
(5) The Convention allocates jurisdiction between specifically identified states who are parties to the Convention.
(6) The Convention imposes a special limitation period.

7.2   Prior to the Warsaw Convention, many carriers had inserted in the contract of carriage conditions which exonerated them completely from all liability towards their customers both for personal injury and for loss of and damage to baggage and cargo. The Warsaw Convention put an end to this practice and specified in some detail the circumstances in which the carrier was to be liable for such injury, loss or damage[1]. It created a presumption against the carrier in case of damage affecting passengers, baggage and cargo, and in the case of delay, in return for which the liability of the carrier was limited[2].

---

[1]   For an explanation of the context in which the Convention was concluded see Lowenfeld and Mendelsohn 'The United States and the Warsaw Convention' [1967] 80 Harv LR 497; *Eastern Airlines v Floyd* 499 US 530 and *El Al v Tseng* 119 S Ct 662 (1999).
[2]   In relation to Community air carriers, the liability limit applicable in passenger cases has been removed and the defences available to carriers in such cases partially withdrawn, see Chapter 12.

7.3   The scheme of the Convention[3] is that in defined circumstances the carrier is liable for personal injury suffered by a passenger (art 17), for loss of or damage to baggage and cargo (art 18) and damage occasioned by delay (art 19), unless the carrier proves (a) that he and his agents took all necessary measures to avoid such injury, loss or damage or that it was impossible to take such measures (art 20) or (b) that the injury, loss or damage was caused in whole or part by the negligence of the injured person (art 21). In return for this presumption of liability, the Convention provides for limits of liability (art 22). It also forbids any attempt on the part of the carrier to contract out of the liability imposed by the Convention (art 23), although it does not forbid agreement of higher limits of liability (art 22). In specified circumstances the limits of liability may not apply, so that the carrier's liability is unlimited (eg arts 3, 4 and 25). The Convention also provides for time limits for the notification of certain types of claim in relation to baggage and cargo (art 26) and imposes a limitation period of two years in relation to all types of claim (art 29).

7.4   In a handful of provisions the Convention thus provides a basic code for claims arising out of the carriage by air. At the heart of this code are arts 17 to 19, which establish the presumption of liability against the carrier and delineate the circumstances in which that presumption applies. These arts are examined in this chapter. Articles 20 and 21, which reveal the nature and strength of the presumption against the carrier by specifying when and how it can be rebutted, are considered in Chapter 9 below.

7.5   Given the level of the limits of liability imposed by the Convention (they were low even by 1929 standards), the balance achieved between the competing interests of carriers on the one hand and passengers and shippers on the other was very much in the favour of carriers[4]. This balance will be altered once the Montreal Convention of 1999 comes into force[5]. That Convention renders the carrier strictly liable for personal injury to passengers not exceeding 100,000 Special Drawing Rights ('SDR'), subject only to reduction of liability for contributory negligence on the part of the claimant. For damages exceeding 100,000 SDR, the carrier is not liable if he proves that the injury was not caused by his negligence or other wrongful act or omission or was solely caused by the negligence or other wrongful act or omission of a third party. The result of this will be that instead of limiting the damages recoverable from the carrier, the occurrence of an accident within the scope of the Montreal Convention will virtually assure a passenger of obtaining compensation in full[6].

---

[3]   Except where otherwise stated or appears from the context, all references to the Convention are references to the amended Convention.

[4]   See Lowenfeld and Mendelsohn [1967] 80 Harv LR 497.

[5]   It is expected that this could be as early as 2001: Tompkins 'The Montreal Convention of 1999: this is the answer' [1999] The Aviation Quarterly 114.

[6]   L Cobbs 'The shifting meaning of 'Accident' under Article 17 of the Warsaw Convention' [1999] 24 Air & Space Law 121, p 122.

7.6   Whereas passengers may previously have sought to argue that their claims did not fall within the Convention so as to avoid its low limits of liability, they are likely to wish to bring themselves within the ambit of the Montreal Convention in order to take advantage of its stricter liability provisions. Carriers, on the other hand, will be more inclined to argue for a restrictive interpretation of the circumstances in which the Convention applies[7].

Interpretation of the Convention

7.7   Although the text discussed in this work is principally the English text of the amended Convention, it should be borne in mind that the French text is authoritative and must be referred to in relation to any issue of construction[8].

7.8   Whilst national courts have recognised that the Convention should not be construed by reference to municipal law concepts or considerations and that decisions in different jurisdictions should so far as possible be kept in line with each other[9], this has not always happened, as the cases examined in this chapter show. On certain controversial questions, such as the recoverability of damages for mental injury, courts in different jurisdictions have come to conflicting conclusions. Where there is no decided case in England on such points, predicting the likely attitude of an English court may be difficult.

Exclusivity of the Convention regime

7.9   Article 24 of the Convention provides that in cases covered by arts 17, 18 or 19, any action for damages however founded can only be brought subject to the conditions and limits set out in the Convention[10]. This means that where there is a claim under the Convention, a claimant has no concurrent remedy at common law[11]. The Convention in those circumstances

---

[7]   L Cobbs [1999] 24 Air & Space Law 121.
[8]   Section 1(2) of the Carriage by Air Act 1961. See also *Corocroft v Pan American Airways* [1969] 1 QB 616; *Adatia v Air Canada* (1992) Times, 4 June; Independent, 10 June, CA.
[9]   *Sidhu v British Airways* [1997] AC 430 per Lord Hope at p 443–4, citing *T v Secretary of State for the Home Department* [1996] AC 742 at p 779A per Lord Lloyd; *El Al v Tseng* 116 S Ct 662 (1999).
[10] Article 24(2) states that in cases covered by art 17 (ie concerning bodily injury suffered by passengers), the Convention conditions and limits apply. However, the action is founded but 'without prejudice to the questions as to who are the persons who have the right to bring suit and what are their respective rights'. Those issues, which are of fundamental importance in the laws of tort and contract, remain governed by the laws of individual jurisdictions. It was neither the purpose nor intention of the Convention to attempt to unify the laws of High Contracting Parties on such matters: *Sidhu v British Airways* [1997] AC 430 at p 447 per Lord Hope.
[11] *Sidhu v British Airways* [1997] AC 430 at p 441 per Lord Hope (in relation to claims under art 17); *Jack v Trans World Airlines* 820 F Supp 1218 (ND Cal 1993).

provides the exclusive cause of action and remedy in respect of personal injury to passengers and loss of and damage to baggage and cargo[12]. The remedies made available by the Convention are to the exclusion of all other remedies[13]. In return for the exclusivity of the Convention, and in order to secure its uniform application, art 23(1), subject to an exception relating to the inherent character of cargo[14], prevents a carrier from trying to exclude or relieve its liability under the Convention either by contractual terms or such other provision[15].

7.10   It follows that a claimant who is injured as a result of an accident occurring on board an aircraft or in the course of any of the operations of embarking or disembarking (and who thus has a claim under art 17) cannot circumvent the limits of liability laid down in the Convention by for example framing his claim in tort and contending that the Convention only applies to claims in contract[16], or claiming damages in a criminal action[17].

7.11   It has been less clear whether carriers may be sued under municipal law rules in cases where they are *not* liable under the Convention because one or more of the pre-conditions for liability under arts 17, 18 and 19 are not satisfied. This question arises where for example a passenger is injured in the course of embarkation but not as a result of an accident[18]. The House of Lords[19] and the Supreme Court of the United States[20] have recently held that in such circumstances the claimant has no remedy.

7.12   In *Sidhu v British Airways*, Lord Hope[21] said that whilst the Convention does not purport to deal with all matters relating to contracts of international carriage by air, in those areas with which it deals (and the liability of the carrier is one of them) it is intended to be exclusive of any resort to the rules of domestic law[22]. There is therefore no scope for allowing claims to be brought against carriers under domestic law for losses sustained in the

---

[12] See *Sidhu v British Airways* [1997] AC 430 at p 437 per Lord Hope.
[13] *Holmes v Bangladesh Biman Corporation* [1989] AC 1112 at p 1129 per Lord Bridge.
[14] Article 23(2) permits a carrier to restrict its liability under the Convention in respect of loss or damage to cargo resulting from the inherent defect, quality or vice of the cargo carried.
[15] In *Corocroft v Pan American Airways Inc* [1969] 1 QB 616, which was reversed on other grounds [1969] 1 IB 641, the first instance judge Donaldson J applied art 23 to reject the contention by the carrier that it was able to rely on its terms to limit its liability, in circumstances where under the Convention its liability would have been unlimited because the air consignment note did not contain the prescribed particulars.
[16] *Santaboni v Japan Airlines Co Ltd* (1985) 1 S & B Av R VII/187 (Rome CA); *Kalivas v Egyptair* (1990) 1 S&B Av R VII/497, affirmed (1991) 1 S&B Av R VII/645 (Athens CA).
[17] *Ministere Public c Audibert* (1981) RFDA 138 (CA Bordeaux 27.2.1980); *Morlevat c Frantz* (1977) RFDA 279 (Cass 10.5.1977).
[18] See eg *El Al v Tseng* 116 S Ct 662 (1999).
[19] In *Sidhu v British Airways* [1997] AC 430.
[20] In *El Al v Tseng* (1999) 116 S Ct 662.
[21] Lord Hope gave the only reasoned speech. Lords Browne-Wilkinson, Jauncey, Mustill and Steyn agreed with him.
[22] *Sidhu v British Airways* [1997] AC 430 at p 453.

course of international carriage by air, even in cases where the Convention does not create any liability on the part of the carrier. To allow such claims outside the Convention would distort the whole system[23].

7.13   Lord Hope recognised this would leave claimants without a remedy in certain cases (*Sidhu* being one such case). However, as he pointed out, the Convention was not designed to provide remedies against carriers for all losses sustained by passengers or in respect of baggage or cargo, or delay. It was instead designed to define those situations in which compensation was to be available. It set out the limits of liability and the conditions under which claims to establish that liability, if disputed, were to be made. A balance was struck, in the interests of certainty and uniformity[24].

7.14   The reasoning in *Sidhu* was followed by the Supreme Court of the United States in *El Al v Tseng*[25]. Ginsburg J noted that recourse to local law remedies 'would undermine the uniform regulation of international air carrier liability that the Warsaw Convention was designed to foster'. In his view, to allow local law claims would encourage 'artful pleading' by claimants seeking to opt out of the Convention's liability scheme when local law promised recovery in excess of that prescribed by the Convention.

7.15   The precise limits of the decision in *Sidhu* are not entirely clear. Lord Hope referred to the Convention being exclusive not only in respect of claims for loss, injury and damage 'in the course of' international carriage by air but also in respect of claims 'arising out of' such carriage[26]. This arguably includes (for example) a claim for damage sustained by a passenger in the terminal building after completing the operation of disembarking, even though the carriage by air would by then have come to an end; such a claim could still be said to be one 'arising out of' the carriage by air. In *El Al v Tseng* Ginsburg J defined the scope of the Convention's exclusivity more precisely. He said that the Convention would not preclude a local law claim for damage sustained before or after the carriage by air because the Convention addressed and concerned, only and exclusively, the airline's liability for passenger injuries occurring on board the aircraft or in the course of any of the operations of embarking or disembarking.

7.16   Courts in a number of other jurisdictions, including Ontario[27], New Zealand[28] and Singapore[29], have also recognised the exclusivity of the

---

23   *Sidhu v British Airways* [1997] AC 430 at pp 447 and 453–4.
24   *Sidhu v British Airways* [1997] AC 430 at p 453.
25   116 S Ct 662 (1999).
26   *Sidhu v British Airways* [1997] AC 430 at pp 437 and 447.
27   *Naval-Torres v Northwest Airlines* (1998) 159 DLR (4th) 67 at pp 73 and 77; *Clark v Royal Aviation Group Inc* (1997) 34 OR (3d) 481.
28   *Emery Air Freight v Nerine Nurseries* [1997] 3 NZLR 723 at p735–7.
29   *Seagate Technology v Changi International Airport Services* [1997] 3 SLR 1 at p 9.

Convention. However, there are certain European jurisdictions where the courts have reached the contrary conclusion and allowed claims under local law where there was no liability under the Convention, notwithstanding that the claims arose in the course of international carriage by air[30]. Uniformity has therefore not been achieved in respect of this issue.

7.17   Where a claim falls outside arts 17, 18 and 19, by reason of it not being a claim for loss or damage sustained in the course of or arising out of international carriage by air, the Convention does not apply and the rights and liabilities of the carrier are governed by the relevant municipal law. This is the case where, for example, passengers are injured, or baggage or cargo lost or damaged, before the carriage by air has commenced or after it has ended[31].

7.18   Thus in *Adatia v Air Canada*, a passenger who was injured by an employee of the carrier in the terminal building after she had disembarked from the aircraft was able to sue the carrier for negligence at common law even though the two-year limitation period provided by the Convention had expired[32]. At the time the passenger was injured, she was not still engaged upon the operation of disembarkation within the meaning of art 17: the international carriage by air had come to an end and the Convention was therefore inapplicable. Similarly, in *Victoria Sales Corpn v Emery Air Freight*[33], cargo which had been flown from Amsterdam to New York was lost from the carrier's warehouse located outside of the confines of JF Kennedy Airport. The claim was not governed by the Convention because art 18 does not apply to cargo in the charge of a carrier outside of an aerodrome[34]. The claim could therefore be brought under local law and was not subject to the limits of liability in the Convention.

7.19   While in the US there was considerable controversy at one time as to whether the provisions of the Warsaw Convention created a cause of action[35], this was largely due to the existence of choice of law and jurisdictional questions in the US[36]. The same problems have not arisen in other

---

30   Perhaps most notable is the decision of the Paris Court of Appeal in *Sté British Airways c Mohamed* (1997) 51 RDFA 155 which arose out of the same facts as gave rise to *Sidhu v British Airways* [1997] AC 430. These decisions are discussed in *Shawcross & Beaumont* at Div VII para 388.

31   Note however the doubt about the precise limits of the exclusivity rule adopted by the House of Lords in *Sidhu v British Airways* [1997] AC 430, as discussed above.

32   *Adatia v Air Canada* [1992] PIQR P238, Times, 4 June, CA.

33   917 F 2d 705 (2nd Cir 1990).

34   See on this aspect of the case, para **8.23** below.

35   See Miller *Liability in International Air Transport* (1977) Ch XII. The latest US cases hold that the Warsaw Convention creates an exclusive cause of action thus excluding any claim for punitive damages under state law: *Re Air Disaster at Lockerbie* 928 F 2d 1267.

36   For a useful discussion see Mankiewicz 'The Judicial Diversification of Uniform Private Law Conventions ' (1972) 21 ICLQ 718 at p741–3.

common law jurisdictions where enabling legislation has emphasised the exclusivity of the Convention regime irrespective of the juridical basis of claim nor in civil law jurisdictions. The Carriage by Air Act 1961 makes it clear that the provisions of the Convention are exclusive irrespective of the basis of claim. Thus a claim rising out of a fatal accident, to which the provisions of art 17 apply, is a claim which may be made under the Fatal Accidents Acts[37] and the limitation of liability contained in art 22 of the Convention applies 'whatever the nature of the proceedings by which liability may be enforced'[38].

The Basis of Liability

Personal Injury

7.20

Rule **19—The carrier is presumed liable for damage sustained as a result of any personal injury suffered by a passenger caused by an accident taking place on board the aircraft or in the course of any of the operations of embarking or disembarking. This presumption may only be rebutted in the circumstances provided in Rule 23 below.**

7.21   Article 17 of the Convention[39] provides that:

'The carrier is liable for damage sustained in the event of the death or wounding of a passenger or any bodily injury suffered by a passenger, if the accident which caused the damage so sustained took place on board the aircraft or in the course of any of the operations of embarking or disembarking.'

There are two essential requirements for founding liability under this Article, namely that:
(i)   the damage claimed must have been caused by the death or wounding of, or other bodily injury suffered by, a passenger; and
(ii)   the death, wounding or other bodily injury must have been caused by an accident which took place on board the aircraft or in the course of any of the operations of embarking or disembarking.

Each of these requirements is examined below.

---

[37]   Section 3 of the 1961 Act.
[38]   Section 4 (1) of the 1961 Act.
[39]   Article 17 (1) of the Montreal Convention is in substantially the same terms.

Death, wounding or other bodily injury

7.22   The cases on art 17 illustrate the diverse nature of injuries suffered by air passengers, ranging from death in a mid-air explosion[40], to food poisoning[41], an allergic reaction to insecticide spray used in the cabin[42] and nervous shock (unaccompanied by any physical injury) after an emergency landing[43]. Whilst death and physical injury are plainly covered by the Article, there is considerable controversy over whether purely mental injury is within its scope.

7.23   Much of the debate has centred around the true interpretation of the phrase 'lesion corporelle' as used in the French text of the Convention[44]. Although this phrase is translated in the English text as 'bodily injury', commentators have argued that in French law the phrase covers any personal injury whatsoever and should therefore not be interpreted as excluding purely mental injury[45]. Municipal courts have not agreed upon an uniform interpretation of the phrase.

7.24   In *Cie Air France v Teichner*[46], a case arising out of the hijacking of an Air France flight to Entebbe in Uganda, the Israeli Supreme Court decided that art 17 does allow recovery for purely mental injuries. It concluded that an expansive interpretation of the Article was required for policy reasons, notably the post-1929 development of the aviation industry and the evolution of Anglo-American and Israeli law allowing recovery for mental injury.

7.25   In *Eastern Airlines v Floyd*[47], the Supreme Court of the United States refused to follow the Teichner decision and held that damages were not recoverable for purely mental injuries under art 17. The US Supreme Court concluded that 'lesion corporelle' was properly translated as bodily injury, which included physical but not purely mental injury. After examining the French legal meaning of 'lesion corporelle', the Supreme Court decided that there was no basis for construing the phrase as encompassing psychological injury. This conclusion was, in the Court's view, consistent with the negotiating history of the Warsaw Convention and with the post Convention conduct and interpretations of the signatories to the Convention.

7.26   *Floyd* was followed by the Court of Appeal of New South Wales in *Kotsambasis v Singapore Air*[48]. The New South Wales Court of Appeal agreed

---

[40]   *Re Lockerbie Air Disaster* 928 F 2d 1267.
[41]   *Abdulrahman Al-Zamil v British Airways* 770 F 2d 3 (1985).
[42]   *Capacchione v Qantas Airways* 25 Avi Cas 17,346 (CD Cal, 1996).
[43]   *Kotsambasis v Singapore Air* (1997) 148 ALR 498.
[44]   The French text is authoritative. See para **7.7** above.
[45]   Mankiewicz *The Liability Regime of the International Air Carrier* (1981) at p 146; and see *Miller* at p 122–128.
[46]   (1985) 39 RFDA 232, (1983) 33 Eur TrL 87.
[47]   499 US 530 (1991).
[48]   (1997) 148 ALR 498.

that the Convention was to be read parsimoniously[49] and that however desirable it was to give a wide interpretation to art 17, the courts could not do so unless that was within the intention of the signatories to the Convention[50].

7.27   There is no English decision on this point. The question was left open in *Sidhu v British Airways*[51], in which passengers suffered psychological injuries when they were apprehended in Kuwait airport and detained by invading Iraqi forces in August 1990. The passengers conceded that their injuries did not come within the scope of art 17, but Lord Hope noted that a suggestion was made in the course of argument that the phrase 'bodily injury' ought now to be construed as including psychological damage[52]. However, since the point did not arise for decision in the case and was not fully argued, he expressed no opinion upon it.

7.28   It is difficult to predict how an English court would decide this question. Given the divergent approach taken to the recovery of damages for mental injury in domestic laws (many jurisdictions not recognising claims for purely psychological injury at the time of the Warsaw Conference), there is force in the view expressed by the Supreme Court of the United States that the drafters of the Convention would most likely have felt compelled to make an unequivocal reference to purely mental injury if they had intended to allow such recovery[53]. Furthermore, as the Supreme Court noted in *Floyd*, a narrow interpretation of art 17 is consistent with the primary purpose of the contracting parties, which was to limit the liability of air carriers in order to foster the growth of the fledgling commercial aviation industry[54]. It is also difficult to avoid the conclusion that literally construed, the term 'lesion corporelle' does not extend to purely mental injury[55]. Indeed, it was only by giving a liberal interpretation to that phrase that the Israeli Supreme Court, and certain US courts prior to *Floyd*[56], were able to construe it as including such injury. An English court may well conclude that to allow recovery for mental injury under art 17 would be overstepping the legitimate bounds of statutory construction (as did the New South Wales Court of Appeal in *Kotsambasis*).

7.29   On 12 July 2000 the Inner House of the Court of Session of Scotland in the case of *Philip King v Bristow Helicopters Ltd*[57] allowed an appeal, and held

---

[49] (1997) 148 ALR 498 at p 506 per Meagher JA.
[50] (1997) 148 ALR 498 at p508 per Stein JA.
[51] [1997] AC 430.
[52] [1997] AC 430 at p 441.
[53] *Floyd* (1991) 499 US 530 at p 545.
[54] *Floyd* (1991) 499 US 530 at p 546.
[55] The meaning of the French phrase is closely examined by *Miller* (1977), especially at pp 122–131.
[56] See eg *Husserl v Swiss Air* 388 F Supp 1238 (SD NY 1975); *Krystal v BOAC* 403 F Supp 1332 (DC Cal 1975) and *Karfunkel v Cie Nationale Air France* 427 F Supp 971 (SD NY 1977).
[57] 12 July 2000, unreported.

that art 17 of the Convention did not preclude recovery for psychological injury alone. The decision was split two in favour and one opposed. The majority appeared to prefer the approach of the Supreme Court of Israel in *Teichner* to that of the Supreme Court of the US in *Floyd*. This case will be persuasive although not binding on an English Court. Of the four judges who have considered this case, two have decided that psychiatric damages are recoverable and two have not[58].

7.30   Damages for psychological injury consequent upon physical injury are probably recoverable under art 17. Although the Supreme Court in *Floyd* did not express a view on this question[59], courts in other cases have accepted that such damages are recoverable and there is no reason to doubt the correctness of those decisions in the light of *Floyd*[60]. In *Kotsambasis v Singapore Air*[61], Stein JA expressed the view (after *Floyd*) that damages for mental injury following physical injury were recoverable under art 17.

7.31   The drafters of the Montreal Convention of 1999 were not able to resolve the debate over the recoverability of damages for purely mental injury. The draft Convention contained a provision allowing recovery of damages for mental injury but this was not agreed and after extensive debate and discussion, it was deleted from the adopted text[62].

Accident

7.32   In order for the carrier to be liable under art 17, the passenger's injury must have been caused by an accident. Although the term 'accident' is not defined in the Convention, it is used in contrast to the term 'occurrence' in art 18. The latter term is wider — every accident is an occurrence, but not every occurrence constitutes an accident[63].

7.33   As a matter of language, the word 'accident' may be used to refer either to the cause of an injury or merely the injury itself, irrespective of its cause[64].

---

[58]   It is not known at the time of writing whether this case will be appealed to the House of Lords.

[59]   (1991) 499 US 530 at p 552–3.

[60]   The editors of *Shawcross* state in Div VII para [521] that where psychic anguish follows and is caused by physical injury, there will be recovery for all types of pain and suffering.

[61]   (1997) 148 ALR 498 at p 508.

[62]   See Tompkins (1999) The Aviation Quarterly 114 at p 115.

[63]   See *Air France v Saks* 470 US 392 (1985) at p 402–3 and 406.

[64]   As was noted by Lord Lindley in *Fenton v J Thorley & Co Ltd* [1903] AC 433, a leading decision on the meaning of the term 'accident' as used in the Workmen's Compensation Act. There is a useful discussion of this and other common law decisions on the meaning of the term 'accident' in R Abeyratne 'Liability for personal injury and death under the Warsaw Convention and its relevance to fault liability in tort law' (1996) 21 Annals of Air and Space Law 1 at p 14–18.

Article 17, however, uses the term to refer to the cause rather than the effect, since it requires the accident to have *caused* the damage[65]. This was recognised by the Supreme Court of the United States in *Air France v Saks*[66], the leading decision on the meaning of the term 'accident' in art 17. Having noted that a distinction was drawn by the draftsmen of the Convention between cause and effect, the Supreme Court observed that it is the cause of an injury that must constitute an accident, rather than the occurrence of the injury alone[67].

7.34   In *Saks*, the Supreme Court defined an accident as being 'an unexpected or unusual event or happening that is external to the passenger'[68]. An injury resulting from the passenger's own internal reaction to the usual, normal and expected operation of the aircraft was thus not caused by an accident within the meaning of art 17[69]. The Court said, however, that its definition was to be applied flexibly, after assessment of all the circumstances surrounding a passenger's injuries[70]. It recognised that there may be room for debate as to where to draw the line between causes that were 'accidents' as opposed to 'occurrences', but nevertheless such distinctions had to be made because of the language of art 17 and 18[71].

7.35   The definition given in *Saks* was endorsed by the English Court of Appeal in *Chaudhari v British Airways*[72]. Leggatt LJ agreed that the word 'accident' in art 17 focuses on the cause and not the effect, and that it therefore did not cover incidents arising as a result of the passenger's own personal, particular or peculiar reaction to the normal operation of the aircraft.

7.36   It is not always possible to reconcile the numerous decided cases on the meaning of 'accident' in art 17. A key consideration emerging from the authorities is whether the event causing the injury results from the usual, normal and expected operation of the aircraft[73]. If it does, it is not an accident for the purposes of art 17.

7.37   On the other hand, where there has been something untoward about the operation of the aircraft, the event is likely to be construed as an accident. The most obvious examples are aircraft crashes, which plainly are 'accidents'. In addition, all of the following incidents have been held to constitute accidents within the meaning of art 17:

---

[65] Similarly, s 75(4) of the Civil Aviation Act 1982, which defines 'accident' (for the purposes of accident investigation) as 'including any fortuitous or unexpected event by which the safety of an aircraft or any person is threatened', focuses on cause rather than effect.
[66] 470 US 392 (1985).
[67] 470 US 392 (1985) at p 398.
[68] 470 US 392 (1985) at p 405.
[69] 470 US 392 (1985) at p 406.
[70] 470 US 392 (1985) at p 405.
[71] 470 US 392 (1985) at p 406.
[72] (1997) Times, 7 May.
[73] See L Cobbs (1999) 24 Air and Space Law 121 at p 123.

- a tyre failure on take-off[74];
- an unusually heavy landing causing a neck injury[75];
- severe turbulence causing loss of hearing and balance and speech abnormality[76];
- an object falling onto a passenger from an overhead locker[77];
- the supply of infected food to passengers causing food poisoning[78];
- cabin crew spilling hot drinks onto passengers[79].

7.38   It is not necessary for the event to be unintentional for it to constitute an accident. Deliberate conduct suffices, so long as it is outside the normal and expected operation of the aircraft. Thus courts in all jurisdictions in which the question has arisen have held that hijackings and terrorist attacks are accidents for the purposes of art 17[80]. The courts have considered these to be risks characteristic of air travel and thus matters for the carrier to control[81].

7.39   The categories of events not constituting accidents include the following:
- Illness or injury caused by a passenger's reaction to the normal operation of the aircraft, such as an allergic reaction to the spraying of insecticide on an aircraft in accordance with government regulations[82] or an ear injury caused by the normal repressurisation of the aircraft cabin in accordance with ordinary and routine operating procedures[83];
- Other incidents arising solely from a passenger's pre-existing medical condition, such as a passenger suffering a hernia attack[84] or thrombophlebitis[85] on a normal flight free of turbulence;
- Incidents resulting from the ordinary and expected behaviour of other passengers, such as where a passenger trips over another passenger's

---

[74]   *Arkin v Trans International Airlines* 19 Avi 18,311 (ED NY, 1985).
[75]   *Salce v Aer Lingus Air Lines* 19 Avi 17,377 (SD NY, 1985).
[76]   *Weintraub v Capital International Airways* 16 Avi 17,911 (NY City Civ Ct, 1980).
[77]   *Charpin v Quarenta* (Aix-en-Provence CA, 9 October 1986) (1987) 40 RFDA 538; *Gezzi v British Airways* 991 F 2d 603 (9th Cir, 1993).
[78]   See *Abdulrahman Al-Zamil v British Airways* 770 F 2d 3 (1985).
[79]   *Lugo v American Airlines* 686 F Supp 373 (DC PR, 1988) 21 Avi 18,020; *Ganzales v Taca International Airlines* 23 Avi 18,431 (Ed La 1992).
[80]   In the US, see *Husserl v Swiss Air* 485 F 2d 1240 (1973); *Day v Trans World Airlines* 528 F 2d 31 (1975); *Evangelinos v Trans World Airlines* 550 F 2d 152 (1976); *People ex rel Compagnie Nationale Air France v Gilberto* 383 NE 2d 977 (1978); *Pflug v Egyptair Corp* 961 F 2d 26 (1992). In France see *Ayache c Air France* (1984) RFDA 450 (T.G.I. Paris, 1984). In Israel see *Air France v Teichner* (1985) RFDA 232 (Supreme Court, 1984).
[81]   See eg *Husserl v Swiss Air* 351 F Supp 702 (1972).
[82]   *Capacchione v Qantas Airways* 25 Avi 17,346 (CD Cal 1996) and *Kleiner v Qantas Airways* 22 Avi 18,179 (SD NY 1990).
[83]   *Warshaw v Trans World Airlines* 442 F Supp 400 (1977). Compare *Weintraub v Trans World Airlines*, referred to in para **7.37** above, where the injury was caused by severe turbulence.
[84]   *Abramson v Japan Airlines* 739 F 2d 130 (1984).
[85]   *Scherer v Pan American World Airways* 387 NYS 2d 581 (1976).

shoes (passengers habitually take off their shoes during a flight)[86] or a passenger hurts himself getting out of his seat because the seat of the passenger in front is fully reclined (a fully reclined seat is not an unusual or unexpected event)[87].

7.40 Cases concerning injuries caused by violent or other abusive conduct on the part of fellow passengers have given rise to considerable controversy in recent years. Such conduct can be characterised as unexpected and unusual, and external to the passenger injured — yet the courts, particularly in the US, have been reluctant to visit upon airlines responsibility for drunken and other offensive behaviour by passengers, which has not been regarded as falling within the sphere of the normal operations of an aircraft[88].

7.41 Thus in *Price v British Airways*[89], an incident in which the claimant was punched in the face by another passenger was not an accident within the meaning of art 17, because it bore no relationship to the carrier's operation of the aircraft. The court rejected an argument by the claimant that there was no basis for distinguishing the type of incident in this case from the violent conduct of a fellow passenger who hijacked an aircraft, which does constitute an accident (as for example in *Husserl v Swiss Air*). In the court's view, hijacking was a characteristic risk of air travel, whereas fist fights between passengers were not. Similarly, in *Wallace v Korean Air*[90], the claimant was sexually molested by the passenger sitting in the seat next to her; this was not an accident because such molestation was neither a risk characteristic of air travel nor an event related to the operation of the aircraft.

7.42 Where, however, airline personnel fail to control another passenger's conduct in circumstances in which they have the opportunity, and can reasonably be expected, to do so, their failure to act may constitute an accident. Thus in *Tsevas v Delta Air Lines*[91], the court found that the failure of flight attendants to reseat a passenger who complained about, and was then molested by, a drunken passenger in the next seat was an accident.

7.43 The burden of proof is on the passenger to prove that an accident has occurred. Where therefore a passenger is injured but cannot prove the cause of his injury, the carrier will not be liable under art 17. A passenger's claim thus failed in *Macdonald v Air Canada*[92] since although she fell and hurt herself

---

[86] *Craig v Compagnie National Air France* 45 F 3d 435 (1994).
[87] *Potter v Delta Airlines* 98 F 3d 881 (1996). Query whether the cabin crew's failure to assist the passenger seeking to get out of his seat could be characterised as an accident.
[88] See generally, L Cobbs (1999) 24 Air and Space Law, 121 at pp 124–6.
[89] 23 Avi 18,465 (SD NY 1992); followed in *Stone v Continental Airlines Inc* 905 F Supp 823 (D Hawaii, 1995).
[90] Unreported, SD NY 6 April 1999; discussed in L Cobbs (1999) 24 Air and Space Law at p 125.
[91] Unreported ND Ill 1 December 1997; discussed in L Cobbs (1999) 24 Air and Space Law at p125.
[92] 11 Avi 18,029 (1st Cir, 1971).

badly in the course of disembarking, she was not able to establish the cause of her fall. She was elderly and the court concluded that it was as reasonable to suppose that some internal condition was the cause of her fall as that the fall was the result of an accident.

Location of the accident: on board the aircraft or in the course of any of the operations of embarking or disembarking

7.44   An accident only falls within the scope of art 17 if it takes place on board the aircraft or in the course of any of the operations of embarking or disembarking.

On board

7.45   There is normally no difficulty about establishing whether an accident occurred on board the aircraft. So long as this 'geographical' requirement is satisfied, the reason for the passenger being on board is irrelevant. Thus in *Herman v Trans World Airlines*[93] the carrier was liable under art 17 for injuries sustained by passengers whilst they were detained by hijackers on board an aircraft in the Jordanian desert for a week, notwithstanding that during that time they were held on board the aircraft without the carrier's consent.

7.46   In another hijacking case, *Husserl v Swiss Air*[94], the New York District Court construed the term 'on board the aircraft' as including all of the time between embarkation at the origin of a flight and disembarkation at a scheduled destination. It thus held the carrier liable for injuries suffered by passengers on a flight which had been hijacked and diverted to a desert airstrip in Jordan, even though the passengers were moved to an hotel after 24 hours on board the hijacked aircraft. The court construed art 17 as applying throughout the period of the alleged injuries, irrespective of the fact that the injuries were suffered (at least in part) after the passengers had been moved from the aircraft to the hotel.

Embarking and disembarking

7.47   Ascertaining whether an accident took place during any of the operations of embarking or disembarking can be more problematic. Of course, if an accident occurs when a passenger is actually entering or alighting from the aircraft, there is no difficulty[95]. Thus art 17 plainly applies where a passenger

---

[93] 12 Avi 17,304 (NY Sup Ct, 1972); 330 NYS 2d 829; reversed 337 NYS 2d 827 (App Div 1972); reversed 34 NY 2d 385 (App Div 1974).
[94] 388 F Supp 1238 (SD NY, 1975), 13 Avi 17,603.
[95] See *Scarf v Trans World Airlines* 4 Avi 17,795 (SD NY, 1955); *Chutter v KLM Royal Dutch Airlines* 132 F Supp 611 (SD NY, 1955); *Gezzi v British Airways* 991 F 2d 603 (9th Cir, 1993).

is injured when climbing up the passenger ramp to board the aircraft: *Scarf v Trans World Airlines*.

7.48   Beyond this, it is not easy to draw the precise limits of the operations of embarking and disembarking. The use of feeder arms in airports means that often there is no break between the airport building and reaching or leaving the aircraft. Determining where the carrier's liability for accidents begins and ends under art 17 can be difficult. Different approaches have been adopted by the courts in the US, civil law jurisdictions and England.

United States cases

7.49   The courts in the US apply a tri-partite test, based on the *Day* and *Evangelinos* cases[96], whereby three factors are relevant to determining whether an accident occurs during the operations of embarking or disembarking, namely:
- the location of the accident;
- the nature of the activity in which the injured passenger was engaged when the accident occurred; and
- the extent of the control exercised by the carrier of the injured passenger at the time of the accident.

7.50   Both the *Day* and *Evangelinos* cases arose out of a terrorist attack which took place in the travel lounge of a Greek airport whilst the passengers (whose flight had been called for boarding) were lining up for a security check at the entrance to the designated departure gate. In both cases, the court concluded that the passengers were in the course of embarking when the attack took place. The courts relied in particular upon the facts that at the time of the attack the passengers were engaged upon activities which were a pre-condition to actual embarkation (ie they were assembled at the departure gate, having been directed to stand in line by the carrier's personnel so as to undergo a weapons search which was a prerequisite to boarding the aircraft), that their movements were restricted (they were not free agents roaming at will through the terminal building but were under the direction of the carrier and were identifiable as a group associated with the particular flight) and that they were physically adjacent to the terminal gate, about to board the aircraft.

7.51   In *Day*[97] the court noted that its decision was in harmony with modern theories of accident cost allocation, since airlines were in a position to distribute among all passengers what would otherwise be a 'crushing burden' upon those few unfortunate to become accident victims. In the court's view,

---

[96] *Day v Trans World Airlines* 528 F 2d 31 (2d Cir, 1975) and *Evangelinos v Trans World Airlines* 550 F 2d 152 (3rd Cir, 1976).
[97] 528 F 2d 31 at p 34.

airlines, in marked contrast to individual passengers, were in a better position to persuade, pressure or if need be compensate, airport managers to adopt more stringent security measures against terrorist attacks.

7.52   In *Hernandez v Air France*[98], the 1st Circuit Court of Appeals applied the tri-partite test in a case concerning disembarking passengers who were attacked whilst waiting to collect their baggage in the baggage retrieval area of an airport by terrorists. The court had regard to the passengers' location, activity and control by the carrier in deciding that they were not involved in any of the operations of disembarking within the meaning of art 17 when the attack occurred. They were not still engaged in the physical activity of separating themselves from the aircraft; the location of the attack was a long way from the aircraft, being well inside the terminal building, and the carrier's personnel were not directing how the passengers went about retrieving their baggage.

7.53   The *Day/Evangelinos* test has since been applied in a large number of cases in the US. A number of these decisions have emphasised the need for there to be a close temporal and spatial relationship with the particular flight itself, as well as a close tie between the accident and the physical act of entering or leaving the aircraft[99]. This is in line with the court's assessment of the intention of the drafters of the Convention; in their view, the delegates to the Warsaw Conference understood embarkation and disembarkation as essentially the physical activity of entering or exiting from an aircraft, rather than a broader notion of initiating or ending a trip[100].

7.54   The requirement for a sufficiently close connection between the accident and the physical act of entering or leaving the aircraft was met when a passenger fell from a bus owned and operated by the airline which was carrying him and other passengers from the aircraft to the airport building: *Ricotta v Iberia*[101]. By contrast, in *McCarthy v Northwest Airlines*[102], a passenger who injured herself on an escalator in the public areas of the terminal building whilst on the way to the departure gate was not in the process of embarking. The accident occurred at a considerable distance from the departure gate and was thus 'far removed from the act of embarkation, both temporally and spatially'[103].

7.55   In other cases, the degree of control exercised by the carrier (or absence thereof) has been a critical factor. In *Upton v Iran National Airlines*[104],

---

[98]   545 F 2d 279 (1977).
[99]   See in particular *Evangelinos, Hernandez* and *McCarthy v Northwest Airlines* 56 F 3d 313 (1st Cir 1995).
[100]   *Hernandez* 545 F 2d 279 at p 283–4.
[101]   482 F Supp 497; affirmed 663 F 2d 206 (2nd Cir 1980).
[102]   56 F 3d 319 (1st Cir 1995).
[103]   56 F 3d 319 (1st Cir 1995).
[104]   450 F Supp 176 (DC NY 1978).

passengers had received boarding passes and were seated in a public area waiting for a delayed flight when the airport roof collapsed on them. The court held that this accident did not take place during any of the operations of embarking because the passengers were free to leave the airport building and were not acting under the control of the carrier. In *Knoll v Trans World Airlines*[105] the court held that an arriving passenger who was injured by slipping on a moving walkway in the terminal building when approaching the immigration area at Heathrow Airport did not fall while in the course of disembarking. At the time of the accident, she was not under the control of the airline or engaged upon any activity imposed by the airline for the purposes of disembarkation. She was instead engaged in activities (passing through immigration and customs control) imposed by the country in which she was travelling. As the court observed in *Knoll*:

> 'The courts have consistently refused to extend coverage of the Warsaw Convention to injuries incurred within the terminal, except in those cases in which plaintiffs were clearly under direction of the airlines.'

7.56   To the same effect are disembarkation cases decided before *Day* and *Evangelinos*, in which the operations of disembarking were held to have ended once a passenger reached 'a safe point inside of the terminal, even though he may remain in the status of a passenger of the carrier while inside the building'[106]. Once the passenger was in such a position, there was no reason to apply the Convention's rules. As the court said in *MacDonald v Air Canada*[107]: 'Neither the economic rationale for liability limits, nor the rationale for the shift in the burden of proof, applies to accidents which are far removed from the operation of aircraft'. The carrier was therefore not liable under art 17 for injuries sustained by a passenger in the baggage pick-up area of an airport arrival hall[108].

Civil law cases

7.57   Courts in civil law jurisdictions have paid particular regard to whether the accident occurred in a location exposed to aviation-related risks and whether the passenger was at the time under the control of the carrier. A leading decision in France is *Mache c Air France*[109], in which the claimant was

---

[105] 610 F Supp 844 (DC Colo, 1985). See also *Rolinck v El Al Israel Airlines* 551 F Supp 261 (passenger who slipped on airport escalator was not disembarking); *Guaridenex de la Cruz v Dominicana de Avacion* 22 Avi Cas 17,639 (slip in hallway between immigration and baggage reclaim area not in the course of disembarking); *Rabinowitz v Scandinavian Airlines* 741 F Supp 441 (injury on moving walkway in terminal building not during disembarkation).

[106] *MacDonald v Air Canada* 439 F 2d 1402 (1st Cir, 1971) at p 1405. See also *Felismina v Trans World Airlines* 13 Avi 17,145 (SD NY, 1974); *Klein v KLM Royal Dutch Airlines* 360 NYS 2d 60 (NY Sup Ct App Div, 1974).

[107] 439 F 2d 1402 (1st Cir, 1971) at p 1405.

[108] *MacDonald v Air Canada* 439 F 2d 1402 (1st Cir, 1971) and *Klein v KLM Royal Dutch Airlines* 360 NYS 2d 60 (NY Sup Ct App Div, 1974).

[109] (1966) 29 RGAE 32 (Cass Civ Lre 18 January 1966); (1966) 20 RFDA 228.

injured whilst being led from the aircraft to the airport terminal building by two of the carrier's hostesses, along with other passengers. The usual entrance used for disembarking passengers was out of order and an alternative route had been arranged. The hostess leading the passengers took an unauthorised shortcut through a garden, where the claimant stepped on a slab of concrete in bad condition, fell into a hole and seriously injured himself. The Cour de Cassation held that in order for a carrier to be liable on the basis of art 17, it was necessary to establish that the accident causing the damage occurred in a place 'exposed to risks inherent to air navigation and exploitation'[110]. The case was remanded to the Rouen Court of Appeal, which found that where the accident happened was not a place exposed to such risks. The Court of Appeal held that the claimant was exposed to those risks whilst on the traffic apron, but not in the garden.

7.58   The 'zone of aviation risk' test has been applied by French courts in other cases concerning accidents occurring outside the terminal building. For example, art 17 was held to apply when a passenger was injured by a train of baggage-wagons which ran into him on the airport apron between the terminal building and the aircraft[111]. The test is, however, less suited to dealing with accidents inside terminal buildings and in such cases the courts have attached more importance to the question of whether at the relevant time the passenger was under the control of the carrier. Thus where passengers were injured falling on an escalator leading to the airport's departure lounges, it was found that they could not rely upon art 17 because the carrier's employees had not yet assumed control of the passengers and the accident occurred in a part of the airport that was used by several carriers[112]. Decisions in other civil law jurisdictions are generally consistent with these French cases[113].

7.59   There is probably little difference in substance between the approaches adopted in the US and the civil law jurisdictions, particularly if, in applying the 'zone of aviation risk' test, one accords proper weight to passengers' exposure not only to the risks inherent to air navigation but also to the risks inherent to the *exploitation* of that means of transport. These arguably include hijacking and terrorism attacks such as were the subject of the *Day* and *Evangelinos* decisions in the US[114]. It is only in marginal cases that the

---

[110] 'expose aux risques inherents a la navigation et a l'exploitation aeriennes' (1966) 29 R.G.A.E. 32 (Cass Civ Lre 18 January 1966) at p 34.

[111] *Cie Air France c Nicoli* (1971) 25 RFDA 173 (CA Paris, 2 April 1971). See also *Fratani-Bassaler c Air France*.

[112] *Zaoui c Aeroport de Paris* (1976) 30 RFDA 394 (Cass Civ Lre, 18 May 1976). See also *Sage c Cie Air Inter* (1976) 30 RFDA 266 (CA Lyon, 10 February 1976); *Forsius c Air France* (1973) 27 RFDA 216 (TGI Paris, 19 February 1973).

[113] See eg *Blumenfeld v BEA* (Berlin CA, 11 March 1961), (1962) 11 ZLW 78; *Richardson v KLM* (Haarlem, 4 May 1991), (1975) 11 Uniform LR 365.

[114] As is pointed out in *Miller* (1977), at p 139, the test laid down by the Cour de Cassation in *Mache c Air France* probably should not be read as restrictively as it has been by most US courts.

tripartite *Day/Evangelinos* test is likely to produce different results to the 'zone of aviation risk' or 'control' tests.

English authority

7.60   The only decision in England on this aspect of art 17 is *Adatia v Air Canada*[115], in which the Court of Appeal declined to adopt any of the tests applied in the US or civil law cases or otherwise put a gloss on the words of art 17. As Sir Christopher Slade said[116], in every case:

> 'the ultimate question is whether, on the wording of [Article 17], the passenger's movements through airport procedures (including his physical location) indicates that he was at the relevant time engaged upon the operation of embarking upon (or disembarking from) the particular flight in question.'

7.61   In *Adatia*, the claimant passenger was injured on a travelator in a corridor in one of the terminal buildings at Heathrow airport. At the time of the accident the passenger and her mother were making their way towards immigration, having recently arrived on a flight from Canada. The passenger's mother was being pushed in a wheelchair by an Air Canada passenger agent and the passenger was walking alongside. The Air Canada agent negligently allowed the wheelchair to become trapped at the end of the travelator, causing the passenger to be crushed between the wheelchair and the side of the travelator. The Court of Appeal concluded that the passenger was not still engaged upon the operation of disembarkation at the time of the accident. As a result, she was able to sue the carrier for negligence at common law, after the expiry of the two-year limitation period allowed by the Convention[117].

Damage

7.62   Under art 17, the carrier is liable for 'damage' sustained in the event of death, wounding or bodily injury to a passenger.

7.63   The term 'damage' is not defined in the Convention. It has been construed in the US as referring to legally cognizable harm, the Convention leaving it to the relevant domestic law to determine what harm is legally

---

[115] [1992] PIQR P238, (1992) Times 4 June, CA.

[116] Agreeing with a submission made in the then current text of *Shawcross*. The reference to a *particular* flight is important. As the editors of *Shawcross* observe, the operations of embarking and disembarking are clearly those relating to a particular flight on a particular aircraft, a point which (they say) seems not to have been emphasised sufficiently in the decided cases. In *Adatia v Air Canada*, the other members of the Court of Appeal (Stocker and Purchas LJJ) agreed with the Judgment of Sir Christopher Slade.

[117] See on this aspect of the case para **7.18** above.

cognizable: *Zicherman v Korean Air Lines*[118]. This was in accordance with the Supreme Court's interpretation of art 24 which in art 17 cases is 'without prejudice to the questions as to who are the persons who have the right to bring suit and what are their respective rights'; this meant that in an action brought under art 17, the Convention did not affect the substantive questions of who may bring suit and what they may be compensated for — those questions were for domestic law[119]. It follows that where the applicable domestic law does not allow recovery of a certain type of loss, no damages are recoverable for that loss under art 17. Thus in *Zicherman*, in which the applicable domestic law was the US Death on the High Seas Act, relatives of passengers killed when a Korean Air flight was shot down after it had strayed into Soviet airspace over the sea of Japan could not recover damages for loss of society, because the Death on the High Seas Act did not allow claims for such non-pecuniary damages.

7.64   However, in *Preston v Hunting*[120] the English High Court awarded the claimant children damages for the loss of the care of their mother who had been killed in an air crash, without reference to domestic law. In making this award, Ormrod J relied only upon the wording of art 17 which, he concluded, was not intended to limit the damages recoverable to the children's financial loss. This decision was criticised in *Zicherman* by the Supreme Court of the United States on the grounds that it gave no consideration to art 24. There is force in this criticism and it is doubtful whether the decision would be followed today.

7.65   US courts have interpreted the term 'damage' in art 17 as including only compensatory damages, with the result that punitive damages (which are not compensatory but are a fine levied on a wrongdoer in order to punish and deter wrongdoing) are not recoverable under art 17[121]. As the court observed in *Re Air Disaster at Lockerbie*[122], there is nothing in the Convention's drafting history suggesting that the drafters contemplated the Convention being used to punish or deter tortious behaviour on the part of airlines, which would in any event defeat the Convention's goals of ensuring a viable airline industry and making international air travel more extensive and accessible.

7.66   Claims arising out of the death of a passenger are governed in England by the Fatal Accidents Act 1976 and subject to the requirements and limitations of that Act.

---

[118] 133 L Ed 2d 596 (1996); 116 S Ct 629.
[119] 133 L Ed 2d at p 605.
[120] [1956] 1 QB 454.
[121] *Re Air Disaster at Lockerbie* 928 F 2d 1267, especially at pp 1280–9. See also *Re Korean Air Lines Disaster* 932 F 2d 1475 at pp 1485–90; *Jack v Trans World Airlines* 854 F Supp 654 at p 663; *Re Air Crash Disaster at Gander, Newfoundland* 684 F Supp 927 at pp 930–3; *Harpalani v Air India* 634 F Supp 797 at p 799; *Pescatore v Pan American Airways* 97 F 3d 1 (2nd Cir 1996) at p 7.
[122] 928 F 2d 1267 at pp 1284–9.

Financial Limit of Liability

7.67

RULE 20—Article 22 of the Warsaw Convention and the Warsaw Convention as amended at the Hague limits the financial liability of the carrier, unless, as is now often the case, the carrier has entered into a special contract with the passenger. The Montreal Convention 1999 will not impose a financial limit on damages payable by the carrier. In the case of a carrier which is subject to European Council Regulation No 2027/97 there will be not be a financial limit of its liability.

7.68   A carrier which is liable to a passenger pursuant to the Warsaw Convention will by reason of art 22(1) be able to restrict its liability to the sum of 125,000 francs[123] or if Montreal Protocol No 2 applies to 8,200 SDRs[124]. Where the liability of the carrier is regulated by the Warsaw Convention as amended by the Hague protocol then the liability of the carrier will be limited to 16,600 SDRs. Where the liability of the carrier is regulated by European Council Regulation No 2027/97 the financial liability will be unlimited, save in respect of any claim in excess of 100,000 SDRs. When the Montreal Convention 1999 takes effect, the carrier's liability will be unlimited.

7.69   It is often the case that the carrier will have agreed by special contract, as permitted by art 22 of the Warsaw Convention and the Warsaw Convention as amended at the Hague, to a higher limit of liability. Carriers which have signed the IATA Intercarrier Agreement and the Intercarrier Implementation Agreement[125] are likely to have altered their terms and conditions so as to agree with passengers a special contract in which there is no limit of liability[126].

---

[123] The value of francs is prescribed by the Carriage by Air (Sterling Equivalents) Order 1996 SI 1996/244, by which 250 francs were deemed to equal 15.89 sterling. For a fuller discussion of currency questions and liability limits, see the comprehensive discussion in *Shawcross* at Div VII paras [422] to [429].

[124] Special Drawing Right, see Div VII para [428] of *Shawcross* for a further reference.

[125] For a fuller explanation of the Intercarrier Agreements see paras **1.41–1.43** above.

[126] Another example of a common special contract to pay higher damages, is the agreement by carriers to pay damages of US$75,000 (inclusive of legal fees and costs) or $58,000 exclusive of legal fees and costs in respect of carriage involving the US. These special contracts stemmed from the Montreal Agreement of 1966. With regard to flights to the US they will be superseded in the future by special contracts which reflect the terms agreed to by carriers in the Intercarrier Agreement.

Chapter 8

The Liability Provisions of the Warsaw Convention (Articles 18 and 19)

Damage to Baggage and Cargo

8.1

RULE 21—**The carrier is presumed liable for damage sustained in the event of destruction or loss of or damage to baggage or cargo occurring during the carriage by air. This presumption may only be rebutted in the circumstances provided in Rule 24 below.**

8.2   Article 18(1) of the Convention[1] provides that:

> 'The carrier is liable for damage sustained in the event of the destruction or loss of, or damage to, any registered baggage or cargo, if the occurrence which caused the damage so sustained took place during the carriage by air.'

This Article thus establishes a presumption that carriers are liable for destruction or loss of, or damage to, registered baggage and cargo occurring in the course of the carriage by air[2]. The period of the carriage by air is defined by arts 18(2) and 18(3). Each of the elements necessary for establishing liability under this article is examined below.

Destruction, loss and damage

8.3   Loss includes a total or partial loss of the contents of the baggage or cargo[3]. Baggage and cargo are 'lost' within the meaning of the Article when stolen by third parties[4].

---

[1]   The text of art 18(1) of the unamended Convention is the same, except that the term 'goods' is used instead of 'cargo'.

[2]   *Kinney Shoe Corpn v Alitalia Airlines* (1980) 15 Avi 18,509 (US DC); *TWA v Franklin Mint* 104 S Ct 1776 (1984), [1984] 2 Lloyd's Rep 432 at p 434.

[3]   *Fothergill v Monarch Airlines* [1980] 2 All ER 696 at p 700 per Lord Wilberforce.

[4]   *Manufacturers Hanover Trust Co v Alitalia* 429 F Supp 964 (1977); *Wing Hang Bank v Japan Airlines* 357 F Supp 94 (1973).

Registered baggage and cargo

8.4   Baggage is registered when it is accepted by the carrier for carriage and a receipt issued to the passenger[5]. The receipt is usually in the form of a baggage check, which provides a means for the carrier to check, regulate and control the carriage of baggage[6].

8.5   In the US, the term 'registered baggage' has been construed as including baggage of which the carrier takes charge for the purposes of carriage by air, even if no receipt or other written record of registration is issued[7]. US courts have thus found that items of hand luggage handed to cabin crew on or after boarding the aircraft constitute registered baggage within the meaning of the Convention[8]. They have regarded the absence of a baggage check as being irrelevant and not altering the status of the baggage as registered baggage of which the carrier has taken charge[9]. If (as is often the case) receipts are not issued in respect of hand luggage handed over to cabin crew, the consequence of these items being treated as registered baggage is that the carrier will be presumed liable for loss or damage under art 18(1) but will, pursuant to art 4(2), be unable to rely on the Convention's limits of liability, by reason of not having delivered a baggage check[10].

8.6   Cargo includes all articles consigned to the carrier for the purposes of transportation by air (other than baggage accompanying passengers). The corresponding term used in art 18(1) of the original Convention, namely 'goods', has been held to constitute virtually anything shippable, including coins[11], a horse[12], bull semen[13] and human remains[14].

Hand luggage

8.7   Article 18(1) does not expressly govern the carrier's liability for unregistered baggage, such as hand luggage carried on board an aircraft by passengers. However, the Convention contemplates liability on the part of the

---

[5]   *Collins v British Airways Board* [1982] QB 734 at p 752 per Kerr LJ; *Martin v Pan American World Airways* 563 F Supp 135 (1983), at p 138.
[6]   *Collins v British Airways Board* [1982] QB 734 at p 747 per Eveleigh LJ.
[7]   See eg *Martin v Pan American World Airways* 563 F Supp 135 (1983).
[8]   *Schedlmayer v Trans International Airlines* 416 NYS 2d 461 (1979); *Hexter v Air France* 563 F Supp 932 (SDNY, 1982); *Gill v Lufthansa German Airlines* 620 F Supp 1453 (1985); and *Chukwima v Groupe Air France Inc* 767 F Supp 43 (1991). A different conclusion has been reached in Germany, where the Bundesgerichtshof has held that hand luggage handed over to cabin crew remains an object of which the passenger takes charge himself and is thus subject to the art 22(3) limit of liability.
[9]   See *Schedlmayer v Trans International Airlines* 416 NYS 2d 461 at p 463–4.
[10] This is the result reached in each of the cases cited in footnote 8 above.
[11] *Trans World Airlines v Franklin Mint Corporation* 104 S Ct 1776 (1984), [1984] 2 Lloyd's Rep 432.
[12] *Stud v Trans International Airlines* 727 F 2d 880 (1984).
[13] *American Breeders Service v KLM Royal Dutch Airlines* 17 Avi 17,103 (1982).
[14] *Johnson v American Airlines* 834 F 2d 721 (1987).

carrier for damage to 'objects of which the passenger takes charge himself', as art 22(3) limits the carrier's liability in respect of such items. What is unclear is whether the carrier is presumed liable for damage to such objects or whether the passenger must establish negligence or fault in accordance with the applicable domestic law.

8.8   US courts have held that the carrier's liability under the Convention for damage to hand luggage is co-extensive with its liability under art 17 (if the luggage was in the charge of the passenger) or art 18 (if the luggage was in the charge of the carrier)[15]. On this basis, a carrier is presumed liable for:

- damage caused to hand luggage in the passenger's charge by an accident on board an aircraft or during any of the operations of embarking or disembarking; and

- damage caused to hand luggage in the carrier's charge on board an aircraft or in an airport.

8.9   This is logical and consistent within the overall framework of the Convention[16]. However, under the Montreal Convention, the carrier will not be presumed liable for damage to unregistered baggage, including personal items; it will instead only be liable for damage to such baggage resulting from its fault or that of its servants or agents[17].

Occurrence

8.10   For the carrier to be liable under art 18, there must be an 'occurrence' giving rise to the damage to the baggage or cargo during the carriage by air. The term 'occurrence' has been broadly construed and is wider than the word 'accident' in art 17. It includes, eg mechanical problems, loss of documentation by the airline[18] and the refusal of the carrier's employees to unload an aircraft[19].

8.11   The burden is on the claimant to prove that the baggage or cargo was not damaged when the carriage began[20]. Where therefore food carried by air arrived at its destination unfit for consumption but there was no evidence of anything having occurred during the carriage by air, the carrier was not liable under art 18(1)[21].

---

[15] *Baker v Landsell Protective Agency* 590 F Supp 165 (1984); see also *Kabbani v International Total Services* 807 F Supp 1073 (1992).

[16] See Reukema 'Hand luggage — passengers love it, the airlines hate it and the Warsaw Convention is not clear on how to handle it' (1987) 12 Annals of Air and Space Law 119, especially at pp 122–3.

[17] Article 17(2).

[18] *Nowell v Quantas* (1990) 22 Avi 18,071.

[19] *Cohen v Varig* 405 NYS 2d 44.

[20] *Boehringer v Pan Am* 531 F Supp 344 (1981).

[21] *Cie La Concorde v Cie Air France* (Paris, 18 May 1988), (1988) 42 RFDA 213.

8.12   So long as the occurrence giving rise to the damage takes place during the carriage by air, it does not matter that the damage may only be sustained or manifest itself later, after the carriage by air has come to an end[22].

The period of the carriage by air

8.13   Article 18(2) provides that 'the carriage by air' comprises:

> 'the period during which the baggage or cargo is in the charge of the carrier, whether in an aerodrome or on board an aircraft, or in the case of a landing outside an aerodrome, in any place whatsoever.'

Except in the case of a landing outside an aerodrome, the carriage by air thus constitutes such time as the baggage or cargo is:
•   in the charge of the carrier; and
•   in an aerodrome or on board an aircraft.

In the case of a landing outside an aerodrome, the carriage by air encompasses the whole time that the baggage or goods are in the charge of the carrier.

In the charge of the carrier

8.14   Clearly, baggage or cargo is in the charge of the carrier when in the carrier's actual possession or control. Article 18(2) thus covers cases where baggage is lost whilst being transferred between flights[23] or cargo is stolen from a carrier's airport warehouse[24]. Ascertaining precisely when the baggage and cargo comes into, and leaves, the carrier's charge may be more difficult, especially in cargo cases. Since the air waybill is prima facie evidence of the receipt of cargo by the carrier, that will often determine when the cargo comes into its charge[25].

8.15   Where cargo is unloaded at an airport by a carrier or its agents, it will come into the carrier's charge at that point in time and the carrier will be liable for damage to the cargo during the period of its unloading[26]. If the carrier or its agents are not solely responsible for unloading the cargo, it may be necessary to examine the facts closely to determine when during the process of unloading the carrier took charge of the cargo.

---

[22] *Nowell v Quantas* (1990) 22 Avi 18,071; *Carnisco International Customs House Brokers v Air China* (1992) 23 Avi 18,491.
[23] *Julius Young Jewellery v Delta Airlines* 414 NYS 2d 528 (1979).
[24] *Westminster Bank v Imperial Airways* [1936] 2 All ER 890; *Corocroft v Pan American Airways Inc* [1969] 1 QB 616; *Wing Hang Bank v Japanese Airlines* (1973) 357 F Supp 94.
[25] Article 11(1) of the Convention; see *El Du Pont de Nemours v Schenkers International Forwarders* (1974) 12 Avi 18,360.
[26] *Deutsche Lufthansa v La Nuechateloise* (Swiss Fed Ct, 26 March 1986), (1989) 43 RFDA 456, 460.

8.16   In *Swiss Bank Corpn v Brink's Mat*[27], three consignments of bank notes were stolen by armed robbers from KLM's warehouse at Heathrow airport when they were in the course of being unloaded from a Brink's Mat security van, weighed and transported by trolley into a strong room in KLM's warehouse. Bingham J (as he then was) held that the consignments came into the charge of the carrier[28] 'at the precise moment when they ceased to be in the custody and control of Brink's Mat'[29]. That moment was when each consignment, having been unloaded, placed on scales and found to conform with the shipping documents, was then placed onto a trolley to be transported to the strong room in the warehouse. Until that point in time, KLM had not accepted the consignment and could have declined to do so had the consignment's weight not accorded with the documents. Acceptance occurred when the consignment was ticked off on the shipping note by the KLM duty officer and moved from the scales onto the trolley[30]. When the robbery took place, two of the three consignments had been checked and weighed, and placed onto the trolley. The third was still in the process of being weighed. It followed that the first two consignments were in the carrier's charge at the time of the loss, but not the third[31].

8.17   In the *Brink's Mat* case, Bingham J rejected an argument by the carrier that a wide construction was to be given to the words 'in charge of the carrier' in art 18(2) and that all three consignments had come into the carrier's charge when the locked security van containing the consignments of bank notes had driven into the warehouse. As he observed, at that point in time the warehouse staff had no control over the consignments (beyond the ability to prevent the van leaving the confines of the warehouse) and no means of access to them; they were therefore not 'in the charge of' the carrier[32].

8.18   The period of the carriage by air ends when the carrier gives up control of the baggage or goods to the passenger or consignee. In the case of baggage, this will generally be when it is collected by the passenger from a luggage carousel in the airport terminal building[33]. In the case of cargo, the carriage by air has been construed as ending when the cargo is delivered to the consignee or his agents[34]. Until then, cargo is generally regarded as being in the carrier's charge, even if required to be handed over to customs officials before actual delivery to the consignee can take place. Although certain earlier

---

[27]   [1986] 2 Lloyd's Rep 79.
[28]   The carrier was Swissair, for whom KLM were acting as ground handling agents.
[29]   [1986] 2 Lloyds Rep 79 at p 96, col 2.
[30]   [1986] 2 Lloyds Rep 79 at p 94, col 1.
[31]   [1986] 2 Lloyds Rep 79 at p 96, col 2.
[32]   [1986] 2 Lloyds Rep 79 at page 96.
[33]   *Berman v TWA* 421 NYS 2d 291 (1979).
[34]   *Alltransport v Seaboard* 349 NYS 2d 277 (1973); *Railroad Salvage of Conn Inc v Japan Freight Consolidators* 556 F Supp 124 (1983); *Sprinks and Cie c Air France* 23 RFDA 405 (CA Paris, 27 June 1969).

authorities[35] found that the carrier ceased to be in charge of cargo once it was handed over to customs officials at the destination airport, the weight of authority in both civil and common law jurisdictions is now to the opposite effect.

8.19   Thus in *Sprinks & Cie c Air France*[36], the carrier was liable when a cargo of machinery was damaged when brought by an employee of the carrier to a loading dock to be placed onto a truck for delivery to the consignee, after it had been cleared through customs and removed from the customs warehouse. The Paris Court of Appeal concluded that the carriage by air ended by the delivery of the cargo to its consignee or to the consignee's agent, or by placing the cargo at their disposal, and no earlier[37]. Similarly, in *Alltransport v Seaboard World Airlines*[38], a New York court held that constructive delivery did not suffice to bring the carriage by air to an end and that the carrier only ceased to be in charge of the goods by physically handing them over to the consignee. The carrier remained in charge of goods so long as it had 'actual custody and control' over them. It was thus irrelevant that the carrier's contractual conditions provided for delivery to the consignee to be complete when the goods were handed over to customs.

8.20   The carrier does not cease to be in charge of cargo where, for the performance of the carriage by air by that carrier, it comes into the actual custody of another carrier. In *Wing Hang Bank v Japan Air Lines*[39], a consignment of bank notes had been carried by JAL to New York, where American Airlines acted as agents for JAL and were responsible for handling the processing through customs and storage of cargo on behalf of JAL. The consignment of bank notes was stolen by armed robbers from American Airlines' storage facility. Although JAL had ceased to have physical control over the cargo, the carriage by air had not yet terminated and they were liable under art 18 for the loss of the cargo, notwithstanding that it was in the actual custody of American Airlines.

8.21   It is not necessary for the carrier to have exclusive or sole control over the baggage or cargo in order for it to have charge within the meaning of art 18(2). In *United International Stables Inc v Pacific Western Airlines*[40] a racehorse being transported from New Zealand to Canada broke out of its stall during the flight and endangered the plane. The captain destroyed the horse. When sued by the horse's owners, the carrier argued that the horse was never

---

[35] See eg *Favre v Belgian State and Sabena* [1950] US Av Rep 392 (CA Brussels, 10 June 1950) and *Cie Air Liban c Cie Parisienne de Res escompte et Cie Air France* (1956) 10 RFDA 320 (CA Paris, 31 May 1956).

[36] (1969) 23 RFDA 405 (CA Paris, 27 June 1969).

[37] (1969) 23 RFDA 405 (CA Paris, 27 June 1969) at p 409.

[38] 12 Avi 18,163 (1973). See also *Railroad Salvage of Conn Inc v Japan Freight Consolidators* 556 F Supp 124 (1983).

[39] 12 Avi 17,884 (SD NY 1973).

[40] 5 DLR 3d 67 (Br Columbia Sup Ct, 1969).

in its charge because the owner's handlers had been on board the aircraft and in charge of the horse throughout. The court rejected this argument, partly in reliance upon contractual and tariff provisions providing for the carrier to be in overall charge of the animals being transported, but also on the basis that art 18(2) of the Convention was not intended to exclude the liability of the carrier in cases in which the consignor or consignee assisted in caring for the cargo. Article 18 did not require the carrier to be in complete control of the cargo.

In an aerodrome or on board an aircraft

8.22   Article 18 does not apply to cargo which is lost or damaged before it reaches an airport or aircraft, even if in the carrier's charge. Thus when cargo was stolen from a carrier's city office before being taken to the airport for loading onto the aircraft, the carrier was not liable under art 18(1)[41]. At the time of the loss, the carriage by air had not yet begun and the Convention was inapplicable.

8.23   The phrase 'in an aerodrome' in art 18(2) has been strictly construed in the US as applying only to baggage or cargo within the physical confines of an airport. Thus in *Victoria Sales Corporation v Emery Air Freight*[42] the Court of Appeals for the Second Circuit (by a majority) held that damage occurring to goods whilst stored in a carrier's warehouse located less than a quarter of a mile outside of the airport did not occur 'in an airport'[43] within the meaning of art 18(2). As Meskill J said, 'the plain language of Article 18 draws the line at the airport's border'[44]. To extend the application of art 18 beyond that point would, in his view, constitute an impermissible judicial amendment of the Convention[45]. Van Graafeiland J dissented. In his view, the term 'airport', which was not defined in the Convention, could be construed as including all cargo handling facilities used by a carrier for the purposes of carrying out the loading and unloading functions normally carried out at an airport, whether or not the facilities were located within the geographical borders of the airport[46].

8.24   Given the large number of freight-handling and storage facilities now located outside the actual confines of airports, the literal construction adopted by the majority in *Victoria Sales* will exclude many claims from the ambit of art

---

[41] *Dabrai v Air India* [1955] All Ind Rep 10
[42] 917 F 2d 705 (1990). Followed and applied in *Hitachi Data Systems Corpn v Nippon Cargo Airlines Co* (1995) 24 Avi 18,433 and *TBI Industrial Corporation v Emery Worldwide* 900 F Supp 687 (1995). See also *General Electric Co v Harper Robinson & Co* 818 F Supp 31 (1993).
[43] The words used in art 18(2) of the original Convention, to which the claim in *Victoria Sales* was subject.
[44] 917 F 2d 705 at p 707.
[45] 917 F 2d 705 at p 708.
[46] 917 F 2d 705 at p 710–11.

18. The editors of *Shawcross* suggest that the wider, functional interpretation adopted by Van Graafeiland J in his dissenting judgment is to be preferred; but, as they admit, once a literal construction is abandoned, it is difficult to see where to draw the line[47].

8.25   Once the carriage by air has come to an end, it cannot be revived for the purposes of establishing liability under art 18. Thus where a passenger retrieved his suitcases from an airport carousel and passed through customs, but then gave them to the carrier's baggage handler to carry out of the terminal building, the carrier was not liable when one of the suitcases was lost[48]. Since the period of the carriage by air had ended, the Convention did not apply even though the baggage was lost when in the carrier's charge, in an airport.

Loading, delivery and transhipment

8.26   Article 18(3) provides that the period of the carriage by air does not extend to any surface carriage performed outside an aerodrome, but that if such carriage takes place in the performance of a contract for carriage by air or for the purpose of loading, delivery or transhipment, any damage is presumed, subject to proof to the contrary, to have been the result of an event which took place during the carriage by air.

8.27   The presumption under this sub-article only applies where the surface transport can be characterised as incidental to the air carriage. In all other cases, the onus is on the claimant to prove that the loss or damage occurred during the carriage by air, as opposed to the surface carriage.

8.28   Where cargo is carried by land in order to suit the carrier's convenience, the surface carriage is likely to be construed as incidental to the carriage by air. In *Cie UTA c Ste Electro-Enterprise*[49] certain equipment had been sent from Le Bourget airport in Paris to Lome airport, in Togo. As the Lome airport was not equipped to handle the jet planes used by the carrier, the equipment was flown to Cotonou airport in the neighbouring state of Benin and transported by truck for 150 kilometres to Lome airport. It was found to be damaged on arrival. The court held that the presumption of art 18(3) applied because the surface carriage was incidental to, and 'in the performance of', the carriage by air, since the carrier had flown the cargo to Cotonou, and then carried it by road to Lome, for its own convenience.

8.29   The presumption under art 18(3) is rebuttable by proof 'to the contrary'. It will therefore not avail a consignee where damage to the cargo can be

---

[47] *Shawcross* Div VII para [602]; cf *Rolls Royce v Heavylift-Volga Dnepr Ltd* (2000) Times, 26 April.
[48] *Berman v TWA* 421 NYS 2d 291 (1979).
[49] (1977) RFDA 79 (CA Paris, 6 May 1976).

shown to have occurred during the surface transportation[50]. Nor can it be relied upon in order to extend the period of the carriage by air.

Recoverable damages

8.30   Under art 18(1), the carrier is liable (subject to Convention limits) for pecuniary or economic loss caused by the destruction or loss of, or damage to, cargo or baggage.

8.31   Whether damages are also recoverable for mental distress has been treated by US and Canadian courts as being a question for the applicable domestic law. On this basis, such damages were allowed by an Ontario court in *Newell v CP Air*[51], where a dog owner suffered grief when his dog was injured while in the charge of the carrier. They were, however, refused by a New York court in *Cohen v Varig*[52], where the claimants suffered distress and embarrassment when their luggage was lost and they were without appropriate clothes for the majority of a 28-day tour of South America[53].

Successive Carriers

8.32   A carriage performed by several successive carriers is deemed, for the purposes of the Convention, to be one undivided carriage if it is regarded by the parties as a single operation[54]. This is so whether there is a single contract or a series of contracts. However, the consignor or consignee of baggage or cargo may not sue all of the successive carriers. In the case of carriage of cargo, the consignor may sue only the first carrier and the carrier who performed the carriage during which the damage occurred[55]. Conversely, the consignee may sue only the last carrier or the carrier who performed the carriage during which the damage occurred[56]. For carriage of baggage, the claimant may sue the first carrier, last carrier or the carrier at the time of the damage[57]. The exception to these principles is where the first carrier has expressly assumed liability for the whole journey[58].

---

[50] *Pick v Lufthansa German Airlines* (1965) 9 Avi 18,077
[51] 74 DLR (3d) 574 (1976).
[52] 405 NYS 2d 44.
[53] See also *Siben v American Airlines* 25 Avi 17,355; compare *Kupferman v Pakistan International Airlines* 438 NYS 2d 189, a delay case under art 19, where *Cohen* was distinguished and damages for inconvenience and distress caused by the late arrival of luggage allowed.
[54] Article 1(3).
[55] Article 30(3).
[56] Article 30(3).
[57] Article 30(3).
[58] Article 30(2).

The Guadalajara Convention

8.33   The Guadalajara Convention 1961[59] deals with a different problem involving multiple carriers: where one carrier makes the contract with the claimant but a different carrier (with authority from the first carrier) actually performs the whole or part of the carriage. In these circumstances, the claimant may sue the contracting carrier in contract (no matter where or when the damage occurred) and the actual carrier, who performed the carriage at the time of the damage, in tort. The Warsaw Convention governs the claim and the aggregate amount claimable from the two carriers may not exceed the highest amount which would be claimable from either of them.

Title to sue

8.34   The general rule at common law is that it is the owner of the cargo or baggage that is entitled to sue for damage or loss; by contrast in civil law jurisdictions, it is generally only the parties to the contract of carriage who have title. Under the Convention, the consignor or the consignee expressly have title to sue. Where the goods have already been sold, it is the consignee who has title to sue and the consignor is considered to have acted as the consignee's agent in arranging the contract for carriage.

8.35   As for the title of third parties to sue the carrier, a number of foreign courts have come to the conclusion that the Convention gives title only to the consignor or consignee and no others. The English court, however, will allow a third party who has a proprietary interest to sue a carrier within the code of liability contained in the Convention. In *Western Digital v British Airways*, a recent decision of the Court of Appeal[60], it was settled that because the Convention does not expressly exclude the rights of action of third parties, the *lex fori* should prevail 'to fill in the gaps'. In the case of English law, this gives the standard common law rights to third parties. The practical consequence of the *Western Digital* decision is that first, an English court will permit the owner of the consignment, who is not named as consignor or consignee, to sue the carrier in accordance with the liability provisions of the Convention for damages caused by the damage or loss to the consignment; and second, where a principal of a consignor or consignee agent has title to the goods, then an English court will permit that principal to sue the carrier under the Convention for damage suffered as a result of loss or damage to the consignment. The decision of Lord Justice Mance in *Western Digital* concluded that the Convention did not exclude claims against an actual carrier based on title to the

---

[59]   Which has force of law in the UK by virtue of the Carriage by Air (Supplementary Provisions) Act 1962.
[60]   *Western Digital Corpn v British Airways plc* [2000] 2 Lloyds Rep 142.

relevant baggage or cargo, but subsumed them within the Convention scheme of liability in Ch III of the Convention. This decision is a welcome response to the doubt on the right of third parties to sue the carrier following the dictum of Lord Hope in *Sidhu v British Airways*[61] which doubted the correctness of the decision of *Gatewhite Ltd v Iberia Airlines Aereas de Espana Societe*[62].

The Montreal Convention

8.36   Certain aspects of the carrier's liability for loss of or damage to baggage and cargo will be clarified when the Montreal Convention comes into force. In particular:

- Article 17(2) of the Montreal Convention provides *inter alia* that the carrier is liable for damages sustained in case of destruction or loss of, or damage to, checked baggage upon condition only that that the event which caused the destruction, loss or damage took place 'on board the aircraft or during any period within which the checked baggage was in the charge of the carrier'. No distinction is drawn between baggage in and outside the airport, or between landings in and outside an airport.
- Under art 17(2), the carrier is not liable if the damage resulted from inherent defect, quality or vice of the checked baggage.
- Article 17(2) also deals expressly with hand luggage and other unchecked baggage. It provides that the carrier is liable for damage to such baggage if the damage resulted from its fault or that of its servants or agents.
- Under art 17(3), checked baggage is presumed to be lost when it does not arrive within 21 days of the date on which it ought to have arrived.
- The destruction or loss of, or damage to, cargo is dealt with separately under art 18, which provides that the carrier is liable for damage sustained in the event of such destruction, loss or damage upon condition only that the event which caused the damage so sustained took place during the carriage by air.
- Under art 18(2), the carrier can escape liability if it can prove that the destruction, or loss of, or damage to, the cargo resulted from inherent defect, quality or vice, defective packing (by someone other than the carrier), an act of war or armed conflict, or an act of public authority carried out in connection with the entry, exit or transit of the cargo.
- Under art 18(3), the carriage by air comprises the period during which the cargo was in the charge of the carrier. No distinction is drawn between cargo inside and outside the airport's perimeter. The precise location of a carrier's warehouse will no longer matter.

---

[61] [1997] AC 430 at pp 450–451.
[62] [1989] 1 Lloyd's Rep 160.

Delay

8.37

RULE 22—**The carrier is presumed liable for damage caused by delay in the carriage by air of passengers, baggage or cargo.**

8.38   Article 19 of the Convention[63] provides that:

> 'The carrier is liable for damage occasioned by delay in the carriage by air of passengers, baggage or cargo.'

Liability under this Article arises where there has been:
*   a delay;
*   in the carriage by air of passengers, baggage or cargo;
*   causing damage.

Each of these elements is considered below.

The meaning of 'delay'

8.39   The notion of delay connotes a discrepancy between the time when the carrier should have delivered the passengers, baggage or cargo to their destination and the time when it actually did so. Since the Convention does not stipulate the time within which carriers must complete the carriage by air or otherwise define what is meant by delay, whether or not there has been 'delay' will *prima facie* fall to be determined by reference to the terms of the contract of carriage pursuant to which the passengers, baggage or cargo were transported. As the court said in *Panalpina International Transport v Densil Underwear*[64], 'delay . . . in the context of Article 19 is a breach of the contractual obligation as to date of delivery'.

8.40   If the contract of carriage specifies a date and time by which the carriage was to be performed, the carrier will be liable for delay in not performing the carriage by that date and time. Such cases are, however, rare. Invariably, the carrier will not contract to deliver passengers, baggage or cargo within a stipulated time and will insert terms designed to ensure it is under no obligation to do so.

8.41   Standard conditions of carriage commonly provide that 'times shown in the ticket, timetable or elsewhere are not guaranteed and [the carrier] assumes no responsibility for making connections'. However, courts in

---

[63] The corresponding wording in art 19 of the Montreal Convention is in identical terms.
[64] [1981] 1 Lloyd's Rep 187 at p 189 per Edgar Fay J.

common law and civil jurisdictions have refused to construe such terms as giving carriers complete freedom as to when to perform the carriage by air; at most, they mean only that no time for performance is stipulated in the contract of carriage[65]. As Luckhoo JA said in *Bart v British West Indian Airways*[66], such provisions do 'not mean and cannot mean that delivery will be permitted to take place however it pleases the carrier'.

8.42   In the absence of an express term specifying the time for performance by the carrier, courts in common law jurisdictions have implied a term (on ordinary contractual principles) requiring the carrier to perform its obligations within a reasonable time[67]. What is reasonable depends upon all the circumstances of the case[68]. A factor likely to be crucial in assessing the reasonableness of the time taken by the carrier to perform its obligations is that one of the principal advantages of air transport, and the reason it is often used instead of generally cheaper forms of surface transport, is its speed[69]. The payment of high rates is likely to be seen as being inconsistent with the absence of an obligation on the part of the carrier to deliver within a short period.

8.43   Courts in common law jurisdictions have been reluctant to find the carrier liable for minor delays and the carrier will, it seems, not be liable for each and every delay, however small. Thus in *Bart v British West Indian Airways*[70], Luckhoo JA said that a delay of seven days beyond the reasonable time for delivery was 'sufficiently long a period . . . to open the doors of liability'. By implication, some lesser delay would not have rendered the carrier liable. In *Panalpina v Densil Underwear*[71], after determining the date by which the cargo should reasonably have arrived, the court went on to consider whether the delay was sufficiently material to be 'actionable'. In the court's view, a delay of 16 days was actionable, whereas a delay of five days would not have been.

8.44   Courts in civil law jurisdictions have generally found the carrier guilty of delay when performance of the carriage by air takes substantially

---

[65] See eg *Bart v British West Indian Airways* [1967] 1 Lloyd's Rep 239 (Guyana Court of Appeal); *Soiullac c Air France* (1965) 28 RGAE 15 (TGI Seine, 26 June 1964); *Ets Peronny c Ste Ethiopian Airlines* (1975) RFDA 395 (CA Paris, 30 May 1975); and *Filion v Suntours* [1980] CP 286.

[66] [1967] 1 Lloyd's Rep 239 at p 289 (Guyana Court of Appeal).

[67] *Bart v British West Indian Airways* [1967] 1 Lloyd's Rep 239 (Guyana Court of Appeal) at pp 251–2 per Sir Kenneth Stoby C and p 289 per Luckhoo JA; *Panalpina v Densil Underwear* [1981] 1 Lloyd's Rep 187 at p 189.

[68] *Bart v British West Indian Airways* [1967] 1 Lloyd's Rep 239 (Guyana Court of Appeal) and *Panalpina v Densil Underwear* [1981] 1 Lloyd's Rep 187.

[69] See in particular *Panalpina v Densil Underwear* [1981] 1 Lloyd's Rep 187 at p190; compare the civil decisions such as *Robert-Houdin v Ste La Panair do Brasil* (1961) 24 RGA 285 (TGI Seine, 9 July 1960) and *Cie General de Geophysique c Cie Iran Air* (1975) 29 RFDA 60 (CA Paris, 14 November 1974).

[70] *Bart v British West Indian Airways* [1967] 1 Lloyd's Rep 239 (Guyana Court of Appeal) at p 289.

[71] *Panalpina v Densil Underwear* [1981] 1 Lloyd's Rep 187 at p 190.

longer than the normal time and was far in excess of what the passenger or shipper could expect from air transportation[72].

8.45   The results achieved by courts using the different approaches adopted in common and civil law jurisdictions are likely to be similar[73]. Under both systems, a carrier is likely to avoid liability for slight delay, either because the delay will not be regarded as unreasonable or actionable (the common law test) or because the carriage did not take substantially longer than normal and was not far in excess of what could be expected (the civil law test). Conversely, a lengthy delay is likely to give rise to liability in both common and civil law jurisdictions.

Delay 'in the carriage by air'

8.46   There has been considerable debate as to what is meant by delay 'in the carriage by air', which is a phrase not defined in art 19.

8.47   No court has ascribed to the narrowest possible construction of these words, namely that the delay must occur while the passengers, baggage or cargo are actually airborne. Such an interpretation seems unduly restrictive and would be inconsistent with the meaning given to the phrase elsewhere in the Convention (notably art 18(2)). It has also been implicitly rejected in cases where art 19 has been found to apply to delays occurring before passengers, baggage or cargo were airborne, eg when a flight has been postponed or cancelled[74].

8.48   An alternative construction has been adopted by courts in France[75], Guyana[76] and the US[77], where the definition of the period of the carriage by air in art 18(2) has been applied to cases of delay under art 19.

8.49   Thus, in *Sté Nouvelle des Transports Mondiaux c Air France*[78], the Paris Court of Appeal said that art 19 'implicitly and rationally' referred to art 18 for the definition of air carriage. Similarly, in *Bart v British West Indian Airways*, Sir Kenneth Stoby C said that it was 'obvious' that the definition of 'carriage by air' in art 18(2) was exhaustive and intended to apply to art 19. He

---

[72] See eg *Ets Peronny v Ste Ethiopian Airlines* (1975) RDFA 395 (CA Paris, 30 May 1975), in which the Paris Court of Appeal summarised the position adopted by French courts in previous cases; *Berube c S. Nordair* (1981) RFDA 157 (C Prov De Chicoutimi, 16 November 1978). The same general rule applies in Germany: see 1984 ZLW 177 (Oberlandesgericht Frankfurt am Main, 26 April 1983).

[73] See Miller *Liability in International Air Transport* (1977) at p 157.

[74] See eg *Robert-Houdin c Ste La Panair do Brasil* (1961) 24 RGA 285 (TGI Seine, 9 July 1960); *Souillac c Air France* (1965) 28 RGAE 15 (TGI Seine, 26 June 1964).

[75] *Sté Nouvelle des Transports Mondiaux c Air France* (1960) 14 RFDA 317 (CA Paris, 14 March 1960).

[76] *Bart v British West Indian Airways* [1967] 1 Lloyd's Rep 239.

[77] *Nowell v Qantas Airways* (1990) 22 Avi 18,072.

[78] (1960) 14 RFDA 317 at p 319.

concluded that the delay in that case had not occurred 'in the carriage by air', because the cargo had been delayed by reason of being mislaid at the carrier's office in Georgetown city, before it was taken to the airport and loaded on the aircraft for carriage to London. It was therefore not in an aerodrome or on board on an aircraft when the delay occurred.

8.50   In *Nowell v Qantas*[79], cargo arrived at its destination on time but could not be released to the consignee from customs because the carrier had lost the relevant customs documents during the transportation. The cargo was only delivered to the consignee nearly one month later, by which time contracts for resale of the cargo had been cancelled. The court held that art 19 applied because although the delay manifested itself after the cargo had arrived at its destination, ie when it could not be released from customs, the event giving rise to the delay (namely, the carrier's loss of documents) had occurred during the transportation by air.

8.51   In the US, in *Brunwasser v Trans World Airlines*[80], the court suggested that the definition of carriage by air in art 18(2) could apply with equal force to art 19 even in a passenger context. In the court's view, the definition of carriage by air in art 18 demonstrated that the term encompassed 'only those activities which were directly associated with the movement of goods and people through the air'[81]. On this basis, the claim by the passenger in that case for damages for delay did not fall within the Convention since her flight had been cancelled some three months before the scheduled departure date. There was, as the court said, no close logical nexus between her injury and international air flight sufficient to establish liability under art 19[82].

8.52   An alternative approach would be to construe the term in a passenger context by reference to art 17, which renders the carrier liable for personal injuries suffered by a passenger as a result of an accident occurring on board the aircraft or during any of the operations of embarking or disembarking. This is, seemingly, the way in which Sir Kenneth Stoby C would have defined the phrase in a passenger context in *Bart v British West Indian Airways*, though the point did not arise for decision in that case[83].

8.53   A further possible construction is that art 19 applies whenever passengers, baggage or cargo do not arrive on time at the point of destination, irrespective of the cause. In her treatise, *Liability in International Air Transport*, Miller argues that this interpretation is supported by those cases (referred to in footnote 65 above) where art 19 was found to apply to postponed or

---

[79]   (1990) 22 Avi 18,072.
[80]   541 F Supp 1338 (1982) at p 1344.
[81]   541 F Supp 1338 (1982) at p 1344.
[82]   541 F Supp 1338 (1982) at p 1345.
[83]   See [1967] 1 Lloyd's Rep 239 at p 258.

cancelled flights, notwithstanding that the claimant passengers had not yet commenced any of the operations of embarking[84]. The advantage of this approach is that it avoids arbitrary results depending upon whether claims can be brought within the limits of arts 17 or 18. Why, for example, should it matter that passengers have not yet started embarking when the delay of their flight is announced? Whether they are checking in their bags at a check-in desk at the terminal building or waiting next to the departure gate about to board the flight, their carriage by air will have been delayed and they will suffer accordingly. In both instances there will, it is submitted, be a sufficiently close nexus between any damage suffered by them as a result of the delay and international air flight to warrant application of the Convention[85].

Recoverable damages

8.54   Article 19 does not specify the nature or extent of the damages recoverable for delay. These have been regarded as matters for applicable domestic laws[86]. What is clear is that damages can only be recovered for loss 'occasioned' by the delay.

8.55   In cargo cases, delay may cause damage to, or loss of, perishable goods. Alternatively, the late arrival of goods may lead to the loss of re-sales and consequent loss of profit, such as where goods intended for pre-Christmas trade arrived 16 days late on 21 December[87].

8.56   In passenger cases, the damages claimed will generally be for consequential losses caused by the delay. A passenger may, for example, miss a show in which he was due to appear and be paid[88]; or a passenger may need to buy replacement clothes, or suffer distress and inconvenience[89], if his luggage does not arrive.

8.57   Difficulties of proof often arise in delay cases and there are a number of reported cases where claims have been rejected because of the claimant's failure to establish that his loss was actually occasioned by the delay[90]. This,

---

[84]   *Miller* (1977) at p 159.
[85]   Cf *Brunwasser v Trans World Airlines* 541 F Supp 1338 at p 1344–5.
[86]   See eg *Panalpina v Densil Underwear* [1981] 1 Lloyd's Rep 187 at p 191, where the court simply had regard to the English rules of remoteness of damage.
[87]   *Panalpina v Densil Underwear* [1981] 1 Lloyd's Rep 187.
[88]   *Robert-Houdin c La Panair do Brasil* (1961) RGA 285 (TGI Seine, 9 July 1960).
[89]   Damages for mental distress and inconvenience due to late arrival of luggage have been refused in France in *Air France c Malbois* (1984) RFDA 287 (Cass. 27 March 1984), but allowed in the US in *Kupferman v Pakistan International Airlines* 438 NYS 2d 189 (1981) (though compare the art 18 cases of *Cohen v Varig* 405 NYS 2d 44 and *Siben v American Airlines* 25 Avi 17,355, where damages for mental distress caused by damage to cargo were not allowed).
[90]   See eg *Vassalo v TCA* (1963) 38 DLR (2d) 383; *Sté National Air France v Ste Arlab* (1985) 39 RFDA 478 (Aix-en-Provence CA, 29 November 1993); *Jamil v Kuwait Airways* 773 F Supp 482 (1991).

however, is not a peculiarity of the Convention but merely reflects the application of general legal principal to Convention cases.

8.58   In the US, art 19 has been construed as only allowing recovery of compensatory, and not punitive, damages[91].

Over-booking of passengers

8.59   There is considerable controversy as to whether passengers who are 'bumped' from a flight due to over-booking have a claim against the carrier for delay under art 19.

8.60   The decisions in the US are conflicting. In *Wolgel v Mexicana Airlines*[92], the Court of Appeals for the Seventh Circuit relied upon the drafting history of art 19 in concluding that claims for damages for the non-performance of the contract of carriage, such as where a passenger was bumped or otherwise refused boarding, were outside the Convention. The court noted that the delegates to the Warsaw conference considered that there was no need for a remedy under the Convention for total non-performance of the contract of carriage because in such a case the injured party had a remedy under the law of his or her home country. A contrary conclusion was reached by a differently constituted Seventh Circuit Court of Appeals in *Sassouni v Olympic Airways*[93], where the claimant (an orthodox Jew) was bumped from a flight to Tel Aviv and had to take the next available flight on the following day, which happened to be Passover. He claimed damages for the emotional distress caused by having to travel on Passover. The court distinguished *Wolgel* on the grounds that the damages claimed by the claimant flowed from the delay in his transportation, as opposed to the bumping itself. Article 19 was thus applicable[94].

8.61   The weight of authority in other jurisdictions, including Canada[95], Germany[96], Italy[97] and France[98], is in line with *Wolgel* in treating bumping and other cases of non-performance of the contract of carriage as outside the scope of the Convention.

8.62   The question of whether bumping falls within the scope of art 19 is of diminished significance in European Community countries since the introduction of a European Community Regulation establishing common rules for

---

[91] *Harpalani v Air India* 634 F Supp 797 (1986).
[92] 821 F 2d 442 (1987).
[93] 769 F Supp 537 (1991).
[94] See also *Mahaney v Air France* 474 F Supp 532 and *Harpalani Air India* 622 F Supp 69.
[95] *Hendler v Cie Iberia* (1980) 34 RFDA 215 (Prov Ct Montreal).
[96] 28 ZLW 134 (1979).
[97] *Imarisio v Trans World Airlines* (1992) 17 Air Law 30 (Turin, 9 May 1974).
[98] *Medical Plus SARL c SA Sabena World Airlines* 36 RFDA 252 (Paris CA, 15 September 1992).

a denied-boarding compensation scheme. The Regulation applies where a passenger is denied access to an over-booked flight departing from an airport in a Member State. It provides for the passenger to elect for reimbursement of the unused ticket or rerouting at the earliest opportunity or at a later date, at the passenger's convenience, and for the immediate payment of minimum compensation of prescribed amounts.

Financial limit of liability

8.63

RULE 22A—**Article 22 of the Warsaw Convention and the Warsaw Convention as amended at the Hague limits the financial liability of the carrier.**

8.64   In the carriage of registered baggage or cargo the liability of a carrier is limited by art 22(2)(a) of the Warsaw Convention to 250 francs[99] or 17 Special Drawing Rights[100] per kilogramme unless a special declaration of value has been made to the carrier, in which case the carrier will be liable to pay a sum not exceeding the declared value. Where the liability of the carrier is regulated by Warsaw Convention as amended by the Hague protocol then the liability of the carrier will be limited to 17 Special Drawing Rights per kilogramme[101].

---

[99] The reference to franc is a reference to a currency unit consisting of sixty-five and a half milligrammes of millesimal fineness nine hundred. See Carriage by Air (Sterling Equivalents) Order 1996, SI 1996/565 for the conversion rate of francs to Sterling. See further *Shawcross* at Div VII paras [422] and [429].

[100] The limit of 17 Special Drawing Rights will apply where the carriage is subject to Additional Protocol No 1 of Montreal 1975.

[101] As a result of the implementation of Montreal Additional Protocol No 2, liability limits under this version of the Warsaw Convention are expressed in Special Drawing Rights.

Chapter 9

Defences Available to the Carrier

9.1   If the carrier is prima facie liable for damage or loss to passengers, baggage or cargo under arts 17, 18 or 19 of the amended or unamended Conventions, the substantive defences available to it are closely circumscribed[1]. In essence[2], they are limited to the narrow defence provided by the two different versions of art 20 contained in the amended and unamended Conventions and to a potentially wider defence of contributory negligence, preserved by art 21 of those Conventions.

9.2   Under the Warsaw Convention as amended by Montreal Protocol (No 4)[3], the carrier is not liable for loss of or damage to cargo, if that loss or damage resulted solely from inherent defect or vice of the cargo, or defective packaging by someone other than the carrier's servants or agents, or an act of war or armed conflict, or an act of a public authority carried out in connection with the entry, exit or transit of the cargo. A similar defence is available to the carrier under the Montreal Convention 1999[4].

Article 20: All Necessary Measures / Impossibility Defence

9.3

Rule 23—**Under both the amended and unamended Conventions the carrier will not be liable for damage if it proves (a) that it and its servants or agents took all necessary measures to avoid the damage or (b) that it was impossible to take such measures.**

---

[1]   Article 20 cannot be relied on as a defence against claims based on arts 10 or 12 of the Convention.
[2]   Another defence is a limitation defence.
[3]   Montreal Protocol (No 4) was given effect in English law by the Carriage by Air Acts (Implementation Protocol No 4 of Montreal, 1975 Order, SI 1999/1312.
[4]   See art 18(2) of the Montreal Convention 1999.

9.4   Article 20 of the amended Convention (and art 20(1) of the unamended Convention) provides as follows:

> 'The carrier is not liable if he proves that he and his servants or agents have taken all necessary measures to avoid the damage or that it was impossible for him or them to take such measures.'

9.5   Drafting background.   The defence provided by art 20 was introduced by British delegates to the 1925 Paris Conference with the intention of applying to the Warsaw convention the concept of 'due diligence' which was well established in international maritime law at the time[5]. The conference reached agreement in principle that the carrier should be liable if it could not establish that it had taken all reasonable and normal measures. The CITEJA draft[6] had spoken in terms of 'reasonable measures'. Many observers have commented, however, on the alien nature in this context of concepts such as reasonableness in civil law codes[7].

9.6   Between the CITEJA draft and the final version of art 20 contained in the unamended Convention, the article underwent an important revision through the introduction of the reference to 'all necessary measures' (*mesures nécessaires*) rather than 'reasonable measures' (*mesures raisonnables*). A certain amount of confusion surrounds this amendment which does not appear to have been adequately debated[8]. As a result of this change, and despite the original intentions of the British delegation, when the Convention came to be translated into English from French, the literal translation which was made did not refer to 'due diligence'. The maritime approach to 'due diligence' has thus played little, if any, part in the interpretation of the necessary measures provision of art 20 in common law jurisdictions[9]. The meaning given to 'all necessary measures' will be discussed in more detail below[10].

9.7   Subsequent changes and proposals.   The amended Convention removed the defence provided by art 20(2) of the unamended Convention[11]. The Guatemala City Protocol[12] has proposed radical changes to the carrier's liability in respect of passengers and baggage. Under its proposed new art 17(1) the only possible defence in relation to the death or injury of a passenger would be to prove that such death or injury resulted solely from the state of health of the passenger; under its proposed new art 17(2) the only possible defence in the case of damage to baggage would be to prove that the damage

---

[5]   See *Miller* pp 66–69.
[6]   See para **1.5** above.
[7]   Eg *Shawcross* Div VII para [408]; *Miller* p 67, p 167.
[8]   See *Miller* p 66.
[9]   See *Miller* p 167.
[10] See paras **9.9** to **9.13**, below
[11] See para **9.43**, below.
[12] See para **1.27**, above.

resulted from inherent defect, quality or vice of the baggage. The Guatemala City Protocol would however, preserve a defence of contributory negligence[13]. The Montreal Protocol No 4[14] has recently introduced radical changes in respect of baggage and cargo: the defence of necessary measures would be limited to cases of delay and more specific liability exceptions would be provided for by the new art 18(3), such as defective packing, inherent vice, acts of war and acts of public authorities.

9.8   The Montreal Convention, 1999.   The Montreal Convention[15] will considerably reduce the importance of the art 20 defence. In the case of passengers having a point of contact with the territory of the US, carriers have waived their right to invoke art 20[16].

9.9   The meaning of 'all necessary measures'.   Clearly, the requirement of a carrier to take 'all necessary measures' to avoid damage cannot be taken literally. There is a fundamental paradox: if *all* necessary measures were taken to prevent the damage then — *ex hypothesi* — the damage would not have occurred in the first place. Conversely, in (almost) any case, *some* measure could have been taken to avoid the damage; ultimately by cancelling the carriage, if necessary.

9.10   The phrase cannot be read literally and its meaning now appears reasonably well established[17], providing a high, though not necessarily insuperable[18], obstacle for the carrier to overcome. A standard formulation is that given in *Goldman v Thai Airways International Ltd*[19]: Chapman J considered that 'all necessary measures' in art 20 meant 'all measures necessary in the eyes of the reasonable man . . . all reasonably necessary measures'. Such an approach does no violence to the language of art 20; as Greer LJ emphasised in *Grein v Imperial Airways*[20] the requirement is to exercise 'all reasonable skill and care in taking *all* necessary measures to avoid causing damage . . .'[21]. The carrier must show that it has taken *all* the necessary measures to avoid the

---

13   Article 21 of the proposed convention.
14   See para **1.33**, above.
15   See para **1.47**, above.
16   The Montreal Convention provides that carriers shall include the following clause in their Conditions of Carriage: 'The Carrier shall not, with respect to any claim arising out of the death, wounding or other bodily injury of any passenger, avail itself of any defence under Article 20(1) of said Convention or said Convention as amended by said Protocol.'
17   See eg *Shawcross* Div VII para [408], Lureau No 204; Zoghibi No 33. Cf *Giemulla & Schmid* Supp.4 Schmid (October 1994) 3.
18   Although, as Phillips J observed in *Antwerp United Diamond BVBA v Air Europe* [1993] 4 All ER 469, 472 it remains 'a rare case when a carrier is able to establish a defence under Article 20.'
19   Unreported, transcript 31 March 1981. There is a short report in (1981) 125 Sol J 413.
20   [1937] 1 KB 50 at 69. It should be noted that Greer LJ was not considering the Warsaw Convention as such but an almost identically worded contractual term. His comments remain authoritative: see *Johnson Estate v Pishke* [1989] 3 WWR 207 at 218, per Halvorson J (Saskatchewan Queen's Bench).
21   Emphasis added.

damage, but its duty is only that of the reasonable carrier in taking such measures[22]. In essence, the carrier must be 'free from fault'[23].

9.11   In *Swiss Bank Corporation v Brink's-Mat Ltd*[24] Bingham J emphasised the necessary measures provision imported a duty on the carrier higher than 'a mere duty to take reasonable care', commenting that this was the price that the carrier had to pay for the limitation of its liability[25]. Bingham J cited with approval[26] the following observations of Judge Connor sitting in the US District Court for the Southern District of New York in *Manufacturers Hanover Trust Company v Alitalia Airlines* [27]:

> 'Both plaintiff and defendant have devoted considerable efforts to explain and support their respective constructions of the phrase "all necessary measures". But, in the end, a common-sense reading serves best. Thus, notwithstanding plaintiff's argument to the contrary, this Court concludes that the phrase "all necessary measures" cannot be read with strict literality, but must, rather, be construed to mean "all *reasonable* measures". After all, there could scarcely be a loss of goods — and consequently no call for operation of Article 20 — were a carrier required to have taken every precaution literally necessary to the prevention of loss. Nor, on the other hand, may a carrier escape liability under Article 20, as Alitalia suggest, by demonstrating no more than its recourse to some — as opposed to all — reasonable measures. In short Article 20 requires of defendant proof, not of a surfeit of preventatives, but rather, of an undertaking embracing all precautions that in sum are appropriate to the risk, i.e., measures reasonably available to defendant and reasonably calculated, in cumulation, to prevent the subject loss.'

9.12   Thus, in the *Swiss Bank* case itself, large consignments of Bank of England bank notes were consigned for carriage by the claimants. While in the defendant's cargo warehouse at Heathrow Airport inter alia the bank notes were stolen by armed robbers, who entered the warehouse. Although there was a strong-room for high value goods in the warehouse, all such goods arriving in the warehouse were unloaded, normally from an armoured van, and checked outside the strong-room. Bingham J considered that if the applicable test had been one of reasonable care he would have found that the defendant had exercised sufficient care to avoid liability[28]. However, the defendant had failed to take *all* necessary measures and so could not rely on the art 20 defence[29]:

---

[22]   See *Miller* p 163.
[23]   *Pierre v Eastern Air Lines* (1957) US & C Av 431.
[24]   [1986] 2 Lloyd's Rep 79.
[25]   At 97.
[26]   At 96–7.
[27]   429 F Supp 964 (1977) 967.
[28]   At 97–8.
[29]   At 97.

'There were some reasonably necessary measures which could have been taken to avoid the damage. I do not include the package by package unloading and storage of the packages among such measures, because such a procedure could reasonably be regarded as dangerous and unlikely to avoid the loss, given the violence which these robbers were evidently willing to use. Nor, in the course of running a busy warehouse, do I regard the routine securing of all doors whenever a security van arrived as such a measure. But it would have been possible to ensure that all doors, if open, were manned and guarded at such times, and if there was no secure area in which the van could be unloaded I think that such a precaution could be regarded as reasonably necessary.'

9.13   Thus, if there were other measures which a reasonable carrier would have taken in order to try to prevent the damage the carrier will not escape liability. In *Rustenburg Platinum Mines Ltd v Pan American World Airways Inc*[30], for example, a consignment of platinum was stolen from the hold of an aircraft. Ackner J commented[31]:

'To my mind it is clear that Pan Am did not take all necessary measures to avoid the damage, nor was it impossible for them to take such measures. A measure would have been to instruct the loaders never to leave a hold which contained valuable cargo unsupervised until it was closed. Another measure which could have been taken was to send this platinum by another flight which could accommodate the valuables in the safety pouch. And yet another was not to have dispatched the platinum on Sept. 8 when the security emergency reduced the number of security guards to such an extent that there was none of duty watching this place.'

General principles

9.14   A number of general principles can be distilled from the abundant case law on art 20.

9.15   **State of Knowledge.**   The measures which are 'necessary' should only be evaluated on the basis of the technical knowledge and standard carrier practice (where relevant) at the time that the damage was caused.

9.16   **Warnings.**   A sufficient warning as to potential dangers may be sufficient to exonerate the carrier even where other measures could have been taken. In *Chisholm v British European Airways*[32], for example, the claimant was

---

[30]   [1977] 1 Lloyd's Rep 564.
[31]   At 577.
[32]   [1963] 1 Lloyd's Rep 626.

injured during a flight from Manchester to Majorca when the aircraft encountered turbulence over the Pyrenees. Passengers had been warned of the risk of turbulence and told to fasten their belts and remain in their seats. The claimant had disregarded the warning and visited the lavatory; on her way back to her seat she had broken her ankle when the plane pitched violently. Fenton Atkinson J considered that the airline had taken all reasonable care and the claim failed[33].

9.17   Another example: in *Air-Inter v Quaranta*[34] a passenger was injured by a falling bag when another passenger opened an overhead luggage locker. The airline staff had made an announcement recommending that passengers take care in opening the lockers and, on appeal, the carrier was held entitled to rely on an art 20 defence.

9.18   On the other hand, a failure to warn passengers of potential risks will not necessarily deprive the carrier of the right to rely on art 20. The Californian Court of Appeals has held that it is not necessary to announce to passengers the potential risk of turbulence either before or during the flight since this is too well known to need announcing[35]. However, the court held the carrier liable on the facts for failing to warn passengers of a bad weather front that the pilot expressly knew the aircraft would have to cross. Similarly, in the *Goldman v Thai Airways* case[36], no warning about the use of seat belts was given despite the known likelihood of clear air turbulence and a defence based on art 20 failed.

9.19   As for warnings by the claimant to the carrier, it is unlikely that the failure of the claimant to alert the carrier to particular risks will exonerate the carrier in circumstances where the carrier itself should have been alerted. For example, in *Boehringer Mannheim Diagnostics Inc v Pan American World Airways Inc*[37] a delicate item of machinery, a 'Super 17' automated blood chemistry analyser, was damaged in transit (probably in being tilted in unloading by the carrier's employees). The claimant succeeded against the carrier. The claimant had made no attempt to mark the crate or otherwise alert the carrier to the nature of its contents. However, the size of the crate in which the analyser was being transported should have alerted the carrier's employees to the risks involved in its normal procedure of tilting crates and the crate could, in any event, have been handled more carefully than it was.

9.20   The nature of the risk.   The measures to be taken by the carrier will clearly depend on the nature and likelihood of the risk to be guarded against.

---

[33] It would appear that the Court applied a simple test of reasonable care (at 628 and 634); and see *Swiss Bank Corporation v Brink's-Mat Ltd* [1986] 2 Lloyd's Rep 79 at 97.

[34] 1 S & B Av R VII/303; See also *Bessis v Air France* (1994) 47 RFDA 173.

[35] *Kohler v Aspen Airways* 19 Avi 18,051.

[36] Unreported, transcript 31 March 1981. There is a short report in (1981) 125 Sol J 413.

[37] 531 F Supp 344 (1981).

The *Manufacturers Hanover* case[38] involved an armed robbery of the carrier's storage facility at Kennedy Airport, New York. The court concluded[39]:

> 'Alitalia . . . did undertake a number of measures, each intrinsically reasonable, to secure high-value cargo . . . The existence and structure of the . . . valuables room; the armed guard hired specially to obstruct illicit access . . . the log book record of high-value cargo, conscientiously maintained; Alitalia's refusal to accept high-value cargo deliveries until an armed guard's arrival; certain precautions taken by Alitalia to prevent undue circulation of documents reflecting a shipment of high-value cargo — all combined to demonstrate that defendant had not been wholly unmindful of nor unmoved by considerations of security. But such precautions would be, predictably enough, likely unavailing in the circumstances of an armed robbery . . . To preserve against such eventuality more could — and should — have been done. With unrestricted access into Building 86 and through it, the armed guard stationed on a chair at the valuables-room entrance was positioned no more securely than the proverbial sitting duck. As Alitalia's own witnesses agreed, restrictions on access to and through Building 86 — or at least, an enclosure about the valuables-room and its guard — might have discouraged or frustrated robbery, if not insured against it. Moreover, armed robbery might have been prevented or ultimately stymied — had a silent alarm system, with direct connection to the Port Authority police station, been installed on the premises . . . The costs involved . . . would have been more than reasonable in the light of its robbery-prevention value. . . .

> That armed robbers had so far spared such facilities could hardly have insulated the reasonably prudent airline carrier from the knowledge that an armed robbery of a cargo warehouse was a likely future contingency. . . .

> Other airlines at Kennedy Airport, at least until January 1974, may well have been less security conscious than was Alitalia; few, if any, may have been more so. . . . [T]hat fact cannot confer added grace to Alitalia's posture herein.'

9.21   Standard carrier practice.   It may in certain cases of reliance on art 20 be of assistance to carriers to refer to the standard practice of airlines. Thus, in *Preyval v Cie Air France*[40], a passenger disembarking from an aircraft fell on its ramp. The ramp was of a normal type, of an international model, nothing indicated that it had not been positioned according to its purpose and the operations of disembarking had been normally attended to by Air France's

---

[38]   See para **9.14**, above.
[39]   At 968–969.
[40]   (1973) 27 RFDA 345.

representatives. Air France was able to rely on art 20 because it had taken all necessary measures.

9.22   By contrast, it did not assist Alitalia in the *Manufacturers Hanover* case to assert that its practices were superior to the norm of airlines operating at Kennedy Airport in 1974. It was not simply a matter for the industry to set its own standards if the court determined that more could and should have been done; 'common prudence' is not to be equated with 'reasonable prudence'[41]. Moreover, the measures taken must be apt in the light of the relevant damage[42]. The carrier will not be assisted by showing that the usual or normal precautions were taken if the circumstances required additional precautions to be taken[43].

Particular instances

9.23   Certain situations commonly recur in which art 20 is relied upon. The following paragraphs provide a brief summary of a number of these situations.

9.24   **Defective construction.**   Where the damage was caused wholly on account of the defective construction of the aircraft, then the carrier will generally be exonerated. This is because (1) in the normal case a reasonable carrier could not have itself have known of the defect and (2) because the manufacturers of the aircraft (who could and should have known) are not treated as the carrier's 'servants or agents' for the purposes of art 20[44]. Clearly, however, where the carrier should have known about the defect (or did know), then art 20 will provide no defence unless the carrier has taken all necessary measures to prevent damage eg regular and proper maintenance and repair of the aircraft[45].

9.25   **Force majeure.**   Where the damage has been caused by force majeure then the carrier will certainly be exonerated if it was impossible to avoid the damage[46]. Where it was theoretically possible to avoid the damage, whether the carrier is nevertheless exonerated will depend in part on the state of knowledge in the industry at the relevant time. Since relatively little is currently known about the occurrence and effects of 'wind-shear', for example, the carrier may well be exonerated for damage arising solely from its effects.

---

[41]   At 968.
[42]   *Shawcross* Div VII para [408].
[43]   See *Boehringer Mannheim Diagnostics Inc v Pan American World Airways Inc* 531 F Supp 344 (1981) at 348; *United International Stables Ltd v Pacific Western Airlines* 5 DLR 3d 67.
[44]   See para **9.42** below.
[45]   *Messeaud v Air Inter* (1995) 48 RFDA 95
[46]   See for example *DeVera v Japan Airlines* 24 Avi Cas 18,317 (SDNY, 1994) where the damage was caused by typhoons and volcanic eruptions.

9.26   By contrast, in cases of thunderstorms (which are reasonably well understood in this context), the pilot will be expected to order passengers to fasten their seat-belts and, where appropriate, to land or change to a different flight level. The carrier will not be able to rely on art 20 where the pilot does not take such evasive action even where air traffic control has ordered him not to; in an emergency, the pilot in command is allowed to (and should) make his own decisions[47]. Thus in *Air Inter c Simon*[48], the pilot had been instructed to remain in a holding position in bad weather to allow another plane to take off. Shortly afterwards, the pilot lost control of the aircraft because of the bad weather. The Cour d'Appel de Paris did not apply art 20 because the pilot had not taken all necessary measures to prevent damage. The court held that the pilot should have taken a stand-by position outside the bad weather or diverted to another airport nearby; he should not have accepted the proposal of the air traffic control.

9.27   Delay.   Article 20 defences may be applicable also in cases of delay under art 19, but the burden on the carrier is, again, a high one. In general, it is not enough to show only that the carrier did all that was necessary to reduce delay once delay became obvious; the carrier must also do all that is necessary to prevent the delay in the first place.

9.28   Where the delay was caused by a technical defect in the aircraft, for the reasons already mentioned[49] this second limb may well be satisfied; but the first may not. In the case of *McMurry v Capitol International Airways*[50], for example, engine trouble led to the cancellation of a particular flight to the US. The fact that all other flights of the defendant carrier were full did not excuse the carrier from liability. Flights by other carriers were available and the carrier could and should have made more effort to find the claimant another flight to the US. By contrast, in the case of *Cenci v Mall Airways Inc*[51], the carrier was able to rely on an art 20 defence in circumstances where it had promptly explained to its passengers the cancellation caused by engine trouble and provided tickets on another airline's flights to the same destination.

9.29   Burden of Proof.   The burden of proof is on the carrier to show that it has taken all necessary measures or that such measures were impossible. It follows when the circumstances of an accident are unknown, it is most unlikely that the carrier will be able to rely on art 20[52]. An inability on the part

---

[47] Schmid 'Ausgewählte internationale Rechtsprechung zum Warschauer Abkommen in den Jahren 1980–1987' [1985] ZLW 123.
[48] 1968 RFDA 198, 198 ULC 90.
[49] See para **9.24**, above.
[50] 424 NYS 2d 88.
[51] 531 NYS 2d 743.
[52] See, for example, *Panalpina International Transport Ltd v Densil Underwear Ltd* [1981] 1 Lloyd's Rep 187, 191; *Boehringer Mannheim Diagnostics v Pan American World Airways Inc* 531 F Supp 344 (1981) especially at 347, where the precise cause of the damage could not be explained. See also *McNair* p 186 and Hjalsted 'The Air Carrier's Liability in cases of Unknown Cause of Damage' (1960) 27 JALC 119, 126. An analogy is with the principles of 'res ipsa loquitur': the carrier is in the best position to explain how the accident occurred.

of the carrier to explain the circumstances in which a theft took place in *Cie Air Liban v Cie Parisienne de Réescompte*[53], for example, precluded any attempt to invoke art 20. Evidence is required that specific measures which could have avoided the damage have been taken. Merely showing that the carrier provided an airworthy aircraft and competent crew is unlikely to be sufficient[54]. If more than one cause of damage is alleged, then the carrier must provide evidence to rebut each one.

9.30   Before art 20 has any application, a passenger must first prove that his claim falls within arts 17, 18 or 19 of the Convention. For example, if a passenger with a pre-existing heart condition suffers a heart attack in a thunderstorm on an aircraft, then the passenger must prove that, given his poor health, the heart attack was not already likely before the flight[55]. He must prove that he has suffered an accident within art 17. If he is able to prove this, then the burden shifts back to the carrier to establish an art 20 defence.

9.31   Foreseeability of risk of damage.   The carrier will not be required to take precautions against risks which are unforeseeable. Only foreseeable risks, which a prudent carrier would have taken measures to prevent, will need to be guarded against[56]. Article 20 is not interpreted so as to consider what precautions were objectively necessary to prevent the damage with the benefit of hindsight[57].

9.32   Causation.   It would appear that if the court determines that a carrier has not taken all necessary measures, it will not be necessary for the claimant to show that such measures would in fact have prevented the accident. In the *Manufacturers Hanover* case the court stated[58]:

> 'We cannot say, of course, that such precautions would necessarily have averted the loss upon which the instant suit is based. Nor, for that matter, can we say that Alitalia's employees, under the circumstances in which they found themselves . . . could and should have acted otherwise for the sake of thwarting their assailants' purpose. We conclude only — but nonetheless fatally for the defense — that Alitalia did not take all reasonable measures that prudent foresight would have envisioned for the securing of high-value cargo.'

9.33   Impossibility.   Article 20 further provides that the carrier may escape

---

[53]   (1956) 10 RFDA 320, 322–3 (CA, Paris).
[54]   *Cie La Jugoslavenki Aéro-Transport v Gati* JCP (1962) II 12596 (CA, Paris).
[55]   *Fleming v Delta Airlines* 12 Avi Cas 18,122 US District Court, SDNY (non-Warsaw case); *Metz v KLM* 15 Avi Cas 17,843 US District Court, DMass.
[56]   See, for example, *McMurry v Capitol International Airways* 424 NYS 2d 88 at 89.
[57]   *Case No 21 U 62/91* (1992) 2 S & B Av R VII/151 at 157–8 (Frankfurt Higher Regional Court).
[58]   At 968.

liability if it can show that it was impossible for it *or* its servants or agents to take such measures. Despite the strict language of the provision it is clear that the carrier must show that it was impossible both for the carrier (usually a corporate body) *and* its servants/agents to take such measures[59].

9.34 Bingham J has stressed that 'impossible' does not mean 'not reasonably possible'[60]:

> ' 'Impossible', even if it cannot be read with complete literalness, is a very strong word. It envisages damage which was inevitable, or at least which no human precaution or foresight would have prevented.'

9.35 Accordingly, cases in which impossibility has been successfully relied on are especially rare. One such case is a case decided in the Frankfurt Higher Regional Court[61], which involved the disappearance of a consignment of carpets from Nepal from an aircraft stranded at Kuwait Airport as a result of the commencement of the Gulf War. The court considered that the only effective measures that the air carrier could have taken would have been the avoidance of Kuwait altogether as the theatre of war or the punctual onward transport out of Kuwait of the rugs; it was unrealistic to expect the carrier to take such precautions if it could not foresee the outbreak of hostilities which took the world by surprise[62].

9.36 A carrier was similarly not liable in respect of goods seized by customs officials in Abu Dhabi. It was impossible for the carrier to avoid the action of the authorities[63].

9.37 The carrier may thus in rare circumstances succeed under art 20 if measures which might have averted the damage were not taken in circumstances where it was not practicable for the carrier to take such measures. Two French cases arising from the 1976 hijacking of an aircraft to Entebbe in Uganda[64] illustrate this principle[65]. Only the authorities at Athens airport, who allowed four heavily armed hijackers to board the aircraft during an intermediate stop, were able to control passengers prior to embarkation. It was held that it would have been impossible for the carrier to take the

---

[59] See *Gurtner v Beaton* (1990) 1 S & B Av R 499 at 518 where Owen J rejected an argument that a carrier could rely on art 20 because it had no knowledge of a particular flight and could not therefore taken any measures in respect of it. This point was not challenged on appeal: [1993] 2 Lloyd's Rep 369.
[60] *Swiss Bank Corporation v Brink's-Mat Ltd.* [1986] 2 Lloyd's Rep 79 at 96.
[61] *Case No 21 U 62/91* (1992) 2 S & B Av R VII/151.
[62] At 158.
[63] *Gulf Air v Sté Romanaise de la Chaussure, UNIC* (1987) 1 S & B Av R VII/265. See also *Najjar v Cie Swissair* (1987) 41 RFDA 232.
[64] The passengers were subsequently released by Israeli military action.
[65] *Haddad v Cie Air France* (1982) 36 RFDA 342; 1 S & B Av R VII/89 and *Ayache v Cie Air France* (1984) 38 RFDA 450.

necessary measures to prevent the hijacking. However, if the court considers that it might have been possible for the carrier to institute an alternative security check it may not avoid liability. The case of *Cie Air-Inter v Bornier*[66] involved the hijacking of an aircraft after take-off from Paris and subsequent injuries to several passengers caused by a grenade brought onto the aircraft by one of the hijackers. The hijacker's weapon might have been detected by a normal security check at the airport, but such a check had not been established for the route in question. Airport security rested with the French police authorities, but the court held that the airline had not discharged its burden of proof under art 20, since it had not established that it was impossible to initiate any alternative kind of security control[67].

9.38   The approach of the US Courts.   Prior to the *Manufacturers Hanover* case the US courts had applied an even more restrictive approach to art 20 defences. It was insufficient for a carrier to show that it had taken all reasonable measures. The carrier had to show that all *possible* measures had been taken[68]. In *Philios v Transcontinetal & Western Air Inc*[69] a passenger suffered ruptured ear-drums when the unpressurised transport plane in which she was travelling descended to land at Athens Airport. The carrier failed in its attempt to invoke art 20 because the use of an aircraft with a pressurised cabin would have averted the damage[70]. The burden placed by such decisions on the carrier had been described as 'almost insurmountable'[71].

9.39   Following the *Manufactures Hanover* case and *dicta* in other cases, such as *Feibelmann v Compagnie Nationale Air France*[72], however, the approach of the US courts is now regarded as broadly in line with that of English and other jurisdictions[73].

9.40   Servants or Agents.   Article 20 refers to necessary measures carried out by the carrier 'and his servants or agents'. The original French text of art 20 uses the word 'préposés' which, according to French law, means persons to whom the principal is entitled to give orders concerning the way in which certain works are to be performed[74]. The following definition is therefore

---

[66] (1983) 37 RFDA 47.
[67] See generally on the issue of liability for lapses of airport security: Gam (1988) LMCLQ 217.
[68] *American Smelting and Refining Co v Phillipine Air Lines Inc* 4 Avi Cas 17, 413. In the case of *Rugani v Royal Dutch Airlines* [1954] US & C Av 74 it was held that the damage could have been avoided had the carrier's cargo room been properly closed and the guard armed with a gun.
[69] (1953) US & C Av 479.
[70] At 482.
[71] *Glassman v The Flying Tiger Line Inc* 9 Avi Cas 18, 295.
[72] 334 NYS 2d 492. The court considered that the Montreal Agreement had 'waiv[ed] the defense of due care (Warsaw Convention, Article 20) . . .' (at 493).
[73] *Shawcross* consider that there is a similar interpretation of the necessary measures provision in England, Canada, Germany, the US and, broadly speaking, in France, with its very different conceptual framework: Div VII para [116]. Cf *Miller* pp 164–166.
[74] Article 1384, Code Civil.

offered by Schmid for the word 'agents' in the Convention: 'all the persons of whom the carrier avails himself in order to perform the carriage, no matter whether they are employed or independent contractors as long as they are acting in performance of work which they have been entrusted with by the carrier'[75].

9.41   Agents of the carrier thus include the agent's employees (eg flight personnel, ground and administrative staff), safety inspectors, handling agents, ground freight carriers[76], air freight forwarders[77], the personnel of the passenger feeder-services on the apron[78], the personnel of private security businesses[79] and temporary crew members[80].

9.42   On the other hand, the following will not be regarded as 'agents': air traffic control authorities, aviation weather service, customs authorities, licensing authorities, the aircraft manufacturer, the operator of the repair and maintenance hangar, the hirer of aircraft or the police authorities in charge of security checks. Nor will a doctor who is a passenger of the aircraft and volunteers to help in an emergency be treated as the carrier's 'agent'.

Article 20(2): The defence of Negligent Pilotage, Handling and Navigation of the Aircraft

9.43

Rule 24—Under the unamended Convention, in respect of baggage and cargo, the carrier will not be liable for damage if it proves (a) that the damage was caused by negligent pilotage or negligent handling of the aircraft or by negligent navigation of the aircraft and (b) that in all other respects the carrier and its servants or agents took all necessary measures to avoid the damage.

9.44   Article 20 of the unamended Warsaw Convention provides an additional defence in the case of baggage and cargo. Article 20(1) of the unamended Convention sets out the provision now found in art 20 of the amended Convention set out above[81]. Article 20(2) of the unamended Convention contains the additional defence:

---

[75] Giemulla/Scmid 'Warsaw Convention' (1992) Supp 1.4 (October 1994) Schmid, 24.
[76] *Jaycees Patou v Pier Air International* 714 F Supp 81 (SDNY 1989).
[77] *Royal Insurance v Amerford Air Cargo* 654 F Supp 679 (SDNY 1987).
[78] *Johnson v Allied Eastern States Maintenance* 19 Avi 17,847 and AL 130 No 22 (US Ct of Apps, DColo 1986).
[79] *Baker v Landsell Protective Agency* 509 F Supp 165 and AL 175 No 38, US District Court (SDNY 1986).
[80] *Handler v ALM and KLM* 14 Avi 17,415 and AL 230, US District Court (EDNY 1976).
[81] See para **9.4** above.

'In the carriage of cargo and baggage the carrier is not liable if he proves that the damage was occasioned by negligent pilotage or negligence in the handling of the aircraft or in navigation and that, in all other respects, he and his servants or agents have taken all necessary measures to avoid the damage.'

9.45   Drafting history.   Article 20(2) of the unamended Convention also finds its origin in maritime law[82]. It is based on art IV, Rule 2(a) of the Hague Rules[83], which provided:

'Neither the carrier nor the ship shall be responsible for loss or damage arising or resulting from -
(a) Act, neglect, or default of the master, mariner, pilot, or the servants of the carrier in the navigation or in the management of the ship.'

9.46   CITEJA experts limited the applicability of the provision to baggage and cargo, although there was a body of opinion at the Warsaw conference which supported its applicability to passengers[84].

9.47   The Hague Conference of 1955 adopted without debate the proposal of the Rio Protocol[85] to delete art 20(2) of the unamended Convention from the amended Convention. It appeared illogical to have different regimes applying to cargo and baggage on the one hand and passengers on the other. Further, the justifications for the provision on maritime law seemed less appropriate to aviation law[86].

9.48   There are very few cases in which art 20(2) of the unamended Convention has been relied on. In *American Smelting and Refining Co v Philipine Airlines Inc*[87] the carrier was held to be entitled to rely on the provision in circumstances where[88]:

'The credible evidence proves that the crash of the defendant's plane was caused by a combination of factors, including negligent piloting, faulty and erroneous instructions from the Kai-Tak Airport control tower, possible failure of the pilot to obey instructions from the control tower and/or to follow defendant's established landing procedures, poor weather conditions and a dangerous landing field and surrounding terrain.'

---

[82] What is described in French textbooks as *faute nautique*: see *Miller* p 69.
[83] Prior to the Warsaw Convention the Hague Rules were given effect in English law pursuant to Carriage of Goods by Sea Act 1924. See now the Carriage of Goods by Sea Act 1971, to which the Hague Rules, as amended by the Brussels Protocol 1968, are scheduled.
[84] *Miller* pp 69–70.
[85] See para **1.12**, above.
[86] *Miller* p 70.
[87] 4 Avi Cas 17,413; See also (1956) US & C Av 387.
[88] At 17,415–6.

9.49 It is clear from maritime cases that if the negligence is primarily in respect of the baggage or cargo the carrier will not be able to rely on it. In *Gosse Millard Ltd v Canadian Government Merchant Marine Ltd*[89] a ship put into port for repairs. The crew opened up the hatches to let in the workmen, but did not close them when it rained causing damage to the cargo. The House of Lords held that this constituted neglect of the cargo rather than neglect of the ship and that the shipowner was liable for the damage. By contrast, in *The British King*[90] the negligent failure of the crew to maintain the ship's pumps constituted negligence in the management of the ship and the shipowner was not liable. It is doubtful whether an air carrier could succeed in the latter type of case, unless it could be shown that the failure was purely operational and the system instituted by the carrier for ensuring proper maintenance was sufficient.

9.50 Article 20(2) is likely to be interpreted very narrowly in an aviation context in the rare case when it is relied on by a carrier. Anything other than a negligent decision taken on the flight deck as to the conduct or course of the flight itself is extremely unlikely to qualify[91]. For example, the negligent failure of the crew to use the apparatus of the plane to protect the cargo is unlikely to be negligence in the handling of the aircraft and the carrier is unlikely to be able to avoid liability[92].

The Defence of Contributory Negligence

9.51

Rule 25—The carrier may be able to avoid or reduce its liability under both the unamended and the amended Convention if the claimant has been guilty of contributory negligence with regard to the damage suffered.

9.52 Article 21 of both the unamended and the amended Convention provides as follows:

> 'If the carrier proves that the damage was caused by or contributed to by the negligence of the injured person the Court may, in accordance with the provisions of its own law, exonerate the carrier wholly or partly from his liability.'

---

[89] [1929] AC 233.
[90] (1898) Fed Rep 872.
[91] See *McNair* pp 185–6, for a discussion as to whether negligence on the part of aircraft mechanics would allow a carrier to invoke the provision.
[92] See *International Packers v Ocean Steamships* [1955] 2 Lloyd's Rep 218.

9.53   The effect of this provision is to apply the rules of contributory negligence of the *lex fori*[93] ie the domestic rules of substantive law, not the
domestic conflict of law rules[94]. In the English context this will mean the
application of the Law Reform (Contributory Negligence) Act 1945[95]. Section
1(1) of the Act provides that:

> 'Where any person suffers damage as the result partly of the fault of any
> other person or persons, a claim in respect of that damage shall not be
> defeated by reason of the fault of the person suffering the damage, but
> the damages recoverable in respect thereof shall be reduced to the extent
> as the court thinks just and equitable having regard to the claimant's
> share in the responsibility for the damage.'

9.54   The claimant will be required to exercise reasonable care to safeguard
his own interests[96]. To the extent that he does not and thereby contributes to
the damage the Court is entitled to apportion damages to the extent that it
holds the claimant thus contributed to the damage.

9.55   Drafting background and proposals for change.   It would appear that
the British delegates to the Warsaw conference were responsible for the introduction of a specific provision dealing with contributory negligence[97]. It
seems that the civil law delegates perceived no need to make a specific provision for the fault of the victim as the carrier is presumed to be at fault and
is only relieved from liability if he proves absence of fault. At the time, prior
to the enactment of the Law Reform (Contributory Negligence) Act 1945,
contributory negligence would have been a complete defence to an action for
negligence in England[98], certain other common law jurisdictions and in some
American states. However, whilst the other delegates accepted that provision
should be made in the Convention for the negligence of the injured party,
they did not accept that it should provide the carrier with a complete defence
in all cases. The final draft of art 21 represented a compromise between the
various states[99]. The resulting solution obviously carries the risk of divergent
solutions by applying the *lex fori* of different states in comparable factual situations[100].

---

[93]   *Shawcross* Div VII para [117]. In the US the relevant *lex fori* is federal common law rather than
the law of the individual state: see *Eichler v Lufthansa German Airlines* 794 F Supp 127 (SDNY
1992) at 129–30.

[94]   *Feibelmann v Compagnie Nationale Air France* 334 NYS 2d 492.

[95]   As expressly determined by the Carriage by Air Act 1961. For details of the 1945 Act, see generally *Clerk & Lindsell on Torts* (16th edn) paras 1–39 ff.

[96]   Eg see *Nance v British Columbia Electric Railway Co Ltd* [1951] AC 601 at 611, per Viscount
Simon.

[97]   *Miller* pp 70–1.

[98]   Eg see *Butterfield v Forrester* (1809) 11 East 60, 61.

[99]   See *Miller* p 71.

[100]   See *Miller* p 168.

9.56   The Guatemala City Protocol[101] and Montreal Protocol No 4[102] have proposed the institution of a substantive provision which would no longer apply the *lex fori*, but provide that if the carrier proves that the damage was caused by or contributed to by the negligence or other wrongful act or omission of the person claiming compensation the carrier shall be wholly or partly exonerated from its liability to the extent that such act or omission caused or contributed to the damage.

9.57   **Conditions of applicability of defence of contributory negligence.** The carrier must prove two things: (1) negligence and (2) the causal role of the negligence in relation to the damage. What amounts to negligence and sufficient causation to invoke art 21 must be decided on the basis of the *lex fori*.

9.58   **The 'injured person'.**   Although some contrary views have been expressed[103] it is clear that the 'injured person' for the purposes of art 21 includes not just those claimants who are physically injured but also claimants who claim by reason of an interest in damaged or lost cargo or goods[104]. 'Person' includes both natural and legal persons[105].

9.59   **Claimant's responsibility to take care of his own interests.**   The courts have developed a common sense approach as to what steps a claimant is obliged to take in his own interests. On the one hand, the primary responsibility for safety is that of the carrier. Thus, in *Goldman v Thai Airways International*[106] it was not negligent of the passenger, injured when the pilot failed to illuminate the seat belt sign during clear air turbulence, to have his seat belt off during the flight.

9.60   On the other hand, the undoubtedly onerous duty on the carrier is not taken to extremes. Thus, a passenger who tripped over a visible piece of luggage left on the tarmac, which she could easily have avoided, would be guilty of contributory negligence[107]. In *Chutter v KLM Royal Dutch Airlines*[108] the claimant left her seat while the 'fasten seat belt' sign was illuminated and went to the open door of the aircraft to wave a farewell to her daughter. At that moment the ramp was being pulled away from the aircraft and she fell to the ground sustaining injuries. Her right to damages was extinguished pursuant to art 21[109].

---

[101] See para **1.27** above.
[102] See para **1.34** above.
[103] Eg Moller *Law of Civil Aviation* (1936) p 307.
[104] *McNair* p 187; See *Rustenburg Platinum Mines v Pan American World Airways Inc.* [1977] 1 Lloyd's Rep 564, where this was assumed to be the case.
[105] *General Aniline and Film Corpn v American Express Co* 12 Avi Cas 17,393.
[106] See para **9.10**, above.
[107] *Eichler v Lufthansa German Airlines* 794 F Supp 127 (SDNY 1992) 130.
[108] 132 F Supp 611.
[109] At 616.

9.61   Claimants would similarly be expected to exercise reasonable care in relation to cargo or baggage. In *AG World Exports v Arrow Air Inc*[110] the shipper negligently failed to provide ground-based air conditioning for a consignment of pigs sent from Florida to Venezuela, some of which were found to be dead on arrival as a result of excessive temperatures. The carrier had kept windows open and fans on during the loading process and had an air conditioning system in operation for the flight, as soon as it was legally permitted to turn it on. It had also recommended a ground-based air-conditioning system to the claimant[111]. The pigs had probably died before the aircraft was airborne. The carrier was completely exonerated from any liability in such circumstances. Conversely in *Boehringer Mannheim Diagnostics Inc v Pan American World Airways Inc*[112] the claimant was held not to be guilty of contributory negligence in failing to mark the crate with warning signs as to the delicate nature of the load which was subsequently damaged by the carrier's operatives[113].

9.62   Burden of Proof.   Irrespective of the provisions of the *lex fori*, art 21 expressly places the burden of proving contributory negligence of the carrier.

9.63   Deduction from which amount?   In cases where the claimant's damages are limited, for example pursuant to art 22, it is not clear whether the deduction for contributory negligence is made from the amount the claimant would have recovered but for the limitation provision or from the capped amount. Drion considers that logic and the scheme of the Convention suggests that the limits should be applied at the end, only after the facts which determine the existence and extent of the liability have been established[114]. This appears to be the better view, but the point has yet to be decided.

9.64

Rule 26—If and when the Montreal Convention applies a defence of exoneration will be available to a carrier in place of defences of 'all necessary measures', impossibility and negligent pilotage.

A carrier will be exonerated in full or in part if it can show that the damage was caused or contributed to by passenger's negligence or other wrongful act or omission.

9.65   The Montreal Convention significantly changes the scope of the Defences available to the carrier. In particular, the defences of 'all necessary

---

[110] 22 Avi Cas 18,221.
[111] At 18,222.
[112] 531 F Supp 344 (1981). See para **9.19**, above.
[113] At 348.
[114] *Drion* pp 110–1. See also *Shawcross* Div VII para [421], which supports Drion's conclusion. In Australia, this approach to art 21 is expressly laid down in domestic legislation: Commonwealth Act 1959, s 16.

measures' (see para **9.9**), 'impossibility' (see para **9.43**) and 'negligent pilotage' (see para **9.43**) are no longer available. In their place is a new provision in a new art 20, entitled 'Exoneration'. This new art 20 provides as follows:

> 'If the carrier proves that the damage was caused or contributed to by the negligence or other wrongful act or omission of the person claiming compensation, or the person from whom he or she derives his or her rights, the carrier shall be wholly or partly exonerated from its liability to the claimant to the extent that such negligence or wrongful act or omission caused or contributed to the damage. When by reason of death or injury of a passenger compensation is claimed by a person other than the passenger, the carrier shall likewise be wholly or partly exonerated from its liability to the extent that it proves that the damage was caused or contributed to by the negligence or other wrongful act or omission of that passenger. This Article applies to all the liability provisions in this Convention, including paragraph 1 of Article 21[115].'

9.66   This appears to limit the carrier's defence to the old art 21 defence of contributory negligence (see **9.51**). The only substantive difference between the new art 20 and the old art 21 is that the question of contributory negligence is no longer based on the *lex fori* but is defined within the article itself. This is in line with proposals made in the Guatemala City Protocol and Montreal Protocol No 4 (see **1.27** and **1.34**). It is to be expected, nevertheless, that previous cases on the old art 21 will, for the most part, still be applied in respect of the new art 20.

9.67   Other general defences, such as force majeure and state-of-knowledge defences would therefore no longer appear to be open to the carrier.

9.68

RULE 27—**Carriage of cargo which is governed by either Montreal Protocol No 4 or Montreal Convention 1999, affords the carrier with the defence that the carrier is not liable if the damage to the cargo was caused by inherent defect, quality or vice of the cargo, defective packing of the cargo by someone other than the carrier, armed conflict or an act by a public authority connected with the entry, exit or transit of the cargo.**

9.69   In the case of carriage of cargo, the Montreal Convention 1999 incorporates certain new defences which were introduced by the Montreal Protocol No 4, but which were not previously available to the carrier under the amended or unamended Warsaw conventions. These are set out in art

---

[115] Paragraph 1 of art 21 deals with compensation in case of death of injury of passengers.

18(2). Article 18, in part, provides as follows:

> '1.   The carrier is liable for damage sustained in the event of the destruction or loss of, or damage to, cargo upon condition only that the event which caused the damage so sustained took place during the carriage by air.
> 2.   However, the carrier is not liable if and to the extent it proves that the destruction, or loss of, or damage to, the cargo resulted from one or more of the following:
>> (a)   inherent defect, quality or vice of the cargo;
>> (b)   defective packing of that cargo performed by a person other than the carrier or its servants or agents;
>> (c)   an act of war or an armed conflict;
>> (d)   an act of public authority carried out in connection with the entry, exit or transit of the cargo.'

The burden of proof will be on the carrier which will escape liability if it is able to satisfy one of the above listed circumstances.

Article 17(2) of the Montreal Convention contains a restricted version of art 18(2) in respect of claims for damage to baggage as opposed to cargo. The defence in art 17(2) is limited to the 'inherent defect, quality or vice' defence in art 18(2)(a).

Chapter 10

Article 25: Breaking the Limits of Liability

Introduction

10.1   The provisions of art 25 of the Warsaw Convention and the Warsaw-Hague Convention seek to define the circumstances in which the respective limits of liability imposed by those Conventions shall not apply. Article 25 applies across the board to all claims relating to injury to passengers, loss of or damage to baggage and cargo, and for delay in the carriage of passengers baggage and cargo[1] and is the subject matter of this Chapter.

10.2   Recent developments which have raised or removed the limits on liability[2] mean that future litigants will need recourse to art 25 even less frequently than at present. Nevertheless, to the extent that the Warsaw and Warsaw-Hague regimes continue to apply, the established law on this topic remains relevant. Furthermore, the wording of the Warsaw-Hague art 25 is preserved in the Montreal Convention in relation to claims for delay, baggage and cargo[3], and will be interpreted in accordance with previous case law.

10.3   While to the litigant in England, it will usually be the amended art 25 in the Warsaw-Hague Convention which is of relevance, art 25 of the Warsaw Convention continues to be of significance not least because it will continue to apply to some flights between the UK and states which are signatories only to the unamended Warsaw Convention. Furthermore, the historical evolution of art 25 remains of importance when seeking to understand the scope of this provision. The discussion which follows therefore encompasses the origins and evolution of the wording of the article before any attempt is made to elucidate the correct meaning of art 25 in the Warsaw Convention and in the Warsaw-Hague Convention.

---

[1]   As to the Arts on which a carrier cannot rely if art 25 is breached, see para **10.14** et seq below.
[2]   Most notably the IATA Intercarrier Agreement of 1995, EC Regulation No 2027/97, and the Montreal Convention of 1999. See para **1.47** et seq above.
[3]   Article 22(5) Montreal Convention 1999.

145

Article 25 of the Warsaw Convention

10.4

RULE 28

(1) Where the Warsaw Convention applies, a claimant can avoid certain limits on recoverable damages if he can show that the damage
was caused by the wilful misconduct of the carrier, his servants or
agents

(2) An act or omission, or series of acts or omissions, will amount to
misconduct for the purposes of paragraph (1), where the conduct
falls outside the range of conduct ordinarily to be expected of a
carrier, his servants or agents in the particular circumstances of
the case having particular regard to the likely consequences of the
acts or omissions in question

(3) 'Misconduct' will be 'wilful' for the purposes of paragraph (1)
where the carrier, his servants or agents either:

   (i) intend to commit a breach of duty knowing that there is a
   risk that injury loss or damage may result

   or

   (ii) know that there is a risk that injury loss or damage may result
   but are recklessly indifferent as to the consequences of their
   actions.

The Drafting History of Article 25 of the Warsaw Convention

10.5   The Warsaw conference of 1929.   In the Warsaw Convention[4] art 25
provides:

> '(1)   The carrier shall not be entitled to avail himself of the provisions
> of this Schedule which exclude or limit his liability, if the damage is
> caused by his wilful misconduct, or by such default on his part as, in
> accordance with the law of the Court seized of the case, is considered to
> be equivalent to wilful misconduct.'[5]

10.6   This peculiar wording was the result of compromise arising out of the
Warsaw conference in 1929 which attempted to reconcile common law and
civil law concepts. The initial proposal of CITEJA presented at the Warsaw
conference provided:

---

[4]   As enacted by Sch 2 of the Carriage by Air Acts (Application of Provisions) Order 1967.
[5]   Article 25(2) provides 'Similarly, the carrier shall not be entitled to avail himself of the said
provisions if the damage is caused as aforesaid by any servant or agent of the carrier acting
within the scope of his employment.'

'If the damage arises from an intentional illicit act for which the carrier is responsible, he will not have the right to avail himself of the provisions of this Convention, which exclude in all or in part his direct liability or that derived from the faults of his servants.'[6]

10.7   The expression 'intentional illicit act'[7] was intended to translate the civil law concept of 'dol', there being no precise analogue in common law jurisdictions for the concept of 'dol'[8]. However, when CITEJA's proposed wording was debated at the Warsaw conference, the German delegation raised the question of whether the concept of 'dol' should be extended to encompass the civil law concept of 'faute lourde'. The British delegation objected to the use of the phrase 'faute lourde' on the basis that it had no precise legal meaning in common law countries (broadly speaking it means gross negligence) and also objected to the proposed CITEJA wording 'intentional illicit act' since it would be difficult for common law systems to know what was intended by this phrase. The British delegation gave the example of a pilot, whose aircraft developed difficulties, landing in a place not authorised for landing in order to avert an accident. The pilot would, strictly speaking, have committed an intentional illicit act, but it was the British delegation's understanding that this was not the type of situation which was intended to fall within art 25. As an alternative the British delegation suggested the use of the phrase 'wilful misconduct' on the grounds that it was an expression which was known to common law systems and that it 'covers not only deliberate acts but also careless acts done without regard for the consequences.[9]' The debate as to whether to include 'faute lourde' in the Warsaw Convention did not reach a definite conclusion. The Italian delegation thought that the British suggestion of 'wilful misconduct' corresponded 'almost entirely' to 'dol' and 'faute lourde', but the French delegation were concerned that the expression 'faute lourde' was too imprecise for use in an international convention which had to be interpreted in common law jurisdictions. The conference therefore approved a course whereby the problem was referred to a drafting committee on the basis that the concept of 'faute lourde' would be included if it was possible to find a formula of words which was satisfactory to the various judicial languages which were represented at the conference.

10.8   The solution hit upon by the drafting committee was intended to please everyone. The French text provided for the limit of liability not to apply 'si le dommage provient de son dol ou d'une faute qui, d'après la loi du

---

[6]   See the CITEJA draft submitted to the Warsaw Convention reproduced at pp 265–6 of the translation of the Minutes of the Second International Conference on Private Aeronautical Law published by Fred B Bothman & Co (1975) (referred to hereafter as 'the Minutes').

[7]   The British delegation solicited an explanation of the meaning attached to this expression in its preliminary comments on the CITEJA draft; see the Minutes of the Warsaw Conference at p 298.

[8]   The Preface to the Minutes of the Warsaw Conference makes specific mention of the difficulty in translating the concept of 'dol' into English.

[9]   Minutes of the Warsaw Conference at pp 59–60.

tribunal saisi, est considerée comme équivalente au dol'[10]. The agreed text thus retained the word 'dol', did not include the expression 'faute lourde' but instead introduced the notion of fault equivalent to 'dol'. The English translation equated 'dol' with 'wilful default' and translated the phrase set out in the text above as 'if the damage is caused by his wilful misconduct or by such default on his part as, in accordance with the law of the court seised of the case, is considered to be equivalent to wilful misconduct'[11].

10.9   While the history of the evolution of art 25 of the Warsaw Convention says a great deal about the difficulty of finding precise equivalent expressions for particular legal concepts, it does also give an indication as to what the scope of disapplication of the limits of liability was intended to be. It is clear that the circumstances in which the limits were to be disapplied extend beyond the cases where the carrier was guilty of the intentional infliction of damage but also include cases where the carrier was careless without regard for the consequences.

10.10   Whereas the decisions of common law courts have shown remarkably little divergence in the interpretation of art 12[12], civil law jurisdictions have differed on whether 'faute lourde' was equivalent to 'dol', ultimately leading to legislation in France defining the fault equivalent to 'dol' as 'faute inexcusable'[13]. In the result there was a widely held perception at the Hague Convention of 1955 that defects in the formulation of art 25 had produced contradictory decisions between civil and common law jurisdictions[14] and given the courts too much scope for disapplying the limits of liability. This resulted in art 25 being reformulated in the Warsaw-Hague Convention[15].

The Interpretation of Article 25 of the Warsaw Convention

10.11   The governing language when interpreting Article 25 of the Warsaw Convention.   Given the difficulties of translation and interpretation which were experienced at the Warsaw conference, it is important to know whether the French text of the Warsaw Convention or the English text takes precedence when art 25 is being interpreted by an English court. The Carriage by Air Act 1961 expressly provides that if there is any inconsistency between the English and French texts of the Warsaw-Hague Convention, the French text

---

[10]   Described by *Drion* as 'probably the most unhappy phrase of the entire Convention' p 197.
[11]   See Carriage by Air (Application of Provisions) Order 1967 Sch 2 Pt B. For criticism of the translation see *Drion* pp 207–8.
[12]   Although not perhaps in the application of the law to the facts of any particular dispute.
[13]   See Mankiewicz [1972] ICLQ 718 at 722–4. For an illustration of the problem in French law see *Broche-Hennessy c Air France* JCP 1952, II, 6985.
[14]   See the cases cited by Mankiewicz [1972] ICLQ 718 at p 723 footnote 10.
[15]   This is curious since according to *Drion*, writing in 1954, in only three cases involving air accidents had art 25 been held to apply and one of the three was reversed on appeal (*Drion* at pp 214–229).

takes precedence[16]. However, the Warsaw Convention is part of English law by virtue of art 2 of the Carriage by Air Acts (Application of Provisions) Order 1967. This incorporates into English law 'the *English* text of the Warsaw Convention' (emphasis added). It is submitted, therefore, that the English text of the Warsaw Convention in Sch 2 to the Carriage by Air (application of Provisions) Order 1967 has precedence in English law[17].

10.12   Causation.   Article 25 of the Warsaw Convention applies where damage is *caused* by the wilful misconduct of a carrier or his agents. The present approach of the English courts to the question of causation is found in the Court of Appeal's decision in *Galoo Ltd v Bright Grahame Murray*[18]. Whilst this case does not concern the Warsaw Convention, it is thought that 'causation' in art 25 would be interpreted in accordance with the guidance given in that judgment, which makes it clear that each case turns on its facts and the question of causation will be determined by the application of common sense[19]. In applying this common sense, the Court must determine whether the matter complained of was an 'effective' or 'dominant' cause of the damage, as opposed to being merely be an opportunity for the damage to occur. An example of a claim under art 25 which failed on the grounds of causation is the US case of *Goepp v American Overseas Airlines*[20] where the alleged wilful misconduct relied upon was the carrier's failure to comply with regulations which required pilots to undertake regular flights accompanied by another pilot who was there to check the pilot's performance. The claimant succeeded in obtaining compensation when the plane crashed in the dark into a mountain, but failed in removing the liability limits since the Court held that her damage had not been caused by the failure of the airline to put its pilots through the accompanied checking flights.

10.13   Quantum of Damages.   It has now been authoritatively settled in English law that in relation to the liability of a carrier arising out of international carriage by air, the Warsaw and Warsaw-Hague Conventions provide the exclusive causes of action against a carrier[21]. The fact that a claim may fall within art 25 of the Warsaw Convention does not give the Claimant a right to rely on causes of action which fall outside the Warsaw Convention, but it does allow the claimant to avoid the limits and exclusions of liability which are contained within the Warsaw Convention, such as art 22 which limits the sums which are recoverable from a carrier. This raises the question of the basis upon which damages are assessed when art 25 applies. In *Re Air Disaster at*

---

[16] Section 1(2) of the Carriage by Air Act 1961 which sets out both the English and the French texts of the Warsaw-Hague Convention in its Schedules.

[17] For a fuller analysis of the choice of prevailing language applicable to the Warsaw Convention and the Warsaw-Hague Convention see Chapter 3 on the Construction of Treaties above.

[18] [1994] 1 WLR 1360.

[19] [1994] 1 WLR 1360 at 1375 per Glidewell LJ.

[20] 3 Avi Cas 18,057.

[21] *Sidhu v British Airways* [1997] AC 430. The US Supreme Court has followed a similar approach in *El Al Israel Airways Ltd v Tseng* (1999) 119 Sct 662.

Lockerbie[22] the US Court of Appeals for the Second Circuit held that even where a carrier was guilty of wilful misconduct under art 25, punitive damages were not recoverable. It was held that damages under the Warsaw Convention were always assessed on a compensatory basis for damage actually suffered and did not permit an award of damages to punish the carrier or show the court's disapproval of what had happened[23]. Furthermore, it is clear that art 25 does not create a cause of action — it merely lifts the limits which are imposed on claims based on other Articles[24]. It is therefore thought that even in a case which falls within art 25, damages will still be assessed on the basis that they are to compensate the claimant for loss actually suffered.

10.14   The provisions of the Warsaw Convention on which the carrier cannot rely when in breach of Article 25.   Article 25 of the Warsaw Convention provides that if that the carrier or his agents cause damage by wilful misconduct, the carrier will not be entitled to 'avail himself of the provisions of this convention which exclude or limit his liability'. This wording obviously raises the question of *which* provisions of the Warsaw Convention 'exclude' or 'limit' a carrier's liability? For example, is art 29 of the Warsaw Convention, which extinguishes the right to damages if the claim is not brought within two years, a provision which 'excludes or limits' a carrier's liability? Unfortunately, under the Warsaw Convention the answer to this question is not certain (and it is worth noting here that the Warsaw-Hague Convention avoids this uncertainty by providing that the limits in art 22, which restrict the sums which are payable in respect of damage caused by the carrier, shall not apply if the carrier's conduct falls within art 25 of that Convention).

10.15   Clearly art 22 in the Warsaw Convention is a provision which limits liability for damage. That article expressly refers to the liability of a carrier being 'limited' to certain sums in respect of liability arising out of the carriage of passengers, registered baggage and cargo[25]. Also, art 20, by which a carrier shall not be 'liable' for damage if it proves, inter alia, that it took all necessary steps to avoid the damage is another provision on which a carrier would not be entitled to rely if its conduct fell with art 25 of the Warsaw Convention[26] (although it is difficult to envisage a claim where a carrier could be found to have 'taken all necessary measures to avoid damage' and caused damage by 'wilful misconduct').

---

[22]   (1991) 23 Avi Cas 17,714.
[23]   The Montreal Convention of 1999 states explicitly in art 29 that punitive, exemplary, or any other non-compensatory damages are not recoverable.
[24]   *Floyd v Eastern Airlines Inc* (1989) 21 Avi Cas 18,401(872 F2d 1462); reversed on other grounds (1991) 23 Avi Cas 17,367 (111Sct1489).
[25]   For the applicable financial limits under art 22 see paras **7.67–7.69** and **8.7**.
[26]   *Rein v Pan American World Airways Inc* (1991) 23 Avi Cas 17,714 at 17,729.

10.16   It is not so clear whether, if the carrier's conduct falls within art 25, it is precluded from relying on art 26(4), which excludes actions against carriers where written notification of damage to baggage or cargo is not given with the prescribed time limits. There is no English authority on point. The preponderance of American cases holds that a carrier is not entitled to rely on art 26(4) if it has caused damage by wilful misconduct[27]. An English court might follow the preponderance of American authority[28]. However, the difficulty with the approach taken in the American cases is that art 26(4) expressly sets out circumstances in which a carrier will not be entitled to rely on the failure to give written notification within the prescribed time limits:

> 'Failing complaint within the times aforesaid, no action shall lie against the carrier, save in the case of fraud on his part.'

10.17   If a carrier has fraudulently caused damage, for example by stealing a passenger's baggage, it will doubtless also be guilty of wilful misconduct. However, there will be cases where a carrier is guilty of wilful misconduct which, due to the absence of dishonesty, does not amount to fraud. There is, therefore, a material distinction between 'wilful misconduct' and 'fraud'. When art 26 was being discussed at the Warsaw conference in 1929 (in the evening of the penultimate session), there was no draft wording for sub-para (4) for the conference to consider, and in these circumstances the President of the drafting committee appears to have assumed that if the carrier was guilty of wilful misconduct, it would not be entitled to rely on prescribed time limits[29]. The conference briefly debated the wording which was available, and left it to the drafting committee to take on board the comments which had been made, and also finish off the drafting of art 26. The drafting committee did produce a completed draft in time for the closing session of the Conference. This draft introduced, for the first time, the exception for fraud, which now appears in art 26(4). The President of the drafting committee reported that the new draft had the unanimous support of the drafting committee, and the new draft was approved by the Conference without any further debate[30]. Thus, there appears to have been a deliberate change of mind (at least by the President of the drafting committee) so that a carrier would only be precluded from relying on art 26 in the case of fraud (as opposed to wilful misconduct). Furthermore, even in the absence of the foregoing account of the drafting of art 26(4), applying ordinary canons of

---

[27] See for example *Excelled Sheepskin Corporation v ATC Services* (1981) 16 Avi 17,069; *Wexler v Eastern Airlines* (1982) 18 Avi Cas 17,155 (concerning the meaning of 'exclude or limit liability' in the context of Arts 4 and 26 of the Warsaw Convention); *Soundwave Electronics v Iberia* (1983) 18 Avi Cas 17,488; cf *Amazon Coffee Co v TWA* (1983) 18 Avi Cas 17,264.

[28] See the comments in *Sidhu v British Airways plc* [1997] AC 430 at 443 and 451 in relation to the readiness of the English courts to use foreign decisions as an aid to interpreting the Convention so as to achieve international uniformity of construction.

[29] Minutes p 216.

[30] Minutes p 230.

construction to arts 25 and 26[31], it is submitted that the correct construction of the Convention is that wilful misconduct which does not amount to fraud does not preclude a carrier from relying on art 26.

10.18   In relation to art 29, which *extinguishes* the right to damages if an action is not brought within the prescribed two year limitation, it is submitted that an English court would hold that this was not excluded by a finding that a carrier's conduct falls within art 25. Although there is no English authority on this point, the overwhelming view of the American courts, demonstrated by a long line of authority, is that the two year limitation period applies regardless of whether the carrier was guilty of wilful misconduct[32]. In short, the American view is that art 25 was never intended to result in periods of limitation which differed according to type of conduct which gave rise to the cause of action. It is submitted that this is correct. If courts in different countries disapplied art 29 to cases falling within art 25 the result would be that they would have to apply their own domestic law of limitation to the claimant's claim. This would defeat one of the main purposes of the Warsaw Convention which was to provide a uniform international code which was not affected by variances between the contracting states' domestic laws. Similarly, art 28, which prescribes the jurisdictions in which a claimant must bring their claim, is not a provision which is affected by art 25[33].

10.19   The meaning of 'wilful misconduct' in English law.   For many years the leading authority in English law on the interpretation of art 25 of the Warsaw Convention was undoubtedly the judgment of Barry J in *Horobin v BOAC*[34]. The phrase has recently been considered again at first instance in the context of art 25 in the case of *Thomas Cook v Air Malta*[35], in which Cresswell J reviewed *Horabin* and subsequent cases, including those decided by the Court of Appeal, which have considered the meaning of 'wilful misconduct' in the context of transport by road under the Convention on the Contract for International Carriage of Goods by Road ('CMR')[36]. It is submitted that *Horabin*, which is nearing its fiftieth anniversary, has stood the test of time and is still the most informative case in English law on the meaning of 'wilful misconduct' in art 25 of the Warsaw Convention. It is also the starting point in the discussion of the meaning of 'wilful misconduct'[37].

---

[31] In particular, the principle *expressio unius est exclusio alterius*, or 'the expression of one thing is the exclusion of another'.

[32] *Bergman v Pan American World Airways Inc* (1969) 32 AD 2d 95,299 NYS 2d 982, 984–85; *Stone v Mexicana Airlines Inc*, 610 F 2.2d 699, 700 (10th Cir, 1979); *Kordich v Butler Aviation Detroit Inc* 103 (Mich App, 1981) 566; *Garlitz v Applied Aviation Services International Corpn* (1982) 17 Avi Cas 17,238; *Wexler v Eastern Airlines* (1982) 18 Avi Cas 17,155; *Magnus Electronics Inc v Royal Bank of Canada* 19 Avi Cas 17,944 (1985).

[33] *Air France v Gilberto* 15 Avi Cas 17,429 (Illinois Supreme Court, 1978).

[34] [1952] 2 All ER 1016.

[35] [1997] 2 Lloyd's Rep 399.

[36] *Sidney G Jones Ltd v Bencher Ltd* [1986] 1 Lloyd's Rep 54 (Popplewell J), *National Semiconductors (UK) Ltd v UPS Ltd* [1996] 2 Lloyd's Rep 212 (Longmore J), *Laceys Footware Ltd v Bowler International Ltd* [1997] 2 Lloyd's Rep 369 (Court of Appeal).

[37] For a discussion of the meaning of wilful misconduct see Bin Cheng [1977] 2 Annals ASL 55.

10.20   'Misconduct'   In *Horabin* the Claimant, who was a passenger on the Defendant's aircraft, was injured when the aircraft ran out of fuel and crashed. He alleged that the carrier was guilty of wilful misconduct in failing, inter alia, to provide a crew sufficiently familiar with the route to be flown, failing to provide a crew sufficiently familiar with the operation of the aircraft in the prevailing conditions, and failing to provide adequate navigational aids and information including airfield maps and charts. He also relied on the failure of the crew to land at various airports in France and their decision to return to England when the fuel level was inadequate. The carrier admitted liability up to the Convention limits but contested that it was guilty of wilful misconduct. In the course of his direction to the jury, Barry J said:

> 'You may think it would be misconduct if anyone employed by the defendants broke, without any justification, some regulation which was designed to ensure the safety of the aircraft and of its passengers; if the pilot departed from the generally accepted standards of safe aerial navigation; or if some official of the defendants failed to supply the pilot of the machine with some map or other information which their rules required him to have, or which any responsible person would realise was part of the necessary equipment of the aircraft. All of those things might amount to misconduct. Carriage by air can be fraught with the gravest danger unless high standards of care are maintained. For that reason, you may feel justified in coming to the conclusion that some relatively minor breach of a safety regulation amounts to misconduct, although it would not do so in places and on occasions when the consequences of such a breach would be much less serious.'

10.21   In considering whether an act or omission amounts to misconduct, therefore, the approach of Barry J involves considering what the consequences of the act or omission are likely to be. The more likely that the act or omission will result in injury, loss or damage the more likely that the act or omission will be found to be misconduct.

10.22   In the *Thomas Cook* case, Cresswell J put it more pithily when he said the starting point was to consider what conduct was ordinarily to be expected in the particular circumstances and then ask whether the acts or omissions complained of were so far outside that range of conduct as to be properly regarded as misconduct. An important circumstance was whether there had been a deliberate disregard of express instructions. Cresswell J went on to hold that it would be wilful misconduct if, aware of a risk that goods would be lost or damaged, a person deliberately went ahead and took that risk *when it was unreasonable in all the circumstances to take that risk*. Clearly, there may be circumstances, such as hijack or extreme weather conditions, which would justify a carrier taking risks in an attempt to avert a greater hazard. Thus, in considering whether there has been misconduct the Court should take account of the circumstances in which the carrier found itself and the likely consequences of the acts or omissions which, in those circumstances, the carrier chose to take.

10.23   **The meaning of 'wilful' in English law.**   In *Horobin v BOAC* Barry J directed the jury as follows in relation to the meaning of wilful:

'Wilful misconduct is misconduct to which the will is a party, and it is wholly different in kind from mere negligence or carelessness, however gross that negligence or carelessness may be. The will must be a party to the misconduct, and not merely to the conduct of which complaint is made. . . To establish wilful misconduct . . . it must be shown, not only that he knowingly (and in that sense wilfully) did the wrongful act, but also that, when he did it, he was aware that it was a wrongful act, i.e., that he was aware that he was committing misconduct.

. . . In order to establish wilful misconduct the claimant must satisfy you that the person who did the act knew at the time that he was doing something wrong and yet did it notwithstanding, or, alternatively that he did it quite recklessly, not caring whether he was doing the right thing or the wrong thing, quite regardless of the effects of what he was doing on the safety of the aircraft and of the passengers for which and for whom he was responsible

To be guilty of wilful misconduct the person concerned must appreciate that he is acting wrongfully, or is wrongfully omitting to act, and yet persists in so acting or omitting to act regardless of the consequences, or acts or omits to act with reckless indifference as to what the results may be.'

10.24   Thus, it is clear from the direction to the jury in the Horobin case that for misconduct to be 'wilful' the actor must intend to do the act and, either know that it is 'wrongful', or be reckless as to whether it is 'wrongful'. However, two questions arise from this part of Barry J's direction:
(1)   What is meant by 'wrongful' — is it enough that the actor appreciated that it was a breach of duty or is it also required that he should have appreciated that it was a breach that carried with it the risk of injury loss or damage?
(2)   What degree of risk of injury loss or damage is required?

10.25   The answer to the first question would appear to be that the actor must appreciate not only that he was acting in breach of duty, but also that there was a risk of injury, loss or damage. As Barry J held, the actor had to realise that he was doing something contrary to the interests of the passengers or his employers or which involved the passengers or the aircraft in a greater risk than if had he acted in accordance with his duty[38].

10.26   As to the second question it is submitted that it is not necessary for the injury, loss or damage to be the *probable* consequence of the act or omission in question and hence for the actor subjectively to appreciate this. This seems to be the correct inference from Barry J's example of the driver approaching red traffic lights who is guilty of wilful misconduct[39]:

---

[38]   See [1952] 2 All ER 1016 at 1023G-H.
[39]   [1952] 2 All ER 1020G-H.

'He knows all about the lights, and he sees in plenty of time that they are changing from yellow to red, but he says to himself: "Hardly any traffic comes out of this side road which I am about to cross. I will go on. I am not going to bother to stop." He does not expect an accident to happen, but he knows that he is doing something wrong. He knows that he should stop, and he is able to stop, but he does not . . . But in that frame of mind no jury would have much difficulty in coming to the conclusion that he had committed an act of wilful misconduct. Of course he did not intend to kill anyone or to injure anyone coming out of the side road. **He thought that in all probability nobody would be coming out of the side road. None the less he took a risk which he knew that he ought not to take.** . . .'(emphasis added)

10.27   The highlighted passage was cited with approval by Mr Justice Longmore in the road transport case of *National Semiconductors (UK) Ltd v UPS Ltd*[40] concerning art 29 of the CMR. In that case it had been argued on behalf of the claimant that complete indifference to the safety of the cargo would have been enough to constitute wilful misconduct. However, the learned Judge rejected this argument on the ground that it lacked the mental element which was inherent in the phrase 'he took a risk which he knew he ought not to take'. In Mr Justice Longmore's view, for wilful misconduct there had to be either (1) an intention to do something which the actor knows to be wrong or (2) a reckless act in the sense that the actor is aware that *loss may result* from his act and yet he does not care whether loss will result or not[41]. Therefore, although there are a number of American decisions which have interpreted 'wilful misconduct' differently, holding that the loss or damage must have been the *probable* result of the act or omission in question[42], it is thought that all that is required as a matter of English law is that damage *might* result[43].

10.28   Recent interpretations of 'wilful misconduct'   Some recent cases on the meaning of wilful misconduct have arguably added an unhelpful gloss to the definitions used in the *Horabin* and *National Semiconductors* cases. Thus, in *Laceys Footware Ltd v Bowler International Ltd*[44], in the context of the CMR, the Court of Appeal held that wilful misconduct included someone who acted

---

[40] [1996] 2 Lloyd's Rep 212.
[41] [1996] 2 Lloyd's Rep 212 at 214.
[42] For example *Pekelis v Transcontinental and Western Air Inc* (1951) 3 Avi Cas 17,440; *Re Korean Airlines Disaster of September 1,* (1983) F 2d 1475; *Pasinato v American Airlines* (1994) 24 Avi Cas 18,081; *Grey v American Airlines* 227 F 2d 282 at 285; cf *Rashap v American Airlines Inc* (1955) US & C Av R 593 ;'The question is whether the pilot wilfully, that is intentionally, failed to balance the gasoline in the tanks, knowing the danger that might be involved, or recklessly disregarding that danger'.
[43] As appears below, art 25 of the Warsaw-Hague Convention specifically requires, in contrast, that the act or omission was done 'recklessly and with knowledge that damage would *probably* result'.
[44] [1997] 2 Lloyd's Rep 369.

with 'reckless carelessness, not caring what the results of his carelessness may be'. It is thought that use of the phrase 'reckless carelessness' [45] hinders rather than helps in understanding the meaning of wilful misconduct. Firstly, the word 'reckless', as defined in a number of criminal cases, requires that the actor took an objectively unjustifiable risk when he was either aware of the existence of the risk (subjective recklessness) or failed to give any thought to the possibility of the risk (objective recklessness)[46]. However, there is a long line of authority which holds that wilful misconduct in art 25 of the Warsaw Convention requires the actor to appreciate that he is doing something wrong. As Ackner J held in *Rustenberg Platinum Mines Ltd v South African Airways*[47]:

> '. . . 'wilful misconduct' goes far beyond negligence, even gross or culpable negligence and involves a person doing or omitting to do that which is not only negligent but which he knows to be wrong, and it is done or omitted regardless of the consequences, not caring what the result of his carelessness may be'

10.29   Thus, it is submitted that the use of the word 'reckless' in *Laceys Footwear* should be interpreted in the sense of subjective recklessness and that objective recklessness is insufficient for a finding of wilful misconduct. Indeed, this appears to have been the sense in which the Court of Appeal was using this word since the finding of wilful misconduct was made on the basis that the actor exposed the goods to 'a risk of which he must have been aware'[48].

10.30   Secondly, it is unclear how the words 'reckless' and 'careless' are to be interpreted together when the word 'reckless' connotes the taking of an objectively unjustifiable risk, whereas 'carelessness' does not necessarily go as far as this. Nevertheless, despite the difficulties with the phrase 'reckless carelessness', it has been adopted in the context of art 25 of Warsaw Convention in the recent first instance decision of *Thomas Cook Group Ltd v Air Malta Co Ltd*[49].

10.31   The question which arises from these recent decisions is whether, by using the phrase 'reckless carelessness', the courts are trying to move away from the definition of 'wilful misconduct' provided by Mr Justice Barry in the *Horabin* case. It is thought that there is no intention to move away from the guidance given in the *Horabin* case and that this can be seen from the elaboration, given in both *Laceys Footwear* and *Thomas Cook*, as to the type of conduct which was considered to amount to reckless carelessness'. In the

---

[45]   The phrase 'reckless carelessness' was taken from the speech of Lord Alverstone in *Forder v Great Western Railway Co* [1905] 2 KB 532.
[46]   *R v Caldwell* [1982] AC 341; *R v Lawrence* [1982] AC 510.
[47]   [1977] 1 Lloyd's Rep 564 at 569 affd; [1979] 1 Lloyd's Rep 19.
[48]   [1997] 2 Lloyd's Rep 369 at 376.
[49]   [1997] 2 Lloyd's Rep 399.

context of goods it was held in both cases that a person acts with reckless care-lessness towards goods in his care if, aware of a risk that the goods may be lost or damaged, he deliberately goes ahead and takes the risk, when it is unreasonable in all the circumstances for him to do so[50]. Comparison of this elaboration with Mr Justice Barry's example, quoted above, of a car driver jumping a red traffic light, shows that 'reckless carelessness' contains the same elements as Mr Justice Barry's definition of wilful misconduct. Thus, the driver of the car was aware that the lights were red and that there was a risk of damage occurring if he did not stop, and yet he went on knowingly to take this risk when he ought not to have done so. Furthermore, large parts of the passages from *Horobin*, cited above, have been referred to with approval in other recent English cases which have dealt with the meaning of wilful mis-conduct in the context of the CMR. In particular, large passages from *Horobin* were cited with approval by Popplewell J in *Sidney G Jones Ltd v Martine Bencher Ltd*[51] which was subsequently followed in *National Semiconductors (UK) Ltd v UPS Ltd*[52]. Therefore, the guidance given by Mr Justice Barry in *Horabin* in 1952 is still applicable today, save, perhaps, in one respect referred to in the next paragraph.

10.32   Series of acts or omissions.   In *Horabin* Barry J directed the jury that they were not entitled to look at the separate acts and omissions relied upon by the claimant and conclude that, although none of the acts or omissions on their own amounted to misconduct, when viewed as a whole they amount to misconduct:

> 'You cannot add up a number of acts and say that, although no one of them really amounts to misconduct, yet put together they show amongst the whole staff of [the carrier], including the pilot, so many small acts of carelessness that in the aggregate they amount to miscon-duct on the part of the [carrier] as a corporation.'

This passage has not been cited in subsequent cases and it is respectfully submitted that it is unlikely that this would be followed by an English court considering a case under art 25 of the Warsaw Convention. It is thought that the correct approach would entitle a court to consider the whole of the con-duct of the carrier in determining whether it is guilty of misconduct. There is an air of unreality in considering acts and omission in isolation without taking account of the surrounding circumstances. Support for the approach suggested is found in American cases such as the decision of the Court of Appeals for the Sixth Circuit in *Re Air Crash Disaster, Polec v Northwest Airlines Inc*[53] where the Court upheld a direction to the jury which had instructed

---

[50]   *Laceys Footwear (Wholesale) Ltd v Bowler International Freight Ltd* [1997] 2 Lloyd's Rep 369 at 374; *Thomas Cook Group Ltd v Air Malta Co Ltd* [1997] 2 Lloyd's Rep 399 at 408.
[51]   [1986] 1 Lloyd's Rep 54 at 59–60.
[52]   [1996] 2 Lloyd's Rep 212.
[53]   25 Avi Cas 17,412 (US CA 6th Cir, 1996) at 17,459–17,461.

them that they were entitled to consider the effect of a series of acts and omissions of the carrier. The Court of Appeals cited with approval *Butler v Aeromexico* [54] in which a finding of wilful misconduct was based on (1) failure to monitor weather reports (2) failure to use the weather radar (3) attempting to land the aircraft in poor weather conditions (3) failure to shut down the engines after the aircraft had crashed (4) failure to evacuate the aircraft properly. Such an approach, which encourages the maintenance of standards throughout all aspects of a carrier's aircraft operation, appears to be that which is now accepted in English law. Thus, although the American cases were not relied on, in *Thomas Cook v Air Malta* Mr Justice Cresswell expressly assessed the conduct of the carrier in the round, taking into account all the acts and omissions which had been alleged amounted to misconduct[55].

10.33   Examples of wilful misconduct.   *Horobin* was decided in 1952 and since then there have been very few reported decisions of English courts on the application of art 25 of the Warsaw Convention[56]. There have, however, been a number of recent cases which have had to decide whether there has been wilful conduct in the context of road transport covered by art 29 of the CMR. There are also a large number of decisions of foreign tribunals on art 25 of the Warsaw Convention. Whilst such cases may be of general guidance in determining whether there has been wilful misconduct in the context of carriage by air, it should be noted that English Courts are reluctant to indulge in a detailed analysis of the facts of other cases in order to determine whether the conduct in the case being tried was the same as, or worse than or better than that in an earlier decided case[57]. The burden of proving that a carrier is guilty of wilful misconduct is on the Claimant who must prove their case on the balance of probabilities[58].

10.34   Pilot error and deviation from route.   The courts have shown themselves willing to make findings of wilful misconduct where a pilot, for no apparently good reason, departs from a route which has been set for the aircraft. Such findings are to be expected since as far as the pilot is aware the route which is set is a safe route and if he departs from it there is a risk of collision. Although this risk may be slight, the consequences of a collision are so serious as to fall within the meaning of wilful misconduct. Thus, in *Berner v British Commonwealth Pacific Airlines Ltd*[59] the carrier was found guilty of

---

[54] 19 Avi 17, 961.

[55] [1997] 2 Lloyd's Rep 399 at 416.

[56] *Rustenburg Platinum Mines Ltd v South Africa Airways* [1977] 1 Lloyd's Rep 564; *Thomas Cook Group Ltd v Air Malta Co* [1997] 2 Lloyd's Rep 399.

[57] *Laceys Footwear (Wholesale) Ltd v Bowler International Ltd* [1997] 2 Lloyd's Rep at 376 per Beldam LJ.

[58] *Horabin v British Overseas Airways Corpn* [1952] 2 All ER 1016 at 1021B.

[59] (1963) 346 F2d 532. See also, in the context of wilful misconduct in the CMR, the decision of *Laceys Footwear (Wholesale) Ltd v Bowler International Freight Ltd* [1997] 2 Lloyd's Rep 369 at 376 for the strict approach taken by the English Court of Appeal in a case where wilful misconduct was found when the driver of a lorry deliberately contravened express instructions as to where to deliver cargo.

wilful misconduct when the pilot descended to a level below that which he had been instructed to maintain and in *Ritts v American Overseas Airlines*[60] wilful misconduct was found where the pilot had been authorised to take off and climb to 7,000 feet when the aircraft in fact crashed into a mountain less than 2,000 feet high which was 7 miles from takeoff. If, however, there is a good reason for a pilot to depart from the set route, the court may refuse to make a finding of wilful misconduct. In *Dame Van Duyvendijic v Air Service*[61] where the pilot decreased altitude in order to get under cloud cover, but in the process crashed the aircraft, on the facts the court refused to make a finding that there had been wilful misconduct. If the route actually plotted by the carrier is inappropriate, this too may lead to a finding of wilful misconduct. In *American Airlines v Ulen*[62], a finding of wilful misconduct was made where, in breach of air regulations, the planned route passed less than 1000 feet over the highest obstacle and the plane crashed into a mountain.

10.35 Instrumentation.   There are a number of cases where carriers have been found guilty of wilful misconduct where either the aircraft has been inadequately equipped or the equipment on the aircraft has been improperly used. In *Butler v Aeromexico*[63] the crew were found guilty of wilful misconduct where it turned off a radar in the aircraft which could have detected bad weather. In *Pekelis v Transcontinental and Western Airlines*[64] the carrier was found guilty of wilful misconduct where the crew switched the hose lines for the altimeters which caused a crash. In *Air Centre v Morland*[65] the inadequate equipment on the aircraft was a material factor in the finding of wilful misconduct. There the pilot attempted to land the aircraft in poor visibility when the altimeter was accurate to only 65 metres.

10.36 Lost and damaged baggage.   It is necessary for a claimant to prove more than just the fact of loss of or damage to baggage in order to prove wilful misconduct against a carrier. If this were not the case the limits of liability provided for in the Warsaw Convention would rarely apply[66]. Often it will be difficult for a claimant to prove the subjective element necessary for a finding of wilful misconduct and the court will be left to infer that baggage was lost or damaged due to the negligence of a carrier's employees which is insufficient to satisfy the requirements of art 25[67]. A case where the claimant was able to prove that the carrier had the requisite state of mind is *Cohen v*

---

[60] [1949] US Av 65.
[61] [1981] RFDA 363.
[62] 186 F 2d 529 (1949).
[63] 19 Avi 17,961; See also *Emery v Sabena* (1960) RGA aff'd 1965 RGAE 331, 1969 RGAE 444.
[64] 187 F2d (1951).
[65] RFDA 415 (1977).
[66] *Iyegha v United Airlines Inc* 24 Avi Cas 18,464 (Ala, 1995).
[67] See, for example *Rolls Royce PLC v Heavylift-Volga Dnepr Ltd* (Commercial Court (Morison J), 3 March 2000), where the judge found that one of the defendants had certainly neglected its statutory safety responsibilities and was clearly negligent, but that the various failures were insufficient, either separately or in the aggregate, to amount to wilful misconduct.

Varig[68] where baggage of passengers who had arrived at Rio de Janeiro was placed on an aircraft bound for New York. The carrier refused to remove the baggage from the aircraft on the grounds that it would be too expensive and time consuming — this was held to amount to wilful misconduct. In *Rymanowski v Pan Am*[69] on the other hand a passenger who was suspicious that his baggage had been misappropriated by a customs officer raised this matter with an agent of the carrier who assured the passenger that his baggage was safely on the aircraft and refused to allow the passenger to inspect his baggage when, in fact, his baggage was not on the aircraft and was never recovered. The passenger's claim that the carrier had committed wilful misconduct failed, the Court holding that the passenger had not proved that there was any collusion between the customs officer and the carrier's agent.

10.37   Delay.   As with loss and damage of baggage, a claimant's greatest difficulty in bringing a case within art 25 is proving that the carrier was more than just negligent. Indeed, in the cases of delay caused by adverse weather conditions it may be that the carrier is wholly innocent. The few cases where a carrier has been found guilty of wilful misconduct for delay have, in the main, involved some disreputable conduct by the carrier's staff. For example, in *Hill v United Airlines*[70] a finding of wilful misconduct was made where the carrier's staff had lied to passengers about the delay in their flight into Seattle, saying that Seattle airport was closed, when in fact the carrier did not have an aircraft available to make that particular flight. Passengers missed onward flights from Seattle which they could have caught had they known that the airport was open, since they could have made alternative arrangements to fly to Seattle. In *Kupferman v Pakistan International Airlines*[71] a finding of wilful misconduct was based on the carrier's failure to properly ticket luggage and confirm that it was on the aircraft, (despite requests for this to be done by the claimant) and the carrier's subsequent false promises that the baggage would arrive the next day, when in fact it arrived over two weeks late.

10.38   Theft.   There have been a number of cases where carriers have been sought to be made liable for the loss of cargo and baggage which has been dishonestly misappropriated. It is in this context that debate has taken place whether, if a carrier's servants or agents are involved in the dishonest misappropriation, they can be said to be acting within the scope of their employment, within the meaning of art 25(2) of the Warsaw Convention. These cases are discussed below under the heading 'Scope of Employment' in the section on art 25 of the Warsaw-Hague Convention. Another way in which a carrier's actions may be brought within art 25 when cargo or baggage is stolen is by showing that the carrier was guilty of wilful misconduct in the design or running of its security systems. In this way a carrier may be made

---

[68] (1975) 380 NYS 2d 450, affd 390 NYS 2d 515; affd NYS 2d 44.
[69] 416 NYS 2d 1018.
[70] 550 F Supp 1048.
[71] (1981) 438 NYS 2d 189.

liable for a theft committed by someone who is not its agent or employee, assuming that causation can be shown. *Thomas Cook Group Ltd v Air Malta Co Ltd*[72] was a case where the claimants alleged that, due to the wilful misconduct of Air Malta in organising their security procedures in relation to the unloading of cargo, the Claimant's cargo of bank notes had been stolen by thieves. It was held that in considering the alleged deficiencies of Air Malta firstly, it was necessary to bear in mind that security measures had to be appropriate to and compatible with the local situation. Thus, it was relevant that prior to the theft which was the subject of the action there had been no other thefts from Malta airport[73]. Secondly, the measures employed by the carrier had to be looked at in the round by balancing its plus points against its minus points. Plus points such as the integration of police and customs guards into the unloading procedure, the use of radios and the use of restricted areas were balanced against the minus points such as the absence of a strong room, open doors and non compliance with the IATA security manual and led to a conclusion on the facts that Air Malta were not guilty of wilful misconduct.

10.39   A carrier may also find himself liable for thefts committed by third parties if his servants or agents have unwittingly facilitated the theft. A recent example is *Laceys Footwear (Wholesale) Ltd v Bowler International Freight Ltd*[74], a road haulage case concerning wilful misconduct in the context of the CMR. In support of a finding that the haulier had been guilty of wilful misconduct, stress was laid on the fact that the relevant employee had breached express instructions as to where the goods should be delivered, and parted with possession of them to a stranger who had no supporting documentation to justify entitlement to the goods.

10.40   Liability of carrier's servants or agents.   In the original text of the Warsaw Convention, there was no express provision made for the servants or agents of a carrier to rely on the limits of liability to which the carrier was entitled. Prior to the Hague conference in 1955 concerns were expressed that, because of the absence of express provision, the original text of the Warsaw Convention was unclear as to whether or not servants or agents of a carrier were entitled to rely on the limits of liability in the Warsaw Convention if sued personally, and therefore it was not clear whether there were any limits of liability to be lost by servants or agents. If it were possible to sue servants or agents personally then the whole scheme of liability under the Warsaw Convention could be avoided by simply suing the carrier's servants or agents instead of the carrier itself. It was in order to avoid such a

---

[72] [1997] 2 Lloyd's Rep 399.
[73] Similarly, in *Rustenburg Platinum Mines Ltd v South African Airways* [1977] 1 Lloyd's Rep 564 affd. [1979] Lloyd's Rep 19, it was relevant that due to a recent spate of hijacks the carrier's security team concentrated on searching passengers and not supervising the hold from which the platinum was stolen.
[74] [1997] 2 Lloyd's Rep 369.

possibility that at the Hague Convention art 25A was agreed in the Hague Protocol 1955 which forms part of the Warsaw-Hague Convention:

> '(1) If an action is brought against a servant or agent of the carrier arising out of damage to which this Convention relates, such servant or agent, if he proves that he acted within the scope of his employment, shall be entitled to avail himself of the limits of liability which that carrier himself is entitled to invoke under Article 22.
> (2) The aggregate of the amounts recoverable from the carrier, his servants or agent, in that case, shall not exceed the said limits.
> (3) The provisions of paragraphs (1) and (2) of this Article shall not apply if it is proved that the damage resulted from an act or omission of the servant or agent done with intent to cause damage or recklessly and with knowledge that damage would probably result.'

10.41   The Warsaw-Hague Convention has the force of law in the UK by virtue of the Carriage by Air Act 1961. However, some states, notably the US, did not ratify the Warsaw-Hague Convention and so the wording of art 25 in the Warsaw Convention may apply to flights to or from such states. In English law art 25 of the Warsaw Convention is given the force of law by the Carriage by Air Acts (Application of Provisions) Order 1967[75] and the Schedules thereto. However, this 1967 Order also included an art 25A which was not in the Warsaw Convention and was identical to the art 25A which appears in the Warsaw-Hague Convention and set out above, (save that the word 'convention' is replaced by 'schedule'). The rather strange result was that a carrier was not entitled to rely on the limits of liability in the Warsaw Convention if it was guilty of 'wilful misconduct' (art 25 in Sch 2 to the 1967 Order) whereas its servants or agents were not able to rely on the limits in art 22 if they caused damage 'intentionally' or 'recklessly with knowledge that damage would probably result' (art 25A in Sch 2 to the 1967 Order)[76]. Article 25A of the 1967 Order was in fact repealed by the Carriage by Air Acts (Application of Provisions) (Fourth Amendment) Order 1998 [77], which in its place introduced the test of wilful misconduct for the acts of servants or agents of the carrier. The effect of this order was therefore to apply a consistent test, namely wilful misconduct for the acts of the carrier as well as those of its servants or agents acting within the scope of their employment. It follows that if a carrier and his servants or agents were sued together in the UK in a case to which Sch 2 to the 1967 Order applied, the Court would apply the same test to determine the liability of the carrier, its servant or agents would obtain a result which meant that the liability of the carrier was no more or no less than the liability of its servants and agents[78]. Such a result is particularly desirable since it is far

---

[75]   SI 1967/480.
[76]   This latter phrase is considered below when discussing art 25 in the Warsaw-Hague Convention.
[77]   SI 1998/1058.
[78]   For a recent example of this approach, see *Rolls Royce plc v Heavylift-Volga Dnepr Ltd* (2000) Times, 26 April.

from clear that art 25A in Sch 2 to the 1967 Order was necessary in order to extend the provisions of the Warsaw Convention to a carrier's servants or agents. In the US (where there is no equivalent to the art 25A found in Schedule 2 to the 1967 Order), it has been held that the true construction of the Warsaw Convention is that its provisions do apply to a carrier's servants or agents[79]. There is great sense in this construction which ensures that the uniformity of the Convention cannot be defeated by suing the carrier's servants or agents individually.

10.42   The meaning of 'servant or agent' and 'within the scope of his employment' are considered below in the context of the Warsaw-Hague Convention, which uses the same terminology.

Article 25 of the Warsaw-Hague Convention

10.43

RULE 29

(1) **Where the Warsaw-Hague Convention applies, a claimant can avoid the limit on recoverable damages in art 22 if he can show that:**
   (i)   **the damage resulted from an act or omission, or series of acts or omissions of either**
      (a)   **the carrier; or**
      (b)   **the carrier's servants or agents acting in the course of their employment;**
   and
   (ii) **the act or omission, or series of acts or omissions was done either**
      (a)   **with intent to cause damage or;**
      (b)   **recklessly and with knowledge that damage of the kind actually suffered would probably result.**

The Drafting History of Article 25 of the Warsaw-Hague Convention

10.44   At the Hague convention, there was produced for the consideration of the delegates a reformulation of art 25 which would have allowed disapplication of the liability limits in only the most limited of circumstances ie a deliberate act or omission done with intent to cause damage. The objective underlying this proposal was to eliminate the perceived risk of uncertainty

---

[79]   *Reed v Wiser* 555 F 2d 1079 (US CA, 2nd Cir, 1977).

as to the circumstances in which the limits of liability might be disapplied; there was a general view that the concepts of 'dol' and 'wilful misconduct' were too vague and allowed claimants to argue in too many cases that the limits of the Warsaw Convention ought to be disapplied[80]. However, it rapidly became apparent that disapplication of the limits in only the very narrow circumstances proposed was generally regarded[81] as unacceptable and that the problem was to define more precisely the circumstances in which, apart from the intentional infliction of damage, unlimited liability should apply.

10.45   The debate at the convention therefore focussed on an alternative text proposed by the Norwegian delegation which read[82]:

> 'The limits of liability specified in Article 22 of the Convention shall not apply if it is proved that the damage resulted from an act or omission of the carrier, his servants or agents, done with intent to cause damage or recklessly by[83] not caring whether or not damage was likely to result; provided that in the case of such act or omission of a servant or agent, it is also proved that he was acting in the course of his employment and within the scope of his authority.'

10.46   This proposal was amended slightly by another proposal put forward by a working party appointed to consider the Norwegian draft. In particular, the working party replaced the phrase 'not caring whether or not damage was likely to result' with 'without caring that damage would probably result'. In commenting on the working party's proposal, the UK delegate stated[84]:

> 'In the text submitted it was stated "recklessly without caring that damage would probably result" and this delegation understood and hoped that these words had been introduced in order to state that the person concerned did know that the probable consequences of his act would be to produce damage.'

10.47   The question of whether knowledge of probable damage was to be objective or subjective was then briefly debated[85] before the delegates were invited to vote on three proposed wordings:

> 'There should be an unlimited liability if the person concerned has committed an intentional act and:

---

[80]   See the Minutes at p 182 recording the observations of the representative from IATA.
[81]   See Minutes p 162–190.
[82]   See Minutes p 166.
[83]   Subsequently amended to 'and'; Minutes p 182.
[84]   Mr Wilberforce, subsequently a Lord of Appeal in Ordinary; Minutes p 196
[85]   Minutes at pp 204–5.

(a) has acted recklessly (3 votes);
(b) has acted recklessly and knew or should have known that damage would probably result (11 votes);
(c) has acted recklessly and knew that damage would probably result (13 votes)'

10.48 Therefore the result by a margin of 2 votes[86] was in favour of the formulation 'and has acted recklessly and knew that damage would probably result'. After some further debate, the problem of redrafting the Norwegian proposal was sent off to a drafting committee[87] which came up with the formula ultimately adopted. The text of the Warsaw-Hague Convention implemented into English law is:

'Article 25
The limits of liability specified in Article 22 shall not apply if it is proved that the damage resulted from an act or omission of the carrier, his servants or agents, done with intent to cause damage or recklessly and with knowledge that damage would probably result; provided that, in the case of such act or omission of a servant or agent, it is proved that he was acting within the scope of his employment.

Article 25A
(1) If an action is brought against a servant or agent of the carrier arising out of damage to which this Convention relates, such servant or agent, if he proves that he acted within the scope of his employment, shall be entitled to avail himself of the limits of liability which that carrier himself is entitled to invoke under Article 22.
(2) The aggregate of the amounts recoverable from the carrier, his servants or agents, in that case, shall not exceed the said limits.
(3) The provisions of paragraphs (1) and (2) of this Article shall not apply if it is proved that the damage resulted from an act or omission of the servant or agent done with intent to cause damage or recklessly and with knowledge that damage would probably result'

10.49   The governing law when interpreting Article 25 of the Warsaw-Hague Convention.   S 1(2) of the Carriage by Air Act 1961 expressly provides that if there is any inconsistency between the English and French texts of the of the Warsaw-Hague Convention the French texts takes precedence.

10.50   Causation and quantum of damages.   Article 25 of the Warsaw-Hague Convention provides that the limits of liability specified in art 22 shall not apply if it is proved that the damage *resulted from* an act or omission of the

---

[86] See Minutes at p 206.
[87] Minutes at p 281.

carrier. The wording used in the Warsaw Convention is that the damage must have been *caused* by the carrier. Despite this change in wording it is thought that there was no intention for there to be a difference in the method of assessing damages under art 25 of the two Conventions and the observations made above in relation to causation and quantum of damages in respect of the Warsaw Convention apply equally to the Warsaw-Hague Convention.

10.51   The provisions of the Warsaw-Hague Convention on which the carrier cannot rely when in breach of Article 25.   The uncertainty created by the Warsaw Convention as to which provisions a carrier cannot rely on if in breach of art 25 does not apply to the Warsaw-Hague Convention which makes it clear that it is only the financial limits in art 22 which are excluded.

10.52   'Recklessly and with knowledge that damage would probably result'. In order to evade the limits of liability specified in art 25 the claimant must prove that:

> '. . . the damage resulted from an act or omission of the carrier, his servants or agents, done with intent to cause damage or recklessly and with knowledge that damage would probably result.'

10.53   In the years after the adoption of this amendment many commentators took the view that the wording adopted had resulted in the adoption of a test for unlimited liability very similar to if not indistinguishable from the common law concept of 'wilful misconduct'[88]. This view appears to have been based on the proposition (of doubtful validity) that the actor guilty of wilful misconduct was required to appreciate that damage was the *probable* consequence of the act in question.

10.54   The first English case to discuss the meaning of the redrafted art 25 was *Goldman v Thai Airways International Ltd*[89]. The Claimant was injured when an aircraft encountered severe turbulence in flight, in an area where moderate turbulence had been forecast. He was not wearing a seatbelt, but the captain had not illuminated the 'fasten seat belts' sign. He relied on art 25 and argued that the captain's failure to illuminate the seatbelt sign was reckless conduct. At first instance Chapman J held[90] that the pilot had acted recklessly in disregarding the instructions in the Flight Operations Manual:

> '10.3 Use of Seat Belts. The passengers must use their seat belts and the sign "FASTEN SEAT BELTS" should be lit-During taxiing, take-off and landing-During all flying in turbulent air and when turbulence can be expected.'

---

[88]   See eg *Miller* p 303 and *McNair* p 247.
[89]   [1983] 3 All ER 693 (Court of Appeal), 1st instance transcript dated 31 March 1981.
[90]   Transcript p 57.

10.55   There were three aspects of the judgment which were all considered on appeal. Firstly, Chapman J held that 'reckless' bore the meaning given to it by Lord Diplock in the criminal case of *R v Caldwell*[91] which concerned the offence of criminal damage under the Criminal Damage Act 1971. A Defendant charged with criminal damage under the 1971 Act would be reckless as to whether or not property would be damaged if (1) he did an act which in fact created an obvious risk that property would be damaged and (2) when he did that act he either did not give any thought to the possibility of there being any such risk or recognized that there was some risk involved and nonetheless went on to do it.

10.56   Secondly, in relation to the requirement that there be 'knowledge that damage would probably result' it was argued on behalf of the carrier that since pilots often fly through areas with forecasts of moderate turbulence without encountering any adverse flying conditions, it could not be said that the pilot knew that damage would *probably* result, merely that there was a *possibility* of damage. Chapman J rejected this argument and held that what was required was the probability of damage eventuating if the risk which was being run materialised. In other words, Chapman J approached the question by asking whether injury was probable when an aircraft was in fact flying through severe turbulence, and concluded on the evidence that it was.

10.57   Thirdly, in relation to the type of damage which had to be probable, Chapman J noted that art 25 of the Warsaw-Hague Convention referred to the probability of 'damage' and not 'the damage' and concluded that 'any sort of damage'[92] was sufficient for art 25. The Claimant had suffered a fracture to his spine and it was sufficient that different sorts of physical injury (such as twisted ankles and cuts) were probable. It is possible, but not clear, that Chapman J also considered that knowledge of probable damage to property would have been sufficient for the claimant to satisfy art 25 in respect of a claim for personal injuries.

10.58   The Court of Appeal took a different approach to Chapman J on all these issues. Chapman J's reliance on the meaning of 'reckless' contained in *R v Caldwell* was criticized on the grounds that what had to be construed in art 25 was a phrase and not an isolated word, and that what was being construed was the meaning of an international convention which had been incorporated into English law. The Court of Appeal noted that in other contexts, an act could be said to be reckless if it involved a risk where the damage was a *possible* consequence and not necessarily a *probable* consequence. However, this was not a permissible interpretation of art 25 since that expressly refers to the probability of damage resulting. Eveleigh LJ held that

---

[91] [1982] AC 341 and see *R v Lawrence* [1982] AC 510, judgment being given by the House of Lords on the same day.
[92] Transcript p 53.

this meant that damage was likely to happen. The Lord Justice went on to state[93]:

> 'As I understand Article 25, it is not sufficient to show that he deliberately broke a regulation, even one which is designed for safety, unless it is also shown that he had knowledge that injury would probably result. While it is not necessary for my decision in this case, I would go further and say that it is in relation to that knowledge (and not to the regulations themselves) that his conduct is to be judged in order to determine whether or not it was reckless.'

10.59   Purchas LJ spoke in similar terms[94]:

> '. . . the true interpretation of Article 25 when it is read as a whole involves the proof of actual knowledge in the mind of the pilot, at the moment at which the omission (which would of course include commission in appropriate cases) occurs, that the omission (or commission) is taking place and that it does involve probable damage of the sort contemplated by the Article.'

10.60   Consistent with this approach is that taken by Kirby P in the Australian case of *SS Pharmaceutical Co Ltd v Qantas*[95], where he held that the phrase 'recklessly and with knowledge that damage would probably result' involves one composite concept.

10.61   It is clear that the Court of Appeal concluded that there had to be subjective knowledge of the probability of damage in the mind of the person committing the act or omission. The Court of Appeal found support for this conclusion in the minutes of the Hague conference (set out above) and rejected Chapman J's approach.

10.62   The Court of Appeal also disagreed with Chapman J that the probability of 'any sort of damage' would satisfy art 25. What had to be shown was the same kind of damage as that suffered, so knowledge of the probability of damage to property would not make the carrier liable for unlimited damages in respect of personal injuries which were not known to be probable. Indeed, Eveleigh LJ was prepared to go as far as requiring that there had to be knowledge of the kind of personal injury suffered; the fact that a cut from a falling wine glass was probable did not mean that the carrier was liable for all unexpected personal injuries which were suffered.

10.63   Therefore, as Eveleigh LJ summarised the position, art 25 requires the Claimant to prove:

---

[93]   [1983] 3 All ER 693 at 703d.
[94]   [1983] 3 All ER 693 at 705.
[95]   [1991] 1 Lloyd's Rep 288.

'(1) that the damage resulted from an act or omission; (2) that it was done with intent to cause damage; or (3) that it was done when the doer was aware that damage would probably result, but he did so regardless of that probability; (4) that the damage complained of is the kind of damage known to be the probable result[96].'

10.64   In *Gurtner v Beaton*[97] the Court of Appeal rejected an argument that the construction of art 25 adopted in *Goldman* impermissibly narrowed the recklessness required and that the Court should first focus on whether the actor was reckless in the sense of having decided unreasonably to take a risk before considering whether the pilot subjectively appreciated the consequences likely to follow if the risk materialised. The Court relied on the decision of the New South Wales Court of Appeal approving *Goldman*[98] in *SS Pharmaceutical Co Ltd v Quantas Airways Ltd*[99]. In the course of his judgment[100] in the latter case having reviewed both the travaux préparatoires and the existing international jurisprudence Kirby P said:

> 'The phrase "recklessly and with knowledge that damage would probably result" therefore involves one composite concept. It requires proof by the claimant seeking the exemption which Article 25 allows that the damage complained of was caused by something significantly more than negligence and carelessness. Even proof of reckless conduct is itself and alone, not enough. It must be shown that, at the time of the reckless conduct, the servants or agents of the carrier concerned knew that such conduct would cause damage but went ahead regardless.'

10.65   The phrase 'with knowledge that damage would probably result' was recently considered again by the Court of Appeal in *Nugent v Michael Goss Aviation Ltd*[101], where the restrictive approaches of *Goldman* and *Gurtner* were endorsed. The action was brought by the executors of Matthew Harding who died in a helicopter crash in 1996; the claim was valued at some £59 million, and art 25 was relied upon to break the limit of approximately £80,000 imposed by art 22. The defendants succeeded in striking out the paragraphs of the statement of claim in which the art 25 case was pleaded and the claimants appealed to Burton J, who refused a re-amendment and upheld the strike out. The claimants appealed to the Court of Appeal; their sought re-amended case was that the pilot, Michael Goss, who also died in the crash, had been reckless in the course of the flight, and that this recklessness was coupled with the background knowledge that damage would probably result.

---

[96] [1983] 3 All ER 693 at 698j.
[97] [1993] 2 Lloyd's Rep 369.
[98] There was a divergence of view as to whether its correctness was challenged; see per the majority at 446 and cf. Kirby P at 460.
[99] 1 S & B Av R VII/443.
[100] At 460. The judge dissented in the result but not on this point.
[101] [2000] 2 Lloyd's Rep 222.

10.66   The pilot had allegedly been reckless by (1) failing to keep his flying skills up to date; (2) failing to acquaint himself with the helicopter's navigational aids; (3) failing to plan the flight properly; and (4) flying when he was tired. However, the claimants faced a considerable hurdle, after *Goldman* and *Gurtner*, in satisfying the 'knowledge of probable loss' criterion. Counsel for the claimants accepted that art 25 was concerned with a carrier's actual knowledge of probable damage, not with knowledge that he ought to have had, and that actual knowledge of probable damage is not established by proving knowledge that damage would probably result if a particular risk materialised. However, he sought to distinguish *Gurtner* by arguing that actual knowledge of probable damage includes 'facts within a pilot's knowledge, even if not present in his mind at the time of the relevant acts or omissions, but which, had he thought about them, would have led him to appreciate the probability of damage', likening such background knowledge to the information stored on the hard disk of a computer. He argued that such a formulation would make sense of the inclusion within art 25 of the recklessness criterion as an alternative to intent to cause damage.

10.67   The Court of Appeal rejected this gloss on 'knowledge of probable loss'. Auld L J dismissed the attempt to argue that 'background knowledge' would count as actual knowledge for the purposes of art 25, holding that such a concept was practically and philosophically indistinguishable from imputed knowledge. He pointed out that it was the clear intention of the contracting states to require proof of an element additional to recklessness, and reiterated that 'the additional ingredient is actual knowledge, in the sense of appreciation or awareness at the time of the conduct in question, that it will probably result in the type of damage caused. Nothing less will do'. It was not possible, on the pleadings in this case, to allow the extreme inference that the pilot knew that he was probably going to kill or seriously injure his passengers and himself[102].

10.68   Pill L J was more sympathetic to the claimants' arguments, opining that, while the court would not impute knowledge to an actor, it was not entitled to ignore his fund of knowledge and experience in assessing his knowledge at the material time; therefore, a pilot would not be able to rely on art 25 if, as a result of alcohol or tiredness, he forgot for a moment his basic training, or made a conscious decision to put it out of his mind. He pointed out that in some situations, he would be prepared to draw inferences that an experienced pilot had the relevant general knowledge which he could be expected to have. However, he rejected the claimants' appeal on the grounds that, on the pleadings and other material before the court, it was not possible

---

[102] Auld L J indicated that to have passed the strike out hurdle, there would have to have been 'some indication in the pleading or outside it of the availability of evidence of facts sufficiently compelling to support such an inference' (ie that the pilot knew he was probably going to kill or seriously injure the passengers or himself).

to infer that the pilot knew that damage would probably result from his conduct.

10.69   Dyson J (sitting in the Court of Appeal) drew a threefold distinction between different types of knowledge; *'actual conscious knowledge'* was knowledge of the type described by Purchas L J in *Goldman*, namely actual knowledge in the mind of the pilot at the time of the relevant act or omission; *'background knowledge'* was knowledge which would be present in the mind of the person if he or she thought about it; *'imputed knowledge'* was that which the person ought to have but does not in fact have. It was clear from *Goldman* and other authorities that imputed knowledge would not suffice for art 25 and that the test was subjective. The question was whether the 'actual knowledge' required by the art could include 'background knowledge' in the sense described. Dyson J highlighted the problems of distinguishing between the concepts of 'background' and 'imputed' knowledge. He concluded that the authors of the Treaty could not have intended such difficult and uncertain questions of classification to apply to art 25, and that therefore nothing other than 'actual conscious knowledge' would suffice. The claimants' appeal therefore failed.

10.70   The problem with the approach adopted in *Goldman* and the subsequent authorities is that in aircraft accident cases it will be almost impossible to escape the limit of liability save where the damage is deliberately inflicted. The adverbial phrase 'and with knowledge that damage would probably result' effectively confines recklessness to cases where the actor thinks that there is a risk of probable damage but decides to take the risk anyway and excludes cases where the risk is obvious but the actor fails to consider it at all. Thus, in crash cases caused by pilot error, in order to bring the case within art 25 of the Warsaw-Hague Convention the claimant will have to prove that the pilot knew that plane would probably crash, such knowledge being actual and conscious at the time of the error causing the crash. Clearly a court will need much convincing that the pilot had such knowledge[103]. Furthermore, the actor who unreasonably believes that, while in most cases there is a probability of damage from the type of action undertaken, but in the particular case he can avoid this consequence, is not caught by art 25.

10.71   The Court of Appeal in *Nugent* gave some limited consideration to the question of whether there were any situations in which art 25 could be relied upon where the damage could *not* be said to be deliberately inflicted. Auld L J, approving Burton J below, ventured the examples of a pilot taking

---

[103] It is submitted that Walsh J in the Canadian case of *Swiss Bank Corpn v Air Canada* (1981) 129 DLR 85 went too far at 100–101 when he said that 'it is evident that a pilot whose own life is at stake when he flies at altitude lower than those permitted, ignores directions from a controller or otherwise by act or omission behaves recklessly, cannot be found to have done so with intent to cause damage or knowledge that damage would probably result'. As Owen J stated in *Gurtner v Beaton* S & B Av R VII/499 at 525, this is a statement of human behaviour, not one of law.

a 'stupid risk', or acting in a rage as conduct which might satisfy the test. Dyson J disagreed with the claimants' submission that art 25 could only be relied on in cases where the pilot was suicidal; he pointed out that the actual conscious knowledge test could be satisfied in cases of reckless manoeuvres in the sky. The problems of proving the requisite level of knowledge would of course still be very considerable. All three judges acknowledged that the threshold set by art 25 was extremely high but opined that this was clearly the intention of the authors of the Treaty.

10.72   The insistence by courts in common law jurisdictions on the subjective appreciation by the actor that the act in question would probably cause damage has been mirrored in most, but not all jurisdictions. Thus, the Belgian[104], Swiss[105], Italian[106], and the German[107] courts have all required proof of actual knowledge of the probability of damage on the part of the actor. Ironically, the one major jurisdiction where a different approach has been adopted is France,[108] whose delegate at the Hague Conference had insisted that the expression 'la conscience' was obviously subjective![109] While the French courts have occasionally adopted a subjective approach, requiring proof of the actual knowledge of the dangers involved[110], in a series of decisions including *Emery v Sabena*[111] and *Moinet v Air France*[112], the Cour de Cassation has explicitly adopted an objective test. There has been some support for this objective approach by a Canadian first instance court in *Swiss Bank Corporation v Air Canada*[113]. The case concerned a theft by the carrier's servant or agents, although it was not possible to identify which one had committed the theft. Walsh J concluded that there was no consistent line of jurisprudence requiring a subjective interpretation and preferred the French cases on the basis that the subjective approach would render art 25 almost nugatory as it required an examination of the intentions of an particular actor,

---

[104] *Consorts Tondriau v Cie Air India* (1977) 31 RFDA 193 in which the Cour de Cassation de Belgique rejected French authorities which adopted an objective approach.

[105] *Lacriox Bartmans v Swiss Air* 28 RFDA 75; *Claudio v Avianca Aerovias Nacionales de Colombia SA* 1987 II BGE 359.

[106] *Belgian International Air Services v Mandreoli* I S & B Av R VII/601.

[107] *Zurich Crash Case* (1981) 30 ZLW 87, Bundersgichtschof.

[108] The approach of the French Courts has been followed in Canada at first instance and in Luxembourg. For a detailed review of the French cases see *Miller* at 206–216.

[109] M. Garnault responding to the question whether in French law the suggested text meant 'actual' knowledge, replied: '. . . in French the expression "la conscience" was really the fullness of the intellectual responsibility of the person committing the act. It was unnecessary to add any adjective at all to this expression and it was even impossible to do so.' Minutes, p 285.

[110] *Cie Air France v Diop* (1968) 22 RFDA 453 Cour de Cassation, although the interpretation of this case is open to question; *Miller* (210) has little doubt that this case demonstrates a subjective approach, but *Mankeiwicz* (118–119) and *Shawcross* (Div VII, para 447) classify this case as another example of the Cour de Cassation adopting an objective approach.

[111] (1969) 32 RGAE 444.

[112] (1976) 30 RFDA105.

[113] (1981) 129 DLR (3d) 85.

which would frequently not be possible, especially in the case of theft where the actor's identity might not be known. However, on appeal[114] it was held that an act of theft necessarily involved a state of mind which was to cause loss or know of the loss which was being caused. It was sufficient therefore to show that the theft was carried out by a carrier's servants or agents acting in the course of their employment and not necessary to identify a particular employee. Therefore, the reasoning of Walsh J was not applied on appeal. Walsh J's decision (along with the French decisions) were cited to the Court of Appeal in *Gurtner v Beaton*[115] in an attempt to obtain leave to appeal to the House of Lords on the basis that art 25 should be given a wider and if necessary an objective interpretation. The Court of Appeal refused leave to appeal. Therefore, as a matter of English law, the position is clear that the test to be applied is a subjective and not an objective one. It is submitted that on the wording of art 25 this is plainly correct.

10.73   'With intent to cause damage'.   The concept of 'intent' is best developed in the criminal law and, in particular, in the law relating to murder. It has been seen above that the English Court of Appeal has criticized the use of the criminal law in determining the meaning of 'recklessly' in art 25. This was because art 25 contains a composite phrase 'recklessly with knowledge that damage would probably result', and it is that phrase which has to be interpreted and not just the word 'recklessly'. However, in relation to 'intent' the criminal courts have had to deal with cases which concern intent to cause damage (or injury) and it is thought that the guidance provided in these cases is helpful in determining the meaning of 'intent to cause damage' in art 25. It should be noted that it is unlikely to be necessary in a case under art 25 to go into great detail as to the meaning of 'intent to cause damage' since there is the alternative of satisfying art 25 by reference to recklessness. The criminal cases have gone to lengths to distinguish intent from recklessness, since it is necessary for some criminal offences, such as murder, to prove intent, with recklessness being insufficient mens rea for such crimes.

10.74   There is no doubt that a person intends to cause damage if he acts with the purpose of causing damage. For example, if a person throws a stone at someone forty yards away and hits them, the hitting of the person is intended even though the thrower thought he was a bad shot and was unlikely to hit his target. However, the courts have given 'intention' a wider meaning than this. A court or jury may infer that a result was intended, although it was not the actor's purpose, if the result is a virtually certain consequence of the act and the actor knows that it is a virtually certain consequence[116]. A notable example of such a case was given in the case of *R v*

---

[114] (1987) 44 DLR (4th) 680.
[115] [1993] 2 Lloyd's Rep 369, although the report of the case does not refer to the fact that these cases were cited in argument.
[116] *R v Hancock, R v Shankland* [1986] AC 455; *R v Nedrick* [1986] 3 All ER 1; *R v Woolin* [1998] 4 All ER 103.

Moloney[117]. There Lord Bridge held that where a man boards a plane for Manchester — the last place he wants to be — for the purpose of escaping pursuit by the police, he intends to go to Manchester. Another apposite example is that given in a Law Commission Working Paper[118] where it was stated that a man would intend to kill those on board an aircraft if he placed a time-bomb on the aircraft for the purpose of causing loss to property and making an insurance claim, when he did not care what would happen to the passengers and crew, but had no substantial doubt that a fatal crash would result from his conduct.

10.75   It will be noted that, on the face of the text, there is no requirement that the act or omission, which is intended to cause damage, is in any way wrongful. The problems which this might create were alluded to by Drion at the Hague Conference in an example of delay which he provided: goods are accepted by the carrier on a flight but at the last minute a passenger is taken seriously ill and has to be carried at once so that the goods are not transported. There would be an act or omission which the carrier intended would delay the transport of the goods. Drion pointed out that this was not the type of situation where the carrier would lose the protection of limited liability[119]. However, no amendment was made to the text to make this clear and as such it appears to be a lacuna in the wording of art 25. It is thought that a Court faced with such an argument would require that the act or omission was done without a valid reason[120].

'Servant or Agent'

10.76   The expression 'servant or agent' is a translation of the French word 'preposés'. In English law servants and agents are usually contrasted with independent contractors, for whose actions an employer is not liable. A large body of case law has grown up on the distinction between who is a servant and who is an independent contractor[121]. A number of tests have been suggested. The recent approach of the Privy Council[122] is to ask whether the person who carried out the services was performing them in business on his own account and if the answer to that question is yes, he will be an independent contractor. In answering this question the following non-exhaustive factors are relevant: whether the person in question provided his own equipment; whether he hired his own helpers; what degree of responsibility for management he had; what degree of control was exercised over him; whether

---

[117] [1985] AC 905.
[118] Working Paper No 31 (1970).
[119] Minutes p 198.
[120] See Bin Chen [1997] 2 Annals ASL 55.
[121] See generally *Clerk & Lindsell* (17th edn 1995) ch 5.
[122] *Lee Ting Sang v Chung Chi-Keung* [1990] 2 AC 374 at 382 approving the dictum of Cooke J in *Market Investigations Ltd v Minister of Social Security* [1969] 2 QB 173.

he had any opportunity to profit from the sound management of the task which he performed. However, it is submitted that both the Warsaw and Warsaw-Hague Conventions appear to displace the ordinary rule of English law that an employer is not liable for the torts of an independent contractor. No English case has yet had to decide this question, but a number of US decisions have given the phrase 'servants or agents' a wide definition. Thus, in *Baker v Lansdell Protective Agency Inc*[123] a firm which manned a security check point for passengers boarding flights at Kennedy Airport were held to be the servants or agents of British Airways, with whom they had a contract to provide such services. Similarly, in *Julius Young Jewelry Manufacturing Co v Delta Airlines*[124] a firm named Allied Aviation Service Company Inc, which was engaged by Delta Airlines and other airlines to perform inter-airline baggage transfer services at Kennedy Airport, was held to be a servant or agent of Delta Airlines and therefore able to rely on the limits of liability in the Warsaw Convention. It is thought that such an approach would be adopted in English law and there is at least some support for this in the case of *Swiss Bank Corporation v Brinks-Mat Ltd and Others*[125]. In that case the Claimant bank sought, inter alia, to make the carrier Swiss Air liable for the theft from an airport warehouse of packages of bank notes. The airport warehouse from which the notes were stolen was in fact that of KLM, and it was staffed by KLM's employees. Swiss Air contracted with KLM to provide these services. Bingham J was content to decide the case, in which Swiss Air and KLM were separate defendants, on the basis that KLM were 'cargo handling agents', and, that both of them together fell within the meaning of 'carrier' in art 25A of the Warsaw Convention.

10.77 **'The Scope of Employment'**[126] The expression 'acting within the scope of his employment' is a translation of 'agissant dans l'éxercise de ses fonctions'[127]. While it is often suggested by common law commentators[128] that the expression 'acting within the scope of his employment' is an inapposite expression to determine the responsibility of an employer for the acts of an agent (in respect of which it is usual to refer to acting within his authority), the formulation does not appear to have given rise to difficulties in practice. The approach of the English courts has been to apply the ordinary common law authorities on the meaning of the expression 'within the scope of his employment'[129]. A test which is frequently cited is that given by Salmond[130]

---

[123] (1984) 18 Avi Cas 18,497 US District Court for Southern District of New York.
[124] (1979) 15 Avi Cas 17,568 New York Supreme Court.
[125] [1986] 2 Lloyd's Rep 79.
[126] For a detailed discussion of the liability of an employer for the torts of his employees see *Clerk & Lindsell* (17th edn 1995) ch 5.
[127] In the Carriage By Air Act 1932 the word 'preposés' was originally translated as 'agents'. However the expression 'servants or agents' was adopted by amendment in 1949. It is the latter translation which has been adopted in relation to art 25 of the amended Convention.
[128] See eg *Shawcross* Div VII para [133].
[129] *Rustenburg Platinum Mines v South African Airways* 1979 1 Ll. R. 19. And see *Clerk and Lindsell* (17th edn 1995) at 5–20 ff.
[130] *Salmond & Heuston on the Law of Torts* (21st edn 1996) 443.

that an act is done in the scope (or course) of employment[131] if it is either (1) a wrongful act authorised by the master, or (2) a wrongful and unauthorised mode of doing some act authorised by the master. Thus, whether an act of wilful misconduct (Warsaw Convention) or an intentional or reckless act or omission (Warsaw-Hague Convention) is within the scope of employment is ultimately a question of fact as to whether the employee has improperly performed his duties.

10.78   This question has been considered by the English courts in the context of art 25 where it has been sought to make carriers liable for the loss of cargo and baggage which has been dishonestly misappropriated by employees and agents. In *Rustenburg Platinum Mines Ltd v South African Airways*[132] a case of platinum was loaded into the hold of an aircraft which was to make a flight from Heathrow to Philadelphia, but before the aircraft took off a cargo loader employed by the carrier stole the case of platinum. At first instance Ackner J referred to *Morris v CW Martin & Sons Ltd*[133] and held the theft by the cargo loader was within the scope of his employment because it was an improper mode of performing the act which he had been authorised to do by the carrier, namely take care of the platinum. In the course of his judgment the Judge explained that art 25 had not applied in the case of *Corocroft Ltd v Pan Am Airways*[134] since in that case the employee of the carrier who carried out the theft, was, unlike the loader in the *Rustenberg* case, not a servant whose duties included looking after goods. In argument for the carrier in the *Rustenberg* case reliance was placed on some US decisions which had held that a theft by an employee was an act which was never one within the scope of his employment. Ackner J referred to Professor Drion's 1954 report to the Hague which referred to the differences of opinion in a number of Convention states and which concluded that theft by a servant or agent of the carrier whose functions in general were connected with the custody of baggage or goods entrusted to the carrier should be considered to be committed in the course of employment. Accordingly Ackner J concluded that his decision that the theft in the *Rustenberg* case was in the scope of the loader's employment was in accordance with the views which prevailed in Convention states. It is submitted that this approach is correct and is to be preferred to those US decisions[135] which hold to the contrary. Ackner J's decision was affirmed on appeal, with Denning LJ[136] stressing the importance of the fact that it was the function of the employee in question to load the item which he in fact chose to steal. According to Denning LJ the carrier would not

---

[131] It has been held by the Northern Ireland Court of Appeal in *McCready v Securicor* [1991] NI 229 that 'acting within the scope of employment' and 'acting within the course of employment' have the same meaning.
[132] [1977] 1 Lloyd's Rep 564; affd [1979] 1 Lloyd's Rep 19.
[133] [1965] 2 Lloyd's Rep 63.
[134] [1968] 2 Lloyd's Rep 459.
[135] Such as *Rymanowski v Pan Am* 416 NYS 2d 1018; affd 427 NYS 2d 795.
[136] [1979] 1 Lloyd's Rep 19 at 23–24.

have been liable if the platinum had been stolen by someone who had nothing to do with the loading at all, such as member of the cabin staff. That employee would not have been discharging their duties in an unauthorised way, but would have been acting outside the scope of their employment on a frolic of their own.

10.79   In *Goldman v Thai Airways International Ltd*[137] Chapman J raised the rhetorical question, (without providing the answer) of whether a carrier would be liable for an assault carried out by one of its crew members on a passenger. It is submitted that the answer would depend on the circumstances surrounding the assault. If the assault is committed in the furtherance of the carrier's business then the carrier is likely to be held vicariously liable[138]. For example, if a member of the cabin crew assaulted a passenger who refused to take his seat during a flight, the carrier would be responsible for any tort committed, whereas if, for example, the assault were carried out in furtherance of a personal act of spite, the carrier would not be liable.

10.80   In relation to the time when an employee is acting within the scope of his employment, as a matter of English law, an employee will be acting within the scope of his employment from the time when he arrives for work until the time that he leaves, as long as he does not arrive unreasonably early or unreasonably late[139]. Thus, if any employee who handles cargo or baggage sneaks into the workplace at night in order to steal valuable cargo or baggage which he became aware of while he was carrying out his work during the day, it is submitted that the carrier would not be liable for this theft[140].

10.81

RULE 30

The standard of proof for a claim under Article 25 will be on a balance of probabilities, but because of the seriousness of the allegation a high degree of probability will be required.

10.82   Whilst the burden of proof for a claim made under art 25 will be the civil standard of a balance of probabilities, a claimant will have to adduce

---

[137] 1st instance transcript dated 31 March 1981; reversed on appeal [1983] 3 All ER 693.
[138] In *Dyer v Munday* [1895] 1 QB 742 a manager of a hire purchase firm was sent to premises to recover arrears of hire payments and when these were not paid he attempted to remove the goods which were on hire purchase in the course of which he committed an assault. His employer was found to be vicariously liable.
[139] *R v National Insurance Comptroller, ex p East* [1976] ICR 206.
[140] For a contrary view see the Canadian case of *Swiss Bank v Air Canada* (1987) 44 DLR (4th) 680 in which Marceau J at 688 disagreed with the judgement in the French case of *Cie St Paul Fire and Marine v Cie Air-France* [1986] RFDA 428 that it had to be proved that the employee had committed the theft during his working hours.

strong evidence in relation to the requisite elements of art 25. The reason is that an English court will generally proceed on the basis that the more serious the allegation the less probable it is and so the more careful the court must be before concluding that it has been proved to that standard[141].

10.83

RULE 31

Article 25 will have a considerably more restricted application to claims subject to Montreal Protocol No 4 and the Montreal Convention 1999.

10.84   In a claim which is regulated by the Montreal Protocol No 4, the application of art 25, as defined in the Warsaw Hague Convention, will be restricted to the carriage of passengers and baggage. In other words it will apply to claims by a passenger made under arts 17 and 19 as well as to claims in respect of baggage made under arts 18 and 19. It has no application to cargo claims because art 25 makes clear that its application applies only to passengers and baggage. A claim by or on behalf of a cargo interest will be subject to the limits imposed in art 22, of 17 SDR per kilogramme, unless a higher limit was agreed by special contract.

10.85   A claim that is regulated by the Montreal Convention 1999, (when it comes into force), will also restrict the application of art 25 (which applies the same test as in the Warsaw Hague Convention) to claims by a passenger for damages for delay as specified in art 19, and for destruction, loss, damage or delay of baggage[142]. In a Montreal Convention claim, it will not be necessary for a passenger or his estate to seek to rely on art 25 for claims for personal injury or death under art 17, as there are no financial limits on the liability of the carrier. As to cargo claims, the Montreal Convention follows the scheme of Montreal Protocol No 4 by not permitting a claim in excess of the limits imposed by art 22(3) unless the consignor has made, at the time when the package was handed over a spacial declaration of interest in delivery at destination, and has paid a supplementary sum if so required, in which case the claim will be limited to the amount of the declared special interest.

---

[141] In the case of *Malca-Amit Ltd v British Airways* (24 April 1999, unreported) (English Commercial Court), which concerned a claim under art 25 of the Warsaw Hague Convention, Lanlgley J applied this test and followed the approach of the Court of Appeal in *Hornal v Neuberger Products Ltd* [1957] 1 QB 247.
[142] Article 22(5) of the Montreal Convention 1999.

Chapter 11

Procedure

Choice of Law

11.1

RULE 32—In relation to issues governed by the Warsaw-Hague Rules, the Convention creates an independent and exclusive cause of action for a passenger who claims for loss, injury or damage sustained in the course of or arising out of international carriage by air, without reference to the rules of his own national law.

11.2 Introduction. One of the principal purposes behind the development of the Warsaw Convention scheme was the unification of the applicable rules concerning cases of carriage by air and the avoidance of issues as to choice of law. In order for the Convention scheme to succeed, it was necessary that the Conventions, as implemented into the national laws of contracting states, were regarded as giving rise to an independent cause of action regulated by the rules contained in the Conventions and not governed by normal conflict of laws rules.

11.3 The Convention Cause of Action. In relation to the Warsaw-Hague Rules, it has been settled by a decision of the House of Lords (exercising its final appellate function both for England and Wales and for Scotland) that the Rules create an independent, and exclusive, cause of action for a passenger who claims against a carrier for loss, injury and damage sustained in the course of, or arising out of, international carriage by air[1]. One of the cases arose in England, the other in Scotland. Both concerned the same British Airways flight from London to Kuala Lumpur via Kuwait. The flight departed on 1 August 1990, just before the Iraqi invasion of Kuwait. By the time that the aircraft landed in Kuwait on 2 August 1990, the invasion had begun. The passengers were taken prisoner by the Iraqi forces. The claimants claimed damages in respect of the consequences of their captivity. It was accepted by all of the claimants that they had no claim under art 17 of the

---

[1] *Sidhu v British Airways plc, Abnett (known as Sykes) v British Airways plc* [1997] AC 430, [1997] 1 All ER 193, [1997] 2 WLR 26, [1997] 2 Lloyd's Rep 76, HL.

Warsaw-Hague Rules, principally because there had been no accident causing damage which took place on board the aircraft or in the course of disembarkation. The question for the House of Lords was whether the passengers could assert any claim at common law in respect of their injuries or whether art 17 created an exclusive cause of action so that the passengers had no remedy at all.

11.4   The House of Lords determined that Sch 1 to the Carriage by Air Act 1961 provided the exclusive cause of action and sole remedy for a passenger who claimed for loss or damage arising out of international carriage by air, even though the consequence of this might be that particular claimants (such as these) would be left without a remedy. The basis of the decision is primarily found in the nature of the objects and structure of the Warsaw-Hague Rules. It was sought to achieve a uniform international code which could be applied by the courts of all of the high contracting parties without reference to the rules of their own domestic law. Although the Convention did not deal with all matters relating to contracts of international carriage by air, in relation to those areas with which it deals (including the liability of the carrier) it was intended to create a uniform code which was exclusive of recourse to the rules of any domestic law.

11.5   **Issues governed by the law of the court seised of the case.**   In relation to some of the issues arising under the Warsaw-Hague Rules, express reference is directed to the law of the court seised of the case (the 'lex fori')[2]. In this respect the Convention provides its own rule on choice of law.

11.6   **Matters not governed by the Convention.**   There are three issues arising out of art 24 where no choice of law rule is provided. Firstly, art 24(1) provides that in the cases governed by arts 18 and 19 any 'action for damages' can only be brought subject to the Convention rules, but does not say which law regulates the heads of damage for which compensation may be claimed.

11.7   Secondly, although art 24 (1) of the Convention does not refer to who has title to sue in respect of a claim governed by arts 18 and 19, the English Court of Appeal has held in *Western Digital Corporation v British Airways*[3] that the identity of who may sue is a matter for domestic law.

11.8   This was a case which concerned the partial loss of cargo. The claimants were not named as consignor or consignee in the air waybill, but brought proceedings either as the principal of the person named as consignor or consignee, or in reliance on their ownership or right to immediate possession of the cargo. The Court of Appeal determined that the references in the Convention to consignor and consignee should be read flexibly so as to

---

[2]   In relation to the effect of contributory negligence (art 21), the form of damages (art 22(1)) questions of procedure (art 28(2)), the calculation of a period of limitation (art 29(2)). In relation to the Warsaw Rules, there is an additional issue governed by the lex fori: the scope of wilful misconduct and equivalent degrees of fault (art 25).

[3]   Unreported; judgment 12 May 2000.

include the principals of persons named in the air waybill as consignor or consignee. The Court of Appeal also determined that the Convention did not preclude a claim against a carrier brought by a party with title to the relevant cargo, although the nature and standard of any liability of the carrier would be governed by the Convention.

11.9   As a result of the decision in the *Western Digital*[4] case, domestic law will be relevant to determine who has the right to sue. Where a claim is asserted in England by a principal of an agent who has contracted with a carrier, principles of English law will determine whether there is a relationship of agency and if so whether the agent or the principal or both may sue the carrier. Under English law and practice the right of suit in contract is commonly associated with ownership of the goods, see *The Albazero*[5]. In respect of tortious claims, English common law recognises that ownership of property or an immediate right to its possession gives rise to a right to sue a person in whose possession or care such property is lost or damaged.

11.10   Thirdly, art 24(2) expressly provides that in cases covered by art 17 the provisions of art 24(1) also apply, but without prejudice to the questions as to who are the persons who have the right to bring suit and what are their respective rights. In these, and any other areas which are not governed by the Convention, the usual English choice of law rules are applicable. In relation to fatal accidents cases, the questions left open by art 24 are covered by the Fatal Accidents Act 1976 which applies to 'any occurrence which gives rise to a liability under art 17'[6].

11.11   The Warsaw Rules.   The position outlined above relates to international carriage governed by the Warsaw-Hague Rules. However, there can be little doubt that the same approach would be adopted in respect of cases covered by the Warsaw Rules. The force of the argument about the need for a uniform code is unaffected by any of the amendments effected by the Hague Convention[7].

11.12   The Rules of Non-International Carriage.   The approach in *Sidhu v British Airways plc*[8] was followed in a later House of Lords decision, involving domestic carriage, *Herd v Clyde Helicopters Ltd*[9]. The Rules of Non-International Carriage are not confined to cases of carriage performed within the UK, but extend to all non-convention carriage involving a place of

---

[4]   (12 May 2000, unreported.)
[5]   [1977] AC 774.
[6]   Carriage by Air Act 1961, s 3; Fatal Accidents Act 1976, Sch 1, para 2.
[7]   In *American Express Co v British Airways Board* [1983] 1 All ER 557, [1983] 1 WLR 701, concerning the loss of a postal packet, carriage of which was governed by Sch 1 to the Carriage by Air Acts (Application of Provisions) Order 1967, Lloyd J (without deciding the point) was prepared to assume that art 18 of the Schedule created a statutory cause of action of a tortious character.
[8]   [1997] AC 430, [1997] 1 All ER 193, [1997] 2 WLR 26, [1997] 2 Lloyd's Rep 76.
[9]   [1997] AC 534, [1997] 1 All ER 775.

departure or destination or an agreed stopping pace in a foreign state and a place of departure or destination or an agreed stopping place in the UK or other British territory. Accordingly, uniformity of interpretation had the same importance in order to eliminate any conflict of laws problems. The Carriage by Air Acts (Application of Provisions) Order 1967 was therefore regarded as providing the exclusive cause of action and sole remedy for the claimants (pursuers).

11.13　Scope of the Rules of Non-International Carriage.　Carriage by air is not governed by the Warsaw-Hague Rules or the Warsaw Rules when it is not international carriage as defined in the Convention. The main cases involve wholly domestic flights, with no agreed stopping place in another state and carriage between two states, one or both of which is not a party to the Convention. An issue which has arisen relates to the scope of Sch 1 to the Carriage by Air Acts (Application of Provisions) Order 1967 which regulates cases of non-convention carriage before the English courts.

11.14　It had been argued by some that the Schedule applied to all cases of non-convention carriage (with limited exceptions concerning gratuitous carriage other than by the Crown or an air transport undertaking). However, in *Holmes v Bangladesh Biman Corpn*[10], the House of Lords held that s 10 of the Carriage by Air Act 1961, under which the 1967 Order was made, and the Order itself were limited in scope to the following two categories of case:
(1)　carriage where the places of departure and destination and any agreed stopping place were all within the UK or other British territory; and
(2)　non-convention carriage with a place of departure or destination or an agreed stopping place in a foreign state and a place of departure or destination or an agreed stopping place in the UK or other British territory.

11.15　The case involved an internal flight in Bangladesh, with no agreed stopping place in another country. The ticket had also been issued in Bangladesh. Both at first instance and in the Court of Appeal, it was nevertheless held that the claimant, the widow of a deceased passenger, could bring her claim in England, so that Sch 1 to the 1967 Order (with a much higher limit of liability) applied. On a straightforward reading of the Order[11], there was no rule against its extra-territorial application.

11.16　However, the basis of the decision of the House of Lords was that s 10 of the Carriage by Air Act 1961 and the 1967 Order had to be given a restricted interpretation, because Parliament could not be taken to have legislated on matters properly within the competence only of a foreign state. Thus the Order excluded all cases of non-convention carriage involving a place of departure or destination in a foreign state and a place of departure or destination in another foreign state, with no agreed stopping places in the UK

---

[10]　[1989] AC 1112, [1989] 1 All ER 852, (1989) 1 S & B Av R VII/355, HL.
[11]　'This order shall apply to all carriage by air, not being carriage to which the amended Convention applies.'

or other British territory, and carriage entirely internal within a foreign state (such as on the facts of the case).

Jurisdiction

11.17

RULE 33—**An action for damages under the Warsaw-Hague Rules or the Warsaw-Rules must be brought, at the option of the claimant, in the territory of one of the high contracting parties either:**

(1)   before the court having jurisdiction where the carrier is ordinarily resident; or

(2)   where the carrier has its principal place of business; or

(3)   where the carrier has an establishment by which the contract of carriage has been made; or

(4)   before the court having jurisdiction at the place of destination.

11.18   General.   Article 28(1) of Sch 1 to the Carriage by Air Act 1961 restricts the jurisdiction of the UK courts to hear an action for damages under the Act. Article 28(1) provides that an action for damages must be brought, at the option of the claimant, in the territory of one of the high contracting parties, in the courts having jurisdiction at one of the following four places:

(1)   where the carrier is ordinarily resident;

(2)   where the carrier has its principal place of business;

(3)   where the carrier has an establishment by which the contract has been made; or

(4)   the place of destination.

11.19   Any clause in the contract of carriage, or any special agreement entered into before the damage occurred, by which the parties purport to vary the rules on jurisdiction is null and void[12].

11.20   Article 28(1) is intended to be strictly applied[13]. Given that carriers by air frequently have branch offices in many countries, a wide interpretation could result in multiple jurisdiction, which would be contrary to the policy of the convention and would leave carriers having to resort to the uncertain defence of forum non conveniens[14].

---

[12]   Carriage by Air Act 1961, Sch 1, art 32. However, in relation to cargo claims, arbitration clauses are permitted, subject to the rules of the convention, provided that the arbitration is to take place within one of the jurisdictions referred to in art 28(1): Carriage by Air Act 1961, Sch 1, art 32.

[13]   *Rotterdamsche Bank NV v BOAC* [1953] 1 All ER 675, [1953] 1 WLR 493.

[14]   *Rothmans of Pall Mall (Overseas) Ltd v Saudi Arabian Airlines Corpn* [1980] 3 All ER 359, (1979) 1 S & B Av R VII/1, at 364, VII/5 (per Mustill J) and at 373, VII/15, per Ormrod LJ (in the Court of Appeal).

11.21   Questions of procedure are to be governed by the law of the court seised of the case[15]. In an English case, therefore, the manner in which the jurisdiction of the court is invoked (by the issue and service of process) is a matter for English law as stated in the relevant procedural rules.

11.22   Exclusion of plea of forum non conveniens. In *Milor Srl v British Airways plc*[16] it was held that the plea of forum non conveniens could not be raised by a defendant where the court had jurisdiction by virtue of the provisions of art 28(1). Valuable loads of jewellery had been consigned Milan-London-Philadelphia and were alleged to have been stolen from a bonded warehouse in Philadelphia. The English courts had jurisdiction by virtue of art 28(1) because the defendants were ordinarily resident and had their principal place of business within the jurisdiction. The defendants sought to argue forum non conveniens, seeking a trial in Pennsylvania. The plea was regarded as not open to the defendants, because of the provisions of art 28(1). If the option given to the claimant were to have value, it could not be regarded as restricted merely to the right to choose the forum in which the proceedings could be commenced. It had to extend to enabling the claimant to choose the forum in which the claim was to be resolved. Forum non conveniens applications were seen to involve significant disadvantages, particularly the incurring of great expense in trying to obtain an improved negotiating position without any intention of allowing the case to be tried in any jurisdiction.

11.23   States involving several jurisdictions. Article 28 deals only with the question of the jurisdiction of the courts of the UK in its international sense, and is not concerned with the issue of the allocation of jurisdiction as between the different parts of the UK. English law, as the law of the court seised of the case, will have to determine whether an English court, as opposed to a Scottish or Northern Irish court, has jurisdiction[17].

11.24   This is the position adopted by the courts of Scotland. In *Abnett v British Airways plc*[18], a passenger bought a ticket in England for a flight with British Airways, a carrier with its principal place of business in England. Her action was brought in Scotland on the basis that the carrier had a place of business in Scotland, which was sufficient to give the courts jurisdiction on the principles of Scottish law. The carrier argued that art 28 allocated jurisdiction only to the English courts. It was held that art 28 allocated jurisdiction to a high contracting party, namely the UK as a whole, and it was for the internal law of that state, and in the particular case the law of Scotland as the law

---

[15] Carriage by Air Act 1961, Sch 1, art 28(2).
[16] [1996] QB 702, [1996] 3 All ER 537, CA.
[17] Carriage by Air Act 1961, Sch 1, art 28(2). By Sch 5, para 6 of the Civil Jurisdiction and Judgments Act 1982, Sch 4 of the latter Act (dealing with the allocation of jurisdiction within the UK) does not apply in this context.
[18] [1994] 1 ASLR 1 (Outer House).

of the court seised of the case, to give effect to its own rules as to the allocation of jurisdiction between the different parts of the UK. The same analysis has been accepted in Italy[19] and in the US[20].

11.25   Where the carrier is ordinarily resident.   The place 'where the carrier is ordinarily resident' is one of the four bases of jurisdiction created by art 28(1). Although the interpretation of this phrase has been considered by the English courts in one case, it remains unclear how it should be construed. In *Rothmans of Pall Mall (Overseas) Ltd v Saudi Arabian Airlines Corpn*[21], there was a contract of carriage made in Amsterdam with a corporate carrier for the carriage of a cargo of cigarettes from Amsterdam to Jeddah. Proceedings in respect of damage to and loss of cargo were commenced in England and the writ served on the London office of the defendant carrier. At first instance (Mustill J) and in the Court of Appeal, it was held that the defendant was not ordinarily resident in England, in that the presence of a branch office, a place of business, in the jurisdiction was not sufficient.

11.26   Mustill J suggested three possible interpretations of the phrase 'ordinarily resident': (i) the words do not apply to corporations at all; (ii) the place where the company is incorporated[22]; or (iii) the place where the central administration and power of decision of the company is located, in accordance with English tax cases concerned with the question of the 'residence' of a company[23]. On the facts of the case, it was not necessary to determine which interpretation was correct. The Court of Appeal, in upholding Mustill J's judgment, did not provide clear guidance on the meaning of the words 'ordinarily resident'. It was indicated that the tax cases were of little assistance in interpreting an international convention. Moreover, analogies with the question of residence for the purposes of the rules regarding service of process were also regarded as irrelevant.

11.27   The issue may arise only rarely in practice: frequently, the place where a carrier is ordinarily resident will be the same place as that in which it has its principal place of business. Jurisdiction can thereby be founded on the latter basis.

---

[19] *Empresa Consolidada Cubana de Aviación* (Court of Cassation, 15 June 1993).
[20] *Smith v Canadian Pacific Airlines Inc* 452 F 2d 798 (2nd Cir, 1971), 12 Avi 17,143; *Eck v United Arab Airlines Inc* [1966] 2 Lloyd's Rep 485, 360 F 2d 804 (2nd Cir, 1966), 9 Avi 18,146; *Hill v United Airlines Inc* 550 F Supp 1048 (SDC Kan, 1982); *Re Air Crash Disaster near New Orelans, Louisiana on July 9 1982, Trivellone-Lorenzi v Pan American World Airways Inc* 821 F 2d 1147 (5th Cir, 1987), 20 Avi 18,179; *Romero v Aerolineas Argentinas* 834 F Supp 673 (DC NJ, 1993).
[21] [1981] QB 368, [1980] 3 All ER 359, (1979) 1 S & B Av R VII/1, CA.
[22] This has been the interpretation adopted in the US, in relation to the different wording of the text of the convention ('domicile of the carrier'): *Wyler v Korean Air Lines Co Ltd* 928 F 2d 1167 (DC Cir, 1991), 23 Avi 17,409, (1991) 1 S & B Av R VII/625.
[23] A company is regarded as being resident for tax purposes where its central management and control actually abides: *De Beers Consolidated Mines Ltd v Howe* [1906] AC 455, 458, HL; *Cesena Sulphur Co Ltd v Nicholson* (1876) 1 Ex D 428; *Egyptian Delta Land and Investment Co Ltd v Todd* [1929] AC 1, HL.

11.28   Where the carrier has its principal place of business.   The second basis of jurisdiction is the place 'where the carrier has his principal place of business'. It is likely that a carrier will be regarded as having only one principal place of business, where the main part of the executive and management work of the business is conducted[24].

11.29   Establishment by which the contract has been made.   The third basis of jurisdiction arises in respect of the courts of the place where the carrier has an 'establishment by which the contract has been made'. This phrase has not been considered by the English courts.

11.30   Normally the contract will be made where the ticket (or air waybill) is issued, but there may be exceptional cases where the contract is regarded as having been made elsewhere. One example is where the agreement to carry the passenger is made in one place but the passenger is permitted to collect the ticket at a different place. In this situation, the place of contracting would be the relevant place. In a case where a passenger's agent tendered cash in New York to purchase a reservation on a flight and was given a receipt, and the ticket was later issued and collected, against the receipt, in Bogota, it was held that the contract was made in New York[25]. In another case, where a ticket was bought from the office of BOAC in New York, that company having been appointed general sales agent for another airline in an agreement which was more extensive in scope than the usual interline sales agency, it was held that the other airline had an establishment by which the contract had been made in New York[26].

11.31   The argument that a travel agent which issues a ticket could constitute an 'establishment' for this purpose has been considered and rejected in a number of French[27] and Canadian[28] cases. In the latter case, this was on the basis that the use of a travel agency appointed to sell tickets on a commission basis did not amount to having an 'establishment' for the purposes of art 28(1).

---

[24] *Eck v United Arab Airlines Inc* 360 F 2d 804 (2nd Cir, 1966), 9 Avi 18,146, [1966] 2 Lloyd's Rep 485; *Recumar Inc v KLM Dutch Airlines* 608 F Supp 795 (SD NY, 1985), 19 Avi 17,292; *Stanford v Kuwait Airways Corpn* 648 F Supp 1158 (SD NY, 1986), 20 Avi 17,393; *Swaminathan v Swiss Air Transport Co Ltd* 962 F 2d 387 (5th Cir, 1992), 23 Avi 18,392.

[25] *Re Air Disaster at Cove Neck, New York, on January 25, 1990, Gutierrez v Avianca (aerovias Nacionales de Colombia SA)* 774 F Supp 718 (ED NY, 1991), 23 Avi 18,017; see also *Campbell v Air Jamaica Ltd* 863 F 2d 1 (2nd Cir, 1988), 21 Avi 17,755.

[26] *Berner v United Airlines Inc* 157 NYS 884 (1956), 5 Avi 17,169, affd 170 NYS 2d 340 (1957).

[27] *Orchestre Symphonique de Vienne v TWA*, IATA ACLR No 418 (1971), (1972) 35 RGAE 202 (TWA had office in Paris and tickets bought in Paris, but through travel agent who dealt directly with Swissair in Geneva, jurisdiction of French courts refused); *Cie d'Assurances Navigation et Transports v Cameroun Airlines* (Paris, 15 December 1989), (1989) 43 RFDA 555 (carrier had office in Paris, but air waybill issued through freight forwarding company in circumstances where that company was not agent of carrier).

[28] *Qureshi v KLM Royal Dutch Airlines* (1979) 102 DLR (3d) 205 (Nova Scotia SC); *Maijala v Pan American World Airways Inc* (Ontario, 20 April 1992) (ticket purchased through American Express; presence of defendant's office in Toronto immaterial).

11.32   In cases where the contract of carriage is varied by subsequent agreement between the passenger or consignor and the carrier, at least where no additional fare has been paid, the variation will not affect the place at which the contract was made for the purposes of art 28, on the basis that the carriage is still provided pursuant to the original contract[29].

11.33   Place of destination.   The fourth basis of jurisdiction is founded on the place of destination. In normal circumstances, this will be the place of destination indicated in the contract of carriage, and particularly that recorded on the passenger ticket, which is required to contain (amongst other things) an indication of the place of destination and which is regarded as prima facie evidence of the terms of the contract of carriage[30].

11.34   This indication will usually be conclusive. Where a passenger purchased a ticket in Kenya, intending to travel to New York, but was only able to obtain a ticket which stated London to be the place of destination, it was held that the New York courts did not have jurisdiction[31]. Where a passenger purchased a return ticket, Bombay-New York-Bombay, but claimed that he did not intend to make the return journey and to obtain a cash refund, it was held that the ticket was determinative and Bombay was the place of destination[32].

11.35   In relation to a return ticket or round trip regarded from the outset as a single operation, the place of destination will be the same as the place of departure[33]. This remains the position even where two passenger tickets are issued, provided that there is still a single contract of carriage[34].

11.36   Exclusivity of Article 28.   The English courts have generally regarded art 28 as creating an exhaustive code in respect of jurisdiction for actions against the carrier. In *Rothmans of Pall Mall (Overseas) Ltd v Saudi*

---

[29] *Boyar v Korean Air Lines* 664 F Supp 1481 (USDC, DC 1987), 20 Avi 18,467; *Nebco International Inc v Iberia Airlines of Spain* 22 Avi 18,341 (SD NY, 1990).

[30] Carriage by Air Act 1961, Sch 1, art 3(1)(a), 3(2).

[31] *McCarthy v East African Airways* 13 Avi 17,385 (DC NY, 1975).

[32] *Solanki v Kuwait Airways* 20 Avi 18,150 (SD NY, 1987); see also *Klos v Polskie Linie Lotnicze* 26 Avi 15,215 (2nd Cir, 1997), where it was argued that two passengers with Warsaw-New York-Warsaw tickets intended to remain in New York, so that New York was their 'destination', but held that the ticket was unambiguous and the agreement clear, that Warsaw was the place of destination.

[33] *Qureshi v KLM Royal Dutch Airlines* (1979) 102 DLR (3d) 205 (round trip to and from Sydney; injury on journey from Amsterdam to Karachi; Sydney nevertheless place of destination); *Podjob v Cie Inex Avio Promet* (Ajaccio, 12 September 1988), (1989) 43 RFDA 142, [1990] Uniform LR 411 (day trip, Ljublana-Ajaccio-Ljublana; Ljublana, not Ajaccio, place of destination).

[34] *Re Air Crash Disaster at Malaga, Spain on September 13, 1982* 577 F Supp 1013 (ED NY, 1984), 18 Avi 17,591, affirmed sub nom *Petrire v Spantax SA* 756 F 2d 263 (2nd Cir, 1985), 19 Avi 17,170, (1985) 1 S & B Av R VII/161, cert den 474 US 846 (1985) (intended flights Madrid-Malaga-New York-Madrid; because only tickets available contained two passenger coupons, return leg New York-Madrid covered by second ticket issued at same time as first; Madrid held to be place of destination).

Arabian Airlines Corpn[35], Roskill LJ stated that art 28 was a 'self-contained code within the limits of which a claimant must found his jurisdiction'. Accordingly, the claimant could not rely on Order 65, rule 3 of the Rules of the Supreme Court (service of process on foreign corporations) so as to extend the scope of the English court's jurisdiction. Similarly, in *Rotterdamsche Bank NV v BOAC*[36], it was held that the procedural rules as to service out of the jurisdiction could not be relied upon so as to widen the scope of the art 28 jurisdiction.

11.37   There may be one exception, arising out of the first instance judgment of Mustill J in *Rothmans Pall Mall (Overseas) Ltd v Saudi Arabian Airlines Corp*[37]. He stated that there may be cases where, although the court could not assert jurisdiction on any of the four bases outlined in art 28, it could nevertheless do so on the basis of an unconditional appearance or submission to the jurisdiction by the defendant, constituting a waiver of any jurisdictional objections.

The Montreal Convention 1999

11.38

Rule 34—Under the Montreal Convention 1999 Jurisdiction is allocated at the option of the claimant to one of the following courts:

(1)   the Court of the domicile of the carrier; or
(2)   the Court of its principal place of business; or
(3)   the Court of a state where the carrier has a place of business through which the contract has been made; or
(4)   before the Court at the place of destination; or
(5)   in respect of damage resulting from the death or injury of a passenger, an action may be brought either before one of the courts listed in (1) to (5) herein, or in the territory of a State Party in which at the time of the accident the passenger has his or her principal and permanent residence and to or from which the carrier operates services for the carriage of passengers by air, either on its own aircraft, or on another carrier's aircraft pursuant to a commercial agreement, and in which that carrier conducts its business of carriage of passengers by air from premises leased or owned by the carrier itself or another carrier with which it has a commercial agreement.

11.39   In addition to the existing four jurisdictions available under the Warsaw Convention[38] where an action for damages must be brought, the

---

[35]   [1981] QB 368, [1980] 3 All ER 359, (1979) 1 S & B Av R VII/1, CA.
[36]   [1953] 1 All ER 675, [1953] 1 WLR 493.
[37]   [1980] 3 All ER 359, (1979) 1 S & B Av R VII/1.
[38]   Article 28 of the Warsaw Convention.

Montreal Convention permits another in respect of an action for damages for the bodily injury or death of a passenger[39]. Specifically a passenger may bring an action in the territory of a State Party in which at the time of the accident the passenger has his or her principal and permanent residence and to or from which the carrier operates services for the carriage of passengers by air, either on its own aircraft, or on another carrier's aircraft pursuant to a commercial agreement, and in which that carrier conducts its business of carriage of passengers by air from premises leased or owned by the carrier itself or by another carrier with which it has a commercial agreement.

11.40   A 'commercial agreement' is defined[40] as an agreement, other than an agency agreement, made between carriers and relating to the provision of their joint services for the carriage of passengers by air. George Tompkins Jr in his article 'The Montreal Convention 1999: this is the answer'[41] states that it is generally accepted that interline agreements, code share agreements, block space agreements and similar intercarrier agreements, fall within the scope of 'commercial agreement' as used in art 33 of the Montreal Convention. This view however has yet to be tested by any court.

11.41   'Principal and permanent residence' is defined as 'the one fixed and permanent abode of the passenger at the time of the accident.'[42] The nationality of the passenger shall not be the determining factor in ascertaining the 'one fixed and permanent abode of the passenger.'

Limitation of Actions

11.42

RULE 35

(1)   The right to damages shall be extinguished if an action is not brought within two years from the date of arrival at the destination, or from the date on which the aircraft ought to have arrived, or from the date on which the carriage stopped.

(2)   The method of calculating the period of limitation is determined by the law of the court seised of the case.

11.43   **The limitation period.**   The right of action under the Convention is extinguished if an action is not brought within two years from the date of arrival at the destination, or from the date on which the aircraft ought to have arrived, or from the date on which the carriage stopped[43]. English law,

---

[39] Article 33(2)(a) of the Montreal Convention: colloquially referred to as the 'fifth jurisdiction'.
[40] Article 33(3)(a) of the Montreal Convention.
[41] 1999 TAQ 114.
[42] Article 33(3)(b) of the Montreal Convention.
[43] Carriage by Air Act 1961, Sch 1, art 29(1).

as the law of the court seised of the case, will determine the method of calculating the period of limitation[44].

11.44   It is the 'right to damages' which is extinguished by the expiry of the relevant limitation period. It is therefore clear that the limitation provisions do not apply to other claims, such as a claim by the carrier for freight. However, they will apply not only to actions brought under the Carriage by Air Act 1961 itself but also to actions brought under the Fatal Accidents Act 1976[45] and the Law Reform (Miscellaneous Provisions) Act 1934.

11.45   It is provided that the right of action is 'extinguished' after the expiry of the limitation period. On this basis, it is the case that the right is completely destroyed and not merely rendered unenforceable (unlike the normal effect of a limitation period under the Limitation Act 1980). As such, it could not be relied on even by way of defence to an action brought by the carrier. In the case of *Aries Tanker Corpn v Total Transport Ltd*[46] a case concerning art III r6 of the Hague Rules, which imposes a similar type of time bar, Lord Wilberforce described this type of time bar as:

> 'a time bar of a special kind, viz one which extinguishes the claim (cf article 29 of the Warsaw Convention 1929) not one which, as most English statutes of limitation (e.g. the Limitation Act 1939, the Maritime Conventions Act 1911), and some international conventions (e.g. the Brussels on Collisions 1910 article 7) do, bars the remedy while leaving the claim itself in existence.'

11.46   In the same way as actions against the carrier itself, no action arising out of the Convention may be brought against a servant or agent of the carrier, acting within the scope of his employment, more than two years after the date of arrival at the destination or from the date at which the aircraft ought to have arrived, or from the date on which the carriage stopped[47].

11.47   Commencement of the limitation period.   The two year period of limitation commences on one of the three dates specified. In most cases, particularly in relation to passengers, the dates will be the same. If there are different dates, it will be the later or latest date which is relevant.

11.48   In *Alltransport Inc v Seaboard World Airlines*[48], damaged goods arrived on 14 October 1970, but were not delivered to the claimant until 16 November

---

[44]   Carriage by Air Act 1961, Sch 1, art 29(2).
[45]   Limitation Act 1980, ss 12(3), 33(2) (the example) and 39 (whereby the rules in the 1980 Act are inapplicable when a limitation period is prescribed by or under any other enactment).
[46]   [1977] 1 WLR 185; [1977] 1 All ER 398; [1977] 1 Lloyd's Rep 334, HL.
[47]   Carriage by Air Act 1961, s 5(1); Carriage by Air Acts (Application of Provisions) Order 1967, SI 1967/480, art 6.
[48]   349 NYS 2d 277 (NY City Ct, 1973), 12 Avi 18,163.

1970. It was held that 'the date on which the carriage stopped' was the date on which the cargo ceased to be in the charge of the carrier[49]. On this basis the limitation period did not commence until 16 November 1972 and the action, commenced on 2 November 1972, was within time.

11.49   In the case where part of a consignment of goods does not arrive, the relevant date is that on which the remainder of the consignment did arrive at the destination or ceased to be in the charge of the carrier[50].

11.50   In relation to baggage, the date of arrival at the destination will involve the destination at which the baggage is returned to the charge of its owner, so that on a return trip London-Paris-London, for this purpose Paris will be a 'destination'[51].

11.51   In *Korba v Trans World Airlines*[52] the claimant passenger should have completed a return journey New York–Tel Aviv–New York on 1 August 1983, but had to return on an earlier flight, arriving in New York on 30 July 1983. It was held that an action commenced on 1 August 1985 was time-barred. This result appears to be correct, on the basis that the 'date on which the aircraft should have arrived' must be taken to refer to the aircraft on which the passenger in fact travelled, rather than (as the claimant contended) the aircraft on which he hoped to travel.

11.52   Addition of defendants after expiry of limitation period. As a procedural issue which is not expressly provided for in the Act, the question of adding a defendant or introducing by amendment a new cause of action after the expiry of the two year limitation period is governed by the law of the court seised of the case. In an English action (whereby the applicable law on this point would be English law), the general rule would be that the court would not permit the addition of a defendant or an amendment that introduced a new cause of action outside the two year limitation period. The reason for this is that the procedural rule by which the addition of a new party or an amendment is deemed to relate back to the date of the original claim does not apply to a claim in which the right to claim damages has been extinguished. The attempt to add a new defendant or to amend to add a new claim after the expiry of two years will be refused by a court on the grounds that as the claim has been extinguished and therefore has ceased to exist no useful purpose would be served by allowing the application[53]. The Court will not permit the application of the procedural rule of relation back of an amendment to a claim to defeat a substantive defence which would have

---

[49] See Carriage by Air Act 1961, Sch 1, art 18(2).
[50] *Srivasta v Alia, The Royal Jordanian Airline* 473 NE 2d 564 (Ill App, 1985). The court rejected the argument that the carriage of the lost goods never stopped.
[51] *Rush v US Air Inc* 19 Avi 18,129 (Ohio App, 1984).
[52] 508 NE 2d 48 (Ind App, 1987).
[53] *Davies v Elsby Bros Ltd* [1960] 3 All ER 672, [1961] 1 WLR 170, CA; *Liff v Peasley* [1980] 1 All E R 623, [1980] 1 WLR 781, CA; *Ketteman v Hansel Properties Ltd* [1987] AC 189, HL.; *The Jay Bola* [1992] 2 Lloyds 62; *Western Digital v British Airways* (12 May 2000, unreported), CA.

accrued to the carrier following the expiry of two years without an action having been brought[54].

11.53   This practice is likely to be applied to any case coming within the scope of the Carriage by Air Act 1961. The provisions of s 35 of the Limitation Act 1980 and Order 15, rule 6 of the Rules of the Supreme Court are applicable only in relation to time-limits governed by the 1980 Act, and so do not apply to carriage by air cases. Whilst the provisions of the Civil Procedure Rules at CPR 17.4 (b) (iv) apply to statutory provisions other than the Limitation Act 1980, their application will be limited to those Acts which bar a remedy whilst leaving the claim in existence, and not to time limits such as that under art 29 which extinguishes the claim. CPR 17.4 cannot deprive a party of a substantive defence. Neither the statutory provisions under which the rule was made nor any general power to regulate the procedure of the Courts can deprive a person of an accrued substantive legal right or create a legal cause of action which did not previously exist[55].

11.54   Contribution proceedings.   It is expressly provided that art 29 is not to be applied to any proceedings for contribution between persons liable for any damage to which the Convention relates[56].

11.55   If the defendant is a carrier, and contribution proceedings are brought either by another carrier or by a third party, s 1(3) of the Civil Liability (Contribution) Act 1978 will apply. By this provision a person ceases to be liable to make contribution if he ceases to be liable on his own account in respect of the damage in question by virtue of the expiry of a limitation period which extinguished the right on which the claim against him would have been based. The carrier's own liability is subject to art 29, the effect of which is to extinguish the right of action after two years from the applicable date. Accordingly, the contribution proceedings will become barred once the original proceedings against the carrier are themselves barred.

11.56   Where contribution is sought against a servant or agent of the carrier acting within the scope of his employment, s 5(1) of the Carriage by Air Act 1961 applies a two year limitation period on the same basis as that provided in art 29.

11.57   Where a carrier brings contribution proceedings against a third party, art 29 does not apply and the relevant provision is s 10 of the Limitation Act 1980. Accordingly, there is a time limit of two years from the date on which the right to recover contribution accrued[57], which will be the date of the relevant judgment or award or of the settlement of the action[58].

---

[54]   *The Jay Bola* [1992] 2 Lloyds 62.
[55]   *The Jay Bola* [1992] 2 Lloyds 62 at p 76.
[56]   Carriage by Air Act 1961, s 5(2), as amended by the Limitation Act 1963, s 4(4) and the Civil Liability (Contribution) Act 1978, Sch 1.
[57]   Limitation Act 1980, s 10(1).
[58]   Limitation Act 1980, s 10(3) and s 10(4).

11.58   Suspension of the limitation period.   By art 29(2) the law of the court seised of the case determines the method of calculating the period of limitation. This provision allocates to the law of the court seised such procedural questions as whether parts of a day are to be disregarded and what steps are required in order to constitute the bringing of the action[59].

11.59   It is unlikely that an English court would permit the suspension or interruption of the limitation period on grounds similar to those applicable under the Limitation Act 1980 (such as on the ground of the infancy or disability of the claimant). The relevant provisions of the Limitation Act 1980 are expressly disapplied where, as in the case of actions governed by the Carriage by Air Act 1961 or the Carriage by Air Acts (Application of Provisions) Order 1967, a period of limitation is prescribed by or under any other enactment. The manner in which art 29(2) is expressed, referring only to 'the method of calculating the period of limitation', also strongly suggests that the role of the law of the court seised is intended to be strictly limited to mechanical and administrative matters, and not to permit extensions of the two year limitation period.

11.60   This is the position adopted by most US decisions on this point[60]. It has also been accepted in numerous other jurisdictions[61]. However, in France a different interpretation has been adopted, holding that the two year period may be suspended in accordance with the provisions of French law[62].

11.61   The Warsaw Rules.   The rules concerning limitation under the 1967

---

[59] *Halmos v Pan American World Airways Inc* 727 F Supp 122 (SD NY, 1989), 22 Avi 17,699 (filing of complaint sufficient for purposes of federal law, but service of summons also required where New York law applied); *Cie Air France v SA Migor* (Pau CA, 23 January 1991), (1991) 44 RFDA 284 (goods arrived on 6 May 1985; under French law (as law of court seised) two years expired on the same date (6 May 1987), so action brought on 7 May 1985 time-barred).

[60] *Kahn v Trans World Airlines Inc* 82 AD 2d 696 (NY AD, 1981) 16 Avi 18,041 (limitation period was condition precedent and not affected by infancy of claimant); *Magnus Electronics Inc v Royal Bank of Canada* 611 F Supp 436 (ND Ill, 1985); 19 Avi 17,944 (alleged fraud did not suspend limitation period); *Data General Corpn v Air Express International Ltd* 676 F Supp 538 (SD NY, 1988) 21 Avi 17,168; *Royal Insurance Co v Emery Freight Corpn* 834 F Supp 633 (SD NY, 1993); *Fishman v Delta Air Lines Inc* 132 F 3d 138 (2nd Cir, 1998); *Castro v Hinson* 959 F Supp 160 (ED NY, 1997), 25 Avi 18,200.

[61] Argentina: *Sud America Terrestre y Maritima Cia de Seguros SA v Scandinavian Airlines System* (Argentine Sup Ct, 13 December 1989), La Ley 1989–B 371; Belgium: *Memorex v Alia and Saudi Arabian Airlines* (1984) 1 S & B Av R VII/137 (Brussels CA, 2 May 1984), [1984] J T 550; India: *Mirza Mohammed Taqui Khan v Air India* (Hyderabad Ct, 1978); Israel: *Daddon v Air France* (1984) 1 S & B Av R VII/141 and (1987) 1 S & B Av R VII/215, (1984) 38(3) PD 785, reported sub nom *Cie Air-France v Teichner* (1985) 39 RFDA 232, (1988) 23 Eur TrL 87; Italy: *Santoboni v Japan Air Lines Co Ltd* (1985) 1 S & B Av R VII/187 (Rome CA, 25 September 1985); *Celada v Aerovias Nacionales de Colombia SA* (Rome, 17 April 1991), 23 Avi 18,128; Malta: *Bennet v Air Malta* (Commercial Ct, 30 May 1988), [1989] Uniform LR 789, (1989) 14 Air L 97; Nigeria: *Oshevire v British Caledonian Airways Ltd* [1990] LRC (Comm) 291 (Nigerian CA), [1990] Uniform LR 424; South Australia: *Timeny v British Airways plc* (1991) 102 ALR 565, (1991) 1 S & B Av R VII/675; Spain: Barcelona CA, 9 October 1973, [1973] Rev Jur Cat 143; and Switzerland: *Mirzan v Air Glaciers SA* (Trib fed, 10 May 1982), (1983) 37 RFDA 365.

[62] *Lorans v Air France* 1977 D 89 (1977) 31 RFDA 268.

Order are the same as those applicable under the 1961 Act. This includes the provisions of the Act as to actions against the servants or agents of a carrier (s 5) and as to contribution proceedings[63].

11.62   Death of party liable.   Where the person liable dies, an action for damages lies against those legally representing his estate, in accordance with the provisions of the Carriage by Air Act 1961[64].

---

[63]   Carriage by Air Acts (Application of Provisions) Order 1967, SI 1967/480, art 6.
[64]   Carriage by Air Act 1961, Sch 1, art 27.

Chapter 12

Air Carrier Liability for Passenger Injury: The EC Dimension

Background

12.1

Rᴜʟᴇ 36—The EU Regulation on Air Carrier Liability in the Event of Accidents was drafted, following some seven years of consultation, with the aim of extending the liability of European Community air carriers (on both domestic and international flights) beyond their existing obligations under the Warsaw Convention.

12.2   Following receipt of the S T Brise Study on the 'Possibilities of Community Action to Harmonise Limits of Passenger Liability and Increase the Amounts of Compensation for International Accident Victims in Air Transport' in 1991, the EC Commission set about actively working on a further scheme to govern air carrier liability within the European Community[1]. In October 1992 the Commission published a Consultation Paper heavily criticising the then existing compensation limits for air carrier liability, recognising the need for a fairer system of compensation and inviting comments as to increased or unlimited liability, the merits of a further system of carrier liability within the confines of the Warsaw Convention and the implementation of new mandatory or self-regulatory rules and procedures. In September 1993, a task force set up by the European Civil Aviation Conference (ECAC) met to discuss the feasibility of an intercarrier agreement increasing the compensation limits. In June 1994 a further task force of Community and ECAC airlines belonging to the Association of European Airlines (AEA) was set up to pursue a recommendation from the ECAC for an intercarrier agreement. However, it became apparent during the course of negotiations that action on the part of the Commission itself might produce

---

[1]   Community legislation already played an important role in the field of aviation including a variety of Council Directives and Regulations governing matters such as the application of art 85 of the Treaty of Rome to the aviation industry, noise emission, access for air carriers to scheduled intra-community air service routes, the harmonization of technical requirements and administrative procedures in the field of civil aviation, the licensing of Community air carriers, the regulation of fares and rates for air services and the principles governing the investigation of civil aviation accidents and incidents.

a more workable system governing air carrier liability within the European Community.

12.3   Following consultation with the then Member States and publication of a report by Frere Chomeley Bischoff on the cost implications of higher compensation limits, on 15 February 1996 the Commission submitted its first proposal for an EC Council Regulation on air carrier liability in case of accidents[2] coupled with an explanatory paper setting out the Commission's assessment of the existing air carrier liability system[3]. The Commission's explanatory paper noted that the Warsaw Convention 'despite its deficiencies, provides a uniform basis enjoying a worldwide recognition for settlement of claims for passengers in aviation accidents' and recommended that any attempts to improve the current system should 'maintain the basic elements of the liability system in force'. However, the paper went on to refer to then current compensation limits as an 'anachronism' which failed to guarantee equal treatment between different carriers and types of operation to avoid the distortion of competition and expressed the view that compensation limits should be in line with levels of compensation paid to victims in non aviation accidents. The Commission also called for 'simple and speedy' procedures, as well as recognition of the need to avoid litigation and for a uniform system of liability. Finally, the Commission recorded its view that the new system should apply to domestic carriage within the Community as well as international carriage by Community air carriers.

12.4   On 26 March 1996, the EC Council consulted[4] the Economic and Social Committee (ESC) under what was then art 84(2) of the EC Treaty (now art 80(2) of the Treaty on European Union) for its views on the proposed draft regulation. The ESC delivered its opinion on 29 April 1996 commenting upon and in certain instances criticising the Commission's proposed draft regulation. Having stated its view that 'the reform of the Warsaw system is long overdue' the ESC highlighted difficulties with the practical application of art 4 of the then draft Regulation imposing an obligation on Community air carriers to make swift lump sum payments to victims and their families and criticised art 5 concerning the provision of information by non-Community carriers and its practical implications for purposes such as enforcement. The ESC also expressed its concern with regard to continued no fault liability in the case of smaller airlines and called for clearer definitions of 'domicile' and 'permanent residence' in the context of the then arts 2 and 7 of the draft regulation and the proposed introduction of a further forum for jurisdiction.

---

[2]   OJ C104 18 10.4.96.
[3]   For summaries of the then proposed provisions and commentary see Harold Caplan 'The Millennium has Arrived: Compensation for Death and Injury in International Air Travel' [1996] ILR 4 (3) p 84–90, Berend Crans and Onno Rijsdijk 'EC Aviation Scene' [1996] Air & Space Law vol XXI no 4/5, and Peter Martin 'The 1995 IATA Intercarrier Agreement: An Update' [1996] Air & Space Law vol XXI no 3.
[4]   OJ C212 22.7.96 p 0038.

12.5   The European Parliament delivered its opinion on the proposed regulation at a first reading on 17 September 1996[5] approving the Commission's
proposed regulation subject to a vast array of amendments. On 11 December
1996, the Commission submitted its Amended Proposal for a Council
Regulation (EC) on air carrier liability in case of accidents[6] to the Council
under what was then art 189a(2) of the EC Treaty (now art 250 of the Treaty on
European Union) ('the Amended Proposal'). The Council reached agreement
on a draft common position with a view to adopting the proposed regulation
on 12 December 1996 and subsequently adopted its common position setting
out a further amended form of the regulation in accordance with art 189c of
the EC Treaty (new art 252) on 24 February 1997[7]. The Council's Common
Position (EC) 16/97 was accompanied by a statement of its reasons[8] which
sets out its understanding of the purpose of the Regulation:

> 'The proposal aims at improving the level of protection of passengers
> involved in air accidents on board a Community air carrier and consti-
> tutes a flanking measure in the context of the third liberalisation
> package on air transport.
>
> The obligations of air carriers in relation to liability in the event of acci-
> dents in international carriage is basically governed by the 1929 Warsaw
> Convention for the Unification of Certain Rules relating to International
> Carriage by Air, of which all Member States are contracting parties, and
> a number of other instruments which, together with the Warsaw
> Convention, are generally referred to as the Warsaw System. However,
> the Warsaw System has not kept pace with the needs of today's aviation
> market. The proposal is therefore intended to introduce at Community
> level some major improvements concerning liability.'

12.6   The Statement of the Council's reasons also identified the numerous
amendments made by it both of its own motion and in adopting certain of the
European Parliament's proposed amendments. As a result the Council
resolved several but not all of the difficulties inherent in the drafting of the
Amended Proposal. The Regulation was finally adopted by the Council on 9
October 1997 under the title 'Council Regulation EC No. 2027/97 of October
1997 on Air Carrier Liability in the Event of Accidents'[9] and came into force on
10 October 1998 in accordance with art 8 of its provisions. The texts of the
Commission's two drafts and the finalised form of the Regulation appear in
the Appendices to this work. As can be seen from the texts substantial amendments were introduced at the Council stage. So for instance, the scope of the
proposed regulation was amended to clarify certain insurance requirements

---

5   OJ C320 28.10.96 p 19.
6   OJ C29 30.1.97 p 10.
7   OJ C123 21.4.97 p 89.
8   OJ C123 21.4.97 p 92.
9   OJ L285 17.10.1997 p 1.

on the part of Community air carriers and a new art 5(2) was inserted concerning a minimum amount of compensation in the event of a passenger's death so as 'to provide a higher level of protection to those entitled to receive it'[10]. Other provisions, including most notably art 7 of the Amended Proposal by which the Commission had sought to convey jurisdiction on the Courts of the Member State where a passenger is domiciled at the date of the accident, were deleted by the Council.

EU Regulations

12.7

RULE 37—**The Regulation has direct effect and does not therefore need to be incorporated into domestic law of Member States in order to give enforceable rights to individuals. Accordingly the effect of UK's Air Carrier Liability Order 1998, purporting to implement the Regulation, has yet to be resolved.**

12.8   The provisions in relation to air carrier liability have taken the form of a Council Regulation. This section deals in outline with the legal effect of such regulations[11] and the relevant legislative procedure that was followed. The relevant provision of art 189 (now art 249 of the Treaty on European Union) concerning regulations states that:

> 'A regulation shall have general application. It shall be binding in its entirety and directly applicable in all Member States.'

A great deal of debate and discussion has surrounded the precise effect of this definition and more particularly whether EC regulations have direct effect and create legal rights in individuals enforceable against Member States or other individuals or whether to achieve such effects regulations require further implementation by means of national legislation, as in the case of EC directives. The answer depends on the wording of the regulation in question. On its true construction, a particular regulation might not itself be capable of giving rise to rights in the individual, for instance where it is expressed to be conditional on national implementation. Some (albeit currently incomplete) guidance has been provided by the European Court of Justice (ECJ) on the legal effect of a regulation as set out in art 189 of the EC Treaty (now art 249). In *Politi SAS v Ministero delle Finanze*[12], the ECJ referred

---

[10] Council's Statement of Reasons at OJ C123 21.4.97 p 92.
[11] A detailed treatment of this subject is beyond the scope of this book and for further reference the reader is referred to Derrick Wyatt and Alan Dashwood *The Substantive Law of the EC* ch 3 and Mark Brealey and Mark Hoskins *Remedies in EC Law* (2nd edn, 1998) ch 4.
[12] Case 43/71 [1971] ECR 1039, [1973] CMLR 60.

to the provisions of the second paragraph of art 189 (as noted above) and concluded that 'therefore, by reason of their nature and their function in the system of the sources of Community law, regulations have direct effect and are as such capable of creating individual rights which national courts must protect'. In *Leonesio v Italian Ministry of Agriculture and Forestry*[13], the ECJ reiterated its view that 'a Community regulation has direct effect and is, as such capable of creating individual rights which national courts must protect'. However, it is noteworthy that the ECJ ruled only that regulations were 'capable of' creating individual rights, they do not inevitably or automatically do so.

12.9   There was nothing in the wording of the drafts of the proposed regulation on air carrier liability to suggest that its provisions were intended to be brought into effect by means of further national implementation, that is by domestic legislation in each Member State. However, the Regulation now expressly states that 'this Regulation shall be binding in its entirety and directly applicable in all Member States'. Thus on coming into force on 10 October 1998 the Regulation gave rise to rights in individuals enforceable against others and which the national courts are bound to protect. Unlike international agreements which though signed and ratified require to be implemented by Act of Parliament or secondary legislation, the Regulation on air carrier liability does not require any further measures to enable it to become law in the UK or any other EC Member State. Indeed, it is likely that it is for this reason that the Commission sought to introduce the new provisions by means of a regulation as opposed to a directive which, as an instrument directed to the governments of the Member States, would have required implementation by the national legislature of each of the Member States for it to create rights enforceable between private individuals[14].

12.10   Whereas in essence policy initiation is the responsibility of the Commission, the Council is the legislature of the European Union or in the case of matters governed by the co-decision procedure (where final decision making is shared with the European Parliament) the co-legislature. Various procedures exist for the introduction of Council Regulations. In this instance the regulation on air carrier liability was subject to what is known as the 'co-operation procedure' introduced by art 6 of the Single European Union 1992. The procedure involves two readings of any proposed regulation by the European Parliament. A proposal subject to the co-operation procedure will once formulated by the Commission pass to the European Parliament prior to making its way to the Council. The Council is then required to adopt a 'common position' by a qualified majority vote on the proposal which is

---

[13]   Case 93/71 [1972] ECR 287.
[14]   Though a directive is capable of creating rights in individuals against a Member State it would not necessarily create such rights against an airline until implemented into the domestic law of the Member States concerned.

then referred back to the European Parliament. The European Parliament then has three months in which to either (a) approve the common position thus requiring the Council to adopt the proposal as set out in the common position, (b) reject the common position in which case the Council may still adopt the proposed regulation but only by an absolute majority vote or (c) propose amendments to the common position thus requiring the Commission to re-examine the proposed regulation prior to returning it to the Council which may adopt it as amended by qualified majority or amend it by unanimity.

12.11   The Council adopted a common position on the proposed regulation on air carrier liability on 24 February 1997. During a plenary session on 29 May 1997, the European Parliament approved at second reading the common position adopted by the Council and also adopted some relatively minor amendments to the proposed test[15]. On 4 July 1997 the Commission accepted all the European Parliament's amendments and forwarded the further amended proposal to the Council. The regulation was then adopted in its amended form by the Council on 9 October 1997.

12.12   Despite the fact that regulations have direct effect, on 21 July 1998 the UK Government made the Air Carrier Liability Order 1998 seeking to implement the Regulation with effect from 17 October 1998. In essence, the Order operates to remove the limits on carrier liability imposed by the Warsaw Convention from the Carriage by Air Act 1961 and the Carriage by Air Acts (Application of Provisions) Order 1967, to delete the minimum liability limit required by reg 11(1)(b) of the licensing of Air Carriers Regulations 1992, to remove the benefit to carriers of art 20 of the Convention (taking all necessary measure to avoid damage or that it was impossible to take such measures) in relation to passenger death, wounding or bodily injury of up to 100,000 SDR and to introduce criminal penalties for breach of certain requirements of art 6 of the Regulation (concerning the provision of information to passengers). For a comprehensive critique of the Air Carrier Liability Order 1998 and its interrelationship with the Regulation the reader is referred to Harold Caplan's article 'The UK Spin on Air Carrier Liability'[16].

12.13   The IATA responded to the coming into force of the Regulation and the making of the Air Carrier Liability Order 1998 with the issue of judicial review proceedings in the High Court for a declaration that the Order was void and seeking a reference to the ECJ under art 177 of the Treaty of Rome (now art 234 of the Treaty on European Union). The

---

[15]   The proposed amendments concerned (1) Recital 13 and art 7 seeking to ensure that third country carriers apply the same levels of liability as Community air carriers while operating to or from the Community and (2) art 6 where it was sought to abolish the need for different types of notice attached to tickets.

[16]   [1998] TAQ 272.

substantive application came before Mr Justice Jowitt in April 1999[17] who held the Order to be a valid application of s 2(2) of the European Communities Act 1972. However, while the Regulation is therefore to be treated as valid in English law, there is a strong case for arguing that the terms of the Order place the UK in breach of its international treaty obligations save to the extent that art 234 of the Treaty of Rome (new art 307)[18] can be called into play. No doubt the conflict between the Member States' international obligations under the Warsaw Convention and their Community obligations has yet to be resolved.

Scope of the Regulation

12.14

RULE 38—The Regulation is superimposed on the Warsaw Convention and intended to be read together with it. The Regulation is narrower than the Warsaw Convention in that it applies only to liability for death or personal injury (and not to damage to baggage or cargo or delay) and only to European Community air carriers. It is wider than the Warsaw Convention in that it applies to domestic as well as international carriage.

12.15   Article 1 of the Regulation provides that:

> 'This Regulation lays down the obligations of Community air carriers in relation to liability in the event of accidents to passengers for damage sustained in the event of death or wounding of a passenger or any other bodily injury suffered by a passenger, if the accident which caused the damage so sustained took place on board an aircraft or in the course of any of the operations of embarking or disembarking.
>
> This Regulation also clarifies some insurance requirements for Community air carriers.
>
> In addition, this Regulation sets down some requirements on information to be provided by air carriers established outside the Community which operate to, from or within the Community.[19']

---

[17] *R v Secretary of State for the Environment, Transport and the Regions, ex p IATA* Queen's Bench Division, 21 April 1999. An application for a reference to the ECJ was refused by Mr Justice Laws on 6 November 1998 (*R v Secretary of State for the Environment, Transport and the Regions, ex p IATA* QBD, 6 November 1998).

[18] Article 234 (now art 307 of the Treaty on European Union) provides that rights and obligations arising from agreements concluded before the entry into force of the Treaty of Rome between one or more Member States and a third country are not to be affected by the Treaty and that to the extent that such agreements are incompatible with the Treaty the Member State concerned must take steps to eliminate the incompatibilities.

[19] OJ C123 21.4.97 p 89.

12.16   These provisions are usefully compared to arts 1(1) and 17 of the Warsaw Convention. Naturally given the jurisdiction of the European Community, the Regulation is concerned solely with the obligations of 'Community air carriers'[20]. However, unlike the Warsaw Convention the provisions of the Regulation are designed to govern both international as well as domestic air carriage undertaken by Community air carriers. Other than this significant extension, the Regulation is essentially narrower in scope than the Convention. So for instance, the Warsaw Convention applies to 'carriage of persons, baggage or cargo'[21] whilst the Regulation is limited to 'liability for damage sustained in the event of death or wounding of a passenger or any other bodily injury suffered by a passenger'[22]. Similarly, there are no provisions in the Regulation governing liability for delay[23] nor as to the applicable limitation periods for the purposes of bringing claims against air carriers[24] nor concerning jurisdiction[25]. More significantly, whilst not expressly stated, the Regulation is designed to be superimposed upon the provisions of the Convention, amending and varying certain of the Convention's provisions where necessary so as to achieve its objects. So for instance one finds express reference to arts 22(1) and 20(1) of the Warsaw Convention at Recitals 7 and 8 of the Preamble to the Regulation respectively. Further, it is clear that the Regulation falls far short of an all inclusive code governing the liability of Community air carriers in cases of accident. Once the Regulation comes into force, the existing regimes governing carriage by air will continue to apply in the case of Community air carriers with the addition of the scheme imposed by the Regulation. As regards domestic application the Regulation should cause little additional difficulty where, as in the UK, domestic legislation on air

---

[20]   The term 'air carrier' is defined at art 2(1)(a) of the Regulation as meaning an air transport undertaking with a valid operating license and by art 2(1)(b) of the Regulation 'Community air carrier' is defined as 'an air carrier with a valid operating license granted by a member State in accordance with the provisions of Regulation (EEC) No. 2407/92'. Accordingly, a Community air carrier is an air carrier whose principal place of business and registered office (if any) are located in a Member State, whose main occupation is air transport (whether in isolation or combined with any other commercial operation of aircraft or repair and maintenance of aircraft) and which is and continues to be owned and effectively controlled directly or through majority ownership by a Member State and/or national(s) of a member State.

[21]   Article 1(1) of the Warsaw Convention.

[22]   Being in itself reminiscent of the wording used in art 17 of the Warsaw Convention.

[23]   See art 19 of the Warsaw Convention.

[24]   See art 29 of the Warsaw Convention which will continue to apply to cases of international carriage undertaken by Community air carriers.

[25]   See art 28 of the Warsaw Convention. Note, however, that the Commission did attempt to further regulate the issue of jurisdiction in its original drafts of the Regulation (art 7) by adding an additional forum to those referred to at art 28 of the Convention, namely the courts of the Member State where the passenger at the time of the accident had his domicile. Regrettably the provision was deleted by the Council though this is not surprising given the inherent difficulties of the proposed clause which failed to define the term 'domicile', failed to deal with the issue of choice of law and could not assist non-EC passengers.

carrier liability reflects the provisions of the Conventions. However, in circumstances in which the liability of air carriers for domestic flights is not so regulated the imposition of the Regulation by reference to the provisions of the Warsaw Convention is likely to make little sense given that its provisions effectively pre-suppose application of the Warsaw Convention in the first instance. No doubt the inter-relationship between the provisions of each have yet to be fully explored in the context of the type of extensive litigation the Commission expressly wished to avoid[26].

12.17   As already noted, the Regulation is concerned with defining 'the obligations of Community air carriers in relation to **liability** in the event of accidents to passengers **for damage**' (emphasis added). Article 1 of the Commission's Amended Proposal (by way of comparison) provided that 'this Regulation defines the obligations of Community air carriers **to cover liability for damage**' (emphasis added). This drafting suggested that unlike the Warsaw Convention the Regulation was not on the face of it aimed at defining the circumstances in which liability arises but with the consequences of liability for the purposes of damages. Though the new drafting does not make the position entirely clear, a brief analysis of the substantive provisions of the Regulation and more particularly arts 3(2), (3) and 5, clearly indicates that the scope of the Regulation goes well beyond issues of quantum and into the realm of the rules governing liability itself.

The Scheme of the Regulation

12.18   Following a detailed Preamble, the Regulation is made up of eight Articles. Other than arts 1(b) and 6 to 8 inclusive, each Article deals with a different aspect of the rules designed to govern air carrier liability within the European Community. The Preamble expressly refers to the Warsaw Convention as amended at the Hague on 28 September 1995 and at Guadalajara on 18 September 1961 as well as to the International Civil Aviation Organisation's (ICAO) review of the Warsaw Convention but states that 'pending the outcome of such review, actions on an interim basis by the Community will enhance the protection of passengers'. Also referred to is the fact that whereas the Warsaw Convention is limited to international carriage, the distinction between domestic and international transport within the Community has been eliminated. More importantly it is stated that 'it is appropriate to remove all monetary limits of liability within the meaning of article 22(1) of the Warsaw Convention or any other legal or contractual limits, in accordance with present trends at international level' as well as the defence available to a carrier under art 20(1) of the Warsaw Convention up to a certain limit. On the other hand, the Regulation expressly retains a carrier's defence of contributory negligence and makes express reference to the right of Community air carriers to claim against third parties.

---

[26]   See Recital 13 of the Commission's original proposed regulations at OJ C29 30.1.97 p 10.

12.19   Article 1 of the Regulation is concerned with the scope of the Regulation and art 2 provides definitions for certain of the terms used. Apart from the specific definitions set out at art 2(1) of the Regulation, any further terminology used in the Regulation is to be equivalent to that used in the Warsaw Convention as amended (art 2(2) of the Regulation). Article 3(1)(a) is the most significant provision as regards compensation since it removes 'any financial limit, be it defined by law, convention or contract' on damages in the event of death, wounding or any other bodily injury suffered by a passenger in case of accident. Article 3(2) effectively creates strict liability on the carrier for about the first ECU 120,000 of any claim by removing, below that sum, the defence afforded to carriers by art 20(1) of the Warsaw Convention. On the other hand art 3(3) retains (without any monetary restriction on its applicability) the carrier's defence of contributory negligence to be defined in accordance with the applicable law. The key provisions of art 3 are then followed by further provisions regarding third party indemnity and contribution (art 4), compulsory and non refundable 'advance payments' of compensation (art 5), the supply of information (art 6), the need for the Commission to report on the application of the Regulation no later than two years after its entry into force taking into account 'economic developments and developments in international forums' (art 7) and the date of entry into force of the Regulation (art 8). In essence, the key provisions of the Regulation as concerns air carrier liability in the event of accidents are to be found in arts 3 and 5.

Disposing with limits on compensation

12.20

RULE **39**—**The Regulation removes any financial limit as defined by 'law, convention or contract' on the liability of Community air carriers for damage arising from death or personal injury. The better view is that this disposes of the limits on compensation set by the Warsaw Convention but not of limits imposed by general principles of English law, such as reasonable foreseeability and mitigation of loss.**

12.21   Article 3(1)(a) of the Regulation provides that:

> 'The liability of a Community air carrier for damages sustained in the event of the death, wounding or any other bodily injury suffered by a passenger in the event of an accident shall not be subject to any financial limit, be it defined by law, convention or contract.'

and reflects the provisions of the Preamble where it is noted that:

> '. . . it is appropriate to remove all monetary limits of liability within the meaning of article 22(1) of the Warsaw Convention or any other legal or contractual limits, in accordance with present trends at international level.'

12.22   Article 3(1) of the Regulation finally ends any limit on quantum in the case of passenger injury introduced by the Warsaw Convention by removing the limitations imposed by art 20 of the Convention altogether in the case of Community air carriers. Yet, the quid pro quo for the limitation of liability under the Warsaw Convention, namely the reversal of the burden of proof so that fault on the part of the carrier is assumed on proof of damage, remains. Indeed, even the circumstances in which a Community air carrier may currently escape liability under the Warsaw Convention by establishing that it took all necessary measures to avoid the damage[27] are further restricted by the terms of the Regulation.

12.23   The measure of damages will now fall to be determined in accordance with the applicable law (being the law of the contract of carriage) so that the level of compensation passengers may recover will vary accordingly, to some extent defeating the aims of harmonization within the Community. More significantly, it is envisaged that the drafting of art 3(1)(a) is likely to cause substantial difficulties given that it purports to remove any financial limit on the liability of a Community air carrier whether that limit be defined 'by law, convention or contract'. In its original form art 3(1) sought to remove any 'statutory or contractual limits'[28] on a Community air carrier's liability. In its final form art 3(1)(a) provides that 'the amount of the pecuniary compensation that a Community air carrier has to sustain . . . shall not be subject **to any legal, conventional or contractual limits**' (emphasis added). The introduction of the term 'convention' is presumably a direct reference to the Warsaw Convention and to the provisions of art 22(1) of the Convention. Nor is the reference to contractual limits surprising. However, what is meant by a limit defined 'by law' is totally unclear. The French text which debars all 'limite pecuniare, même si celle-ci est fixée par voie législative, conventionelle ou contractuelle' suggests an attempt to exclude only statutory limits (in addition to conventional or contractual limits) as opposed to any legal limit as is suggested by the English text. The English version of the Preamble to the Regulation which refers to 'all monetary limits of liability within the meaning of Article 22(1) of the Warsaw Convention **or any other legal or contractual limits**' (emphasis added) does nothing to clarify the position but more accurately reflects 'toute autre limitation juridique ou contractuelle' as referred to in the French text. Under English law the first legal limits on loss and damage that immediately spring to mind are the requirements that these be reasonably foreseeable and that a claimant take steps to mitigate his or her loss. Reference in art 3(1)(a) of the Regulation to the removal of any financial limit be it defined by law, convention or contract certainly implies that traditional legal limits on the recoverability of damages are not to apply though one assumes that this cannot have been the Council's true intention and that the reference to financial limits defined by law is not in fact intended to add anything to the prohibition on financial limits defined by convention, contract or legislation. This interpretation of art 3(1)(a) falls into

---

[27]   Article 20(1) of the Warsaw-Hague Convention.
[28]   OJ C104 10.4.1996 p 18.

line with the Commission's original explanatory paper[29] which referred to the fact that compensation amounts 'should probably be in line with the level of compensation actually paid to victims in non-aviation accidents in industrialized countries' and to which a variety of rules apply to the measure of damages.

12.24   The removal of any limits on a Community air carrier's liability in monetary terms removes the need to consider the application of art 25 of the Warsaw Convention designed to restrict the scope of the cap on damages applied by art 22(1) of the Convention by dissapplying the financial limits in cases in which it is proved that 'the damage resulted from an act or omission of the carrier, his servants or agents, done with intent to cause damage or recklessly and with knowledge that damage would probably result . . .'. The removal of any limit on the amount of damages recoverable by way of compensation against a Community air carrier necessarily removes the need to consider issues such as whether there was recklessness or deliberate fault on the part of the carrier. On the other hand, the scope of the Regulation is limited to the liability of Community air carriers and there are no provisions nor references to proceedings which may be brought against a servant or agent of the carrier arising out of damage to which the Warsaw Convention relates. Accordingly, art 25A of the Convention should continue to apply to limit the liability of a servant or agent of a Community air carrier in accordance with the provisions of arts 22 and 25A(3) of the Convention.

Limiting the defences available to Community air carriers

12.25

RULE 40—The Regulation removes the carrier's defence under Article 20(1) of the Convention that it had taken all reasonable measures to avoid the damage or that it was impossible for him to have taken those steps for the first 100,000 SDR of damages

12.26   Article 20(1) of the Warsaw Convention offers a carrier a means of avoiding liability in circumstances in which 'he proves that he and his servants or agents have taken all necessary measures to avoid the damage or that it was impossible for him or them to take such measures'. The availability of this defence has already been curtailed and was (for instance) waived by all carriers party to the 1966 Montreal Agreement with regard to international carriage which has a point in the US as its point of origin, destination or agreed stop over, and in some instances by carriers who enter into special contracts with their passengers excluding the defence. However, art 3(2) of the Regulation goes well beyond the current limitations on the application of the art 20(1) defence by excluding it in the case of Community air carriers for

---

0.4.96 p 18.

any damages 'up to the equivalent in ecus of 100,000 SDR'[30]. Specifically, art 3(2) reads:

> 'For any damages up to the sum of the equivalent in ecus of 100 000 SDR, the Community air carrier shall not exclude or limit his liability by proving that he and his agents have taken all necessary measures to avoid the damage or that it was impossible for him or them to take such measures.'

12.27   The justification and reasoning behind this provision is found in the Preamble to the Regulation which provides:

> 'Whereas in order to avoid situations where victims of accidents are not compensated, Community air carriers should not, with respect to any claim arising out of the death, wounding or other bodily injury of a passenger pursuant to article 17 of the Warsaw Convention, avail themselves of any defence under Article 20(1) of the Warsaw Convention up to a certain limit.'

12.28   The provision does not make it clear whether it is intended to remove the art 20(1) defence on the first SDR 100 000 worth of a claim or only in relation to claims worth up to SDR 100 000. On the other hand, the terminology used in the Preamble and more particularly the words 'in order to avoid situations where victims of accidents are not compensated' suggests that the former construction of art 3(2) of the Regulation is the correct one. Plainly, the terms of art 3(2) of the Regulation go well beyond matters concerning quantum and into the realm of defining the circumstances in which liability will arise. Indeed, the provisions of the Regulation are a major step towards the imposition not only of unlimited liability but of no fault liability though capped at the sum of SDR 100,000. The aim, it would appear, is essentially a social one namely to ensure that the victims of air accidents recover some compensation (subject only to the issue of contributory negligence) whether or not the accident itself was preventable. Further, it is in this context that the Council extended the scope of the Regulation to include reference to a Community air carrier's obligation to carry insurance set out in art 7 of Regulation (EEC) 2407/92 'to cover liability in case of accidents in respect of passengers . . .' which provision is by virtue of art 3(1)(b) of the Regulation to be 'understood as requiring that a Community air carrier shall be insured up to the limit of the liability required pursuant to' art 3(2) of the

---

[30] This figure was increased from SDR 100,000 in the Commission's original proposed Regulation (EC) on air carrier liability in case of accidents to SDR 120,000 in the Commission's Amended Proposal. The definition of a special drawing right at art 2(1)(e) of the Regulation and to sums expressed in that unit at arts 3 and 5 were inserted by the Council to be consistent with the monetary unit used in the Warsaw Convention and other international intercarrier agreements under the aegis of the IATA. The sum of SDR 100 000 was broadly equivalent to ECU 120 000.

Regulation ie up to the sum of the equivalent in ECUs 100 000 SDR 'and thereafter up to a reasonable level'. What it is intended should amount to a 'reasonable level' is not indicated.

Contributory negligence

12.29

RULE 41—The Regulation preserves the defence of contributory negligence on the part of the passenger.

12.30   Article 3(3) of the Regulation expressly retains the defence of contributory negligence on the part of the passenger[31] by broadly repeating the terms of art 21 of the Warsaw Convention. In turn, the Preamble expressly recognizes that despite the new limitation on the defence afforded to air carriers by art 20 of the Warsaw Convention, 'Community air carriers may be exonerated from their liability in cases of contributory negligence of the passenger concerned'. One assumes that the express inclusion of the contributory negligence defence in the Regulation is designed to bring the position in relation to domestic carriage by Community air carriers into line with that governing their liabilities under the Warsaw Convention. In other words, express reference to the defence is necessary by reference to a set of rules designed to govern both domestic as well as international carriage.

12.31   Incorporation of the provisions of art 21 of the Warsaw Convention into the Regulation will make little difference to the liability of carriers on domestic flights in the UK where the defence of contributory negligence has always been available as a matter of law. Moreover, similarly to that of art 21 of the Warsaw Convention, the wording of art 3(3) of the Regulation expressly provides that a Community air carrier 'may be exonerated wholly or partly from its liability **in accordance with the applicable law**' (emphasis added). Thus a carrier sued in the Courts of the UK will have the benefit of the defence of contributory negligence as provided under English law or Scottish law, and indeed s 6 of the Carriage by Air Act 1961 expressly refers to the application of the Law Reform (Contributory Negligence) Act 1945. However, divergences are likely to continue to arise in the application of this defence depending on the detailed provisions concerning contributory negligence under the applicable domestic law.

12.32   It is envisaged that difficulties are likely to arise in the interrelationship between the defence of contributory negligence and the

---

[31]   This is a substantial revision to the Commission's original proposed Regulation (EC) on air carrier liability in case of accidents (OJ C104 10.4.96 p 18) which made no reference to the defence of contributory negligence afforded to a carrier under art 21 of the Warsaw Convention.

provisions of art 3(2) of the Regulation the question being whether a deduction for contributory negligence should be made before or after the ceiling on no fault liability has been reached. In other words, is the ceiling imposed by art 3(2) of the Regulation on a no fault defence under art 20(1) of the Warsaw Convention intended to apply to the award of damages before or after a deduction has been made for contributory negligence? It is suggested that the introductory words of art 3(3) which state 'notwithstanding the provisions of paragraph 2' indicate that any finding of contributory negligence should operate to reduce any award including the first 100,000 SDR provided for under art 3(2).

12.33   Lastly, in the context of the effect of the Regulation on the defences available to Community air carriers, it should be noted that express provision has been made at art 4 of the Regulation to the effect that nothing in the Regulation is to imply that a Community air carrier is the sole party liable to pay damages or to restrict its rights to a contribution or indemnity from any other party in accordance with the applicable law.

Advance payments

12.34

RULE 42—**The Regulation provides a new system of advance payments to every passenger killed or injured within 15 days of their being identified 'to meet immediate economic needs on a basis proportional to the hardship suffered'. In the case a death, a minimum of 15,000 SDR per passenger is stipulated. These payments are non-refundable save in limited circumstances.**

12.35   One of the most innovative provisions of the Regulation is art 5 which allows for a type of 'interim payment' to those entitled to claim compensation from a Community air carrier[32]. Specifically art 5 provides:

> '1. The Community air carrier shall without delay, and in any event not later than 15 days after the identity of the natural person entitled to compensation has been established, make such advance payments as may be required to meet immediate economic needs on a basis proportional to the hardship suffered.

---

[32] The need and reasoning behind the provisions of art 4 as originally envisaged is set out in the Commission's original explanatory paper (OJ C104 10.4.96 p 18) in the following terms:

> 'Simple and speedy procedures should be guaranteed. It is intolerable that victims or their relatives should have to wait for the results of lengthy litigations. Therefore, passengers or next of kin should receive from the carrier on the one hand, the uncontested part of the claim and on the other hand, a lump sum (a certain percentage liability limit) as soon as possible.'

2. Without prejudice to paragraph 1, an advance payment shall not be less that the equivalent in ecus of 15 000 SDR per passenger in the event of death.

3. An advance payment shall not constitute recognition of liability and may be offset against any subsequent sums paid on the basis of Community air carrier liability, but is not returnable, except in the cases prescribed in Article 3(3) or in circumstances where it is subsequently proved that the person who received the advance payment caused, or contributed to, the damage by negligence or was not the person entitled to compensation.'

12.36   In its original draft form, this provision required payment of 'a lump sum of up to ECU 50,000 in proportion to the injury sustained and in any event a sum of ECU 50,000 in case of death' whereas the Commission's Amended Proposal anticipated 'advance payments as may be required to meet economic needs'[33]. The Council opted for a mix of these provisions retaining the reference to such advance payments 'as may be required to meet economic needs' whilst also defining the minimum level for an advance payment in the event of a passenger's death. Further, in its original form art 5 required payment to be made at the latest 10 days after the event during which the damage occurred. Now payment is required not later than 15 days[34] after the identity of the natural person entitled to compensation has been established. In the event of injury to a passenger the new formulation of the provision is likely to make little difference as to the date by which an advance payment must be made, but in the case of death art 5(1) now antici-pates the possibility of difficulties arising in establishing the identity of the persons entitled to compensation.

12.37   It is assumed that the redrafting of the provision was designed to address some of the concerns and criticisms raised by the ESC[35] which com-mented on the original formulation of art 5 (previously art 4 of the draft regulations) in the following terms:

'4.3. Article 4

4.3.1 The Committee welcomes the concept of swift payment of a lump sum to deal with immediate costs. However, the Committee is con-cerned that the proposal will be unworkable unless it is clear as to how certain difficulties will be met. For example, it can take time to identify victims and trace relatives. In addition, in the case of injury rather than death, what proportion of the advance payment is to be made? Who

---

[33] OJ C104 10.4.96; OJ C29 30.11.97 p 10.
[34] These are defined as current and not working days by art 35 of the Warsaw Convention.
[35] OJ C212 22.7.96 p 38.

decides? The Committee accepts the need to set aside money within ten days of an accident, but the Commission should provide more detail of how and when payments are to be made.

4.3.2 The Committee welcomes the move to unlimited liability for passenger accidents. However, as the proposal will have some effect on costs — particularly for smaller airlines — the Committee considers that, for higher levels of payment, proof of fault may be justified.'

However, neither the Commission's Amended Proposal nor the Regulation in its final form address such issues in the case of injury claims as who is to determine the amount of the advance payment and how such payments are to be made.

12.38   The first apparent difficulty likely to arise on the application of art 5(1) lies in the need to determine what sum may be required to meet 'immediate economic needs', what is meant by 'immediate economic needs' and how the sums in question are to be calculated with reference to 'the hardship suffered'. No guidance is provided by the Regulation. Further there is no reason to suppose that the sums concerned might not be substantial should they for instance include medical expenses. The situation is likely to be further complicated by the fact that art 5(1) contemplates several advance payments which lies ill with the need for those payments to be made not later than 15 days after the identity of the person entitled to compensation has been established. An alternative and more logical construction is that art 5(1) contemplates payments to several persons in respect of a passenger's death as opposed to several payments for one claimant. Moreover, the contents of sub-paragraph (3) of art 5 are likely to ensure that disputes will arise as to the amount of the advance payments given that these are non-refundable save in limited circumstances.

12.39   By making the advance payments it requires under arts 5(1) and (2) non refundable save in limited circumstances, art 5 might in practice affect the liability of Community air carriers who will find themselves effectively subject to strict liability at least in the amount of the advance payments made. However, art 5 was substantially amended at the Council stage so that whereas the Commission's Amended Proposal[36] provided that the advance payments were 'not returnable under any circumstances' (then art 4(2) of the proposed regulation), art 5(3) now provides for repayment in cases of contributory negligence on the part of the injured or deceased passenger 'or in circumstances where it is subsequently proved that the person who received the advance payment caused, or contributed to, the damage by negligence or was not the person entitled to compensation'. These amendments to the

---

[36]   OJ C29 30.11.97 p 10.

Commission's Amended Proposal should ensure that Community air carriers will not find themselves subject to strict liability up to the amount of an advance payment in cases of substantial contributory negligence on the part of the victim. Further, the final form of the provision also anticipates refunds in the event of contributory negligence/fault on the part of persons entitled to compensation other than the victim and in circumstances in which the person who received the advance payment was not the person entitled to compensation. No exception has been made for circumstances in which the carrier is subsequently found not to have been liable, though art 5(3) expressly states that 'an advance payment shall not constitute recognition of liability'. The absence of any exception to the non-refundable character of an advance payment with reference to liability is not surprising given that art 3(2) of the Regulation operates to create strict liability up to the sum of SDR 100 000. The provisions of art 5 are it seems unlikely to extend that strict liability any further unless the advance payments required exceeds the sum of SDR 100,000.

12.40   Certain difficulties in the practical application of art 5 remain despite the substantial redrafting at the Council stage. As already noted art 5 is concerned with payments to natural persons entitled to compensation ie 'a passenger or any person entitled to claim in respect of that passenger, in accordance with applicable law'[37]. No difficulty is likely to arise in cases of injury to a passenger[38], but what of the position in the event of death? The Commission's original explanatory paper[39] indicated that art 5 was intended to refer to the relatives of victims of air accidents. However, under the law of England and Wales, on strict interpretation those entitled to claim in respect of a death are the executor or administrator of the deceased's estate for the six months following the death and thus not necessarily those likely to require advance payments 'to meet immediate economic needs'. Further, though it is for the executor or administrator to bring proceedings in the first instance, in the case of an administrator he or she must first have obtained the grant of letters of administration before proceedings are commenced. Thus it can be seen that the mechanics of art 5 of the Regulation are likely to give rise to litigation if they are to operate to enable (amongst others) dependents to recover payments to cover their immediate economic needs shortly following the death of a passenger.

---

[37] Article 2(1)(c) of the Regulation. Unlike the Warsaw Convention which only deals with the matter by way of inference, the Regulation seeks to define those persons who are entitled to claim compensation under its provisions. Specifically art 2(1)(c) of the Regulation defines 'persons entitled to compensation' as 'a passenger or any person entitled to claim in respect of that passenger, in accordance with applicable law'.

[38] The amended definition of 'persons entitled to compensation' at art 2(1)(c) no longer limiting the definition of persons entitled to claim 'in the event of the death of the passenger' opens the way to including claims brought by a relative for nervous shock other than in the event of a passenger's death.

[39] OJ C104 10.4.96 p 18.

Information and Documents of Carriage

12.41

R**ULE** **43—The Regulation requires air carriers to inform passengers in plain and intelligible language of Article 3 (removal of limitations on liability) and Article 5 (advance payments) in the conditions of carriage and the ticket document.**

12.42   Chapter II of the Warsaw Convention contains certain provisions in connection with documents of carriage. To this must now be added the requirements of art 6 of the Regulation. In particular, art 6 requires a Community air carrier to include the provisions of arts 3 and 5 of the Regulation in its conditions of carriage, to provide adequate information concerning those Articles and to print a summary of the provisions 'in plain and intelligible language' on the ticket document. It is not at all clear whether the provisions in fact mean that a Community air carrier must merely refer passengers to the contents of arts 3 and 5 of the Regulation or whether it is required to explain the legal effect of those provisions.

12.43   Further, by art 6(3) of the Regulation, non Community air carriers operating to, from and within the Community and not applying the provisions of arts 3 and 5 of the Regulations are required to 'expressly and clearly inform passengers' of that fact at the time of purchase of tickets at the carrier's agencies, travel agencies or check-in counters located in the territory of a Member State[40]. All air carriers are also required by art 6(3) to provide passengers with a form setting out their conditions of carriage. Further, it is provided that mere reference to a liability limit on the ticket document or an equivalent will not constitute sufficient information. Clearly, the aim of these provisions is to ensure that passengers should be fully aware before purchasing tickets whether or not the carrier in question is subject to the provisions of arts 3 and 5 of the Regulation. No doubt whether or not wording is 'in plain and intelligible language' is likely to give rise to debate and consequent litigation.

---

[40] Note that there is no reference in the Regulation to any sanction being imposed on a non-community air carrier who fails to comply with these provisions.

Chapter 13

Carriage by Air: Common Law of Carriage

13.1

RULE 44—Carriage by Air will be governed by the common law only rarely. In practice, it will normally be limited to (1) gratuitous carriage by a non-air transport undertaking (eg gratuitous carriage by a private individual) or (2) carriage in extraordinary circumstances outside the normal scope of the carrier's business.

Introduction

13.2 In cases where there is no applicable statutory regime, the common law will govern exclusively[1]. However, in practice, the occasions when the relationship between the carrier and passenger or consignor of goods will be governed by the common law and not subject to the exclusive provisions of one or other of the statutory regimes will be rare[2]. Even gratuitous carriage performed by an air transport undertaking will be subject to the amended or unamended Convention, or in the case of non-international carriage, aspects of the unamended Convention[3]. However, there may be some occasions when carriage subject purely to the common law occurs, probably the most important of which is the case of a private individual carrying his friends and their luggage in his own aircraft without payment (ie gratuitous carriage not performed by an air transport undertaking). In this situation, were an accident to

---

[1] It should be noted that many of the principles relating to common law carriage derive from cases relating to land and sea carriage.

[2] This Chapter considers the liability of *carriers* only. Accordingly it excludes the liability of third parties who may cause injury to passengers or goods. Further, the liability considered is the liability of the carrier *as carrier*. For example, there can be no contract of carriage as regards employees of a carrier actually carrying on work while the carriage is being effected — ie pilots, flight attendants etc. See **4.20** above. The responsibilities of the aircraft operator in such a case are as employer and will determined by principles applicable to employer and employee rather than by rules relating to carriage. Similarly while an operator might owe limited common law duties to a stowaway on board a flight without permission that liability is not as a carrier.

[3] See para **4.8** above.

occur, the aircraft owner might be liable as a gratuitous bailee in the case of luggage and for the tort of negligence in the case of passengers. Another situation when the common law may apply is carriage performed by way of experimental trial prior to the introduction of a regular service or carriage performed in extraordinary circumstances outside the normal scope of the carrier's business.

Sources of the Carrier's Obligations

13.3   A carrier at common law is a person who transports goods or passengers or both from any place to any place in the manner agreed with the passenger or owner of the goods to be carried[4]. A carrier's duty in relation to goods or passengers may arise in contract, tort or bailment or by virtue of his occupation of the vehicle in question. In addition, a carrier may be a 'common carrier' or a private carrier. A common carrier will be subject to additional duties.

The Carriage of Goods

13.4

RULE 45—A carrier of goods may be either a 'common carrier' or a 'private carrier':

(a)   **A common carrier is a carrier who publicly professes to carry for reward. His duties and liabilities include:**
  (i)   **a duty to accept all goods tendered with the appropriate freight unless they are (1) not of the class he carries, (2) are dangerous or exceptional, (3) are tendered an unreasonable time before the journey or (4) are inadequately packed;**
  (ii)   **a duty to charge only a reasonable rate for the carriage of goods;**
  (iii)   **a duty to deliver the goods within a reasonable time; and**
  (iv)   **strict liability for all loss and damage to goods in the course of transit save for (1) act of God, (2) acts of the Queen's enemies, (3) inherent vice, or (4) consignor's fault.**

(b)   **A private carrier is any carrier who is not a common carrier. His duties and liabilities include:**

---

[4]   The carrier need not be paid for this service. The test is whether the person said to be the carrier is in fact accepting the responsibility of the carriage — *Aqualon (UK) Ltd v Vallana Shipping Corpn* [1994] 1 Lloyds Rep 669 where the critical question was said to be what role and responsibility was in fact undertaken, per Mance J at p 673.

    (i)   **a common law duty as bailee;**

    (ii)   **a duty to take reasonable care;**

   (iii)   **a duty to deliver the goods within a reasonable time; and**

   (iv)   **(where goods are carried for reward) a duty to use reasonable care to provide an aircraft which is fit for the carriage in question.**

13.5   **Common Carrier.**   A special category of carrier is the common carrier[5]. A common carrier is a person who carries as a public employment, and holds himself out to undertake for reward to transport the goods of all those who wish to employ him[6]. Whether or not a person is a common carrier is in every case a question of fact[7] and is tested objectively, that is, it does not depend on his private intentions[8]. The following have been held to be common carriers: masters and owners of general ships[9]; railway companies and their successor the British Transport Commission[10]; and carriers by road[11].

---

[5] While the position of common carriers is dealt with briefly in his chapter, it is difficult to imagine a situation when carriage by a 'common carrier' will fall outside the statutory regime. As discussed in para **13.2** above, the two main cases not covered by the Conventions are gratuitous bailment not by an air transport undertaking and carriage in extraordinary circumstances outside the carrier's normal business. In neither of these cases could the carrier be a common carrier: it is a requirement of common carriage that the carriage must be for reward (*Tyler v Morrice* (1699) Carth 485) and the carrier must engage in the business habitually (*Watkins v Cottell* [1916] 1 KB 10 — where the following definition of common carrier set out in Macnamara on Carriers by Land 2nd edn p 11, was approved by Avory J at p 14 'he must hold himself as ready to engage in the transportation of goods for hire as a business and not merely as an occupation pro hac vice'.).

[6] *Belfast Ropework Co Ltd v Bushell* [1918] 1 KB 210.

[7] *Belfast Ropework Co Ltd v Bushell* [1918] 1 KB 210 per Bailhache J at p 215 citing *Brind v Dale* (1837) 8 C&P 207, 212 per Lord Abinger CB.

[8] *A. Siohn & Co Ltd and Academy Garments (Wigan) Ltd v R H Hagland & Sons (Transport) Ltd* [1976] 2 Lloyds Rep 428. The defendant company were road carriers. The director of the company gave evidence that he did not always accept customers who wished to come to him as his plan was to have regular customers and accept only those who were sound financially. According to him he did not accept casual trade. However, relying in particular on a advertisement placed by the company, Cusak J held (at p 430): 'it seems to me that the nature of the service which [the defendants] held themselves out to provide, which is indicated in their price list and in the document "Just lift the phone", does provide very cogent evidence that they were in fact, though perhaps unbeknown to themselves because [the director] is not a lawyer, common carriers'.

[9] *Nugent v Smith* (1876) 1 CPD 423 and see Halsbury's Laws Vol 5(1) 4th edn, reissue para 403.

[10] See *Chitty on Contracts* 28th edn at para 36–010. Before 1963 the railway companies, and their successor the British Transport Commission, were undoubtedly common carriers of most kinds of goods. But under the Transport Act 1962, s 43(6) and Railways Act 1993, neither the British Railways Board nor any other Board set up under that Act nor any of the privatised railway undertakings is a common carrier.

[11] *Bretherton v Wood* (1821) 3 Brod & B 54 where the owner of a stage coach was held to be a common carrier. Today most carriers of goods by road are private carriers and under the Road Haulage Associations Conditions of Carriage of 1991, the carrier stipulates that he is not a common carrier — *Chitty* at para 36–010.

13.6   No English authority decides whether a carrier by air is capable of being a common carrier[12]. However, given that other carriers by sea, road and rail are capable of being common carriers, it would be odd if a carrier by air were ruled out simply by the fact that the carriage is performed by air rather than road[13]. This reasoning was adopted, albeit *obiter*, by Mackinnon J in *Aslan v Imperial Airways*[14]:

> 'I see no reason why a man who carries goods by a machine that travels through the air should not be a common carrier or assume the liabilities of a common carrier if he acts in a certain way . . . If a man who owned an aeroplane or a seaplane chose to engage in the trade of carrying goods as a regular business and to hold himself out ready to carry for any who wished to employ him so far as he had room in his airship or aeroplane for their goods, very likely he would become a common carrier or be under the various liabilities of a common carrier.'

13.7   Duties of a Common Carrier.   The common carrier's duties are imposed by the common law and arise by virtue of his status as a common carrier rather than from any contract (whether express or implied) with those whose goods he carries[15]. In addition to the carrier's duties in relation to the goods while in transit which are discussed in para **13.8** below, the common carrier is subject, at common law, to two peculiar obligations: in the absence of a lawful ground for refusal he must accept for transport goods tendered with the appropriate freight[16] and he must charge only a reasonable rate for their carriage. If he breaches either of these duties (subject to limited defences), the

---

[12]   It was assumed without deciding the issue that a carrier by air could be a common carrier by the Privy Council in *Ludditt v Ginger Cootes Airways* [1947] AC 233. In *Aslan v Imperial Airways* (1933) 45 Lloyds Law Rep 322, Mackinnon J proceeded on the assumption that a carrier by air could be a common carrier although finding the defendant not to be a common carrier on the facts of the case. For a contrary view see Fletcher 'Carriage of Goods by Air' (1934) 50 LQR 329 criticized by *McNair*, p 139.

[13]   See the discussion in *McNair* pp 138–144. It has been accepted in Canada and the US that an air carrier may be a common carrier: see the Canadian cases of *Nysted v Wings* [1942] 3 DLR 336 and *Ludditt v Ginger Coote Airways Ltd* [1942] DLR 29 (as set out in *Shawcross* Div VII para [78] and the American cases listed in *Shawcross* Div VII para [78].

[14]   (1933) 45 Lloyds Law Rep 316 at p 322.

[15]   See, for example, *Eastman Chemical v NMT Trading Ltd* [1972] 2 Lloyds Rep 25 — the claimants contracted with the first defendants who were haulage contractors and carriers, and who agreed to carry goods by road from London to Wellesbourne. The first defendants employed the second defendants, who were also haulage contractors and carriers to carry the goods for them. It was held that both the first and second defendants were common carriers. See also Halsbury's Laws Vol 5(1) at para 402. See also *Clarke v West Ham Corporation* [1909] 2 KB 858 — having confirmed that a carrier of passengers could be a common carrier, Farwell L J went on to say that once it has been determined that a person is a common carrier of passengers 'all the provisions which by law affect common carriers of goods, not as bailees, but as carriers by reason of their public profession, are equally applicable to carriers of passengers mutatis mutandis.' at p 878–879.

[16]   An action for damages lies against a common carrier for refusing to carry a passenger's luggage — *Munster v South Eastern Rly Co* (1858) 4 CBNS 676.

common carrier commits the tort of wrongful refusal of goods. The following defences are open to the common carrier[17]: first, the goods are not of the class that he carries[18]; second, the goods are dangerous[19] or exceptional in character[20]; third, the goods were tendered an unreasonable time before the journey[21]; and fourth, the goods consigned were inadequately packed[22].

13.8   Common carriers are usually bailees of the goods they carry and as such owe the duty of care discussed at para **13.13** below. However, the duties owed by common carriers go further than this. By long-established custom common carriers, unlike private carriers, are, prima facie, strictly responsible for all loss or damage which occurs in the course of transit[23]. The liability of the common carrier is thus often described as an 'insurer's liability'. To escape liability the common carrier must prove both that the loss or damage was caused by one of the 'four excepted perils' discussed below and further that no negligence on the part of the carrier or his employees contributed to the loss and damage[24].

---

[17] See in general *Chitty* at para 36–018.

[18] *Johnson v The Midland Railway Company* (1849) 4 Ex 367: 'At common law a carrier is not bound to carry for every person tendering goods of any description, but his obligation is to carry according to his public profession . . . . A person may profess to carry a particular description of goods only . . . in which case he will not be compelled to carry any other kind of goods; or he may limit his obligation to carrying from one place to another . . . and then he would not be bound to carry to or from the intermediate places.' pp 372–373 per Parke B.

[19] *Bamfield v Goole and Sheffield Transport Co Ltd* [1910] 2 KB 94 — the defendants delivered a quantity of chemicals stored in casks. The chemicals gave off poisonous fumes during carriage. It was held that 'where a man calls upon a common carrier to carry general cargo, thus relying simply upon the common law duty of the carrier so to do, and without informing the carrier of the nature of those goods so as to enable him to judge of their fitness, there is implied by law a contract by the person making the request to keep indemnified the person having the duty against damages arising from the fact that the goods are not such that he had the right this to call upon the common carrier to carry', at p 108 per Fletcher Moulton LJ and per Farwell LJ at p 115 'It may also be put thus: a common carrier is bound to carry according to his profession, but he does not profess to carry goods dangerous to life or limb: he is bound, to use Lord Holt's phrase in *Lane v Cotton* (1700) 12 Mod 473 to carry "packets proper to be sent by a carrier."'

[20] *Date and Cocke v G W Sheldon & Co (London) Ltd* (1921) 7 Lloyd's Rep 53 — ' it does not follow that a person is not a common carrier because he refused to accept certain classes of goods. He may be a common carrier and yet restrict his carrying of goods to a particular class, or, at any rate, he may exclude a particular class of goods' at p 54.

[21] *Lane v Cotton* (1701) 12 Mod 473 — 'it is true, it is said in [*Mosse and Slew* 3 Keb 72, 112, 135], that if the owners of the goods had brought them before such time as was convenient before the ship was ready to sail, he might refuse to receive them; and that may be: and it is so in the case of a carrier; if goods be brought to his inn before the convenient time for him to be gone, he may refuse to take them. . .'.

[22] *LNWR Co v Richard Hudson and Sons Ltd* [1920] AC 324 at p 340 — 'in *Sutcliffe v Great Western Railway Co* [1910] 1 KB 478, 503, Kennedy LJ said that a common carrier may refuse to carry goods which are tendered to him for carriage without such protection as would be necessary to enable the carrier to carry them to their destination with a reasonable prospect of security during the transit'.

[23] See the judgment of Holt CJ in *Coggs v Bernard* (1703) 2 Ld Raym 909 where he identified a number of forms of bailment, listing a common carrier and master of a ship as among those 'bound to answer for the goods at all events' at p 917.

[24] See, in general, *Chitty* at paras 36–019–36–023 and Halsburys Laws Vol 5(1) at paras 446–451.

13.9   The 'four excepted perils' at common law are as follows: first, *Act of God* — which means an operation of natural forces which it was not reasonably possible to foresee and guard against[25]; second, *Act of the Queen's enemies* — that is, acts of the armed forces of a foreign power with which the country is at war[26]; third, *Inherent vice* — that is some latent characteristic of the goods which by its development in the course of transit, tends to their injury, deterioration or destruction[27]; and fourth, *Consignor's fault* — if loss, damage or destruction is due solely to the fault of the consignor (or his agent) the common carrier is free from liability[28].

13.10   Private carriers.   Carriers who are not common carriers will be private carriers:

> 'There seems to be a general agreement, whether one consults the authorities or the text-books, that to make a man a common carrier he must carry out a public employment; he must carry for all indifferently; he must hold himself out as ready to carry for hire as a business and not as a casual occupation pro hac vice. He is sometimes described as a person who undertakes for reward to carry the goods of such as choose to employ him from place to place. To this I think it would be safe to add the words "at a reasonable rate". All other carriers are private carriers.[29]'

13.11   Duties of Private Carrier.   Unlike a common carrier, a private carrier is free to decide whether to agree to carry passenger, baggage or cargo[30]. The private carrier will be under a duty in relation to the goods he carries while in transit. Unlike the common carrier, the private carriers obligations in relation to the goods he carries are not imposed by law; rather, his obligations arise

---

[25]   For example, *Nugent v Smith* (1876) 1 CPD 423 — where a horse was injured while being carried on a vessel during a storm which was described as 'more than ordinary bad weather', Cleasby B held at p 411 'the words Act of God, comprehend no doubt such events as earthquakes and all other convulsions of nature' for example violent storms and tempests.

[26]   This does not include hijack or robbery. See *Barcaly v Cuculla Y Gana* (1784) 3 Doug 389.

[27]   See *Lister v Lancashire and Yorkshire Railway* [1903] 1 KB 878 — damage was caused to an engine being carried by the defendant common carrier. As the engine was not in fact fit to be carried in the way in which it was intended to be carried, and the damage resulted in consequence of that unfitness, the defendants were excused.

[28]   This may include, for example, improper packing or misleading address on the goods. In *Bradley v Waterhouse* (1828) 3 C & P 318 a consignor hid a bag of gold coins in a consignment of tea: he was not entitled to recover because he had misled the carrier as to the nature and value of the consignment and brought the loss on himself.

[29]   *Belfast Ropework Company v Bushell* [1918] 1 KB 210 at p 212 per Bailhache J.

[30]   Subject to statutory provisions preventing discrimination in the provision of goods and services on the grounds of sex, race or disability; see race Relations Act 1976, s 20, Sex Discrimination Act 1975, s 29 and possibly the Discrimination Disability Act 1995 — although by sub-section 19(5) the Act does not apply to 'any service so far as it consists of the use of any means of transport'.

either from a contract to carry particular goods or from his acceptance of particular goods. In either case the duties of a private carrier are more limited than those of a common carrier.

13.12   Bailment.   A bailment comes into existence 'whenever one is knowingly and willingly in possession of goods which belong to another'[31]. A private carrier of goods is a bailee[32]. The bailment may be pursuant to a contract to which the carrier is a party but the bailment is separate from the contract and a bailment can arise independently of any contract. A gratuitous, non-contractual, bailment might arise, for example, where a carrier agrees to transport goods free of charge or where an item is lent to the carrier without charge. As a bailee, the carrier's obligation at common law is to take reasonable care of his bailors goods and not to convert them[33].

13.13   Duty to take reasonable care.   The private carrier's fundamental duty, whether as bailee or pursuant to a contract of carriage, is to take reasonable care to carry goods safely and deliver them intact[34]. Thus, the private carrier's liability extends only to loss or damage caused by his own or his employee's negligence or deliberate wrongdoing[35]. However, while as a matter of law the bailor must prove negligence, the fact of loss, damage or non-delivery is prima facie evidence of negligence on the part of the carrier or his employees and the burden of disproving negligence is on the carrier as bailee:

> 'once the bailment had been established, and once the failure of the bailee to hand over the articles in question has been proved, there is a prima facie case, and the claimant is entitled to recover, unless the defendant can establish to the satisfaction of the court a defence . . . it is a good answer for him to say that the goods were stolen without any default on his part . . . but it is, of course, in those circumstances for the defendants to establish affirmatively, not only that the goods were

---

[31] See *Palmer on Bailment* (2nd edn) p 3. While a contract for the carriage of goods would be a bailment for reward, liability in bailment is distinct from liability in contract and tort: *The Kapetan Marcos (No 2)* [1987] 2 Lloyd's Rep 321.

[32] *Albarcruz (Cargo Owners) v Albazero (Owners), The Albazero* [1977] AC 774 at 841 'the contract for the carriage of goods involves a bailment' per Lord Diplock.

[33] *Morris v C W Martin & Sons Ltd* [1966] 1 QB 716 — 'One of the common law duties owed by a bailee of goods is not to convert them. . . This duty, which is common to all bailments as well as to other relationships which do not amount to bailment, is independent of and additional to the other common law duty of a bailee for reward to take reasonable care of his bailor's goods' per Diplock LJ at p 732.

[34] See *Travers v Cooper* [1915] 1 KB 73 at 88; *Aslan v Imperial Airways* [1933] All ER Rep 567; and see Supply of Goods and Services Act 1982 s 13 under which, in a contract for the supply of a service where the supplier is acting in the course of a business, there is an implied term that the supplier will carry out the service with reasonable care and skill.

[35] Unless, of course, a contractual bailee has contracted for a higher duty.

stolen, but that they were stolen without default on their part; in other words, there was no negligence on their part in the care which they took of the goods'[36].

13.14   The same duty to take reasonable care of the goods in his possession applies to a bailee for reward and to a gratuitous bailee[37].

13.15   Where goods are carried for reward, as well as the duty of care in relation to the goods while in transit, the carrier is obliged to use reasonable care to provide a vehicle, in the case of carriage by air an aircraft, which is fit for the carriage in question[38].

13.16   **Liability for servants and independent contractors.** Difficult questions may arise where carriage is actually performed by an employee or independent contractor of the carrier. The strict liability of the common carrier means that the question of whether damage was caused by a servant of the carrier or by an independent sub-contractor does not arise. In relation to claims in negligence or contract against a private carrier the rules discussed in para **13.40** below in the context of the carriage of passengers apply. Cases involving the carriage of goods will also usually involve the bailment for reward of the goods to the carrier. In the absence of an express term to the contrary, a contractual bailee is liable for loss or damage caused by his

---

[36]   *Houghland v R.R. Low Luxury Coaches Ltd* [1962] 1 QB 694 at pp 698–699 per Ormerod LJ.

[37]   *Houghland v R.R. Low Luxury Coaches Ltd* [1962] 1 QB 694. This case, which concerned a gratuitous bailment, confirmed that the same principles apply to cases of gratuitous bailment as apply to bailment for reward: 'it seems to me that to try and put a bailment, for instance, into a watertight compartment — such as gratuitous bailment on the one hand, and bailment for reward on the other — is to overlook the fact that there might well be an infinite variety of cases, which might come into one or the other category. The question that we have to consider in a case of this kind, if it is necessary to consider negligence, is whether in the circumstances of this particular case a sufficient standard of care has been observed by the defendants or their servants' per Ormerod LJ at p 698. See also *Port Sweetenham Authority v T W Wu and Co* [1979] AC 580. However, it may well be that the degree of care required of a gratuitous carrier will not be as great as that of a carrier for reward. In particular, in the case of gratuitous carriage it seems that there is no duty to exercise reasonable care in the provision of a fit vehicle — see *Haseldine v Daw* [1941] 2 KB 343 at p 373 — 'a person who asks for and is given a gratuitous ride in a vehicle, whether in the horizontal or vertical plane, takes the vehicle as he finds it and is only entitled to warning of danger of which the owner is aware . . . Of course, if I give a person a lift in my car I must drive with due care, but that is very different from being under a duty to use care to see that the car is in a safe condition before I let him get in when I have no reason to believe that it is not.'

[38]   See *Aslan v Imperial Airways* [1933] All ER Rep 567. The carrier does not warrant the safety of the vehicle, but is under a duty to use reasonable care to provide a fit vehicle. Unlike the carrier of goods at sea who warrants not merely to do his best to make the ship fit but that the ship should really be fit, there is no warranty of airworthiness: see *McNair* pp 144–148. See *John Carter (Fine Worsteds) Ltd v Hanson Haulage (Leeds) Ltd* [1965] 2 QB 495 where it was held that the warranty of seaworthiness applied in cases of carriage of goods by sea does not apply to carriage by road, where the standard of liability is not that of warranty but of reasonable care (per Sellers LJ at p 517 Davies LJ at p 529 and per Russell LJ at p 535). A similar duty will apply to a carrier by air — there will be no warranty of airworthiness.

independent contractors[39]. Even if there is no direct contractual relationship between bailor and bailee, it is likely that the bailee's duty is non-delegable and that the carrier will be liable where he has entrusted the goods to someone else for safekeeping[40].

13.17   Who can sue the Carrier?   Generally, the person to whom the carrier is liable in respect of goods lost or damaged during transit is their owner[41] — because the goods are at his risk and therefore it is him who has suffered the loss. There is a rebuttable presumption that the owner of goods is a party to the contract of carriage[42], but even if the owner is not a party to the contract of carriage, if any, he will usually be the party who brings the claim[43].

13.18   In a case where the goods have been sold, the owner of the goods will usually be the consignee as risk in the goods passes on delivery to the carrier[44]. If the goods are damaged in transit, since the risk is on the consignee, it will usually be the consignee who can bring a cause of action against the carrier.

13.19   Although generally only the owner may sue, this position may be varied by contract: for example, an agreement between the consignor and consignee of the goods (that risk will remain with the former) or an agreement between the consignor and the carrier. In the latter case the consignor will be liable to the true owner if he recovers damages from the carrier[45].

---

[39] *Riverstone Meat Co Pty Ltd v Lancashire Shipping Co Ltd* [1961] AC 807 — the claimant's goods were damaged while on board the defendant's ship by reason of the unseaworthiness of the ship. It was proved that this unseaworthiness was due to the negligence of an employee of an independent firm of ship repairers employed by the defendant. The House of Lords held the defendant liable.

[40] *Morris v CW Martin & Sons* [1966] 1 QB 716.

[41] Or, in relation to a claim in tort the person enjoying possessory title to the goods: see *The Aliakmon* [1986] AC 785 at 809 per Lord Brandon.

[42] See *Coombes v Bristol and Exeter Rly Co* (1858) 3 H & N 510 and *Cork Distilleries Co v GS and W Rly* (1874) LR 7 HL 269 — per Mellor J at p 277 'there is evidence in the present case that these goods were, with the consent or by the authority of the purchaser, consigned by the vendors, as consignors, to be carried by the defendants as common carriers, to be delivered to the purchaser as consignees, and that the name of the consignee was made known to the defendants at the time of delivery. Under such circumstances the ordinary inference is that the contract of carriage is between the carrier and the consignee, the consignor being the agent for the consignee to make it' — approved by the House of Lords per the Lord Chancellor at p 278.

[43] *Dawes v Peck* (1799) 8 TR 330 — 'this question must be governed by the consideration in whom the legal right was vested; for he is the person who has sustained the loss, if any, by the negligence of the carrier; and whoever has sustained the loss is the proper party to call for compensation from the person by whom he has been injured.' per Lord Kenyon Ch J at p 332.

[44] See *The Albazero* [1977] AC 774 — 'It was well established by the end of the eighteenth century that the ordinary implication in a contract for the sale of goods was that the place of delivery of the goods to the buyer was the seller's place of business and that if the seller made a contract with a carrier for onward delivery he did so on the buyer's behalf' per Lord Diplock at p 842.

[45] See *Dunlop v Lambert* (1839) 6 Cl & F 600; cf *The Albazero* [1977] AC 774 at 844 and 847.

13.20   Choice of claims.   The owner of goods is likely to be a party to the contract of carriage and thus have a contractual claim. Even if it cannot be established that an owner of goods is party to a contract of carriage, it is open to the owner to sue the carrier in either tort or in bailment[46]. Given a choice of claims, it will usually be more advantageous to sue in bailment than in contract or tort. This is because once the claimant can prove loss of or damage to the goods in transit the burden of disproving negligence falls on the carrier[47].

13.21   Time of delivery.   Unless a particular time for delivery is agreed, both a common and a private carrier must deliver the goods within a reasonable time. However, the carrier is not responsible for loss caused by delay which is not due to his own or his employee's negligence[48].

13.22   Counterclaim to claim for freight.   It is likely, as in the case of carriage of goods by sea and land[49], that a claim in respect of loss or damage to cargo cannot be made by way of counterclaim to a claim by a carrier for freight[50].

13.23   The contract of carriage — exclusion of liability.   In cases where a contract to carry is established, the carriers' duties will, prima facie, be determined by that contract[51]. A carrier may attempt to exclude or limit his liabilities under that contract by some form of exclusion clause. However, an attempt by contract to exclude or limit a carrier's liability for negligence or misconduct will be strictly construed against the carrier[52]: unless the words used clearly and unequivocally apply to liability for negligence or misconduct the Court will assume that there was no intention to exclude or limit such

---

[46] *Lee Cooper v Jeakins* [1967] 2 QB 1.

[47] See para **13.18** above.

[48] So, the carrier is not responsible for delay caused by something outside his foresight or control, such as an act of God or the act of a third party. See *Taylor v Great Northern Rly Co* (1866) LR 1 CP 385 where a railway company was prevented from carrying goods within the usual time by an unavoidable obstruction on their line caused by an accident resulting solely from the negligence of another company. The railway company was not liable for loss caused by the delay.

[49] See *Aries Tanker Corpn v Total Transport* [1977] 1 WLR 185 — when this 'long established rule of English law' in relation to carriage by sea was affirmed by the House of Lords; in *RH & D International v IAS Animal Air Services* [1984] 1 WLR 573 the rule was applied to carriage by road.

[50] See *Shawcross* Div VII para [85].

[51] Where a contract is silent appropriate terms may be implied eg under Supply of Goods and Service Act 1982 s 13 (duty to use reasonable care and skill) and s 14 (performance of the service within a reasonable time).

[52] There is a general rule that an exclusion clause will be construed against the party relying on it. An example of this general rule is that exceptions from liability provided for in the contract of carriage (eg 'at customer's risk') will qualify the duty to take care *during the transit*, but will not qualify the duty of supplying a fit aircraft, unless expressly excluded — see in relation to carriage by sea *The Christel Vinnen* [1924] P 208 and *McNair* at p 148.

liability[53]. The principle was referred to in the Scottish aviation case of *M'Kay v Scottish Airways Ltd*[54]:

> 'It is well settled that clauses exempting a carrier from liability fall to be construed strictly and *contra proferentem* . . . Only clear and unambiguous language will suffice to exclude a common law liability, and, as the language used in conditions expressed on a ticket is language framed and devised by the carriers themselves, it will *in dubio* fall to be construed in the sense most unfavorable to the carrier who sells the ticket and most favorable to the passenger who buys it.'

13.24   The application of these principles may have a different result in relation to common as opposed to private carriers. If, for example, a clause says that the carrier will not be liable for loss and damage caused by fire, this will not exempt a common carrier from liability where the fire is caused by his negligence. However, in the case of a private carrier such a clause would exempt the carrier from liability for negligence because otherwise the words could have no effect:

> 'A common carrier is liable for the acts of his servants whether they are negligent or not; an ordinary bailee is not liable for the acts of his servants unless they are negligent. If a common carrier would protect himself from responsibility for all acts of his servants he must use words which will include those acts which are negligent; because words which would suffice to protect him from acts properly done by his servants in the course of their service may fall short of protecting him from their negligent acts. But if an ordinary bailee uses words applicable to the acts of his servants, inasmuch as he is not liable for their acts unless negligent, the words will generally cover negligent acts, although such acts

---

[53]   In *Steinman v Angier Line* [1891] 1 QB 619 the court applied the principle that 'words of general exemption from liability are only intended (unless the words are clear) to relieve the carrier from liability where there has been no misconduct or default on his part or that of his servants.' per Bowen LJ at p 623. See also *Neilson v LNWR* [1922] 2 AC 263 at p 217 'I agree entirely with the view expressed by Scrutton LJ, and I venture to borrow his language: "If a carrier wishes to exempt himself from liability for the negligence of his servants he must do it in clear and unambiguous language" and "he must use ordinary English and not inventive words of doubtful meaning"' per Lord Dunedin at pp 271–272.

[54]   [1948] SC 254 at 256 per Lord Mackintosh. See also *Smith v South Wales Switchgear* [1978] 1 WLR 165 where the House of Lords (Sc) applied to an exemption clause the test summarised as follows in *Canada Steamship Lines Ltd v R* [1952] AC 192, 208 (per Lord Fraser of Tullybelton at p 172): '(1) If the clause contains language which expressly exempts the person in whose favour it is made (hereafter called the "proferens") from the consequences of the negligence of his own servants, effect must be given to that provision . . . (2) If there is no express reference to negligence, the court must consider whether the words used are wide enough, in their ordinary meaning, to cover negligence on the part of the servants of the proferens . . . (3) If the words used are wide enough for the above purpose, the court must then consider whether "the head of damage may be based on some ground other than that of negligence."'

are not specifically mentioned, because otherwise the words would have no effect.[55']

13.25   Incorporation of Terms.   Before a carrier can rely on an exclusion clause he must establish that the clause is part of the contract of carriage. Where a carrier relies on standard conditions, he must show that he did all that was reasonably necessary to bring the conditions to the notice of the customer before the journey commenced[56]. The more unusual the term, the greater the degree of notice likely to be required[57].

13.26   If an exclusion clause is incorporated into the contract between the carrier and the owner of the goods, the owner of the goods might chose to sue an employee of the carrier who is actually responsible for the damage and/or a sub-contractor who actually carried out the carriage. The question may arise whether an employee of the carrier can rely on an exemption clause in the contract of carriage between the owner of goods and his employer. Prima facie, the employee is a not a party to the contract and cannot rely on an exemption in favour of his employer[58] or even a provision purporting to exclude his own liability[59]. An employee will only be able to rely on an

---

[55]   *Rutter v Palmer* [1922] 2 KB 87 at p 90 per Barnes LJ. See further *Chitty* at para 36–028 and compare, for example, *Price & Co v Union Lighterage Company* [1903] 1 KB 750 where a clause exempting a barge owner from liability for 'any loss or damage to goods which can be covered by insurance' was held not to exempt the common carrier from loss and damage caused by the negligence of his servants — affirmed by CA [1904] 1 KB 412 and *Rutter v Palmer* [1922] 2 KB when in the case of an ordinary bailee the term 'customers' cars are driven by your staff at customer's sole risk' was held to protect the defendant from liability for the negligence of his servants. See also *Harris Ltd v Continental Express Ltd* [1961] 1 Lloyd's Rep 251 and *Alderslade v Hendon Laundry Ltd* [1945] KB 189.

[56]   *Fosbroke-Hobbes v Airwork* [1937] 1 All ER 108 — the second defendant's aircraft was hired under a contract of hire entered into with the first defendant. Just as the aeroplane was preparing to leave, an envelope containing a 'ticket' was handed to the hirer by the pilot. The 'ticket' was a document called a special charter and contained a number of conditions, including, inter alia, an exemption clause. Before the hirer read the document the plane crashed. The exemption clause could not be relied on as it was not communicated to the hirer before the journey started. It was held that there was no reason to suppose that there would be conditions other than those contained in the letters by which the original contract was made.

[57]   *Interfoto Picture Library v Stiletto Visual Programmes* [1989] QB 433 — 'It is, in my judgment, a logical development of the common law into modern conditions that it should be held, as it was in *Thornton v Shoe Lane Parking Ltd* [1971] 2 QB 163, that, if one condition in a set of printed conditions is particularly onerous or unusual, the party seeking to enforce it must show that that particular condition was brought to the attention of the other party' — per Dillon LJ at pp 437–438.

[58]   See *Adler v Dickson* [1955] 1 QB 158 — the claimant was injured while a passenger in a liner due to the negligence of the master and boatswain whom she sued. The defendants were held liable notwithstanding clauses in the contract of carriage with the shipping company who employed the defendants which exempted the company from liability for the negligence of its servants.

[59]   *Adler v Dickson* [1955] 1 QB 158 per Jenkins LJ at p 186 and Morris LJ at p 200.

exemption clause if it can be shown that his employer was acting as his agent in entering into the contract[60]. Alternatively, if a clause can be construed as a promise not to sue, the employer could choose to enforce this promise not to sue for the benefit of his employee[61]. Finally, in an action brought by the owner of goods against someone to whom part of the contract of carriage has been sub-contracted the owner may be bound by the terms of the sub-contract including an exclusion of liability if he expressly or impliedly consented to the carrier sub-contracting in those terms.

13.27   Reasonableness.   Even if a term of the contract is apt to cover negligence, any attempt to restrict the carrier's duty must satisfy statutory controls: in particular, under the Unfair Contract Terms Act 1977[62]. Under that Act, where a contract is entered into in the course of business, a person cannot exclude or restrict his liability for loss and damage (other than in relation to death or personal injury resulting from negligence which cannot be excluded at all) except in so far as the term or notice satisfies the requirement of reasonableness[63]. Further, when one contracting party deals as a consumer or on the other's written standard terms of business the other cannot when he himself is in breach of contract exclude or restrict any liability of his in respect of the breach or claim to be entitled to render a contractual performance substantially different from that which was reasonably expected of him except in so far as the contract satisfies the requirements of reasonableness[64].

13.28   In determining whether or not a term is reasonable, the court must have regard to the matters set out in Sch 2 to the Act. These guidelines set out the following factors which are relevant to the consideration of reasonableness: (a) the strength of bargaining positions of the parties; (b) whether the customer received an inducement to enter into the term; (c) whether the customer knew or ought reasonably to have known of the existence and extent of the term; (d) where the term excludes or restricts liability by reference to compliance with a condition, whether it was reasonable to expect that compliance with that condition would be practicable.

13.29   Council Directive (EEC) 93/13 on Unfair Terms in Consumer

---

[60]   See *Chitty* paras 14–043–14–046 and *New Zealand Shipping Co Ltd v AM Sattherthwaite and Co Ltd* [1975] AC 154.
[61]   See *Chitty* para 14–047 and *European Asian Bank AG v Punjab and Sind Bank* [1982] 2 Lloyd's Rep 356.
[62]   Supply of Goods and Services Act 1982 s 16 provides that although the terms which would otherwise be implied by law may be negatived or varied by express agreement, or by course of dealing between the parties, this is expressly subject to the Unfair Contract Terms Act 1977.
[63]   Unfair Contract Terms Act 1977 s 2.
[64]   Unfair Contract Terms Act 1977 s 3.

Contracts[65] is also applicable to all contracts (including contracts of carriage[66]) concluded after 1 July 1995. The Directive applies to contracts entered into between a supplier and a consumer[67]. Article 3 of the Directive defines 'unfair terms' as follows:

> 'A contractual term which has not been individually negotiated shall be regarded as unfair if, contrary to the requirement of good faith, it causes a significant imbalance in the parties' rights and obligations arising under the contract, to the detriment of the consumer.'

13.30   The requirement of good faith is unlikely to differ materially from the test of 'reasonableness' under the 1977 Act[68]. The Annex to the Directive lists a number of terms which may be regarded as unfair, including, 'irrevocably binding the consumer to terms with which he had no real opportunity of becoming acquainted before the conclusion of the contract.'

The Carriage of Passengers

13.31

RULE 46—A carrier of passengers may either be a 'common carrier' or a 'private carrier':

(a)   A 'common carrier' is a carrier who publicly professes to carry for reward. His duties and liabilities include:
   (i)   a duty to carry any person not in an unfit condition for whom he has accommodation upon tender of the proper fare without imposition of any unreasonable condition; and
   (ii)   a duty to see reasonable care is taken for the safety of passengers;

(b)   A private carrier is any carrier who is not a common carrier. His duties and liabilities include:

---

[65]   Implemented into English law initially by the Unfair Terms in Consumer Contracts Regulations 1994, SI 1994/3159 made under the European Communities Act 1972. These regulations were revoked and replaced by the Unfair Terms in Consumer Contracts Regulations 1999. Formally the provisions of the 1994 Regulations apply to contracts made between 1 July 1995 and the coming into force of the 1999 Regulations. However, given the general requirement to interpret in accordance with the Directive, in practice there is unlikely to be any difference.

[66]   The operative parts of the Directive do not state to which types of contact the Directive applies, but it clearly extends to contracts for the supply of services and the Preamble states that transport contracts fall within its scope (Article 1(2)).

[67]   'Seller or supplier' is defined to mean 'any natural or legal person who is acting for purposes relating to his trade, business or profession' and 'consumer' as 'any natural person who is acting for purposes outside his trade, business or profession.'

[68]   In particular, there are specific references made in the Preamble to certain matters which appear as guidelines in Sch 2 to the 1977 Act. See *Chitty* para 15–044.

(i)   a duty to see reasonable care is taken for the safety of passengers.

13.32   As with carriers of goods, carriers of passengers can be either common or private carriers. The common carrier of passengers, like the common carrier of goods, is a carrier who holds himself out as willing to carry members of the public generally. All carriers who are not common carriers will be private carriers.

13.33   Duties of a common carrier.   A common carrier of passengers, like a common carrier of goods, offers to carry anyone who chooses to use his service and he is there is therefore bound to carry any person not in an unfit condition for whom he has accommodation upon tender of his proper fare, without the imposition of any unreasonable condition[69]. There seems to be no reason why a carrier of passengers by air should not be subject to the same common law obligation to carry as any other carrier exercising public employment as a carrier of passengers[70]. In contrast, a private carrier will of course be free to decide who to carry as a passenger subject to statutory constraints against discrimination on grounds of sex, race or disability.

13.34   Duties of common and private carriers.   Unlike a carrier of goods, a common carrier of passengers is not treated as an 'insurer' of the safety of the passengers carried and is not subject to the strict form of liability which applies to the common carrier of goods.

13.35   Both common and private carriers of passengers are under a duty to see that reasonable care is taken for the safety of their passengers:

> 'The liability of a common carrier of passengers was settled by the decision of the Exchequer Chamber in 1869 in *Readhead v Midland Railway Co* (1869) LR 4 QB 379. It was there held that the liability of a general or

---

[69] See *Clarke v West Ham Corpn* [1909] 2 KB 858 'a common carrier of goods comes under two distinct duties or liabilities: he is liable to carry according to his profession, and he is also liable as bailee of chattels . . . . A carrier of passengers comes under the first duty or liability, and for the same reason, namely, that he is bound to carry according to his profession.' per Farwell LJ at p 877 and at p 878 'Adapting to carriers of passengers what was said as to carriers of goods by Cockburn CJ in *Garton v Bristol and Exeter Rly Co* (1861) 1 B & S 112 at p 162, persons holding themselves out to the world as common carriers are bound to act as such in respect to all persons not in an unfit condition for whom they have accommodation, on having tendered to them the legal fare, without subjecting the person tendering to any unreasonable condition.' See further *Ludditt v Ginger Coote Airways Ltd* [1947] AC 233 at p 241, where Lord Wright held that carriers of goods and passengers are both 'subject to the obligations which arise from their exercising a public profession which requires them to carry for all sundry, subject to obvious limiting conditions.' Therefore, a common carrier of passengers can be sued for an unjustifiable refusal to carry passengers — *Benett v The Peninsular and Oriental Steam-Boat Co* (1848) 6 CB 775.

[70] *McNair* at p 143. See also *Bennett v The Peninsular and Oriental Steam-Boat Co* (1848) 6 CB 775 which confirms (per Wilde CJ at p 787) that those engaged in international carriage could be common carriers.

public or common carrier of passengers is more limited than that of a common carrier of goods. By the custom of the realm a common carrier of goods was at common law 'bound to answer for the goods at all events . . . The law charges this person thus entrusted to carry goods against all events but acts of God and of enemies of the King' (ibid 382). The carrier of passengers is not subjected to a duty so stringent. His obligation at common law, as was held in the leading case just cited, is to carry 'with due care'. One reason for the distinction, no doubt, is that the carrier of goods is a bailee of the goods which he carries, whereas a carrier of passengers is not a bailee of his passengers.[71']

13.36   The duty to take reasonable care.   'A carrier's obligation to his passengers, whether it be expressed in contract or in tort, is to provide a carriage that is as free from defects as the exercise of all reasonable care can make it'[72] and to take and use reasonable care to carry passengers safely[73]. The carrier does not, in the absence of express agreement, warrant the safety or fitness of the vehicle and, therefore, he is not liable for any inherent defect in the vehicle which could not reasonably be detected[74].

---

[71] *Ludditt v Ginger Coote Airways Ltd* [1947] AC 233 per Lord Wright at pp 240–241.

[72] *Barkway v South Wales Transport Co Ltd* [1950] 1 All ER 392 per Lord Radcliffe at pp 403–404 and see *Hyman v Nye* (1881) 4 QBD 685 at 687 per Lindley J — 'a person who lets out carriages is not, in my opinion, responsible for all defects discoverable or not; he is not an insurer against all defects; nor is he bound to take more care than coach proprietors or railway companies who provide carriages for the public to travel in; but in my opinion, he is bound to take as much care as they; and although not an insurer against all defects, he is an insurer against all defects which care and skill can guard against.'

[73] See *Aston v Heaven* (1797) 2 Esp 533 — 'the question therefore depends on the consideration of whether there was any negligence in the driver? It is said that he was driving with reins so loose that he could not readily command his horses: if that was the case, the defendants are liable; for a driver is answerable for the smallest negligence. But if this does not appear, and the accident appears to have arisen from any unforeseen accident or misfortune, as from the horses suddenly taking fright; in such case the defendants are not liable.' per Eyre CJ at pp 535–536; *Christie v Griggs* (1809) 2 Camp 79 at 80 per Mansfield CJ 'I think the claimant has made a prima facie case by proving his going on the coach, the accident, and the damage he has suffered. It now lies on the other side to shew that the coach was as good a coach as could be made, and that the driver was as skillful a driver as could anywhere be found.'

[74] *Readhead v Midland Rly Co* (1869) LR 4 QB 379 — a passenger on the defendant's railway was injured due to a latent defect [in a tyre] which was not attributable to any fault on the part of the manufacturer and could not be detected previously to the breaking. In order for the claimant to succeed he would have had to have established either that there was a warranty, by way of insurance on the part of the carrier to convey the passenger safely to his journey's end, or, a warranty that the carriage in which he travels shall be in all respects perfect for its purpose, that is to say, free from all defects likely to cause peril. It was held that no such warranty was placed on a carrier of passengers, whose obligation was to take due care to carry the passenger safely. See also the decision of the New Zealand Court of Appeal in *Dominion Air Lines Ltd v Strand* [1933] NZLR as set out in *McNair* at p 145. Liability may also attach to a carrier as a result of the application of the provisions of the Occupiers Liability Act 1957, but it is difficult to see what this would add in an aviation context to the common law duty of care, where applicable: see generally *Shawcross* Div VII para [89] and *Clerk & Lindsell* (17th edn) Chapter 10. See para **13.39** below in relation to duties owed to trespassers under Occupiers Liability Act 1984.

13.37   Choice of claims.   A passenger who has paid for his ticket has the choice between suing for breach of contract or for the tort of negligence[75]. In cases where there is no contract between passenger and carrier it is sufficient that the passenger was being carried with the carrier's permission[76]. Apart from the exceptional case of a trespasser (for example a stowaway) the standard of care in tort is the same for passengers who have paid for their tickets as it is for those who, for one reason or another, have made no contract with the carrier and/or are traveling for nothing[77]. The carriage of passengers cannot be regarded as bailment as a human being cannot be the subject of a bailment[78].

13.38   Trespassers.   Trespassers, including stowaways, may in limited circumstances have a cause of action against the carrier if he is injured whilst on board an aircraft. Until recently, trespassers, including stowaways, could only sue where they were injured willfully or recklessly[79].

13.39   The common law rules in relation to occupiers (which apply to aircraft operators who are for these purposes occupiers of the aircraft) have now been replaced by the Occupiers Liability Act 1984 s 1(4): the occupier owes a trespasser a duty to take such care as is reasonable in all the circumstances of the case to see that the trespasser does not suffer injury on the premises by reason of any danger on them, provided three conditions are met: first that the occupier knows or ought to know of the existence of the danger on his land; that he knows or ought to know that the trespasser is in the vicinity of the danger, or is likely to come into it; and that the risk is one against which in all the circumstances of the case, he may reasonably be expected to offer some protection.

---

[75] The estate and/or dependents of a passenger killed during transit can claim, in relation to claims in tort, under the Fatal Accidents Act 1976 and the Law Reform (Miscellaneous Provisions) Act 1934. An action for breach of contract would survive the death of the passenger: *The Greta Holme* [1897] AC 596 at 601.

[76] Although the carriage of passengers cannot be regarded as bailment as a human being cannot be the subject of a bailment — *Clarke v West Ham Corpn* [1909] 2 KB 858 at 877.

[77] See, for example, *Harris v Perry & Co* [1903] 2 KB 205 — where it was held that the principle in all cases is that reasonable care must be exercised. However, the standard of reasonableness naturally must vary according to the circumstances of the case, the trust reposed and the skill and appliances at the disposal of the person to whom another confers a duty (at p 226).

[78] *Clarke v West Ham Corpn* [1909] 2 KB 858 at 877.

[79] This rule was applied by the Court of Appeal in *British Railways Board v Herrington* [1972] AC 877. The House of Lords affirmed the decision of the Court of Appeal but based liability on a finding of negligence, having found that British Rail were not reckless. However, the House of Lords also emphasised that the duty of care owed to a trespasser was not the same as is owed to a person invited onto the land. The duty owed to trespassers was a duty to take such steps as common sense or common humanity would dictate to exclude or warn or otherwise, within reasonable and practical limits to reduce or avert danger. However, the precise level of duty owed remained obscure. It was suggested that the duty was limited in two respects: that the defendant could not be liable without actual knowledge that trespassers were likely to be on his land, and that the defendant's assets were taken into account in assessing what he was expected to do — but both these distinctions have subsequently been doubted. See *Clerk and Lindsell* (17th edn) at para 10–73.

13.40   Liability for servants and independent contractors.   Carriers of passengers will be vicariously liable for the negligent acts of their servants acting in the course of their employment[80]. In such a case, an injured passenger can sue not only the carrier who is vicariously liable for the negligence of his employees acting within the scope of their employment, but also the negligent employee himself[81].

13.41   The liability of a carrier for the negligence of an independent contractor who is carrying out the carriage is more difficult[82]. In general[83], a carrier would not be responsible for the negligent acts of independent contractors unless the wrongful act or omission can be attributed to the negligence or other personal fault of the employer himself[84]. For example, if an employer negligently selected an incompetent contractor he will himself have committed a tort. Similarly, if the employer has authorised or ratified the independent contractor's tort he will be jointly liable for it[85].

---

[80]   *Ricketts v Thomas Tilling* [1915] 1 KB 644 — the driver of an omnibus belonging to the defendants allowed the conductor to drive the vehicle. The conductor drove negligently and injured a pedestrian. It was held that there was evidence that the driver was negligent in allowing the conductor to drive the bus and the defendant employer was liable. The defendants were not directly responsible for the acts of the conductor as he was not authorised to drive the vehicle and therefore was not acting within the scope of his employment.

[81]   See *Adler v Dickson* [1955] 1 QB 158, the claimant, who was injured when mounting the gangway of the ship, brought an action in negligence against the master and boatswain of the ship; *Gore v Van Der Lann* [1967] 2 QB 31 — the claimant who fell while attempting to board a bus claimed damages against the bus conductor claiming that the accident was due to his negligence.

[82]   For the distinction between an employee and an independent contractor see *Clerk & Lindsell* (17th edn) paras 5–02–5–19.

[83]   There are however, some 'non-delegable duties' whereby the law imposes on an employer a strict or absolute duty which he cannot discharge by delegating the work to an independent sub-contractor. The existence of such duties at common law is unclear. However, it may be that the duty to take reasonable care to ensure an aircraft is fit to fly is one of there absolute non-delegable duties — see *Rogers v Night Riders* [1983] RTR 324 — the defendants operated a mini-cab service. They hired radios to car-hire drivers, although the car itself was owned and controlled by the driver. The claimant was injured by the negligent maintenance of one of the cabs. The Court of Appeal held that as the defendants had held themselves out to the general public as a car-hire firm and had undertaken to provide a mini-cab for the claimant and the claimant relied on them to do so, they owed her a non-delegable duty of care to take reasonable steps to ensure that the vehicle so provided was well maintained.

[84]   See *Reedie v LNWR* (1849) 4 Ex 244; *D & F Estates Ltd v Church Comrs* [1989] AC 777, affirming the general rule that a main contractor does not in general assume a duty of care to any person who might be injured by a dangerous defect caused by the negligence of an apparently competent sub-contractor. This is also the position under the Occupiers Liability Act 1957 s 2(4)(b) which provides: where damage is caused to a visitor by a danger due to the faulty execution of any work of construction, maintenance or repair by an independent contractor employed by the occupier, the occupier is not to be treated without more as answerable for the danger if in all the circumstances he had acted reasonably in entrusting the work to an independent sub-contractor and had taken such steps (if any) as he reasonable ought in order to satisfy himself that the contractor was competent and that the work had been properly done.

[85]   See *Ellis v Sheffield Gas Consumer's Co* (1853) 2 E & B 767, a gas company employed a contractor to dig up the street and lay pipes (having no statutory or other right to do so). The contractor negligently reinstated the surface and the claimant was injured. The company was responsible as the accident was caused by the very thing which the contractor was employed to do.

13.42   The position is different if a passenger is in a contractual relationship with the carrier: if the passenger is injured in transit by an accident caused by the negligence of an independent contractor the carrier would be in breach of a contractual duty to ensure that due care was used in transporting the passenger[86].

13.43   *Res ipsa loquitur.*   Unlike in a case of bailment (as to which see para **13.8** above), the burden is on the passenger to show that the carrier or his servants or agents were negligent. However, the otherwise heavy burden of proof thus imposed on passengers is alleviated in one important respect. The principle of *res ipsa loquitur* may apply in which case the burden may be on the carrier to disprove negligence[87]. The doctrine comes into play if it is shown that:

(a)   the thing causing the accident (such as the aircraft itself) was under the exclusive control of the carrier or his servants;

(b)   the accident was of a type which does not normally happen if reasonable care is used; and

(c)   the exact cause of the accident is unexplained[88].

13.44   Provided each of these conditions is met there is a presumption of negligence and the burden will be on the carrier to show that he took all reasonable care. In practice, it will often be the case that where goods are damaged or passengers injured during transit, that there is a presumption of negligence[89]. Examples of when the principle of *res ipsa loquitur* has been applied are: allowing an underground train to depart from a station with the doors open[90]; allowing an omnibus to brush into the branches of an over-

---

[86] *Great Western Railway v Blake* (1862) 7 H & N 987, a passenger held a ticket issued by the Great Western Railway and was injured in an accident caused by the negligence of the South Wales Railway, on whose lines the journey was partly run. It was held that the Great Western Railway was liable to the passenger as there was an implied term in the contract that the Great Western Railway undertook that due care would be used in carrying the passenger throughout the journey and in maintaining the lines for the entirety of the journey. The principle was confirmed and applied in *Thomas v Rhymeny Rly Co* (1871) LR 6 QB 266.

[87] See, for example, the statement of the principle in *Barkway v South Wales Transport* [1950] 1 All ER 392 — 'the maxim is no more than a rule of evidence affecting *onus*. It is based on commonsense, and its purpose is to enable justice to be done when the facts bearing on causation and on the care exercised by the defendant are at the outset unknown to the claimant and are or ought to be within the knowledge of the defendant.' per Lord Normand at p 399 and per Lord Radcliffe at p 403 — 'I find nothing more in that maxim than a rule of evidence, of which the essence is that an event which in the ordinary course of things is more likely than not to have been caused by negligence is by itself evidence of negligence.'

[88] If the cause of the accident is known, the doctrine of *res ipsa loquitur* has no application — *Barkway v South Wales Transport* [1950] 1 All ER 392.

[89] See *Barkway v South Wales Transport* [1950] 1 All ER 392 'the fact that an omnibus leaves the roadway and so causes injury to a passenger or to someone on the pavement is evidence relevant to infer that the injury was caused by the negligence of the owner, so that, if nothing more were proved, it would be a sufficient foundation for a finding of liability against him.' per Lord Normand at p 399. In fact, in this, case the actual cause of the accident was known and therefore the maxim did not apply.

[90] *Brookes v London Passenger Transport Board* [1947] 1 All ER 506.

hanging tree as it proceeded down a country lane[91]; the fact that part of a lorry intruded onto the pavement killing a pedestrian[92]; the door of a railway carriage flying open when pressure put on the window bar[93]; and the collision of two trains belonging to the same company[94].

13.45   Exclusion or limitation of liability for personal injury or death.   A carrier will be unable to rely on any contractual terms to exclude or limit liability in respect of death or personal injury to passengers caused by its negligence[95].

---

91   *Radley v London Passenger Transport Board* [1942] 1 All ER 433.
92   *Laurie v Raglan Building Co Ltd* [1942] 1 KB 152.
93   *Gee v Metropolitan Rly Co* (1873) LR 8 QB 161.
94   *Skinner v LB & SC Ry* (1850) 5 Exch 787.
95   Unfair Contract Terms Act 1977, s 2(1). See also art 3(3) and the Annex to Directive (EC) 93/13.

Chapter 14

Contract Relationships

Introduction

14.1

RULE 47—The Warsaw Convention regime exclusively governs claims by passengers in respect of loss, injury and damage sustained in the course of, or arising out of, carriage by air. Other causes of action arising out of the contract of carriage will, save exceptionally, be governed by the general principles of contract law.

14.2 In all but the most exceptional cases the carriage of passengers or goods by air will be effected pursuant to a contract and the respective rights of carrier and passenger or consignor will in the first instance be defined by the contract[1]. The contractual rights and obligations of the parties are in most fundamental respects overlain by the provisions of the Warsaw Convention regime discussed in other chapters of this book. But those provisions do not govern every aspect of the relationship between the parties. As a matter of English law, the Convention regime provides the exclusive cause of action and remedy in respect of claims for loss, injury and damage sustained in the course of, or arising out of, the carriage in question[2]. However, not every claim arising out of a contract of carriage by air falls within the Convention regime. For example, a passenger may purport to cancel the contract and seek a full or partial refund of any price paid. Or the carrier may, whether because of overbooking or for some other reason, refuse to carry a passenger to whom a ticket has been issued, or may refuse to carry his baggage, or may offer to carry him only in a different class; and the passenger may seek compensation. Or there may be a dispute between carrier and passenger as to the

---

[1] Questions of potential liability in tort or under the common law of carriage will accordingly only arise in practice extremely rarely. They are not considered in this book.
[2] See the decision of the House of Lords in *Sidhu v British Airways plc* [1997] AC 430. The same approach has been followed by the US Supreme Court in *Tseng v El Al Israel Airlines Ltd* 119 Sct 662 (1999) but not in some other jurisdictions. This book is concerned with the position under English law.

price of carriage performed but not paid for. In none of these cases does the claim relate to loss or damage sustained in the course of, or arising out, of carriage.

14.3   The purpose of this chapter is to analyse the contractual rights and obligations of the parties to a contract of carriage apart from the impact of the Warsaw Convention regime, though at various points the provisions of the Convention will have to be referred to. The position is analysed as a matter of English law, which will normally be the applicable law in any English Court[3].

The Contractual Framework: Passengers

How flights are sold

14.4   It may be helpful to set out by way of preliminary the principal methods by which flights are sold in the UK.

Scheduled flights

14.5   **Direct sale.**   All UK airlines sell flights directly, both over the counter (at airports from which they operate and usually at other offices) and remotely (whether by post, telephone, fax or over the internet). Likewise, many foreign-based airlines maintain sales offices in the UK, in addition to their desks at airports, from which sales can be made. Others make direct sales through 'general sales agents' ('GSAs'), who may be companies specialising in that role or travel agents or other travel companies: their offices are often presented to the public as the offices of the airline. Airline offices and GSAs will be in a position to make reservations and issue tickets (on that airline's own ticket stock) instantaneously.

14.6   **Sale through travel agents.**   Travel agents can make flight reservations with an airline either directly through a computer reservation service ('CRS'), or by telephone, fax or correspondence. Not all, however, can issue tickets. 'IATA-registered' travel agents are authorised to issue tickets for flights with airlines who are members of IATA, using IATA ticket stock which is not specific to any particular airline but on which the carrier on whose behalf the ticket is issued is identified by the use of a carrier identification plate which prints the carrier's name on the ticket coupon. IATA-registered agents enter into a standard form of agreement with IATA (a 'Passenger Sales

---

[3]   See para **14.60** below. It should not be taken for granted that Scottish law is identical in all respects. For convenience, however, reference is sometimes made to the 'UK' position.

Agency Agreement') setting out ticketing and accounting procedures[4]. Other agents may be authorised by particular carriers to issue tickets on their behalf under ad hoc agreements and supplied with ticket stock for the purpose. But in the absence of such authority an agent, having made a reservation, will have to obtain the ticket from the airline or its GSA. Travel agents are paid commission, typically 9% on published prices, for seats sold. A travel agent does not of course contract with the passenger as a principal.

14.7   Sale through consolidators.   Over the last two decades an increasingly sophisticated market has developed under which airlines make seats on scheduled flights available to so-called consolidators ('bucket shops') at special prices, for supply to the public: there is no commission, and it is for the consolidator to decide what mark-up it should apply. Arrangements between airlines and consolidators can be both complex and protean; but, although economically they deal with one another as principals, in selling seats to the public consolidators act as agents for the airline — without (save in particular circumstances) assuming any contractual liability to the passenger. Consolidators may also sell seats on charter flights (as to which see below), in which case again they will generally be acting as agents and not principals.

14.8   Package tours.   Many package tours involve carriage on scheduled flights. In such a case the tour operator will have to make a reservation with the carrier in the ordinary way and obtain a ticket. Some tour operators hold ticket stock for the airlines with whom they deal regularly and are authorised to issue tickets themselves; in other cases tickets will have to be obtained from the airline itself or its GSA. As a matter of general law the correct analysis is that the tour operator acts as the agent of the passenger in contracting with the airline. That contractual position is now overlain by the Package Travel, Package Holidays and Package Tours Regulations 1992 (which implement Council Directive 90/314/EEC) ('the Package Travel Regulations'): by reg 15 the tour operator is rendered liable for the defaults of the suppliers of the various services comprised in the package. But such liability is by way of addition, not substitution, so that package tour customers retain their independent contractual rights against the airline, such as they are, as well of course as their rights under the Warsaw Convention regime.

14.9   'Ticketless' travel.   Full development of electronic ticketing may have to await the coming into force of the Montreal Convention 1999, which will substantially relax the requirements of the current Warsaw Convention

---

[4]   The terms of the Agreement were recently the subject of litigation: see *Associated British Travel Agents Ltd v British Airways plc* [2000] 2 Lloyd's Rep 209. The particular issue concerned whether airport charges at BAA airports were to be treated as part of the ticket price for the purpose of calculating commission; but the background to the Agreement is usefully described. IATA also offers a clearing house system which provides a mechanism for monthly settlement of debts and credits between IATA members: as to this, see *British Eagle International Airlines Ltd v Cie Air France* [1975] 1 WLR 758 (HL).

regime as regards passenger documentation[5]. But already airlines are, within the constraints of the current regime, increasingly making use of procedures which dispense with the conventional form of ticket. On booking a flight, typically by telephone or on-line, the passenger is supplied simply with a document confirming his reservation, which is exchanged for a boarding-pass at check-in.

Charter flights

14.10   In the case of a charter flight, the operator of the aircraft has contracted with the charterer to carry the charterer's passengers. Thus seats are not sold by the carrier, or by travel agents, directly to passengers. Seats will be sold by the charterer, typically a tour operator, or by other tour operators, consolidators or others to whom the charterer has sub-sold space. Cases will depend on their particular facts. In some cases the contract will be between the passenger and the charterer (or intermediary). It is to be noted that the existence of a contract as between charterer and passenger will not necessarily mean that the operator of the aircraft will not be considered to be a carrier for the purposes of the Warsaw Convention regime[6]. In any event where the Guadalajara Convention is applicable, the operator of the aircraft will be the actual carrier for the purposes of the Warsaw Convention regime.

Formation of the contract

14.11

RULE 48—Subject to any express agreement to the contrary, a contract of carriage by air is formed when the essential terms of the contract are concluded and not (if later) on the delivery of the ticket or any other subsequent event.

14.12   The question of at what point a contract of carriage by air is concluded is important principally because it is central to the question of the incorporation of the airline's standard terms. However, the various ways in which purchasers arrange for flights, as reviewed above, may produce varying legal results; and there is no clear authority on the correct legal analysis. It is necessary to distinguish a number of different situations.

14.13   It is convenient to start with the paradigm case of an intending passenger buying a ticket direct from the airline office, and being issued there

---

[5]   Contrast art 3 of the Warsaw Convention (as amended at the Hague) with art 3 of the Montreal Convention.

[6]   See for example *Block v Compagnie Nationale Air France* 386 F 2d 323 (5th Cir 1967).

and then, in return for payment, with a ticket containing what purports to be a reservation for a specific flight.

14.14   Subject to any express term to the contrary, the natural analysis of such a transaction is, it is submitted, that a contract is concluded at the moment that the passenger accepts the ticket: the carrier, in return for the payment received, promises to carry the passenger (and his baggage) on the specified flight. It is at that point that, in commercial terms, a deal has been struck. Even in this straightforward situation, however, the position is surprisingly unclear. In *MacRobertson Miller Airline Services v Comr of State Taxation (Western Australia)*[7] the High Court of Australia had to consider whether an airline ticket was 'an agreement or memorandum of agreement' for the purposes of stamp duty. The ticket in question was bought over the counter at the office of the airline and delivered in exchange for payment of the fare. It was held that the ticket was not such an agreement or memorandum. In view of the high persuasive authority of decisions of the High Court of Australia, the decision requires careful consideration. The reasoning of the three members of the Court was not identical and is not entirely easy to follow. In summary:

(1)   Barwick CJ based himself primarily on the detailed wording of the Conditions of Carriage printed on the ticket: these contained such swingeing exemptions that they 'fully occup[ied] the whole area of possible obligation, leaving no room for the existence of a contract of carriage' (p 133)[8]. However, he also put forward (at pp 133–4) a general proposition that, in the absence of an *express* promise to carry, an airline ticket 'is to be regarded as doing no more than denominate the carriage which, if performed, will earn the prepaid fare . . . [and if it contains terms of carriage] regulate the relationship of the parties during and in connexion with such carriage'. The issue of the ticket is on this analysis no more than a receipt for a prepaid fare, which will (subject to conditions) be refundable if the passenger is not, in the event, carried. This is because 'having regard to the known contingencies of airline operation it would be incongruous to infer the making of a promise to carry from the mere payment of the fare and its acknowledgment by the issue of a ticket'. A contract would only arise at the point that the carrier provides the passenger with a seat on the aeroplane — typically at check-in.

(2)   Stephen J considered the question purely in general terms. In his view the issue of a ticket constituted a contractual offer but not one which was immediately accepted so as to give rise to a contract. A contract would arise only when the passenger indicated acceptance by his conduct, 'for instance by immediately boarding the vehicle or . . . when a reasonable

---

[7]   (1975) 133 CLR 125.
[8]   In particular, the airline reserved the right at any time to abandon any flight or cancel any ticket — without any limitation on the circumstances in which the right might be exercised.

time has passed during which the passenger has had an opportunity of reading the conditions appearing on the ticket and has not then rejected the offer and demanded the return of his fare' (p 139): at least in the latter case acceptance is not immediate. Stephen J's view was based on an analysis of how the Courts have treated the problem of the incorporation of standard terms in the so-called 'ticket cases', which he believed compelled the conclusion that no contract could come into being until an opportunity to read the terms in question had been afforded.

(3)   Jacobs J by way of general analysis distinguished the existence of two separate contracts — the first 'an executory contract when the ticket was issued', made between the airline and the purchaser of the ticket (the airline being the offeror and the passenger the offeree); and the second the actual contract of carriage made when the passenger named in the ticket (who may or may not be the purchaser) presents it and embarks on the carriage. The ticket was thus not itself the agreement nor a memorandum of it. Jacobs J did, however, as an alternative endorse Barwick CJ's reasoning based on the particular terms of the ticket.

14.15   It does not therefore seem that either Stephen J or Jacobs J fully adopted the general analysis of Barwick CJ as to the effect of the issue of an airline ticket. But in any event it is submitted that to the extent that *MacRobertson Miller* decides or suggests that, even apart from any express exemptions, no contract arises at the moment of the delivery of the ticket, it is wrong[9]. The purchaser will, it is submitted, naturally regard the delivery of the ticket as the assumption of an obligation on the part of the carrier to carry the named passenger(s) on the flight specified, and he will have made payment in consideration of that obligation. He will expect, and need, to be able to arrange his affairs on the basis of that undertaking. It is inherently undesirable that the legal analysis should be at odds with the natural expectation of the parties. The 'known contingencies of airline operation' relied on by Barwick CJ may well justify the incorporation of terms qualifying what would otherwise be an absolute obligation to carry, but they do not justify the conclusion that there should be no contract at all, leaving the airline free to repudiate its apparent promise for whatever reason it chooses or none.

14.16   The alternative analysis adopted by Barwick CJ and Jacobs J based on the width of the exemptions employed by the carrier in the particular case is unlikely to have any relevance to any contracts of carriage that might

---

[9]   It was later distinguished by the High Court of Australia, in a case concerning carriage by sea, *Oceanic Sun Line Special Shipping Co Inc v Fay* (1988) 165 CLR 197, although the reasoning evades rather than confronts the difficulties — see per Wilson and Toohey JJ at pp 204–5 and per Brennan J at pp 226–7.

be considered in an English Court. It is true that the IATA Conditions of Contract (as to which see para **14.24** below), do purport to qualify any absolute obligation to carry the passenger at the times or by the routes identified in the ticket. But there is no equivalent in the IATA conditions (or, almost certainly, in any other standard conditions in use by domestic or international carriers operating in the UK) to the swingeing terms considered in *MacRobertson Miller*.

14.17   Thus far only the paradigm case identified in para **14.13** has been considered. But it is of course now very common for the sale of a seat to take place over the telephone, or on-line, or by exchange of faxes or email or even by exchange of correspondence, with immediate payment occurring by the giving of authority to debit a credit or charge card. In these cases a ticket (or other documentary confirmation) will not be delivered at the moment of agreement: it may be sent on by post or courier, or collection may be arranged at the airport of departure. It may of course be that one or other party makes clear at the moment of booking that no contract will arise until the ticket is sent or received. But in the absence of such express stipulation (which will in practice be rare), when is the contract formed? The point is not authoritatively settled. There are, broadly, two possibilities (assuming that the 'Barwick analysis' is wrong).

(1)   It may be argued that no contract comes into existence until the ticket is delivered[10]. The argument would be that the ordinary understanding of both carriers and passengers is that a ticket is the essential evidence of a right to be carried and thus they would not expect an obligation to arise until a ticket had been delivered. Some limited support could be gained for this argument from the provision of art 3(2) of the Convention to the effect that 'the passenger ticket shall constitute *prima facie* evidence of *the conclusion* and conditions of the contract of carriage': although the ticket could of course evidence a pre-existing contract, this provision does emphasise its special status under the Convention regime.

(2)   It is submitted, however, that plainly the better view is that the delivery of the ticket is not essential to the conclusion of a contract[11]. Once the essential terms have been agreed (typically: place of departure and destination, reserved flight(s) (if any), the price and any special conditions applicable to cancellation) then as a matter of ordinary contractual principles, a contract has been concluded — and a fortiori where the price is not only agreed but paid. The ticket is evidence of that contract, and will

---

[10]   Or indeed until the ticket had been retained by the purchaser for a sufficient time for his acceptance of the conditions to be inferred — cf the argument of Stephens J in *MacRobertson Miller*.

[11]   This appears to be the view also of John Balfour, who has given particular attention to this and related questions — see his article 'Electronic Ticketing: A Bonfire of Verbiage?' [1996–7] TAQ 89. See also Martin 'Phone in, Turn up, Take-off, A Look at the Legal Implications of Self-service Ticketing' [1995] 20 Air & Space Law 189.

normally be needed in order to procure a boarding pass; but its actual delivery need not be a condition of a contract being formed. A businessman who has paid for a ticket over the phone and arranged to pick it up at the airport of departure is not likely to accept that the airline remains free to change its mind and deny him his booking simply because he has not yet taken physical delivery of the ticket. In *Daly v General Steam Navigation Co. Ltd*[12] a booking for a cross-Channel ferry journey had been made and confirmed in writing, and a deposit paid, on the basis that a ticket would be issued subsequently. Brandon J held that it was wholly unrealistic to regard the confirmed booking as no more than a step in negotiations, under which the ferry company could have walked away at any time until it chose to issue the ticket (see at p 262)[13]. There is no distinction from the case of the reservation of a flight, with ticket to follow.

14.18   It follows from this analysis that in principle a passenger who books a seat — even if not yet issued with a ticket — but cancels or otherwise fails to travel on the flight reserved is in breach of contract. But there will in general be in place an express contractual regime governing the passenger's entitlement to the refund of any price paid — from full flexibility in the case of full-price tickets to conditional or partial refunds in the case of cheaper tickets. If there is no such regime, the ordinary common law rules as to the restitution of pre-payments to a party in breach will apply.

14.19   Of course a number of other variations will occur. But none of them should affect the fundamental analysis of when the contract is formed. Specifically:
(1)   The purchase may be effected through a travel agent. But the travel agent is (in this respect) simply an agent for the airline. Once the passenger has been told that he has been booked on a flight (which will in practice only occur once the agent has communicated with the carrier by computer or telephone), the reasonable understanding is that a binding obligation has been assumed — whether or not at that point an actual ticket is issued (which will depend on whether the agent has the ability to issue tickets itself).
(2)   In cases of telephone or on-line booking, the analysis is even clearer. Payment will almost certainly be effected by credit card at the point of booking. Even if the purchaser is told, as is routine, that a written 'confirmation' will follow, that would not prevent a contract arising.
(3)   In the case of an 'open' ticket, ie one where no specific flight is reserved,

---

[12] [1979] 1 Lloyd's Rep 257.
[13] Brandon J was following the decision of Michael Ogden QC in *Hollingworth v Southern Ferries Ltd* [1977] 2 Lloyd's Rep 70 and declining to follow the earlier decision in *Cockerton v Naviera Aznar SA* [1960] 2 Lloyd's Rep 450. His approach was in turn followed by the High Court of Australia in *Oceanic Sun Line* above (1988) 165 CLR 197. See also *Dillon v Baltic Shipping Co* [1991] 2 Lloyd's Rep 155 (Supreme Court of New South Wales).

the carrier's obligation is only to carry the passenger on the route identified, for the agreed price, on the flight of his choice — *subject to
availability*. That is obviously a less specific obligation than that where a
particular flight is identified; nevertheless, it is a perfectly effective contract and there is no reason why it should be dependent on the issue of
a ticket.

Parties

14.20

Rule **49—The identities of the parties to the contract of carriage will
depend on the ordinary principles of the law of contract; but a passenger who is not a party to the contract will generally be entitled by
statute to enforce its terms.**

14.21   The Carrier.   In the ordinary case of carriage by scheduled flight the
carrier, in the sense of the party contracting to perform the carriage, will (subject to the points made below) be the airline by whom the flight is operated,
whose identity will be shown on the ticket. There are, however, four situations which require special mention.
(1)   The carrier will, as set out above, very often contract through an agent.
       The ordinary principles of agency apply. The agent will normally have
       actual authority for any contract which it may purport to enter on the
       carrier's behalf. Where it does not, the question will be whether it has
       ostensible authority. That question cannot be answered in the abstract:
       it will depend on the facts of the particular case whether a holding out
       by the carrier, and reliance by the purchaser, can be established.
(2)   A ticket may be purchased for a journey with more than one leg, where
       carriage on the different legs is performed by different carriers. In such
       a case condition 5 of the IATA Conditions of Contract (considered
       below) provides that:

> 'An air carrier issuing a ticket for carriage over the lines of another
> air carrier does so only as its Agent.'

There is no reason to doubt the effectiveness of that provision where the
IATA Conditions are incorporated (as to which, see below); and even
where they are not it would no doubt be taken as best evidence of the
basis on which airlines act in such cases — absent any reason to suppose
a different result was intended in the particular case. Thus the purchaser will in such a case be contracting with two or more carriers in
respect of the journey covered by the ticket.
(3)   Quite apart from the question of a multi-leg journey, the identified car-
       rier may not be the actual operator of the flight booked. This may occur
       if it has entered into a code-sharing arrangement with another airline.
       The existence of such an arrangement should not of itself affect the con-
       tractual position. The obligation to carry is undertaken by the airline
       with whom (or with whose agent) the purchaser has dealt as principal;

and the fact that it has arranged for the carriage to be performed by another airline is immaterial[14]. This is almost certainly so even where the fact of code-sharing is disclosed to the purchaser at the time of booking, though there might be room for argument in such a case, depending on the precise facts, that the actual operator was a party to the contract alongside or instead of the airline issuing the ticket.

(4)   In the case of charter flights the charterer may be the contractual carrier.

14.22   The Passenger.   In the paradigm case the person whom the carrier contracts to carry is the other party to the contract of carriage. But in many instances this will not be the case — as where an employer buys a ticket for his employee or the head of a family for other family members. In such cases the passenger will not be in any contractual relationship with the carrier. This should rarely give rise to any problem in practice, since the passenger will enjoy under the Convention all rights necessary to protect his principal interests. But occasionally a 'non-party passenger' may be denied a right for which the purchaser of the ticket contracted — most obviously in the case of denied boarding (see below). In such a case the passenger identified at the moment of booking will in all ordinary circumstances be entitled to enforce the contract under the Contracts (Rights of Third Parties) Act 1999: he will be a person on whom the contract purports to confer a benefit within the meaning of s 1 (1) (b)[15]. This appears to be recognised in the terminology of art 1 of the IATA Conditions of Carriage, where 'you' is defined as 'any person . . . carried or to be carried . . . pursuant to a Ticket'. At common law, there would seem to be no reason why a passenger's rights to be carried should not be assignable; but in practice transfer of tickets is likely to be prohibited by the carrier's standard terms: see para **14.52** below.

Incorporation of standard conditions

14.23

Rᴜʟᴇ 50—**The following rules will determine the incorporation of the carrier's standard terms into the contract of carriage (apart from those fully set out in a contractual document):**

---

[14]   IATA airlines have now undertaken to disclose the existence of any code-sharing arrangements at the time of reservation: see Conditions of Carriage art 2.3. It is a nice point whether, absent such express disclosure, the fact of carriage by another carrier represents a breach by the contracting airline. The starting-point is that while in ordinary circumstances the passenger may expect that carriage will be performed by the airline with which he has contracted, the identity of the actual operator is not a contractual stipulation: the observations of Goddard J in *Fosbroke-Hobbs v Airwork Ltd* [1937] 1 All ER 108 at p 111 E–F, probably still represent the law. But there may be cases where the purchaser has made it plain that the identity of the operator is important to him.

[15]   The coming into force of the Act should make it unnecessary to resort to the doubtful line of authority initiated by the Court of Appeal in *Jackson v Horizon Holidays Ltd* [1975] 1 WLR 1468, as explained by the House of Lords in *Woodar Investment Development Ltd v Wimpey Construction UK Ltd* [1980] 1 WLR 277.

(1)   **Where there is express reference to such terms in a ticket or other contractual document (or in any on-line booking procedure), the passenger will be bound by any conditions of the kind which might reasonably be expected to apply to a contract of the type in question.**

(2)   **In the absence of such reference at the time of contract, any standard terms contained in or references by the document will only be incorporated if the purchaser can be taken to have notice of them by some other means. A modern court is likely to regard a purchaser as fixed with knowledge of standard terms provided that they were of a kind which might reasonably be expected to apply to a contract of the type in question.**

14.24   In all but the most exceptional case the ticket, or other documentation issued to the passenger, will incorporate, or purport to incorporate, the carrier's standard terms. The principal standard conditions so referred to will generally (but not always — see below) comprise:

(a)   the Conditions of Contract which IATA requires its members to print on all tickets ('the IATA Conditions of Contract') — these are 'short-form' conditions which set out a limited number of particular terms but also purport to incorporate by reference the carrier's full general conditions of carriage[16], being (normally):

(b)   the General Conditions of Carriage (Passenger and Baggage) recommended by IATA, by way of a formal Recommended Practice, for use by its members ('the IATA Conditions of Carriage') — the use of these is *not* compulsory on IATA members, but most members do in fact employ them, subject in some cases to a degree of adaptation, and seek to incorporate them by reference on the ticket.

The Conditions of Contract and the Conditions of Carriage are referred to collectively in this chapter as 'the IATA Conditions'.

14.25   The IATA Conditions of Carriage have very recently been the subject of a major overhaul as a result of pressure from the UK Office of Fair Trading. The revised Recommended Practice 1724 was adopted by the IATA Passenger Services Conference in August 2000, subject to receipt of various governmental approvals[17]. It is outside the scope of this work to provide a full

---

[16]   See Condition 3 (iii) of the IATA Conditions of Contract. Article 3.1.1 of the Conditions of Carriage refers to the Conditions of Contract as being 'a summary of some of the provisions of these Conditions of Carriage'.

[17]   The necessary approvals are expected to have been obtained, and RP 1724 thus to be in force, by the date of publication of this book. That does not automatically mean that they will be incorporated into individual contracts with immediate effect, and it will be up to individual airlines to amend their documentation. But for practical purposes the majority of airlines will almost certainly now be dealing on the basis of the new Conditions, and this book proceeds on that basis.

commentary on the IATA Conditions; but since in most cases the parties' rights and obligations will be defined by reference to them they are referred to at some points below.

14.26   The main cases in which the IATA Conditions may not be incorporated are as follows:
(a)   A significant minority of carriers (particularly charter airlines) are not members of IATA and so are not subject to either the requirement to employ the Conditions of Contract or the recommendation to employ the Conditions of Carriage. There is of course nothing to stop such carriers employing them as a matter of choice, either wholesale, or subject to modification, and many, but not all, do so.
(b)   The IATA Conditions of Carriage do not apply to flights to from or via the US or Canada. This does *not* affect the Conditions of Contract.

14.27   Some carriers will have additional standard rules or regulations, over and above the IATA Conditions, which are arguably incorporated in the contract[18]; these are generally concerned with matters of detail but may sometimes be of significance.

14.28   It cannot however be taken for granted in every case that the purported incorporation of standard conditions via the ticket or other purportedly contractual documentation will be effective. On the analysis given above, in many situations a contract will have been formed before any ticket or other such document is received by the passenger[19]. The applicable principles will be those set out in the numerous 'ticket cases', which are mostly concerned with carriage by rail or by ship — there are no reported English cases dealing expressly with the incorporation of standard conditions in contracts for carriage by air. Not all the cases can easily be reconciled, but the broad position can be summarised as follows:
(1)   Where at the moment of contract the purchaser is given a ticket (or other document confirming his booking) he will be bound by any conditions of the kind which might reasonably be expected to apply to a contract of the type in question. This is because a ticket is plainly a contractual document and would reasonably be expected to contain, or contain reference to, standard-form contractual terms. The purchaser has, at least notionally, the opportunity to inspect any conditions printed on (or

---

[18]   Condition 3 (iii) of the Conditions of Contract purports to incorporate 'carrier's conditions of carriage *and related regulations*': these are also referred to in art 2.5 of the Conditions of Carriage, which makes clear that in the event of any inconsistency the Conditions prevail, and in art 17. But only a limited number of carriers have published 'regulations' to which these words might apply.
[19]   Article 3 (2) of the Convention provides that the ticket shall constitute prima facie evidence of the conditions of the contract. However, the words 'prima facie' (in French 'jusqu'à preuve du contraire') mean that it remains open to a purchaser or passenger to seek to show that the contract was in fact in different terms.

referred to in) the ticket before indicating his definitive acceptance. Thus in the paradigm case considered in para **14.13** above there should be no difficulty about incorporation. The same result is achievable in the case of a well-designed on-line booking service, which ensures that the purchaser has explicitly to acknowledge acceptance of the airline's standard conditions before the purchase is complete — and has the opportunity to access them[20].

(2)   Where, however, the contract is made in advance of the delivery of a ticket or other contractual document, or, in the case of an on-line booking, without any explicit acceptance of standard terms being obtained, any standard terms contained or referred to in the ticket will only be incorporated to the extent that the purchaser has had notice of them by some other means. This may or not be the case. One such means would be course of dealing — ie in the present context, where the purchaser had flown with that carrier before and had accordingly seen from the ticket that standard conditions of carriage applied. But even in the unusual case of a purchaser who had never flown before it is submitted that a modern Court should take the view that it was sufficiently obvious that any contract of carriage would incorporate standard terms and that the purchaser should be treated as fixed with notice of them[21].

(3)   Incorporation by either of the routes discussed above will not apply where the clause in question is particularly onerous or unusual.

14.29   Generally, the strict approach to incorporation adopted by some Courts in the past, often in cases involving unreasonable exclusions or limitations of liability, is less likely to be followed in modern conditions. Standard conditions are a commercial necessity, and their wholesale exclusion would lead to real difficulty. The potential unfairness of some standard terms is nowadays addressed not by adopting artificial rules to restrict incorporation but by means of legislation of the type considered in the following paragraphs. The truth is that the ordinary reasonable purchaser buying an airline ticket in modern conditions, whatever the precise sequence of events, can fairly be taken to appreciate that the offer of carriage is made on the basis that the carrier's standard conditions should apply — provided that they are of a kind which might reasonably be expected and subject to the various statutory protections in place. The fact that the IATA Conditions have now been modified in response to regulatory pressure will probably further incline the Courts to wish to find them incorporated.

---

[20]   This is the procedure followed by, for example, British Airways.
[21]   Again, a similar view is (tentatively) expressed by Balfour, loc cit. He expresses concern about the effect of the decision of the House of Lords in *McCutcheon v David MacBrayne Ltd*. [1964] 1 WLR 125; but that case turned on its particular facts.

Regulation of contract terms

14.30

Rᴜʟᴇ 51—**Contracts for carriage of passengers by air will generally fall within the terms of the Unfair Contract Terms Act 1977 and will fall within the terms of the Unfair Terms in Consumer Contracts Regulations 1999 if the purchaser was acting as a consumer (but in neither case so as to affect the provisions of the Warsaw Convention regime).**

14.31   In English law (apart, of course, from the Convention) there are two pieces of legislation which may restrict the effectiveness of the contractual terms applying to a contract of carriage by air.

(1)   The Unfair Contract Terms Act 1977

14.32   The Unfair Contract Terms Act applies as between contracting parties:
(a)   where one of them 'deals as consumer', ie is not himself acting in the course of a business while the other party is; or
(b)   the contract is made on one of the parties' standard terms — a phrase which is not defined in the Act but as to which no issue is likely to arise in cases of contracts for carriage by air[22].

14.33   The purchaser of a passenger ticket may or may not be a consumer within the meaning of the Act, depending on whether he is buying the ticket in the course of a business. But since virtually all carriage by air will take place on the carrier's standard terms s 3 will apply to virtually all contracts for carriage by air.

14.34   The effect of s 3 is that the party whose standard terms are incorporated cannot rely on any term of the contract to exclude or restrict any liability for a breach on his part or claim to be entitled to render a contractual performance substantially different from that which was reasonably expected of him, or render no performance at all, unless the 'requirement of reasonableness' is satisfied. That requirement is that 'the term shall have been a fair and reasonable one to be included having regard to the circumstances which were, or ought to have been, known to or in the contemplation of the parties when the contract is made' (s 11). It is outside the scope of this work to discuss the effect of this provision in general.

14.35   Section 29 provides that nothing in the Act shall prevent a party relying on provisions required or authorised by statute or made in

---

[22]   See s 3.

compliance with an international convention. This provision prevents the Act biting on the limitations of liability under the Warsaw Convention; but it has no application to standard terms of the type considered in this chapter, since an IATA resolution does not have the force of an international convention.

(2)   Unfair Terms in Consumer Contracts Regulations 1999

14.36   The Unfair Terms in Consumer Contracts Regulations 1999[23] are intended to give effect in domestic law to Council Directive 93/13 on Unfair Terms in Consumer Contracts ('the 1993 Directive'). The Regulations apply to terms which have not been 'individually negotiated' in contracts concluded between a seller or supplier and a consumer. Regulation 5 contains various detailed provisions glossing the concept of 'individual negotiation'. Regulation 3 (1) defines a consumer as 'any natural person who, in making contracts covered by [the Regulations], is acting for purposes which are outside his trade, business or profession'. As with the 1977 Act, purchasers of passenger tickets may or may not be consumers for the purpose of the Regulations.

14.37   It will be seen that there is a considerable overlap between the application of the 1999 Regulations and the 1977 Act, but the latter has the wider application since if standard terms are employed it is unnecessary to consider whether the purchaser is a consumer.

14.38   Where the Regulations apply, the principal consequence is that any unfair term in the contract 'shall not be binding on the consumer' (reg 5). A term is unfair:

> 'if, contrary to the requirement of good faith, it causes a significant imbalance in the parties' rights and obligations arising under the contract, to the detriment of the consumer.'

Regulation 4 gives further guidance on how the test of unfairness is to be applied. Regulation 6 (2) excludes from the effect of regulation 5 any term defining the main subject matter of the contract and the adequacy of the price.

14.39   The other substantive provision of the Regulations is that a seller or supplier is obliged to ensure that any written term 'is expressed in plain, intelligible language': if there is doubt about the meaning of a written term the interpretation most favourable to the consumer is to prevail (reg 7).

---

[23] The 1999 Regulations (SI 1999/2083) replace the Unfair Contract Terms in Consumer Contracts Regulations 1994 (SI 1994/3159). The 1994 Regulations were thought not sufficiently to reflect the requirements of the 1993 Directive. The differences in wording are significant, and there are more extensive enforcement procedures; but the overall effect is broadly the same.

14.40   The Regulations do not apply to contractual terms which reflect the provisions or principles of international conventions. The intention of this provision is to exclude the application of the regulations to terms in the Warsaw Convention[24]. As with s 29 of the 1977 Act (see above), this provision has no application to the standard terms of the type considered in this chapter, since an IATA resolution does not have the force of an international convention.

14.41   Following an inconclusive review by the European Commission in 1997/8 the UK Office of Fair Trading in June 1999 initiated action under enforcement powers in the 1994 Regulations raising questions as to the fairness of a wide range of the IATA Conditions[25]. This led to the adoption of the revised IATA Conditions of Carriage referred to in para **14.25** above. The Office of Fair Trading has, in cautious terms, pronounced itself satisfied with the changes made[26]; and, while that does not preclude challenge by individual passengers under either the 1977 Act or the 1999 Regulations, it seems unlikely that any challenge to the fairness of the revised IATA Conditions of Carriage would succeed. Conversely, any other forms of standard condition are likely to be highly vulnerable to such challenge to the extent that they give passengers less protection than the IATA Conditions.

Substantive Terms: Passengers

14.42   It is not within the scope of this chapter to give a complete review of the 'non-Convention' contractual rights and obligations of carrier and passenger, which will inevitably depend on the standard terms and conditions of the carrier in question. But it may be useful to review briefly how the IATA Conditions — which should apply in at least the majority of cases — deal with some of the carrier's and passenger's principal rights and obligations.

The carrier's obligation to carry

14.43

Rᴜʟᴇ 52—**The extent of the carrier's obligations, including the circumstances in which it is entitled to refuse to carry the passenger, will be defined by the terms of the contract, subject to the provisions of the Unfair Contract Terms Act 1977 and the Unfair Terms in Consumer Contracts Regulations 1999.**

---

[24]   See art 1 (2) of the 1993 Directive.
[25]   The impact of the 1994 Regulations (as they then were) on the old IATA Conditions was reviewed in Grant 'The Unfair Terms in Contract Regulations and the IATA General Conditions of Carriage — A United Kingdom Consumer's Perspective' [1998] JBL 123.
[26]   See press release dated 14 September 2000.

Refusal to carry

14.44   The primary obligation of a carrier under a contract of carriage must be to allow the passenger and his baggage to board the flight for which he has made a reservation (or, in the case of an open ticket, a flight for which there is availability within the terms of the ticket). If, once the passenger has been admitted, there is a delay or the passenger suffers injury or loss, his rights are governed by the Convention. But where the carrier refuses to carry the passenger at all, or rejects his baggage, the Convention has no application; and the passenger has a prima facie claim for breach of contract (as well as, in an appropriate case, 'denied boarding compensation' — see para **14.49** below). However, that right is qualified by the IATA Conditions of Carriage in a number of respects.

14.45   First, the obligation to carry is conditional on the passenger (a) presenting himself by the check-in deadline (art 6.1); (b) tendering a valid ticket — see art 3.1.6[27]; and (c) presenting himself at the boarding gate by the time advised to him at check-in (art 6.3).

14.46   Secondly, art 7 of the IATA Conditions of Carriage gives carriers the right to refuse carriage in a number of specified circumstances, including legal compulsion, risk to other passengers, previous misconduct and refusal to submit to a security check. There is no express provision in such a case for a refund, and whether one is due will depend on the general law relating to deposits and pre-payments. In addition carriers are given a general discretion, to be exercised reasonably, to give notice to a particular passenger that he will not be carried in future — ie in respect of carriage to which he would otherwise be entitled under a ticket issued to him. In such a case he will be entitled to a refund. No indication is given of the likely grounds for such a notice, but no doubt it is aimed principally at passengers who have misconducted themselves on an earlier flight. Article 8 specifies a number of grounds on which baggage may be refused. Article 8.6.3 also gives a wide discretion to the carrier to carry checked baggage on another flight 'for safety, security or operational reasons'.

14.47   Thirdly, art 9.1 gives the carrier an apparently unfettered right to change the times of scheduled flights after the issue of a ticket with a confirmed reservation. The only obligations which it accepts are (a) to endeavour to notify the passenger of the change (if it has contact details); and (b) to give a refund if it is unable to book the passenger on an alternative flight acceptable to him.

14.48   Fourthly, in the case of non-Convention cancellations, delays etc (ie

---

[27] However the carrier will, on certain conditions, issue a new ticket to replace one that is lost or mutilated 'provided there is evidence, readily ascertainable at the time, that a ticket valid for the flight(s) in question was duly issued' and provided the passenger gives an indemnity (art 3.1.7 (a)).

occurring before the carriage has commenced), art 9.2 gives the passenger the choice of (a) carriage at the earliest opportunity on another flight operated by the carrier; (b) carriage by another route or on the services of another carrier, at no extra cost; or (c) a refund. These are exclusive remedies.

14.49   Overbooking.   Most airlines overbook, in order to cover the likelihood of 'no-shows'[28]. Almost all will offer 'denied boarding compensation' to passengers who, as a result, cannot be carried on the flight for which they are booked. Since 1991 the EU has prescribed minimum rules for denied boarding compensation where there has been overbooking in the case of any flight departing from a member state (Council Regulation 295/91). It is open to carriers to incorporate those, or other more generous, rules in their standard conditions; but the passengers will be entitled to the minimum rights in any event[29].

Some other conditions

14.50   Fares.   The fare will almost invariably have been agreed at the date of contract and will most commonly have been paid on that date. But in the unusual case where payment is deferred art 4.1 of the IATA Standard Conditions provides that the fare will be calculated in accordance with the carrier's tariff as at the date of payment.

14.51   Changes/refunds.   Whether flights can be changed or tickets cancelled and the passenger refunded (in whole or in part) depends on the conditions agreed at the time that the contract was made. There are a wide variety of fares, with different conditions as to changes and refunds attached, and the passenger will generally be bound by what was agreed at the time of booking. However, in the case of a non-refundable ticket a passenger who is prevented from travelling by *force majeure* is entitled to a credit for travel with that carrier to the value of the non-refundable amount (art 3.1.4). *Force majeure* is defined (see art 1) as 'unusual and unforeseeable circumstances beyond [the passenger's] control, the consequences of which could not have been avoided even if all due care had been exercised'[30].

14.52   Transferability.   Article 3.1.1 of the IATA Conditions of Carriage provides that carriage will only be provided to the passenger named on the ticket; and art 3.1.2 provides that tickets are not transferable. However, the

---

[28]   The policy of overbooking was the subject of the decision of the House of Lords in *British Airways Board v Taylor* [1976] 1 WLR 13; but the appeal concerned a prosecution under the Trade Descriptions Act, and the speeches contain nothing of direct relevance on the contractual analysis.

[29]   Article 9.2.4 of the IATA Standard Conditions of Carriage is simply a blanket provision referring to the particular airline's policy and any requirements of the applicable law.

[30]   The definition is taken from the Package Travel Regulations.

Package Travel Regulations entitle a passenger who is prevented from travelling by *force majeure* to transfer his right to a third party. And a credit granted under art 3.1.4 of the IATA Conditions of Carriage may be used to buy travel for someone other than the original passenger.

14.53   Validity of ticket.   In the case of an open ticket, art 3.2 provides for a period of validity of one year from date of issue or date of first travel under the ticket (if itself occurring within the first year). However, there are provisions for extension or refund in the event of failure to travel as a result of illness.

14.54   Refunds.   Article 10 prescribes the refund regime, both in cases where the carrier has failed to carry and in cases where the passenger wishes to cancel.

14.55   Misconduct by the passenger.   Article 11 deals with misconduct by the passenger.

Cargo

14.56   In general terms most air cargo is consigned through freight forwarders/forwarding agents. Forwarders may act as true agents, leaving the carrier as the principal, or they may themselves contract to carry the goods as principals. Deciding which is the position in a given case may not be straightforward. It is in no way decisive that the forwarder may describe itself as an agent or otherwise use the language of agency. The capacity in which the forwarder acts can only be decided on a detailed review of the documents in the light of the overall commercial context and the dealings between the parties.

14.57   The contracting carrier of goods consigned by air, whether contracting with the actual consignor (directly or through a forwarder acting as agent) or with a forwarder as principal, will typically contract on its standard terms for the carriage of cargo as set out, or referred to, in the air waybill. Article 11 of the Warsaw Convention provides that the air waybill provides prima facie evidence of the terms of the contract of carriage, and in practice issues as to incorporation are far less likely to arise than in the case of passenger carriage; when they do they will fall to be determined according to ordinary contractual principles[31].

14.58   The contractual position is of course in most important respects overlain by the Convention regime discussed elsewhere. As regards those

---

[31] It should be noted that it is not uncommon for a forwarder to seek to incorporate by reference in its own terms the applicable terms of the carrier by whom the goods are in the event to be carried or to limit its liability so that it is co-extensive with that of the carrier.

aspects which the Convention does not affect, it is not possible to undertake any general analysis. IATA has adopted Conditions of Contract for the carriage of cargo, which its members are required to set out on all air waybills: these deal with a limited number of matters. It has not, as in the case of passengers, adopted any wider-ranging recommended Conditions of Carriage. These remain a matter for individual carriers. It is fair to say, however, that many airlines' standard terms for the carriage of cargo do have a strong family resemblance by being derived more or less closely from draft standard terms which IATA sought, ultimately unsuccessfully, to introduce in the mid-1950s.

14.59   Airlines' standard conditions of cargo are in principle subject to the provisions of the Unfair Contract Terms Act 1977 and the Unfair Terms in Consumer Contracts Regulations 1999, discussed in paras **14.30–14.41** above. It will be fairly rare for a consumer to consign goods by air, so that the 1999 Regulations will have a more limited application than the 1977 Act (which, as noted, operates even where both parties are dealing in the course of a business, provided that the contract is on one party's standard terms).

Conflict of Laws

Jurisdiction

14.60

Rule 53—Where the Convention does not govern, the English courts will apply their ordinary rules of jurisdiction, namely:

(1)   Where the defendant is domiciled in a country which is a signatory to the Brussels or Lugano Convention, a person wishing to pursue a contractual claim against the defendant can do so:
  (i)   in the defendant's country of domicile; or
  (ii)   in the courts for the place of performance of the obligation in question; or
  (iii)   where the claim arises out of the operations of a branch, agency or other establishment, in the courts of the state where that branch, agency or other establishment is situated.
(2)   Where the defendant is domiciled in a non-contracting state, the English courts will have jurisdiction if the defendant is present in the jurisdiction. For a company, this means incorporated in England or with a registered office in England or carrying on business within the jurisdiction.

14.61   Claims within the scope of the Convention are of course governed by the provisions of the Convention as to forum[32]. In the case of other claims

---

[32] See para **11.17**.

an English Court would apply its ordinary rules as to jurisdiction, which can be briefly summarised as follows.

14.62   Where the defendant, typically the carrier, is domiciled in a country which is a signatory to the Brussels or Lugano Convention, the relevant rules will be those under the Convention in question (applied by the Civil Jurisdiction and Judgments Act 1982, as amended). The basic rule is that a person wishing to pursue a contractual claim against a person domiciled in a Convention state will have to do so in that state[33]. That course will frequently be unattractive to a party wishing to proceed against a carrier. However, he can also sue:

(a)   *In the courts for the place of performance of the obligation in question*[34]. It is necessary to identify the particular obligation giving rise to the dispute. In a case of failure to carry, it is not at all clear how this provision would apply: what, for example, is the 'place of performance' of an obligation to carry passengers or goods from one country to another? The question is not easy: the Convention appears to envisage that there will be a single 'place of performance'[35], which is particularly hard to reconcile with a transaction whose purpose is to transport goods or persons from one place to another. However, it is submitted that the place of performance is to be treated as the destination country. It is the 'delivery' of the passenger (or goods) which appears to be the essence of the obligation.

(b)   *Where the claim can be said to 'aris[e] out of the operations of a branch, agency or other establishment' of another state, in the courts of the state where that branch, agency or establishment is situated*[36]. 'Operations' would appear to cover ticket sales. An office maintained by a carrier would plainly be a 'branch' within the meaning of the article. The application of the term 'agency' is less clear. It is submitted that it would cover the situation where an airline has appointed a general sales agent in a particular country who makes sales direct to the public — certainly where (as commonly occurs) the agent promotes itself as the office of the airline; but not an ordinary travel agent.

14.63   It should be noted that the provisions of the Brussels and Lugano Conventions permitting consumers to sue in their own country of domicile do not apply to 'contracts of transport'[37].

14.64   The position where the Convention does not apply is less restrictive.

---

[33] See art 2 of the Brussels and Lugano Conventions.
[34] See art 5(1) of the Brussels and Lugano Conventions.
[35] See the observation in the Jenard Report that 'the Committee considered that it would be unwise to give jurisdiction to a number of Courts' (Commentary on art 5 and 6, under the head 'Forum Contractus').
[36] See art 5(5) of the Brussels and Lugano Conventions.
[37] See art 13 of the Brussels and Lugano Conventions.

The English Courts will have jurisdiction where the defendant is present within the jurisdiction. In the case of a company that means (in effect) if it is incorporated in England or has a registered office or carries on business within the jurisdiction. It is irrelevant whether the contract was made through that office. And even where the defendant is not present within the jurisdiction, permission to serve out of the jurisdiction may be sought under Civil Procedure Rule 6.20.

Proper law

14.65

RULE 54—**Where the Convention does not govern, the English courts will apply their ordinary rules as to proper law, namely:**

(1) **Where there is an express choice of law clause by the parties, that law will apply;**

(2) **Otherwise, the contract will be governed by law of the country with which it is most closely connected:**

    (i) **In the case of carriage of goods, the country where the carrier has its principal place of business if it is also the country for the loading or discharge is to take place or the principal place of business of the consignor;**

    (ii) **In other cases, the country in which the carriage is to commence.**

14.66 Again, the question of proper law will be irrelevant where the carriage falls within the Warsaw Convention regime. But in those cases where it is relevant, it is governed by the Rome Convention (as applied by the Contracts (Applicable Law) Act 1990). In the absence of any express choice of law by the parties (and the IATA Conditions provide for none), the contract is to be governed by the law of the country with which it is most closely connected: art 4 (1). In the case of the carriage of goods, if the country where, at the time that the contract is made, the carrier has its principal place of business is also the country in which loading or discharge is to take place or the consignor has *its* principal place of business, that is presumed to be the country with which the contract is most closely connected. In other cases, the Convention gives no guidance, and there is as yet no authority; but it is submitted that in the usual case the closest connection will be with the country in which the carriage is to commence[38]. Even if this is not where the contract is made, which it will most often be, the place of embarkation is where passenger and carrier are likely to have the most significant dealings.

---

[38] This was the tentative view of Dicey & Morris under the broadly equivalent common-law test: *The Conflict of Laws* (11th edn, p 1270). Clearly there may be exceptional cases which might point to a different conclusion; but the Courts are likely to favour development of a straightforward rule.

Appendix 1a

Carriage by Air Act 1961

(1961 c 27)

An Act to give effect to the Convention concerning international carriage by air known as "the Warsaw Convention as amended at The Hague, 1955", to enable the rules contained in that Convention to be applied, with or without modification, in other cases and, in particular, to non-international carriage by air; and for connected purposes

[22nd June 1961]

1. Convention to have the force of law.   [(1) Subject to this section:

(a)   the provisions of the Convention known as "the Warsaw Convention as amended at The Hague, 1955" as set out in Schedule 1 to this Act ("the Convention"); and

(b)   the provisions of that Convention as further amended by Protocol No 4 of Montreal, 1975 and as set out in Schedule 1A to this Act ("the Convention as amended"),

shall, so far as they relate to the rights and liabilities of carriers, carriers' servants and agents, passengers, consignors, consignees and other persons, and subject to the provisions of this Act, have the force of law in the United Kingdom in relation to any carriage by air to which they apply, irrespective of the nationality of the aircraft performing that carriage.

(2)   In relation to Community air carriers:

(a)   in respect of damages up to the equivalent in euros of 100,000 Special Drawing Rights arising from the death, wounding or other bodily injury suffered by a passenger, the provisions of Article 20 of the Convention or the Convention as amended; and

(b)   in respect of damages arising from the death, wounding or other bodily injury suffered by a passenger, the provisions of Articles 21 and 22(1) of that Convention,

do not have the force of law in the United Kingdom.

(3)   If there is any inconsistency between the text in English in Part I of Schedule 1 or 1A to this Act and the text in French in Part II of that Schedule, the French text shall prevail.".

(3)   In section 2(1):

    (a)   after the words "High Contracting Parties to the Convention" there shall be inserted the words "or the Convention as amended"; and

    (b)   for the words "the Convention as set out in the First Schedule" there shall be substituted the words "that Convention as set out in Schedule 1 or 1A".

(4)   In sections 2(2), 3, 4(1), 4A(2), 5(2), 6, 7(2), 10(1) and 11(b) for the words "the First Schedule" there shall be substituted the words "Schedule 1 or 1A".

(5)   In sections 5(1) and (2) and 10(1) after the words "the Convention" there shall be inserted the words "or the Convention as amended".

(6)   After Schedule 1 there shall be inserted, as Schedule 1A, the provisions set out in the Schedule to this Order.]

Notes   Substituted by SI 1999/1312, art 2(1), (2). Date in force: 21 May 1999 (except in relation to rights and liabilities arising out of an occurrence which took place before that date): see SI 1999/1312, art 1.

---

2. Designation of High Contracting Parties.   (1) Her Majesty may by Order in Council from time to time certify who are [, either generally or in respect of specified matters,] the High Contracting Parties to the Convention [or the Convention as amended], in respect of what territories they are respectively parties and to what extent they have availed themselves of the provisions of the Additional Protocol at the end of [that Convention as set out in Schedule 1 or 1A] to this Act.

(2)   Paragraph (2) of Article 40A in [Schedule 1 or 1A] to this Act shall not be read as extending references in that Schedule to the territory of a High Contracting Party (except such as are references to the territory of any State, whether a High Contracting Party or not) to include any territory in respect of which that High Contracting Party is not a party.

(3)   An Order in Council under this section shall, except so far as it has been superseded by a subsequent Order, be conclusive evidence of the matters so certified.

(4)   An Order in Council under this section may contain such transitional and other consequential provisions as appear to Her Majesty to be expedient.

Notes   Sub-s (1): words ', either generally or in respect of specified matters,' in square brackets prospectively inserted by the Carriage by Air and Road Act 1979, s 1(2), Sch 2, para 2, as from a day to be appointed.

    Sub-s (1): words 'or the Convention as amended' in square brackets inserted by SI 1999/1312, art 2(1), (3)(a). Date in force: 21 May 1999 (except in relation to rights and liabilities arising out of an occurrence which took place before that date): see SI 1999/1312, art 1.

    Sub-s (1): words 'that Convention as set out in Schedule 1 or 1A' in square brackets substituted by SI 1999/1312, art 2(1), (3)(b). Date in force: 21 May 1999 (except in relation to rights and liabilities arising out of an occurrence which took place before that date): see SI 1999/1312, art 1.

    Sub-s (2): words 'Schedule 1 or 1A' in square brackets substituted by SI 1999/1312, art 2(1), (4). Date in force: 21 May 1999 (except in relation to rights and liabilities arising out of an occurrence which took place before that date): see SI 1999/1312, art 1.

---

3. Fatal Accidents.   References in section one of the Fatal Accidents Act 1846, as it applies in England and Wales, and [in Article 3(1) of the Fatal Accidents (Northern Ireland) Order 1977], to a wrongful act, neglect or default shall include references to any occurrence which gives rise to a liability under *Article 17* [Article 17(1)] in [Schedule 1 or 1A] to this Act.

Notes   Words 'in Article 3(1) of the Fatal Accidents (Northern Ireland) Order 1977' in square brackets substituted by the Fatal Accidents (Northern Ireland) Order 1977, SI 1977/1251, art 8, Sch 1.

Words 'Article 17' in italics prospectively repealed and subsequent words in square brackets prospectively substituted by the Carriage by Air and Road Act 1979, s 1(2), Sch 2, para 3, as from a day to be appointed.

Words 'Schedule 1 or 1A' in square brackets substituted by SI 1999/1312, art 2(1), (4). Date in force: 21 May 1999 (except in relation to rights and liabilities arising out of an occurrence which took place before that date): see SI 1999/1312, art 1.

---

4. Limitation of liability.   (1) It is hereby declared that the limitations on liability in Article 22 [and Article 22A] in [Schedule 1 or 1A] to this Act apply whatever the nature of the proceedings by which liability may be enforced and that, in particular:

(a)   . . .

(b)   the limitation for each passenger in *paragraph (1)* [paragraph 1(a)] of the said Article 22 applies to the aggregate liability of the carrier in all proceedings which may be brought against him under the law of any part of the United Kingdom, together with any proceedings brought against him outside the United Kingdom.

(2)   A court before which proceedings are brought to enforce a liability which is limited by the said Article 22 [or Article 22A] may at any stage of the proceedings make any such order as appears to the court to be just and equitable in view of the provisions of the said Article 22 [or Article 22A], and of any other proceedings which have been, or are likely to be, commenced in the United Kingdom or elsewhere to enforce the liability in whole or in part.

(3)   Without prejudice to the last foregoing subsection, a court before which proceedings are brought to enforce a liability which is limited by the said Article 22 [or Article 22A] shall, where the liability is, or may be, partly enforceable in other proceedings in the United Kingdom or elsewhere, have jurisdiction to award an amount less than the court would have awarded if the limitation applied solely to the proceedings before the court, or to make any part of its award conditional or the result of any other proceedings.

(4)   *The Minister of Aviation may from time to time by order made by statutory instrument specify the respective amounts which for the purposes of the said Article 22, and in particular of paragraph (5) of that Article, are to be taken as equivalent to the sums expressed in francs which are mentioned in that Article.*

(5)   References in this section to the said Article 22 [and Article 22A] include, subject to any necessary modifications, references to that Article as applied by Article 25A.

Notes   Sub-s (1): words 'and Article 22A' in square brackets inserted by the Carriage by Air and Road Act 1979, s 1(2), Sch 2, para 4.

Sub-s (1): words 'Schedule 1 or 1A' in square brackets substituted by SI 1999/1312, art 2(1), (4). Date in force: 21 May 1999 (except in relation to rights and liabilities arising out of an occurrence which took place before that date): see SI 1999/1312, art 1.

Sub-s (1): para (a) repealed by the Civil Liability (Contribution) Act 1978, s 9(1), (2), Sch 1, para 5(1), Sch 2.

Sub-s (1): in para (b) words 'paragraph (1)' in italics prospectively repealed and subsequent words in square brackets prospectively substituted by the Carriage by Air and Road Act 1979, s 1(2), Sch 2, para 4, as from a day to be appointed.

Sub-ss (2), (3), (5): words in square brackets inserted by the Carriage by Air and Road Act 1979, s 1(2), Sch 2 para 4(a), as from a day to be appointed.

Sub-s (4): prospectively repealed by the Carriage by Air and Road Act 1979, s 1(2), Sch 2 para 4(c), as from a day to be appointed.

[4A. Notice of partial loss. [(1) In Article 26(2) the references to damage shall be construed as including loss of part of the baggage or cargo in question and the reference to the receipt of baggage or cargo shall, in relation to loss of part of it, be construed as receipt of the remainder of it.

(2) It is hereby declared, without prejudice to the operation of any other section of this Act, that the reference to Article 26(2) in the preceding subsection is to Article 26(2) as set out in Part I and Part II of [Schedule 1 or 1A] to this Act.

Notes Inserted by the Carriage by Air and Road Act 1979, s 2.

Sub-s (2): words 'Schedule 1 or 1A' in square brackets substituted by SI 1999/1312, art 2(1), (4). Date in force: 21 May 1999 (except in relation to rights and liabilities arising out of an occurrence which took place before that date): see SI 1999/1312, art 1.

5. Time for bringing proceedings. (1) No action against a carrier's servant or agent which arises out of damage to which the Convention [or the Convention as amended] relates shall, if he was acting within the scope of his employment, be brought after more than two years, reckoned from the date of arrival at the destination or from the date on which the aircraft ought to have arrived, or from the date on which the carriage stopped.

(2) Article 29 in [Schedule 1 or 1A] of this Act shall not be read as applying to any proceedings for contribution between [persons liable for any damage to which the Convention [or the Convention as amended] relates], . . .

(3) The foregoing provisions of this section and the provisions of the said Article 29 shall have effect as if references in those provisions to an action included references to [arbitral proceedings]; [and the provisions of section 14 of the Arbitration Act 1996 apply to determine when such proceedings are commenced.]

Notes Sub-s (1): words 'or the Convention as amended' in square brackets inserted by SI 1999/1312, art 2(1), (5). Date in force: 21 May 1999 (except in relation to rights and liabilities arising out of an occurrence which took place before that date): see SI 1999/1312, art 1.

Sub-s (2): words 'Schedule 1 or 1A' in square brackets substituted by SI 1999/1312, art 2(1), (4). Date in force: 21 May 1999 (except in relation to rights and liabilities arising out of an occurrence which took place before that date): see SI 1999/1312, art 1.

Sub-s (2): words 'persons liable for any damage to which the Convention relates' in square brackets substituted by the Civil Liability (Contribution) Act 1978, s 9(1), Sch 1, para 5(2).

Sub-s (2): words 'or the Convention as amended' in square brackets inserted by SI 1999/1312, art 2(1), (5). Date in force: 21 May 1999 (except in relation to rights and liabilities arising out of an occurrence which took place before that date): see SI 1999/1312, art 1.

Sub-s (2): words omitted repealed by the Limitation Act 1963, s 4(4).

Sub-s (3): words in square brackets substituted by the Arbitration Act 1996, s 107(1), Sch 3, para 13(2).

6. Contributory negligence. It is hereby declared that for the purposes of Article 21 in [Schedule 1 or 1A] to this Act the Law Reform (Contributory Negligence) Act 1945 (including that Act as applied to Scotland), and section two of the Law Reform (Miscellaneous Provisions) Act (Northern Ireland) 1948, are provisions of the law of the United Kingdom under which a court may exonerate the carrier wholly or partly from his liability.

Notes Words 'Schedule 1 or 1A' in square brackets substituted by SI 1999/1312, art 2(1), (4). Date in force: 21 May 1999 (except in relation to rights and liabilities arising out of an occurrence which took place before that date): see SI 1999/1312, art 1.

7. Power to exclude aircraft in use for military purposes. (1) Her Majesty may from time to time by Order in Council direct that this section shall apply, or shall cease to apply, to the United Kingdom or any other State specified in the Order.

(2)   The Convention as set out in [Schedule 1 or 1A] to this Act shall not apply to the carriage of persons, cargo and baggage for the military authorities of a State to which this section applies in aircraft registered in that State if the whole capacity of the aircraft has been reserved by or on behalf of those authorities.

Notes Sub-s (2): words 'Schedule 1 or 1A' in square brackets substituted by SI 1999/1312, art 2(1), (4). Date in force: 21 May 1999 (except in relation to rights and liabilities arising out of an occurrence which took place before that date): see SI 1999/1312, art 1.

8. Actions against High Contracting Parties. Every High Contracting Party to the Convention who has not availed himself of the provisions of the Additional Protocol at the end of the Convention as set out in the First Schedule to this Act shall, for the purposes of any action brought in a court in the United Kingdom in accordance with the provisions of Article 28 in the said Schedule to enforce a claim in respect of carriage undertaken by him, be deemed to have submitted to the jurisdiction of that court, and accordingly rules of court may provide for the manner in which any such action is to be commenced and carried on; but nothing in this section shall authorise the issue of execution against the property of any High Contracting Party.

[8A. Amendments consequential on revision of Convention. (1) If at any time it appears to Her Majesty in Council that Her Majesty's Government in the United Kingdom have agreed to a revision of the Convention, Her Majesty may by Order in Council [make such amendments of this Act, the Carriage by Air (Supplementary Provisions) Act 1962 and section 5(1) of the Carriage by Air and Road Act 1979] as Her Majesty considers appropriate in consequence of the revision.

(2)   In the preceding subsection "revision" means an omission from, addition to or alteration of the Convention and includes replacement of the Convention or part of it by another convention.

(3)   An Order in Council under this section shall not be made unless a draft of the Order has been laid before Parliament and approved by a resolution of each House of Parliament.]

Notes Inserted by the Carriage by Air and Road Act 1979, s 3(1). Date in force: 22 October 1998: see SI 1998/2562, art 2.
     Sub-s (1): words in square brackets substituted by the International Transport Conventions Act 1983, s 9, Sch 2, para 1.

9. Application to British possessions, etc.   (1) Her Majesty may by Order in Council direct that this Act shall extend, subject to such exceptions, adaptations and modifications as may be specified in the Order, to:

    (a)   the Isle of Man;

    (b)   any of the Channel Islands;

    (c)   any colony or protectorate, protected state or United Kingdom trust territory.

The references in this subsection to a protectorate, to a protected state and to a United Kingdom trust territory shall be construed as if they were references contained in the British Nationality Act 1948.

(2)   An Order in Council under this section may contain such transitional and other consequential provisions as appear to Her Majesty to be expedient, and may be varied or revoked by a subsequent Order in Council.

10. Application to carriage by air not governed by Convention.   (1) Her Majesty may by Order in Council apply [Schedule 1 or 1A] to this Act, together with any other provisions of this Act, to carriage by air, not being carriage by air to which the Convention [or the Convention as amended] applies, of such descriptions as may be specified in the Order, subject to such exceptions, adaptations and modifications, if any, as may be so specified.

(2)   An Order in Council under this section may be made to apply to any of the countries or places mentioned in paragraphs (a), (b) and (c) of subsection (1) of the last foregoing section.

(3)   An Order in Council under this section may contain such transitional and other consequential provisions as appear to Her Majesty to be expedient, and may confer any functions under the Order on a Minister of the Crown in the United Kingdom or on any Governor or other authority in any of the countries or places mentioned in paragraphs (a), (b) and (c) of subsection (1) of the last foregoing section, including a power to grant exemptions from any requirements imposed by such an Order.

(4)   An Order in Council under this section may be varied or revoked by a subsequent Order in Council.

(5)   An Order in Council under this section shall not be made unless a draft of the Order has been laid before Parliament and approved by a resolution of each House of Parliament:

Provided that this subsection shall not apply to an Order which applies only to the Isle of Man or all or any of the Channel Islands.

Notes   Sub-s (1): words 'Schedule 1 or 1A' in square brackets substituted by SI 1999/1312, art 2(1), (4). Date in force: 21 May 1999 (except in relation to rights and liabilities arising out of an occurrence which took place before that date): see SI 1999/1312, art 1.

    Sub-s (1): words 'or the Convention as amended' in square brackets inserted by SI 1999/1312, art 2(1), (5). Date in force: 21 May 1999 (except in relation to rights and liabilities arising out of an occurrence which took place before that date): see SI 1999/1312, art 1.

---

13. Application to Crown.   This Act shall bind the Crown.

14. Short title, interpretation and repeals.   (1) This Act may be cited as the Carriage by Air Act 1961.

[(2)   In this Act:

"the Council Regulation" means Council Regulation (EC) No 2027/97 of 9th October 1997 on air carrier liability in the event of accidents;

"Community air carrier", "SDR" and "ecu" have the meaning given by Article 2 of the Council Regulation; and

"court" includes (in an arbitration allowed by the Convention) an arbitrator.]

(3)   On the date on which section one of this Act comes into force the Acts specified in the Second Schedule to this Act shall be repealed to the extent specified in the third column of that Schedule:

Provided that, without prejudice to section thirty-eight of the Interpretation Act 1889 (which relates to the effect of repeals), this subsection shall not affect any rights or liabilities arising out of an occurrence before that date.

Notes   Sub-s (2): substituted by SI 1998/1751, art 3(2). Date in force: 17 October 1998: see SI 1998/1751, art 1.

Appendix 1b

Schedule 1

The Warsaw Convention With The Amendments Made in it By The Hague Protocol

Part I   The English Text

Convention For the Unification of Certain Rules Relating to International Carriage by Air

Chapter I   Scope—Definitions

Article 1

(1)   This Convention applies to all international carriage of persons, baggage or cargo performed by aircraft for reward. It applies equally to gratuitous carriage by aircraft performed by an air transport undertaking.

(2)   For the purposes of this Convention, the expression *international carriage* means any carriage in which, according to the agreement between the parties, the place of departure and the place of destination, whether or not there be a break in the carriage or a transhipment, are situated either within the territories of two High Contracting Parties or within the territory of a single High Contracting Party if there is an agreed stopping place within the territory of another State, even if that State is not a High Contracting Party. Carriage between two points within the territory of a single High Contracting Party without an agreed stopping place within the territory of another State is not international carriage for the purposes of this Convention.

(3)   Carriage to be performed by several successive air carriers is deemed, for the purposes of this Convention, to be one undivided carriage if it has been regarded by the parties as a single operation, whether it had been agreed upon under the form of a single contract or of a series of contracts, and it does not lose its international character merely because one contract or a series of contracts is to be performed entirely within the territory of the same State.

Article 2

(1)   This Convention applies to carriage performed by the State or by legally constituted public bodies provided it falls within the conditions laid down in Article 1.

(2)   This Convention shall not apply to carriage of mail and postal packages.

Chapter II   Documents of Carriage

Section 1   Passenger Ticket

Article 3

(1)   In respect of the carriage of passengers a ticket shall be delivered containing

    (a)   an indication of the places of departure and destination;

    (b)   if the places of departure and destination are within the territory of a single High Contracting Party, one or more agreed stopping places being within the territory of another State, an indication of at least one such stopping place;

    (c)   a notice to the effect that, if the passenger's journey involves an ultimate destination or stop in a country other than the country of departure, the Warsaw Convention may be applicable and that the Convention governs and in most cases limits the liability of carriers for death or personal injury and in respect of loss of or damage to baggage.

(2)   The passenger ticket shall constitute prima facie evidence of the conclusion and conditions of the contract of carriage. The absence, irregularity or loss of the passenger ticket does not affect the existence or the validity of the contract of carriage which shall, none the less, be subject to the rules of this Convention. Nevertheless, if, with the consent of the carrier, the passenger embarks without a passenger ticket having been delivered, or if the ticket does not include the notice required by paragraph (1) (c) of this Article, the carrier shall not be entitled to avail himself of the provisions of Article 22.

Section 2   Baggage Check

Article 4

(1)   In respect of the carriage of registered baggage, a baggage check shall be delivered, which, unless combined with or incorporated in a passenger ticket which complies with the provisions of Article 3, paragraph (1), shall contain:

    (a)   an indication of the places of departure and destination;

    (b)   if the places of departure and destination are within the territory of a single High Contracting Party, one or more agreed stopping places being within the territory of another State, an indication of at least one such stopping place;

    (c)   a notice to the effect that, if the carriage involves an ultimate destination or stop in a country other than the country of departure, the Warsaw Convention may be applicable and that the Convention governs and in most cases limits the liability of carriers in respect of loss of or damage to baggage.

(2)   The baggage check shall constitute prima facie evidence of the registration of the baggage and of the conditions of the contract of carriage. The absence, irregularity or loss of the baggage check does not affect the existence of the validity of the contract of

carriage which shall, none the less, be subject to the rules of this convention. Nevertheless, if the carrier takes charge of the baggage without a baggage check having been delivered or if the baggage check (unless combined with or incorporated in the passenger ticket which complies with the provisions of Article 3, paragraph (1) (c)) does not include the notice required by paragraph (1) (c) of this Article, he shall not be entitled to avail himself of the provisions of Article 22, paragraph (2).

Section 3   Air Waybill

Article 5

(1)   Every carrier of cargo has the right to require the consignor to make out and hand over to him a document called an "air waybill"; every consignor has the right to require the carrier to accept this document.

(2)   The absence, irregularity or loss of this document does not affect the existence or the validity of the contract of carriage which shall, subject to the provisions of Article 9, be none the less governed by the rules of this Convention.

Article 6

(1)   The air waybill shall be made out by the consignor in three original parts and be handed over with the cargo.

(2)   The first part shall be marked "for the carrier," and shall be signed by the consignor. The second part shall be marked "for the consignee"; it shall be signed by the consignor and by the carrier and shall accompany the cargo. The third part shall be signed by the carrier and handed by him to the consignor after the cargo has been accepted.

(3)   The carrier shall sign prior to the loading of the cargo on board the aircraft.

(4)   The signature of the carrier may be stamped; that of the consignor may be printed or stamped.

(5)   If, at the request of the consignor, the carrier makes out the air waybill, he shall be deemed, subject to proof to the contrary, to have done so on behalf of the consignor.

Article 7

The carrier of cargo has the right to require the consignor to make out separate waybills when there is more than one package.

Article 8

The air waybill shall contain:

(a)   an indication of the places of departure and destination;

(b)   if the places of departure and destination are within the territory of a single High Contracting Party, one or more agreed stopping places being within the territory of another State, an indication of at least one such stopping place;

(c)   a notice to the consignor to the effect that, if the carriage involves an ultimate destination or stop in a country other than the country of departure,
the Warsaw Convention may be applicable and that the Convention governs and in most cases limits the liability of carriers in respect of loss of or
damage to cargo.

Article 9

If, with the consent of the carrier, cargo is loaded on board the aircraft without an air
waybill having been made out, or if the air waybill does not include the notice
required by Article 8, paragraph (c), the carrier shall not be entitled to avail himself of
the provisions of Article 22, paragraph (2).

Article 10

(1)   The consignor is responsible for the correctness of the particulars and statements relating to the cargo which he inserts in the air waybill.

(2)   The consignor shall indemnify the carrier against all damage suffered by him, or
by any other person to whom the carrier is liable, by reason of the irregularity, incorrectness or incompleteness of the particulars and statements furnished by the
consignor.

Article 11

(1)   The air waybill is prima facie evidence of the conclusion of the contract, of the
receipt of the cargo and of the conditions of carriage.

(2)   The statements in the air waybill relating to the weight, dimensions and packing of the cargo, as well as those relating to the number of packages, are prima facie
evidence of the facts stated; those relating to the quantity, volume and condition of the
cargo do not constitute evidence against the carrier except so far as they both have
been, and are stated in the air waybill to have been, checked by him in the presence of
the consignor, or relate to the apparent condition of the cargo.

Article 12

(1)   Subject to his liability to carry out all his obligations under the contract of carriage, the consignor has the right to dispose of the cargo by withdrawing it at the
aerodrome of departure or destination, or by stopping it in the course of the journey
on any landing, or by calling for it to be delivered at the place of destination or in the
course of the journey to a person other than the consignee named in the air waybill, or
by requiring it to be returned to the aerodrome of departure. He must not exercise this
right of disposition in such a way as to prejudice the carrier or other consignors and
he must repay any expenses occasioned by the exercise of this right.

(2)   If it is impossible to carry out the orders of the consignor the carrier must so
inform him forthwith.

(3)   If the carrier obeys the orders of the consignor for the disposition of the cargo
without requiring the production of the part of the air waybill delivered to the latter,
he will be liable, without prejudice to his right of recovery from the consignor, for any
damage which may be caused thereby to any person who is lawfully in possession of
that part of the air waybill.

(4)   The right conferred on the consignor ceases at the moment when that of the consignee begins in accordance with Article 13. Nevertheless, if the consignee declines to accept the waybill or the cargo, or if he cannot be communicated with, the consignor resumes his right of disposition.

Article 13

(1)   Except in the circumstances set out in the preceding Article, the consignee is entitled, on arrival of the cargo at the place of destination, to require the carrier to hand over to him the air waybill and to deliver the cargo to him, on payment of the charges due and on complying with the conditions of carriage set out in the air waybill.

(2)   Unless it is otherwise agreed, it is the duty of the carrier to give notice to the consignee as soon as the cargo arrives.

(3)   If the carrier admits the loss of the cargo, or if the cargo has not arrived at the expiration of seven days after the date on which it ought to have arrived, the consignee is entitled to put into force against the carrier the rights which flow from the contract of carriage.

Article 14

The consignor and the consignee can respectively enforce all the rights given them by Articles 12 and 13, each in his own name, whether he is acting in his own interest or in the interest of another, provided that he carries out the obligations imposed by the contract.

Article 15

(1)   Articles 12, 13 and 14 do not affect either the relations of the consignor or the consignee with each other or the mutual relations of third parties whose rights are derived either from the consignor or from the consignee.

(2)   The provisions of Articles 12, 13 and 14 can only be varied by express provision in the air waybill.

(3)   Nothing in this Convention prevents the issue of a negotiable air waybill.

Article 16

(1)   The consignor must furnish such information and attach to the air waybill such documents as are necessary to meet the formalities of customs, octroi or police before the cargo can be delivered to the consignee. The consignor is liable to the carrier for any damage occasioned by the absence, insufficiency or irregularity of any such information or documents, unless the damage is due to the fault of the carrier or his servants or agents.

(2)   The carrier is under no obligation to enquire into the correctness or sufficiency of such information or documents.

Chapter III   Liability of the Carrier

Article 17

The carrier is liable for damage sustained in the event of the death or wounding of a passenger or any bodily injury suffered by a passenger, if the accident which caused the damage so sustained took place on board the aircraft or in the course of any of the operations of embarking or disembarking.

Article 18

(1)   The carrier is liable for damage sustained in the event of the destruction or loss of, or of damage to, any registered baggage or any cargo, if the occurrence which caused the damage so sustained took place during the carriage by air.

(2)   The carriage by air within the meaning of the preceding paragraph comprises the period during which the baggage or cargo is in charge of the carrier, whether in an aerodrome or on board an aircraft, or, in the case of a landing outside an aerodrome, in any place whatsoever.

(3)   The period of the carriage by air does not extend to any carriage by land, by sea or by river performed outside an aerodrome. If, however, such a carriage takes place in the performance of a contract for carriage by air, for the purpose of loading, delivery or transhipment, any damage is presumed, subject to proof to the contrary, to have been the result of an event which took place during the carriage by air.

Article 19

The carrier is liable for damage occasioned by delay in the carriage by air of passengers, baggage or cargo.

Article 20

The carrier is not liable if he proves that he and his servants or agents have taken all necessary measures to avoid the damage or that it was impossible for him or them to take such measures.

Article 21

If the carrier proves that the damage was caused by or contributed to by the negligence of the injured person the court may, in accordance with the provisions of its own law, exonerate the carrier wholly or partly from his liability.

Article 22

(1)   In the carriage of persons the liability of the carrier for each passenger is limited to the sum of [16,600 special drawing rights]. Where, in accordance with the law of the court seised of the case, damages may be awarded in the form of periodical payments the equivalent capital value of the said payments shall not exceed francs [this limit]. Nevertheless, by special contract, the carrier and the passenger may agree to a higher limit of liability.

(2)   (a)   In the carriage of registered baggage and of cargo, the liability of the carrier is limited to a sum of [17 special drawing rights] per kilogramme, unless the passenger or consignor has made, at the time when the package

was handed over to the carrier, a special declaration of interest in delivery at destination and has paid a supplementary sum if the case so requires. In that case the carrier will be liable to pay a sum not exceeding the declared sum, unless he proves that that sum is greater than the passenger's or consignor's actual interest in delivery at destination.

(b) In the case of loss, damage or delay of part of registered baggage or cargo, or of any object contained therein, the weight to be taken into consideration in determining the amount to which the carrier's liability is limited shall be only the total weight of the package or packages concerned. Nevertheless, when the loss, damage or delay of a part of the registered baggage or cargo, or of an object contained therein, affects the value of other packages covered by the same baggage check or the same air waybill, the total weight of such package or packages shall also be taken into consideration in determining the limit of liability.

(3) As regards objects of which the passenger takes charge himself the liability of the carrier is limited to [332 special drawing rights] per passenger.

(4) The limits prescribed in this Article shall not prevent the court from awarding, in accordance with its own law, in addition, the whole or part of the court costs and of the other expenses of the litigation incurred by the plaintiff. The foregoing provision shall not apply if the amount of the damages awarded, excluding court costs and other expenses of the litigation, does not exceed the sum which the carrier has offered in writing to the plaintiff within a period of six months from the date of the occurrence causing the damage, or before the commencement of the action, if that is later.

[(5) The sums mentioned in terms of the special drawing right in this Article shall be deemed to refer to the special drawing right as defined by the International Monetary Fund. Conversion of the sums into national currencies shall, in case of judicial proceedings, be made according to the value of such currencies in terms of the special drawing right at the date of the judgment.]

Article 23

(1) Any provision tending to relieve the carrier of liability or to fix a lower limit than that which is laid down in this Convention shall be null and void, but the nullity of any such provision does not involve the nullity of the whole contract, which shall remain subject to the provisions of this Convention.

(2) Paragraph (1) of this Article shall not apply to provisions governing loss or damage resulting from the inherent defect, quality or vice of the cargo carried.

Article 24

(1) In the case covered by Articles 18 and 19 any action for damages, however founded, can only be brought subject to the conditions and limits set out in this Convention.

(2) In the cases covered by Article 17 the provisions of the preceding paragraph also apply, without prejudice to the questions as to who are the persons who have the right to bring suit and what are their respective rights.

Article 25

The limits of liability specified in Article 22 shall not apply, if it is proved that the damage resulted from an act or omission of the carrier, his servants or agents, done with intent to cause damage or recklessly and with knowledge that damage would probably result; provided that, in the case of such act or omission of a servant or agent, it is also proved that he was acting within the scope of his employment.

Article 25A

(1)   If an action is brought against a servant or agent of the carrier arising out of damage to which this Convention relates, such servant or agent, if he proves that he acted within the scope of his employment, shall be entitled to avail himself of the limits of liability which that carrier himself is entitled to invoke under Article 22.

(2)   The aggregate of the amounts recoverable from the carrier, his servants and agents, in that case, shall not exceed the said limits.

(3)   The provisions of paragraphs (1) and (2) of this Article shall not apply if it is proved that the damage resulted from an act or omission of the servant or agent done with intent to cause damage or recklessly and with knowledge that damage would probably result.

Article 26

(1)   Receipt by the person entitled to delivery of baggage or cargo without complaint is prima facie evidence that the same has been delivered in good condition and in accordance with the document of carriage.

(2)   In the case of damage, the person entitled to delivery must complain to the carrier forthwith after the discovery of the damage, and, at the latest, within seven days from the date of receipt in the case of baggage and fourteen days from the date of receipt in the case of cargo. In the case of delay the complaint must be made at the latest within twenty-one days from the date on which the baggage or cargo have been placed at his disposal.

(3)   Every complaint must be made in writing upon the document of carriage or by separate notice in writing despatched within the times aforesaid.

(4)   Failing complaint within the times aforesaid, no action shall lie against the carrier, save in the case of fraud on his part.

Article 27

In the case of the death of the person liable, an action for damages lies in accordance with the terms of this Convention against those legally representing his estate.

Article 28

(1)   An action for damages must be brought, at the option of the plaintiff, in the territory of one of the High Contracting Parties, either before the court having jurisdiction where the carrier is ordinarily resident, or has his principal place of business, or has an establishment by which the contract has been made or before the court having jurisdiction at the place of destination.

(2)   Questions of procedure shall be governed by the law of the court seised of the case.

Article 29

(1)   The right to damages shall be extinguished if an action is not brought within two years, reckoned from the date of arrival at the destination, or from the date on which the aircraft ought to have arrived, or from the date on which the carriage stopped.

(2)   The method of calculating the period of limitation shall be determined by the law of the court seised of the case.

Article 30

(1)   In the case of carriage to be performed by various successive carriers and falling within the definition set out in the third paragraph of Article 1, each carrier who accepts passengers, baggage or cargo is subjected to the rules set out in this Convention, and is deemed to be one of the contracting parties to the contract of carriage in so far as the contract deals with that part of the carriage which is performed under his supervision.

(2)   In the case of carriage of this nature, the passenger or his representative can take action only against the carrier who performed the carriage during which the accident or the delay occurred, save in the case where, by express agreement, the first carrier has assumed liability for the whole journey.

(3)   As regards baggage or cargo, the passenger or consignor will have a right of action against the first carrier, and the passenger or consignee who is entitled to delivery will have a right of action against the last carrier, and further, each may take action against the carrier who performed the carriage during which the destruction, loss, damage or delay took place. These carriers will be jointly and severally liable to the passenger or to the consignor or consignee.

Chapter IV   Provisions relating to Combined Carriage

Article 31

(1)   In the case of combined carriage performed partly by air and partly by any other mode of carriage, the provisions of this Convention apply only to the carriage by air, provided that the carriage by air falls within the terms of Article 1.

(2)   Nothing in this Convention shall prevent the parties in the case of combined carriage from inserting in the document of air carriage conditions relating to other modes of carriage, provided that the provisions of this Convention are observed as regards the carriage by air.

Chapter V   General and Final Provisions

Article 32

Any clause contained in the contract and all special agreements entered into before the damage occurred by which the parties purport to infringe the rules laid down by this Convention, whether by deciding the law to be applied, or by altering the rules as to jurisdiction, shall be null and void. Nevertheless for the carriage of cargo arbitration clauses are allowed, subject to this Convention, if the arbitration is to take place within one of the jurisdictions referred to in the first paragraph of Article 28.

Article 33

Nothing contained in this Convention shall prevent the carrier either from refusing to enter into any contract of carriage, or from making regulations which do not conflict with the provisions of this Convention.

Article 34

The provisions of Articles 3 to 9 inclusive relating to documents of carriage shall not apply in the case of carriage performed in extraordinary circumstances outside the normal scope of an air carrier's business.

Article 35

The expression "days" when used in this Convention means current days not working days.

Article 36

The Convention is drawn up in French in a single copy which shall remain deposited in the archives of the Ministry for Foreign Affairs of Poland and of which one duly certified copy shall be sent by the Polish Government to the Government of each of the High Contracting Parties.

Article 40A

(1)   (This paragraph is not reproduced. It defines "High Contracting Party".)

(2)   For the purposes of the Convention the word territory means not only the metropolitan territory of a State but also all other territories for the foreign relations of which that State is responsible.

(Articles 37, 38, 39, 40 and 41 and the concluding words of the Convention are not reproduced. They deal with the coming into force of the Convention.)

Notes   Article 22: in para (1) words "16,600 special drawing rights" in square brackets substituted by the Carriage by Air and Road Act 1979, s 4(1)(a)(i).
Article 22: in para (1) words "this limit" in square brackets substituted by the Carriage by Air and Road Act 1979, s 4(1)(a)(ii).
Article 22: in sub-para (2)(a) words "17 special drawing rights" in square brackets substituted by the Carriage by Air and Road Act 1979, s 4(1)(a)(i).
Article 22: in para (3) words "332 special drawing rights" in square brackets substituted by the Carriage by Air and Road Act 1979, s 4(1)(a)(i).
Article 22: para (5) substituted by the Carriage by Air and Road Act 1979, s 4(1)(a)(iii).

Part II   The French Text

Convention Pour l'Unification de Certaines Règles Relatives au Transport Aérien International

Chapitre 1er   Objet—Définitions

Article 1er

(1)   La présente Convention s'applique à tout transport international de personnes, bagages ou marchandises, effectué par aéronef contre rémunération. Elle s'applique également aux transports gratuits effectués par aéronef par une entreprise de transports aériens.

(2)   Est qualifié transport international, au sens de la presénte Convention, tout transport dans lequel, d'après les stipulations des parties, le point de départ et le point de destination, qu'il y ait ou non interruption de transport ou transbordement, sont situés soit sur le territoire de deux Hautes Parties Contractantes, soit sur le territoire d'une seule Haute Partie Contractante si une escale est prévue sur le territoire d'un autre Etat, même si cet Etat n'est pas une Haute Partie Contractante. Le transport sans une telle escale entre deux points du territoire d'une seule Haute Partie Contractante n'est pas considéré comme international au sens de la présente Convention.

(3)   Le Transport à exécuter par plusieurs transporteurs par air successifs est censé constituer pour l'application de la présente Convention un transport unique lorsqu'il a été envisagé par les parties comme une seule opération, qu'il ait été conclu sous la forme d'un seul contrat ou d'une série de contrats, et il ne perd pas son caractère international par le fait qu'un seul contrat ou une série de contrats doivent être exécutés intégralement dans le territoire d'un même Etat.

Article 2

(1)   La Convention s'applique aux transports effectués par l'Etat ou les autres personnes juridiques de droit public, dans les conditions prévues à l'article 1er.

(2)   La présente Convention ne s'applique pas au transport du courrier et des colis postaux.

Chapitre II   Titre de Transport

Section 1   Billet de Passage

Article 3

(1)   Dans le transport de passagers, un billet de passage doit être délivré, contenant:

   (a)   l'indication des points de départ et de destination;

   (b)   si les points de départ et de destination sont situés sur le territoire d'une même Haute Partie Contractante et qu'une ou plusieurs escales soient prévues sur le territoire d'un autre Etat, l'indication d'une de ces escales;

(c) un avis indiquant que si les passagers entreprennent un voyage comportant une destination finale ou une escale dans un pays autre que le pays de départ, leur transport peut être régi par la Convention de Varsovie qui, en général, limite la responsabilité du transporteur en cas de mort ou de lésion corporelle, ainsi qu'en cas de perte ou d'avarie des bagages.

(2) Le billet de passage fait foi, jusqu'à preuve contraire, de la conclusion et des conditions du contrat de transport. L'absence, l'irrégularité ou la perte du billet n'affecte ni l'existence ni la validité du contrat de transport, qui n'en sera pas moins soumis aux règles de la présente Convention. Toutefois, si, du consentement du transporteur, le passager s'embarque sans qu'un billet de passage ait été délivré, ou si le billet ne comporte pas l'avis prescrit à l'alinéa 1(c) du présent article, le transporteur n'aura pas le droit de se prévaloir des dispositions de l'article 22.

Section 2   Bulletin de Baggages

Article 4

(1) Dans le transport de bagages enregistrés, un bulletin de bagages doit être délivré qui, s'il n'est pas combiné avec un billet de passage conforme aux dispositions de l'article 3, alinéa 1er, ou n'est pas inclus dans un tel billet, doit contenir:

(a) l'indication des points de départ et de destination;

(b) si les points de départ et de destination sont situés sur le territoire d'une même Haute Partie Contractante et qu'une ou plusieurs escales sont prévues sur le territoire d'un autre Etat, l'indication d'une de ces escales;

(c) un avis indiquant que, si le transport comporte une destination finale ou une escale dans un pays autre que le pays de départ, il peut être régi par la Convention de Varsovie qui, en général, limite la responsabilité du transporteur en cas de perte ou d'avarie des bagages.

(2) Le bulletin de bagages fait foi, jusqu'à preuve contraire, de l'enregistrement des bagages et des conditions du contrat de transport. L'absence, l'irrégularité ou la perte du bulletin n'affecte ni l'existence ni la validité du contrat de transport, qui n'en sera pas moins soumis aux règles de la présente Convention. Toutefois, si le transporteur accepte la garde des bagages sans qu'un bulletin ait été délivré ou si, dans le cas où le bulletin n'est pas combiné avec un billet de passage conforme aux dispositions de l'article 3, alinéa 1 (c), ou n'est pas inclus dans un tel billet, il ne comporte pas l'avis prescrit à l'alinéa 1 (c) du présent article, le transporteur n'aura pas le droit de se prévaloir des dispositions de l'article 22, alinéa 2.

Section 3   Lettre de Transport Aérien

Article 5

(1) Tout transporteur de marchandises a le droit de demander à l'expéditeur l'établissement et la remise d'un titre appelé: "lettre de transport aérien"; tout expéditeur a le droit de demander au transporteur l'acceptation de ce document.

(2)   Toutefois, l'absence, l'irrégularité ou la perte de ce titre n'affecte ni l'existence, ni la validité du contrat de transport qui n'en sera pas moins soumis aux règles de la présente Convention, sous réserve des dispositions de l'article 9.

Article 6

(1)   La lettre de transport aérien est établie par l'expéditeur en trois exemplaires originaux et remise avec la marchandise.

(2)   Le premier exemplaire porte la mention "pour le transporteur"; il est signé par l'expéditeur. Le deuxième exemplaire porte la mention "pour le destinataire"; il est signé par l'expéditeur et le transporteur et il accompagne la marchandise. Le troisième exemplaire est signé par le transporteur et remis par lui à l'expéditeur après acceptation de la marchandise.

(3)   La signature du transporteur doit être apposée avant l'embarquement de la marchandise à bord de l'aéronef.

(4)   La signature du transporteur peut être remplacée par un timbre; celle de l'expéditeur peut être imprimée ou remplacée par un timbre.

(5)   Si, à la demande de l'expéditeur, le transporteur établit la lettre de transport aérien, il est considéré, jusqu'à preuve contraire, comme agissant pour le compte de l'expéditeur.

Article 7

Le transporteur de marchandises a le droit de demander a l'expéditeur l'établissement de lettres de transport aérien différentes lorsqu'il y a plusieurs colis.

Article 8

La lettre de transport aérien doit contenir:

   (a)   L'indication des points de départ et de destination;

   (b)   si les points de départ et de destination sont situés sur le territoire d'une même Haute Partie Contractante et qu'une ou plusiers escales sont prévues sur le territoire d'un autre Etat, l'indication d'une de ces escales;

   (c)   un avis indiquant aux expéditeurs que, si le transport comporte une destination finale ou une escale dans un pays autre que le pays de départ, il peut être régi par la Convention de Varsovie qui, en général, limite la responsabilité des transporteurs en cas de perte ou d'avarie des marchandises.

Article 9

Si, du consentement du transporteur, des marchandises sont embarquées à bord de l'aéronef sans qu'une lettre de transport aérien ait été établie ou si celle-ci ne comporte pas l'avis prescrit à l'article 8, alinéa (c), le transporteur n'aura pas le droit de se prévaloir des dispositions de l'article 22, alinéa 2.

Article 10

(1)   L'expéditeur est responsable de l'exactitude des indications et déclarations concernant la marchandise qu'il inscrit dans a la lettre de transport aérien.

(2)   Il supportera la responsabilité de tout dommage subi par le transporteur ou par toute autre personne à l'égard de laquelle la responsabilité du transporteur est engagée à raison de ses indications et déclarations irrégulières, inexactes ou incomplétes.

Article 11

(1)   La lettre de transport aérien fait foi, jusqu'à preuve contraire, de la conclusion du contrat, de la réception de la marchandise et des conditions du transport.

(2)   Les énonciations de la lettre de transport aérien, relatives au poids, aux dimensions et à l'emballage de la marchandise ainsi qu'au nombre des colis, font foi jusqu'à preuve contraire; celles relatives à la quantité, au volume et à l'état de la marchandise ne font preuve contre le transporteur qu'autant que la vérification en a été faite par lui en présence de l'expéditeur, et constatée sur la lettre de transport aérien, ou qu'il s'agit d'énonciations relatives à l'état apparent de la marchandise.

Article 12

(1)   L'expéditeur a le droit, sous la condition d'exécuter toutes les obligations résultant du contrat de transport, de disposer de la marchandise, soit en la retirant a l'aérodrome de départ ou de destination, soit en l'arrêtant en cours de route lors d'un atterrissage, soit en la faisant délivrer au lieu de destination ou en cours de route à une personne autre que le destinataire indiqué sur la lettre de transport aérien, soit en demandant son retour à l'aérodrome de départ, pour autant que l'exercice de ce droit ne porte préjudice ni au transporteur, ni aux autres expéditeurs et avec l'obligation de rembourser les frais qui en résultent.

(2)   Dans le cas où l'exécution des ordres de l'expéditeur est impossible, le transporteur doit l'en aviser immédiatement.

(3)   Si le transporteur se conforme aux orders de disposition de l'expéditeur, sans exiger la production de l'exemplaire de la lettre de transport aérien délivré à celui-ci, il sera responsable, sauf son recours contre l'expéditeur, du préjudice qui pourrait être causé par ce fait à celui qui est régulièrement en possession de la lettre de transport aérien.

(4)   Le droit de l'expéditeur cesse au moment ou celui du destinataire commence, conformément à l'article 13 ci-dessous. Toutefois, si le destinataire refuse la lettre de transport ou la marchandise, ou s'il ne peut être atteint, l'expéditeur reprend son droit de disposition.

Article 13

(1)   Sauf dans les cas indiqués à l'article précédent, le destinataire a le droit, dès l'arrivée de la marchandise au point de destination, de demander au transporteur de lui remettre la lettre de transport aérien et de lui livrer la marchandise contre le paiement du montant des créances et contre l'exécution des conditions de transport indiquées dans la lettre de transport aérien.

(2)   Sauf stipulation contraire, le transporteur doit aviser le destinataire dès l'arrivée de la marchandise.

(3)   Si la perte de la marchandise est reconnue par le transporteur ou si, à l'expiration d'un délai de sept jours après qu'elle aurait dû arriver, la marchandise n'est pas arrivée, le destinataire est autorisé à faire valoir vis-à-vis du transporteur les droits résultant du contrat de transport.

Article 14

L'expéditeur et le destinataire peuvent fair valoir tous les droits qui leur sont respectivement conférés par les articles 12 et 13, chacun en son propre nom, qu'il agisse dans son propre intérêt ou dans l'intérêt d'autrui, à condition d'exécuter les obligations que le contrat impose.

Article 15

(1)   Les articles 12, 13 et 14 ne portent aucun préjudice ni aux rapports de l'expéditeur et du destinataire entre eux, ni aux rapports des tiers dont les droits proviennent, soit de l'expéditeur, soit du destinataire.

(2)   Toute clause dérogeant aux stipulations des articles 12, 13 et 14 doit être inscrite dans la lettre de transport aérien.

(3)   Rien dans la présente Convention n'empêche l'établissement d'une lettre de transport aerien négociable.

Article 16

(1)   L'expéditeur est tenu de fournir les renseignements et de joindre à la lettre de transport aérien les documents qui, avant la remise de la marchandise au destinataire, sont nécessaires à l'accomplissement des formalités de douane, d'octroi ou de police. L'expéditeur est responsable envers le transporteur de tous dommages qui pourraient résulter de l'absence, de l'insuffisance ou de l'irrégularité de ces renseignements et pièces, sauf le cas de faute de la part du transporteur ou de ses préposés.

(2)   Le transporteur n'est pas tenu d'examiner si ces renseignements et documents sont exacts ou suffisants.

Chapitre III   Responsabilité du Transporteur

Article 17

Le transporteur est responsable du dommage survenu en cas de mort, de blessure ou de toute autre lésion corporelle subie par un voyageur lorsque l'accident qui a causé le dommage s'est produit à bord de l'aéronef ou au cours de toutes opérations d'embarquement et de débarquement.

Article 18

(1)   Le transporteur est responsable du dommage survenu en cas de destruction, perte ou avarie de bagages enregistrés ou de marchandises lorsque l'événement qui a causé le dommage s'est produit pendant le transport aérien.

(2)   Le transport aérien, au sens de l'alinéa précédent, comprend la période pendant laquelle les bagages ou marchandises se trouvent sous la garde du transporteur, que

ce soit dans un aérodrome ou à bord d'un aéronef ou dans un lieu quelconque en cas d'atterrissage en dehors d'un aérodrome.

(3) La période du transport aérien ne couvre aucun transport terrestre, maritime ou fluvial effectué en dehors d'un aérodrome. Toutefois lorsqu'un tel transport est effectué dans l'exécution du contrat de transport aérien en vue du chargement, de la livraison ou du transbordement, tout dommage est présumé, sauf preuve contraire, résulter d'un évènement survenu pendant le transport aérien.

Article 19

Le transporteur est responsable du dommage résultant d'un retard dans le transport aérien de voyageurs, bagages ou marchandises.

Article 20

Le transporteur n'est pas responsable s'il prouve que lui et ses préposés ont pris toutes les mesures nécessaires pour éviter le dommage ou qu'il leur était impossible de les prendre.

Article 21

Dans le cas où le transporteur fait la preuve que la faute de la personne lésée a causé le dommage ou y a contribué, le tribunal pourra, conformément aus dispositions de sa propre loi, écarter ou atténuer la responsabilité du transporteur.

Article 22

(1) Dans le transport des personnes, la responsabilité du transporteur relative à chaque passager est limitée à la somme de deux cent cinquante mille francs. Dans le cas où, d'après la loi du tribunal saisi, l'indemnité peut être fixée sous forme de rente, le capital de la rente ne peut dépasser cette limite. Toutefois par une convention spéciale avec le transporteur, le passager pourra fixer une limite de responsabilité plus élevée.

(2) (a) Dans le transport de bagages enregistrés et de marchandises, la responsabilité du transporteur est limitée à la somme de deux cent cinquante francs par kilogramme, sauf déclaration spéciale d'intérêt à la livraison faite par l'expéditeur au moment de la remise du colis au transporteur et moyennant le paiement d'une taxe supplémentaire éventuelle. Dans ce cas, le transporteur sera tenu de payer jusqu'à concurrence de la somme déclarée, à moins qu'il ne prouve qu'elle est supérieure à l'intérêt réel de l'expéditeur à la livraison.

   (b) En cas de perte, d'avarie ou de retard d'une partie des bagages enregistrés ou des marchandises, ou de tout objet qui y est contenu, seul le poids total du ou des colis dont il s'agit est pris en considération pour déterminer la limite de responsabilité du transporteur. Toutefois, lorsque la perte, l'avarie ou le retard d'une partie des bagages enregistrés ou des marchandises, ou d'un objet qui y est contenu, affecte la valeur d'autres colis couverts par le même bulletin de bagages ou la même lettre de transport aérien, le poids total de ces colis doit être pris en considération pour déterminer la limite de responsabilité.

(3) En ce qui concerne les objets dont le passager conserve la garde, la responsabilite du transporteur est limitée à cinq mille francs par passager.

(4)   Les limites fixées par le présent article n'ont pas pour effet d'enlever au tribunal la faculté d'allouer en outre, conformément à sa loi, une somme correspondant à tout ou partie des dépens et autres frais du procès exposés par le demandeur. La disposition précédente ne s'applique pas lorsque le montant de l'indemnité allouée, non compris les dépens et autres frais de procès, ne dépasse pas la somme que le transporteur a offerte par écrit au demandeur dans un delai de six mois à dater du fait qui a causé le dommage ou avant l'introduction de l'instance si celle-ci est postérieure à ce délai.

(5)   Les sommes indiquées en francs dans le présent article sont considérées comme se rapportant à une unité monetaire constituée par soixante-cinq milligrammes et demi d'or au titre de neuf cents millièmes de fin. Ces sommes peuvent être converties dans chaque monnaie nationale en chiffres ronds. La conversion de ces sommes en monnaies nationales autres que la monnaie-or s'effectuera en cas d'instance judiciaire suivant la valeur de ces monnaies à la date du jugement.

Article 23

(1)   Toute clause tendant à exonérer le transporteur de sa responsabilité ou à établir une limite inférieure à celle qui est fixée dans la présente Convention est nulle et de nul effet, mais la nullité de cette clause n'entraîne pas la nullité du contrat qui reste soumis aux dispositions de la présente Convention.

(2)   L'alinéa 1er du présent article ne s'applique pas aux clauses concernant la perte ou le dommage résultant de la nature ou du vice propre des marchandises transportées.

Article 24

(1)   Dans les cas prévus aux articles 18 et 19, toute action en responsabilité, à quelque titre que ce soit, ne peut être exercée que dans les conditions et limites prévues par la présente Convention.

(2)   Dans les cas prévus à l'article 17, s'appliquent également les dispositions de l'alinéa précédent, sans préjudice de la détermination des personnes qui ont le droit d'agir et de leurs droits respectifs.

Article 25

Les limites de responsabilité prévues à l'article 22 ne s'appliquent pas s'il est prouvé que le dommage résulte d'un acte ou d'une omission du transporteur ou de ses préposés fait, soit avec l'intention de provoquer un dommage, soit témérairement et avec conscience qu'un dommage en résultera probablement, pour autant que, dans le cas d'un acte ou d'une omission de préposés, la preuve soit également apportée que ceux-ci ont agi dans l'exercice de leur fonctions.

Article 25A

(1)   Si une action est intentée contre un préposé du transporteur à la suite d'un dommage visé par la présente Convention, ce préposé, s'il prouve qu'il a agi dans l'exercice de ses fonctions, pourra se prévaloir des limites de responsabilité que peut invoquer ce transporteur en vertu de l'article 22.

(2)   Le montant total de la réparation qui, dans ce cas, peut être obtenu du transporteur et de ses préposés ne doit pas dépasser lesdites limites.

(3)   Les dispositions des alinéas 1 et 2 du présent article ne s'appliquent pas s'il est prouvé que le dommage résulte d'un acte ou d'une omission du préposé fait, soit avec l'intention de provoquer un dommage, soit témérairement et avec conscience qu'un dommage en résultera probablement.

Article 26

(1)   La réception des bagages et marchandises sans protestation par le destinataire constituera présomption, sauf preuve contraire, que les marchandises ont été livrées en bon état et conformément au titre de transport.

(2)   En cas d'avarie, le destinataire doit adresser au transporteur une protestation immédiatement après la découverte de l'avarie et, au plus tard, dans un délai de sept jours pour les bagages et de quatorze jours pour les marchandises à dater de leur réception. En cas de retard, la protestation devra être faite au plus tard dans les vingt et un jours à dater du jour où le bagage ou la marchandise auront été mis à sa disposition.

(3)   Toute protestation doit être faite par réserve inscrite sur le titre de transport ou par un autre écrit expédié dans le délai prévu pour cette protestation.

(4)   A défaut de protestation dans les délais prévus, toutes actions contre le transporteur sont irrecevables, sauf le cas de fraude de celui-ci.

Article 27

En cas de décès du débiteur, l'action en responsabilité, dans les limites prévues par la présente Convention, s'exerce contre ses ayants droit.

Article 28

(1)   L'action en responsabilité devra être portée, au choix du demandeur, dans le territoire d'une des Hautes Parties Contractantes, soit devant le tribunal du domicile du transporteur, du siège principal de son exploitation ou du lieu où il possède un établissement par le soin duquel le contrat a été conclu, soit devant le tribunal du lieu de destination.

(2)   La procédure sera réglée par la loi du tribunal saisi.

Article 29

(1)   L'action en responsabilité doit être intentée, sous peine de déchéance, dans le délai de deux ans à compter de l'arrivée à destination ou du jour où l'aéronef aurait dû arriver, ou de l'arrêt du transport.

(2)   Le mode de calcul du délai est déterminé par la loi du tribunal saisi.

Article 30

(1)   Dans les cas de transport régis par la définition du troisième alinéa de l'article 1er, à exécuter par divers transporteurs successifs, chaque transporteur acceptant des voyageurs, des bagages ou des marchandises est soumis aux règles établies par cette Convention, et est censé être une des parties contractantes du contrat de transport, pour autant que ce contrat ait trait à la partie du transport effectueé sous son contrôle.

(2)   Au cas d'un tel transport, le voyageur ou ses ayants droit ne pourront recourir que contre le transporteur ayant effectué le transport au cours duquel l'accident ou le retard s'est produit, sauf dans le cas où, par stipulation expresse, le premier transporteur aura assuré la responsibilité pour tout le voyage.

(3)   S'il s'agit de bagages ou de marchandises, l'expéditeur aura recours contre le premier transporteur et le destinataire qui a le droit à la délivrance contre le dernier, et l'un et l'autre pourront, en outre, agir contre le transporteur ayant effectué le transport au cours duquel la destruction, la perte, l'avarie ou le retard se sont produits, Ces transporteurs seront solidairement responsables envers l'expéditeur et le destinataire.

Chapitre IV   Dispositions Relatives aux Transports Combinés

Article 31

(1)   Dans le cas de transports combinés effectués en partie par air et en partie par tout autre moyen de transport, les stipulations de la présente Convention ne s'appliquent qu'au transport aérien et si celui-ci répond aux conditions de l'article 1er.

(2)   Rien dans la présente Convention n'empêche les parties, dans le cas de transports combinés, d'insérer dans le titre de transport aérien des conditions relatives à d'autres modes de transport, à condition que les stipulations de la présente Convention soient respectées en ce qui concerne le transport par air.

Chapitre V   Dispositions Générales et Finales

Article 32

Sont nulles toutes clauses du contrat de transport et toutes conventions particulières antérieures au dommage par lesquelles les parties dérogeraient aux règles de la présente Convention soit par une détermination de la loi applicable, soit par une modification des règles de compétence. Toutefois, dans le transport des marchandises, les clauses d'arbitrage sont admises, dans les limites de la présente Convention, lorsque l'arbitrage doit s'effectuer dans les lieux de compétence des tribunaux prévus à l'article 28, alinéa 1.

Article 33

Rien dans la présente Convention ne peut empêcher un transporteur de refuser la conclusion d'un contrat de transport ou de formuler des règlements qui ne sont pas en contradiction avec les dispositions de la présente Convention.

Article 34

Les dispositions des articles 3 à 9 inclus relative aux titres de transport ne sont pas applicables au transport effectué dans des circonstances extraordinaires en dehors de toute opération normale de l'exploitation aérienne.

Article 35

Lorsque dans la présente Convention il est question de jours, il s'agit de jours courants et non de jours ouvrables.

Article 36

La présente Convention est rédigée en français en un seul exemplaire qui restera déposé aux archives du Ministère des Affaires Etrangerès de Pologne, et dont une copie certifiée conforme sera transmise par les soins du Gouvernement polonais au Gouvernement de chacune des Hautes Parties Contractantes.

Article 40A

(1)   ...

(2)   Aux fins de la Convention, le mot territoire signifie non seulement le territoire métropolitain d'un Etat, mais aussi tous les territoires qu'il représente dans les relations extérieures.

Appendix 1c

Schedule 1A   The Warsaw Convention with the Amendments made in it by The Hague Protocol and Protocol no 4 of Montreal, 1975

Part I   The English Text

Convention for the Unification of Certain Rules Relating to International Carriage by Air

Chapter I   Scope—Definitions

Article 1

(1)   This Convention applies to all international carriage of persons, baggage or cargo performed by aircraft for reward. It applies equally to gratuitous carriage by aircraft performed by an air transport undertaking.

(2)   For the purposes of this Convention, the expression international carriage means any carriage in which, according to the agreement between the parties, the place of departure and the place of destination, whether or not there be a break in the carriage or a transhipment, are situated either within the territories of two High Contracting Parties or within the territory of a single High Contracting Party if there is an agreed stopping place within the territory of another State, even if that State is not a High Contracting Party. Carriage between two points within the territory of a single High Contracting Party without an agreed stopping place within the territory of another State is not international carriage for the purposes of this Convention.

(3)   Carriage to be performed by several successive air carriers is deemed, for the purposes of this Convention, to be one undivided carriage if it has been regarded by the parties as a single operation, whether it had been agreed upon under the form of a single contract or a series of contracts, and it does not lose its international character merely because one contract or a series of contracts is to be performed entirely within the territory of the same State.

Article 2

(1)   This Convention applies to carriage performed by the State or by legally constituted public bodies provided it falls within the conditions laid down in Article 1.

(2)   In the carriage of postal items the carrier shall be liable only to the relevant postal administration in accordance with the rules applicable to the relationship between the carriers and the postal administrations.

(3)   Except as provided in paragraph (2) of this Article, the provisions of this Convention shall not apply to the carriage of postal items.

Chapter II   Documents of Carriage

Section 1   Passenger Ticket

Article 3

(1)   In respect of the carriage of passengers a ticket shall be delivered containing:

    (a)   an indication of the places of departure and destination;

    (b)   if the places of departure and destination are within the territory of a single High Contracting Party, one or more agreed stopping places being within the territory of another State, an indication of at least one such stopping place;

    (c)   a notice to the effect that, if the passenger's journey involves an ultimate destination or stop in a country other than the country of departure, the Warsaw Convention may be applicable and that the Convention governs and in most cases limits the liability of carriers for death or personal injury and in respect of loss of or damage to baggage.

(2)   The passenger ticket shall constitute prima facie evidence of the conclusion and conditions of the contract of carriage. The absence, irregularity or loss of the passenger ticket does not affect the existence or the validity of the contract of carriage which shall, none the less, be subject to the rules of this Convention. Nevertheless, if, with the consent of the carrier, the passenger embarks without a passenger ticket having been delivered, or if the ticket does not include the notice required by paragraph (1)(c) of this Article, the carrier shall not be entitled to avail himself of the provisions of Article 22.

Section 2   Baggage Check

Article 4

(1)   In respect of the carriage of registered baggage, a baggage check shall be delivered, which, unless combined with or incorporated in a passenger ticket which complies with the provisions of Article 3, paragraph (1), shall contain:

    (a)   an indication of the places of departure and destination;

    (b)   if the places of departure and destination are within the territory of a single High Contracting Party, one or more agreed stopping places being within the territory of another State, an indication of at least one such stopping place;

    (c)   a notice to the effect that, if the carriage involves an ultimate destination or stop in a country other than the country of departure, the Warsaw Convention may be applicable and that the Convention governs and in most cases limits the liability of carriers in respect of loss or damage to baggage.

(2)   The baggage check shall constitute prima facie evidence of the registration of the baggage and of the conditions of the contract of carriage. The absence, irregularity or loss of the baggage check does not affect the existence or the validity of the contract of

carriage which shall, none the less, be subject to the rules of this Convention. Nevertheless, if the carrier takes charge of the baggage without a baggage check having been delivered or if the baggage check (unless combined with or incorporated in the passenger ticket which complies with the provisions of Article 3, paragraph (1)(c)) does not include the notice required by paragraph (1)(c) of this Article, he shall not be entitled to avail himself of the provisions of Article 22, paragraph (2).

Section 3   Documentation Relating to Cargo

Article 5

(1)   In respect of the carriage of cargo an air waybill shall be delivered.

(2)   Any other means which would preserve a record of the carriage to be performed may, with the consent of the consignor, be substituted for the delivery of an air waybill. If such other means are used, the carrier shall, if so requested by the consignor, deliver to the consignor a receipt for the cargo permitting identification of the consignment and access to the information contained in the record preserved by such other means.

(3)   The impossibility of using, at points of transit and destination, the other means which would preserve a record of the carriage referred to in paragraph (2) of this Article does not entitle the carrier to refuse to accept the cargo for carriage.

Article 6

(1)   The air waybill shall be made out by the consignor in three original parts.

(2)   The first part shall be marked "for the carrier"; it shall be signed by the consignor. The second part shall be marked "for the consignee"; it shall be signed by the consignor and the carrier. The third part shall be signed by the carrier and handed by him to the consignor after the cargo has been accepted.

(3)   The signature of the carrier and that of the consignor may be printed or stamped.

(4)   If, at the request of the consignor, the carrier makes out the air waybill, he shall be deemed, subject to proof to the contrary, to have done so on behalf of the consignor.

Article 7

Where there is more than one package:

(a)   the carrier of the cargo has the right to require the consignor to make out separate air waybills;

(b)   the consignor has the right to require the carrier to deliver separate receipts when the other means referred to in paragraph (2) of Article 5 are used.

Article 8

The air waybill and receipt for the cargo shall contain:

(a)   an indication of the places of departure and destination;

(b)   if the places of departure and destination are within the territory of a single High Contracting Party, one or more agreed stopping places being within the territory of another State, an indication of at least one such stopping place; and

(c)   an indication of the weight of the consignment.

Article 9

Non-compliance with the provisions of Articles 5 to 8 shall not affect the existence or the validity of the contract of carriage, which shall, none the less, be subject to the rules of this Convention including those relating to limitation of liability.

Article 10

(1)   The consignor is responsible for the correctness of the particulars and statements relating to the cargo inserted by him or on his behalf in the air waybill or furnished by him or on his behalf to the carrier for insertion in the receipt for the cargo or for insertion in the record preserved by the other means referred to in paragraph (2) of Article 5.

(2)   The consignor shall indemnify the carrier against all damage suffered by him, or by any other person to whom the carrier is liable, by reason of the irregularity, incorrectness or incompleteness of the particulars and statements furnished by the consignor or on his behalf.

(3)   Subject to the provisions of paragraphs (1) and (2) of this Article, the carrier shall indemnify the consignor against all damage suffered by him, or by any other person to whom the consignor is liable, by reason of the irregularity, incorrectness or incompleteness of the particulars and statements inserted by the carrier or on his behalf in the receipt for the cargo or in the record preserved by the other means referred to in paragraph (2) of Article 5.

Article 11

(1)   The air waybill or the receipt for the cargo is prima facie evidence of the conclusion of the contract, of the acceptance of the cargo and of the conditions of carriage mentioned therein.

(2)   Any statements in the air waybill or the receipt for the cargo relating to the weight, dimensions and packing of the cargo, as well as those relating to the number of packages, are prima facie evidence of the facts stated; those relating to the quantity, volume and condition of the cargo do not constitute evidence against the carrier except so far as they both have been, and are stated in the air waybill to have been, checked by him in the presence of the consignor, or relate to the apparent condition of the cargo.

Article 12

(1)   Subject to his liability to carry out all his obligations under the contract of carriage, the consignor has the right to dispose of the cargo by withdrawing it at the airport of departure or destination, or by stopping it in the course of the journey on any landing, or by calling for it to be delivered at the place of destination or in the

course of the journey to a person other than the consignee originally designated, or by requiring it to be returned to the airport of departure. He must not exercise this right of disposition in such a way as to prejudice the carrier or other consignors and he must repay any expenses occasioned by the exercise of this right.

(2)   If it is impossible to carry out the orders of the consignor the carrier must so inform him forthwith.

(3)   If the carrier obeys the orders of the consignor for the disposition of the cargo without requiring the production of the part of the air waybill or the receipt for the cargo delivered to the latter, he will be liable, without prejudice to his right of recovery from the consignor, for any damage which may be caused thereby to any person who is lawfully in possession of that part of the air waybill or the receipt for the cargo.

(4)   The right conferred on the consignor ceases at the moment when that of the consignee begins in accordance with Article 13. Nevertheless, if the consignee declines to accept the cargo, or if he cannot be communicated with, the consignor resumes his right of disposition.

Article 13

(1)   Except when the consignor has exercised his right under Article 12, the consignee is entitled, on the arrival of the cargo at the place of destination, to require the carrier to deliver the cargo to him, on payment of the charges due and on complying with the conditions of carriage.

(2)   Unless it is otherwise agreed, it is the duty of the carrier to give notice to the consignee as soon as the cargo arrives.

(3)   If the carrier admits the loss of the cargo, or if the cargo has not arrived at the expiration of seven days after the date on which it ought to have arrived, the consignee is entitled to enforce against the carrier the rights which flow from the contract of carriage.

Article 14

The consignor and the consignee can respectively enforce all the rights given them by Articles 12 and 13, each in his own name, whether he is acting in his own interest or in the interest of another, provided that he carries out the obligations imposed by the contract of carriage.

Article 15

(1)   Articles 12, 13 and 14 do not affect the relations of the consignor and the consignee with each other or the mutual relations of third parties whose rights are derived either from the consignor or from the consignee.

(2)   The provisions of Articles 12, 13 and 14 can only be varied by express provision in the air waybill or the receipt for the cargo.

Article 16

(1)   The consignor must furnish such information and such documents as are necessary to meet the formalities of customs, octroi or police before the cargo can be

delivered to the consignee. The consignor is liable to the carrier for any damage occasioned by the absence, insufficiency or irregularity of any such information or documents, unless the damage is due to the fault of the carrier, his servants or agents.

(2)   The carrier is under no obligation to enquire into the correctness or sufficiency of such information or documents.

Chapter III   Liability of the Carrier

Article 17

The carrier is liable for damage sustained in the event of the death or wounding of a passenger or any other bodily injury suffered by a passenger, if the accident which caused the damage so sustained took place on board the aircraft or in the course of any of the operations of embarking or disembarking.

Article 18

(1)   The carrier is liable for damage sustained in the event of the destruction or loss of, or damage to, any registered baggage, if the occurrence which caused the damage so sustained took place during the carriage by air.

(2)   The carrier is liable for damage sustained in the event of the destruction or loss of, or damage to, cargo upon condition only that the occurrence which caused the damage so sustained took place during the carriage by air.

(3)   However, the carrier is not liable if he proves that the destruction, loss of, or damage to, the cargo resulted solely from one or more of the following:

    (a)   inherent defect, quality or vice of that cargo;

    (b)   defective packing of that cargo performed by a person other than the carrier or his servants or agents;

    (c)   an act of war or an armed conflict;

    (d)   an act of a public authority carried out in connection with the entry, exit or transit of the cargo.

(4)   The carriage by air within the meaning of the preceding paragraphs of this Article comprises the period during which the baggage or cargo is in the charge of the carrier, whether in an airport or on board an aircraft, or, in the case of a landing outside an airport, in any place whatsoever.

(5)   The period of the carriage by air does not extend to any carriage by land, by sea or by river performed outside an airport. If, however, such carriage takes place in the performance of a contract for carriage by air, for the purpose of loading, delivery or transhipment, any damage is presumed, subject to proof to the contrary, to have been the result of an event which took place during the carriage by air.

Article 19

The carrier is liable for damage occasioned by delay in the carriage by air of passengers, baggage or cargo.

Article 20

In the case of passengers and baggage, and in the case of damage occasioned by delay in the carriage of cargo, the carrier shall not be liable if he proves that he and his servants and agents have taken all necessary measures to avoid the damage or that it was impossible for them to take such measures.

Article 21

(1)   In the carriage of passengers and baggage, if the carrier proves that the damage was caused by or contributed to by the negligence of the person suffering the damage the Court may, in accordance with the provisions of its own law, exonerate the carrier wholly or partly from his liability.

(2)   In the carriage of cargo, if the carrier proves that the damage was caused by or contributed to by the negligence or other wrongful act or omission of the person claiming compensation, or the person from whom he derives his rights, the carrier shall be wholly or partly exonerated from his liability to the claimant to the extent that such negligence or wrongful act or omission caused or contributed to the damage.

Article 22

(1)   In the carriage of persons the liability of the carrier for each passenger is limited to the sum of 16,600 Special Drawing Rights. Where, in accordance with the law of the court seised of the case, damages may be awarded in the form of periodical payments, the equivalent capital value of the said payments shall not exceed this limit. Nevertheless, by special contract, the carrier and the passenger may agree to a higher limit of liability.

(2)   (a)   In the carriage of registered baggage, the liability of the carrier is limited to a sum of 17 Special Drawing Rights per kilogramme, unless the passenger or consignor has made, at the same time when the package was handed over to the carrier, a special declaration or interest in delivery at destination and has paid a supplementary sum if the case so requires. In that case the carrier will be liable to pay a sum not exceeding the declared sum, unless he proves that that sum is greater than the passenger's or the consignor's actual interest in delivery at destination.

(b)   In the carriage of cargo, the liability of the carrier is limited to a sum of 17 Special Drawing Rights per kilogramme, unless the consignor has made, at the same time when the package was handed over to the carrier, a special declaration of interest in delivery at destination and has paid a supplementary sum if the case so requires. In that case the carrier will be liable to pay a sum not exceeding the declared sum, unless he proves that that sum is greater than the consignor's actual interest in delivery at destination.

(c)   In the case of loss, damage or delay of part of registered baggage or cargo, or of any object contained therein, the weight to be taken into consideration in determining the amount to which the carrier's liability is limited shall be only the total weight of the package or packages concerned. Nevertheless, when the loss, damage or delay of a part of the registered baggage or cargo, or of an object contained therein, affects the value of other packages covered by the same baggage check or the same air waybill, the total weight of such package or packages shall also be taken into consideration in determining the limit of liability.

(3)   As regards objects of which the passenger takes charge himself the liability of the carrier is limited to 332 Special Drawing Rights per passenger.

(4)   The limits prescribed in this Article shall not prevent the court from awarding, in accordance with its own law, in addition, the whole or part of the court costs and of the other expenses of the litigation incurred by the plaintiff. The foregoing provision shall not apply if the amount of the damages awarded, excluding court costs and other expenses of the litigation, does not exceed the sum which the carrier has offered in writing to the plaintiff within a period of six months from the date of the occurrence causing the damage, or before the commencement of the action, if that is later.

(5)   The sums mentioned in terms of the Special Drawing Right in this Article shall be deemed to refer to the Special Drawing Right as defined by the International Monetary Fund. Conversion of the sums into national currencies shall, in case of judicial proceedings, be made according to the value of such currencies in terms of the Special Drawing Right at the date of judgment.

(6)   The value of a national currency, in terms of the Special Drawing Right, of a High Contracting Party which is a Member of the International Monetary Fund, shall be calculated in accordance with the method of valuation applied by the International Monetary Fund, in effect at the date of the judgment for its operations and transactions. The value of a national currency, in terms of the Special Drawing Right, of a High Contracting Party which is not a Member of the International Monetary Fund, shall be calculated in a manner determined by that High Contracting Party. Nevertheless, those States which are not Members of the International Monetary Fund and whose law does not permit the application of the provisions of paragraph (2)(b) of Article 22 may, at the time of ratification or accession or at any time thereafter, declare that the limit of liability of the carrier in judicial proceedings in their territories is fixed at a sum of two hundred and fifty monetary units per kilogramme. This monetary unit corresponds to sixty-five and a half milligrammes of gold of millesimal fineness nine hundred. This sum may be converted into the national currency concerned in round figures. The conversion of this sum into national currency shall be made according to the law of the State concerned.

Article 23

(1)   Any provision tending to relieve the carrier of liability or to fix a lower limit than that laid down in this Convention shall be null and void, but the nullity of any such provision does not involve the nullity of the whole contract, which shall remain subject to the provisions of this Convention.

(2)   Paragraph (1) of this Article shall not apply to provisions governing loss or damage resulting from the inherent defect, quality or vice of the cargo carried.

Article 24

(1)   In the carriage of passengers and baggage, any action for damages, however founded, can only be brought subject to the conditions and limits set out in this Convention, without prejudice to the question as to who are the persons who have the right to bring suit and what are their respective rights.

(2)   In the carriage of cargo, any action for damages, however founded, whether under this Convention or in contract or in tort or otherwise, can only be brought subject to the conditions and limits of liability set out in this Convention without prejudice to the question as to who are the persons who have the right to bring suit and what are

their respective rights. Such limits of liability constitute maximum limits and may not be exceeded whatever the circumstances which give rise to the liability.

Article 25

In the carriage of passengers and baggage, the limits of liability specified in Article 22 shall not apply if it is proved that the damage resulted from an act or omission of the carrier, his servants or agents, done with intent to cause damage or recklessly and with knowledge that damage would probably result; provided that, in the case of such act or omission of a servant or agent, it is also proved that he was acting within the scope of his employment.

Article 25A

(1)   If an action is brought against a servant or agent of the carrier arising out of damage to which this Convention relates, such servant or agent, if he proves that he acted within the scope of his employment, shall be entitled to avail himself of the limits of liability which that carrier himself is able to invoke under Article 22.

(2)   The aggregate of the amounts recoverable from the carrier, his servants or agents, in that case, shall not exceed the said limits.

(3)   In the carriage of passengers and baggage, the provisions of paragraphs (1) and (2) of this Article shall not apply if it is proved that the damage resulted from an act or omission of the servant or agent done with intent to cause damage or recklessly and with knowledge that damage would probably result.

Article 26

(1)   Receipt by the person entitled to delivery of baggage or cargo without complaint is prima facie evidence that the same have been delivered in good condition and in accordance with the document of carriage.

(2)   In the case of damage, the person entitled to delivery must complain to the carrier forthwith after the discovery of the damage, and, at the latest, within seven days from the date of receipt in the case of baggage and fourteen days from the date of receipt in the case of cargo. In the case of delay the complaint must be made at the latest within twenty-one days from the date on which the baggage or cargo has been placed at his disposal.

(3)   Every complaint must be made in writing upon the document of carriage or by separate notice in writing despatched within the times aforesaid.

(4)   Failing complaint within the times aforesaid, no action shall lie against the carrier, save in the case of fraud on his part.

Article 27

In the case of the death of the person liable, an action for damages lies in accordance with the terms of this Convention against those legally representing his estate.

Article 28

(1)   An action for damages must be brought, at the option of the plaintiff, in the territory of one of the High Contracting Parties, either before the court having

jurisdiction where the carrier is ordinarily resident, or has his principal place of business, or has an establishment by which the contract has been made or before the court having jurisdiction at the place of destination.

(2)   Questions of procedure shall be governed by the law of the court seised of the case.

Article 29

(1)   The right to damages shall be extinguished if an action is not brought within two years, reckoned from the date of arrival at the destination, or from the date on which the aircraft ought to have arrived, or from the date on which the carriage stopped.

(2)   The method of calculating the period of limitation shall be determined by the law of the court seised of the case.

Article 30

(1)   In the case of carriage to be performed by various successive carriers and falling within the definition set out in the third paragraph of Article 1, each carrier who accepts passengers, baggage or cargo is subjected to the rules set out in this Convention, and is deemed to be one of the contracting parties to the contract of carriage in so far as the contract deals with that part of the carriage which is performed under his supervision.

(2)   In the case of carriage of this nature, the passenger or his representative can take action only against the carrier who performed the carriage during which the accident or the delay occurred, save in the case where, by express agreement, the first carrier has assumed liability for the whole journey.

(3)   As regards baggage or cargo, the passenger or consignor will have a right of action against the first carrier, and the passenger or consignee who is entitled to delivery will have a right of action against the last carrier, and further, each may take action against the carrier who performed the carriage during which the destruction, loss, damage or delay took place. These carriers will be jointly and severally liable to the passenger or to the consignor or consignee.

Article 30A

Nothing in this Convention shall prejudice the question whether a person liable for damage in accordance with its provisions has a right of recourse against any other person.

Chapter IV   Provisions Relating to Combined Carriage

Article 31

(1)   In the case of combined carriage performed partly by air and partly by any other mode of carriage, the provisions of this Convention apply only to the carriage by air, provided that carriage by air falls within the terms of Article 1.

(2)   Nothing in this Convention shall prevent the parties in the case of combined carriage from inserting in the document of air carriage conditions relating to other modes of carriage, provided that the provisions of this Convention are observed as regards the carriage by air.

Chapter V   General and Final Provisions

Article 32

Any clause contained in the contract and all special agreements entered into before the damage occurred by which the parties purport to infringe the rules laid down by this Convention, whether by deciding the law to be applied, or by altering the rules as to jurisdiction shall be null and void. Nevertheless for the carriage of cargo arbitration clauses are allowed subject to this Convention, if the arbitration is to take place within one of the jurisdictions referred to in the first paragraph of Article 28.

Article 33

Except as provided in paragraph (3) of Article 5, nothing in this Convention shall prevent the carrier either from refusing to enter into any contract of carriage or from making regulations which do not conflict with the provisions of this Convention.

Article 34

The provisions of Articles 3 to 8 inclusive relating to documents of carriage shall not apply in the case of carriage performed in extraordinary circumstances outside the normal scope of an air carrier's business.

Article 35

The expression "days" when used in this Convention means current days not working days.

Article 36

The Convention is drawn up in French in a single copy which shall remain deposited in the archives of the Ministry of Foreign Affairs of Poland and of which one duly certified copy shall be sent by the Polish Government to the Government of each of the High Contracting Parties.

Article 40A

(1)   [This paragraph is not reproduced. It defines "High Contracting Party".]

(2)   For the purposes of the Convention the word territory means not only the metropolitan territory of a State but also all other territories for the foreign relations of which that state is responsible.

[Articles 37, 38, 39, 40 and 41 and the concluding words of the Convention are not reproduced. They deal with the coming into force of the Convention.]

[Part II   The French Text]

[Convention Pour l'Unification de Certaines Régles Relatives au Transport Aérien International

Chapitre 1er Objet—Définitions

Article 1er

(1)   La présente Convention s'applique à tout transport international de personnes, bagages ou marchandises, effectué par aéronef contre rémunération. Elle s'applique également aux transports gratuits effectués par aéronef par une entreprise de transports aériens.

(2)   Est qualifié transport international, au sens de la présente Convention, tout transport dans lequel, d'après les stipulations des parties, le point de départ et le point de destination, qu'il y ait ou non interruption de transport ou transbordement, sont situés soit sur le territoire de deux Hautes Parties Contractantes, soit sur le territoire d'une seule Haute Partie Contractante si une escale est prévue sur le territoire d'un autre Etat, même si cet Etat n'est pas une Haute Partie Contractante. Le transport sans une telle escale entre deux points du territoire d'une seule Haute Partie Contractante n'est pas considéré comme international au sens de la présente Convention.

(3)   Le transport à exécuter par plusieurs transporteurs par air successifs est censé constituer pour l'application de la présente Convention un transport unique lorsqu'il a été envisagé par les parties comme une seule opération, qu'il ait été conclu sous la forme d'un seul contrat ou d'une série de contrats, et il ne perd pas son caractère international par le fait qu'un seul contrat ou une série de contrats doivent être exécutés intégralement dans le territoire d'un même Etat.

Article 2

(1)   La Convention s'applique aux transports effectués par l'Etat on les autres personnes juridiques de droit public, dans les conditions prévues a l'article 1er.

(2)   Dans le transport des envois postaux, le transporteur n'est responsable qu'envers l'administration postale compétente conformément aux règles applicables dans les rapports entre les transporteurs et les administrations postales.

(3)   Les dispositions de la présente Convention autres que celles de l'alinéa 2 ci-dessus ne s'appliquent pas au transport des envois postaux.

Chapitre II   Titre de Transport

Section I—Billet de Passage

Article 3

(1)   Dans le transport de passagers, un billet de passage doit être délivré, contenant:

    (a)   l'indication des points de départ et de destination;

    (b)   si les points de départ et de destination sont situés sur le territoire d'une même Haute Partie Contractante et qu'une ou plusieurs escales soient prévues sur le territoire d'un autre Etat, l'indication d'une de ces escales;

    (c)   un avis indiquant que si les passagers entreprennent un voyage comportant une destination finale on une escale dans un pays autre que le pays de départ, leur transport peut être régi par la Convention de Varsovie qui, en général, limite la responsabilité du transporteur en cas de mort ou de lésion corporelle, ainsi qu'en cas de perte ou d'avarie des bagages.

(2)   Le billet de passage fait foi, jusqu'à preuve contraire, de la conclusion et des conditions du contrat de transport. L'absence, l'irrégularité ou la perte du billet n'affecte ni l'existence ni la validité du contrat de transport, qui n'en sera pas moins soumis aux règles de la présente Convention. Toutefois, si, du consentement du transporteur, le passager s'embarque sans qu'un billet de passage ait été delivré, ou si le billet ne comporte pas l'avis prescrit à l'alinéa 1(c) du présent article, le transporteur n'aura pas le droit de se prévaloir des dispositions de l'article 22.

Section II—Bulletin de Bagages

Article 4

(1)   Dans le transport de bagages enregistrés, un bulletin de bagages doit être délivré qui, s'il n'est pas combiné avec un billet de passage conforme aux dispositions de l'article 3, alinéa ler, ou n'est pas inclus dans un tel billet, doit contenir:

    (a)   l'indication des points de départ et de destination;

    (b)   si les points de départ et de destination sont situés sur le territoire d'une même Haute Partie Contractante et qu'une ou plusieurs escales soient prévues sur le territoire d'un autre Etat, l'indication d'une de ces escales;

    (c)   un avis indiquant que, si le transport comporte une destination finale ou une escale dans un pays autre que le pays de départ, il peut être régi par la Convention de Varsovie qui, en général, limite la responsabilité du transporteur en cas de perte ou d'avarie des bagages.

(2)   Le bulletin de bagages fait foi, jusqu'à preuve contraire de l'enregistrement des bagages et des conditions du contrat de transport. L'absence, l'irrégularité ou la perte du bulletin n'affecte ni l'existence ni la validité du contrat de transport, qui n'en sera pas moins soumis aux règles de la présente Convention. Toutefois, si le transporteur accepte la garde des bagages sans qu'un bulletin ait été délivré ou si, dans le cas où le bulletin n'est pas combiné avec un billet de passage conforme aux dispositions de l'article 3, alinéa I(c), ou n'est pas inclus dans un tel billet, il ne comporte pas l'avis prescrit a l'alinéa I(c) du présent article, le transporteur n'aura pas le droit de se prévaloir des dispositions de l'article 22, alinéa 2.

Section III—Documentation Relative aux Marchandises

Article 5

(1)   Pour le transport de marchandises une lettre de transport aérien est émise.

(2)   L'emploi de tout autre moyen constatant les indications relatives au transport à

exécuter peut, avec le consentement de l'expéditeur, se substituer à l'emission de la lettre de transport aérien. Si de tels autres moyens sont utilisés, le transporteur délivre à l'expéditeur, à la demande de ce dernier, un récépissé de la marchandise permettant l'identification de l'expédition et l'accès aux indications enregistrées par ces autres moyens.

(3)   L'impossibilité d'utiliser, aux points de transit et de destination, les autres moyens permettant de constater les indications relatives au transport, visés a l'alinéa 2 ci-dessus, n' autorise pas le transporteur à refuser l'acceptation des marchandises en vue du transport.

Article 6

(1)   La lettre de transport aérien est établie par l'expéditeur en trois exemplaires originaux.

(2)   Le premier exemplaire porte la mention "pour le transporteur"; il est signé par l'expéditeur. Le deuxième exemplaire porte la mention "pour le destinataire"; il est signé par l'expéditeur et le transporteur. Le troisième exemplaire est signé par le transporteur et remis par lui à l'expéditeur après acceptation de la marchandise.

(3)   La signature du transporteur et celle de l'expéditeur peuvent être imprimées ou remplacées par un timbre.

(4)   Si, à la demande de l'expéditeur, le transporteur établit la lettre de transport aérien, il est considéré, jusqu'à preuve contraire, comme agissant au nom de l'expéditeur.

Article 7

Lorsqu'il y a plusieurs colis:

(a)   le transporteur de marchandises a le droit de demander à l'expéditeur l'établissement de lettres de transport aérien distinctes;

(b)   l'expéditeur a le droit de demander au transporteur la remise de récépissés distincts, lorsque les autres moyens visés à l'alinéa 2 de l'article 5 sont utilisés.

Article 8

La lettre de transport aérien et le récépissé de la marchandise contiennent:

(a)   l'indication des points de départ et de destination;

(b)   si les points de départ et de destination sont situés sur le territoire d'une même Haute Partie Contractante et qu'une ou plusieurs escales soient prévues sur le territoire d'un autre Etat, l'indication d'une de ces escales;

(c)   la mention du poids de l'expédition.

Article 9

L'inobservation des dispositions des articles 5 à 8 n'affecte ni l'existence ni la validité du contrat de transport, qui n'en sera pas moins soumis aux règles de la présente Convention, y compris celles qui portent sur la limitation de responsabilité.

Article 10

(1)   L'expéditeur est responsable de l'exactitude des indications et déclarations concernant la marchandise inscrites par lui ou en son nom dans la lettre de transport aérien, ainsi que de celles fournies et faites par lui ou en son nom au transporteur en vue d'être insérées dans le récépissé de la marchandise ou pour insertion dans les données enregistrées par les autres moyens prévus à l'alinéa 2 de l'article 5.

(2)   L'expéditeur assume la responsabilité de tout dommage subi par le transporteur ou par toute autre personne à l'égard de laquelle la responsabilité du transporteur est engagée, à raison des indications et déclarations irrégulières, inexactes ou incomplètes fournies et faites par lui ou en son nom.

(3)   Sous réserve des dispositions des alinéas 1 et 2 du présent article, le transporteur assume la responsabilité de tout dommage subi par l'expéditeur ou par toute autre personne à l'égard de laquelle la responsabilité de l'expéditeur est engagée, à raison des indications et déclarations irrégulières, inexactes ou incomplètes insérées par lui ou en son nom dans le récépissé de la marchandise ou dans les données enregistrées par les autres moyens prévus à l'alinéa 2 de l'article 5.

Article 11

(1)   La lettre de transport aérien et le récépissé de la marchandise font foi, jusqu'à preuve contraire, de la conclusion du contrat, de la réception de la marchandise et des conditions du transport qui y figurent.

(2)   Les énonciations de la lettre de transport aérien et du récépissé de la marchandise, relatives au poids, aux dimensions et à l'emballage de la marchandise ainsi qu'au nombre des colis font foi jusqu'à preuve contraire; celles relatives à la quantité, au volume et à l'état de la marchandise ne font preuve contre le transporteur qu'autant que la vérification en a été faite par lui en présence de l'expéditeur, et constatée sur la lettre de transport aérien, ou qu'il s'agit d'énonciations relatives à l'état apparent de la marchandise.

Article 12

(1)   L'expéditeur a le droit, sous la condition d'exécuter toutes les obligations résultant du contrat de transport, de disposer de la marchandise, soit en la retirant à l'aérodrome de départ ou de destination, soit en l'arrêtant en cours de route lors d'un atterrissage, soit en la faisant délivrer au lieu de destination ou en cours de route à une personne autre que le destinataire initialement désigné, soit en demandant son retour à l'aérodrome de départ, pour autant que l'exercice de ce droit ne porte préjudice ni au transporteur, ni aux autres expéditeurs et avec l'obligation de rembourser les frais qui en résultent.

(2)   Dans le cas où l'exécution des ordres de l'expéditeur est impossible, le transporteur doit l'en aviser immédiatement.

(3)   Si le transporteur se conforme aux ordres de disposition de l'expéditeur, sans exiger la production de l'exemplaire de la lettre de transport aérien ou du récépissé de la marchandise délivré à celui-ci, il sera responsable, sauf son recours contre l'expéditeur, du préjudice qui pourra être causé par ce fait à celui qui est régulièrement en possession de la lettre de transport aérien ou du récépissé de la marchandise.

(4)   Le droit de l'expéditeur cesse au moment où celui du destinataire commence,

conformément à l'article 13. Toutefois, si le destinataire refuse la marchandise, ou s'il ne peut être atteint, l'expéditeur reprend son droit de disposition.

Article 13

(1)   Sauf lorsque l'expéditeur a exercé le droit qu'il tient de l'article 12, le destinataire a le droit, dès l'arrivée de la marchandise au point de destination, de demander au transporteur de lui livrer la marchandise contre le paiement du montant des créances et contre l'exécution des conditions de transport.

(2)   Sauf stipulation contraire, le transporteur doit aviser le destinataire dès l'arrivée de la marchandise.

(3)   Si la perte de la marchandise est reconnue par le transporteur ou si, à l'expiration d'un délai de sept jours après qu'elle aurait dû arriver, la marchandise n'est pas arrivée, le destinataire est autorisé à faire valoir vis-à-vis du transporteur les droits résultant du contrat de transport.

Article 14

L'expéditeur et le destinataire peuvent faire valoir tous les droits qui leur sont respectivement conférés par les articles 12 et 13, chacun en son propre nom, qu'il agisse dans son propre intérêt ou dans l'intérêt d'autrui, à condition d'exécuter les obligations que le contrat de transport impose.

Article 15

(1)   Les articles 12, 13 et 14 ne portent aucun préjudice ni aux rapports de l'expéditeur et du destinataire entre eux, ni aux rapports des tiers dont les droits proviennent, soit de l'expéditeur, soit du destinataire.

(2)   Toute clause dérogeant aux stipulations des articles 12, 13 et 14 doit être inscrite dans la lettre de transport aérien ou dans le récépissé de la marchandise.

Article 16

(1)   L'expéditeur est tenu de fournir les renseignements et les documents qui, avant la remise de la marchandise au destinataire, sont nécessaires à l'accomplissement des formalités de douane, d'octroi ou de police. L'expéditeur est responsable envers le transporteur de tous dommages qui pourraient résulter de l'absence, de l'insuffisance ou de l'irrégularité de ces renseignements et pièces, sauf le cas de faute de la part du transporteur ou de ses préposés.

(2)   Le transporteur n'est pas tenu d'examiner si ces renseignements et documents sont exacts ou suffisants.

Chapitre III   Responsabilité du Transporteur

Article 17

Le transporteur est responsable du dommage survenu en cas de mort, de blessure ou de toute autre lésion corporelle subie par un voyageur lorsque l'accident qui a causé le dommage s'est produit à bord de l'aéronef ou au cours de toutes opérations d'embarquement et de débarquement.

Article 18

(1)   Le transporteur est responsable du dommage survenu en cas de destruction, perte ou avarie de bagages enregistrés lorsque l'événement qui a causé le dommage s'est produit pendant le transport aérien.

(2)   Le transporteur est responsable du dommage survenu en cas de destruction, perte ou avarie de la marchandise par cela seul que le fait qui a causé le dommage s'est produit pendant le transport aérien.

(3)   Toutefois, le transporteur n'est pas responsable s'il établit que la destruction, la perte ou l'avarie de la marchandise résulte uniquement de l'un ou de plusieurs des faits suivants:

   (a)   la nature ou le vice propre de la marchandise;

   (b)   l'emballage défectueux de la marchandise par une personne autre que le transporteur ou ses préposés;

   (c)   un fait de guerre ou un conflit armé;

   (d)   un acte de l'autorité publique accompli en relation avec l'entrée, la sortie ou le transit de la marchandise.

(4)   Le transport aérien, au sens des alinéas précédents, comprend la période pendant laquelle les bagages ou marchandises se trouvent sous la garde du transporteur, que ce soit dans un aérodrome ou à bord d'un aéronef ou dans un lieu quelconque en cas d'atterrissage en dehors d'un aérodrome.

(5)   La période du transport aérien ne couvre aucun transport terrestre, maritime ou fluvial effectué en dehors d'un aérodrome. Toutefois, lorsqu'un tel transport est effectué dans l'exécution du contrat de transport aérien en vue du chargement, de la livraison ou du transbordement, tout dommage est présumé, sauf preuve contraire, résulter d'un événement survenu pendant le transport aérien.

Article 19

Le transporteur est responsable du dommage résultant d'un retard dans le transport aérien de voyageurs, bagages ou marchandises.

Article 20

Dans le transport de passagers et de bagages et en cas de dommage résultant d'un retard dans le transport de marchandises, le transporteur n'est pas responsable s'il prouve que lui et ses préposés ont pris toutes le mesures nécessaires pour éviter le dommage ou qu'il leur était impossible de les prendre.

Article 21

(1)   Dans le transport de passagers et de bagages, dans le cas où le transporteur fait la preuve que la faute de la personne lésée a causé le dommage ou y a contribué, le tribunal pourra, conformément aux dispositions de sa propre loi, écarter ou atténuer la responsabilité du transporteur.

(2)   Dans le transport de marchandises, le transporteur est exonéré, en tout ou en

301

partie, de sa responsabilité dans la mesure où il prouve que la faute de la personne qui demande réparation ou de la personne dont elle tient ses droits a causé le dommage ou y a contribué.

Article 22

(1)   Dans le transport des personnes, la responsabilité du transporteur relative à chaque passager est limité à la somme de 16.000 Droits de Tirage spéciaux. Dans le cas où, d'après la loi du tribunal saisi, l'indemnité peut être fixée sous forme de rente, le capital de la rente ne peut dépasser cette limite. Toutefois par une convention spéciale avec le transporteur, le passager pourra fixer une limite de responsabilité plus élevée.

(2)   (a)   Dans le transport de bagages enregistrés, la responsabilité du transporteur est limitée a la somme de 17 Droits de Tirage spéciaux par kilogramme, sauf déclaration spéciale d'intérêt à la livraison faite par l'expéditeur au moment de la remise du colis au transporteur et moyennant le paiement d'une taxe supplémentaire, éventuelle. Dans ce cas, le transporteur sera tenu de payer jusqu'à concurrence de la somme déclarée, à moins qu'il ne prouve qu'elle est supérieure à l'intérêt réel de l'expéditeur à la livraison.

(b)   Dans le transport de marchandises, la responsabilité du transporteur est limitée à la somme de 17 Droits de Tirage spéciaux par kilogramme, sauf déclaration spéciale d'intérêt à la livraison faite par l'expéditeur au moment de la remise du colis au transporteur et moyennant le paiement d'une taxe supplementaire, éventuelle. Dans ce cas, le transporteur sera tenu de payer jusqu'à concurrence de la somme déclarée, à moins qu'il ne prouve qu'elle est supérieure à l'intérêt réel de l'expéditeur à la livraison.

(c)   En cas de perte, d'avarie ou de retard d'une partie des bagages enregistrés ou des marchandises, ou de tout objet qui y est contenu, seul le poids total du ou des colis dont il s'agit est pris en considération pour déterminer la limite de responsabilité du transporteur. Toutefois, lorsque la perte, l'avarie ou le retard d'une partie des bagages enregistrés ou des marchandises, ou d'un objet qui y est contenu, affecte la valeur d'autres colis couverts par le même bulletin de bagages ou la même lettre de transport aérien, le poids total de ces colis doit être pris en considération pour déterminer la limite de responsabilité.

(3)   En ce qui concerne les objets dont le passager conserve la garde, la responsabilité du transporteur est limitée à 332 Droits de Tirage spéciaux par passager.

(4)   Les limites fixées par le présent article n'ont pas pour effet d'enlever au tribunal la faculté d'allouer en outre, conformément à sa loi, une somme correspondent à tout ou partie des dépens et autres frais du procès exposés par le demandeur. La disposition précédente ne s'applique pas lorsque le montant de l'indemnité allouée, non compris les dépens et autres frais de procès, ne dépasse pas la somme que le transporteur a offerte par écrit au demandeur dans un délai de six mois à dater du fait qui a causé le dommage ou avant l'introduction de l'instance si celle-ci est postérieure à ce délai.

(5)   Les sommes indiquées en Droits de Tirage spéciaux dans le présent article sont considérées comme se rapportant au Droit de Tirage spécial tel que défini par le Fonds Monétaire International. La conversion de ces sommes en monnaies nationales s'effectuera en cas d'instance judiciaire suivant la valeur de ces monnaies en Droit de Tirage spécial à la date du jugement.

(6)   Les sommes indiquées en Droits de Tirage spéciaux dans le présent article sont considérées comme se rapportant au Droit de Tirage spécial tel que défini par le Fonds Monétaire International. La conversion de ces sommes en monnaies nationales s'effectuera en cas d'instance judiciaire suivant la valeur de ces monnaies en Droit de Tirage spécial à la date du jugement. La valeur, en Droit de Tirage spécial, d'une monnaie nationale d'une Haute Partie Contractante qui est membre du Fonds Monétaire International, est calculée selon la méthode d'évaluation appliquée par le Fonds Monétaire International à la date du jugement pour ses propres opérations et transactions. La valeur, en Droit de Tirage spécial, d'une monnaie nationale d'une Haute Partie Contractante qui n'est pas membre du Fonds Monétaire International, est calculée de la façon déterminée par cette Haute Partie Contractante.

Toutefois, les Etats qui ne sont pas membres du Fonds Monétaire International et dont la législation ne permet pas d'appliquer les dispositions de l'alinéa 2(b) de l'article 22, peuvent au moment de la ratification ou de l'adhésion, ou à tout moment par la suite, déclarer que la limite de responsabilité du transporteur est fixée, dans les procédures judiciaires sur leur territoire, à la somme de deux cent cinquante unités monétaires par kilogramme, cette unité monétaire correspondant à soixante-cinq milligrammes et demi d'or au titre de neuf cents millièmes de fin. Cette somme peut être convertie dans la monnaie nationale concernée en chiffres ronds. La conversion de cette somme en monnaie nationale s'effectuera conformément à la législation de l'Etat en cause.

Article 23

(1)   Toute clause tendant à exonérer le transporteur de sa responsabilité ou à établir une limite inférieure à celle qui est fixée dans la présente Convention est nulle et de nul effet, mais la nullité de cette clause n'entraîne pas la nullité du contrat qui reste soumis aux dispositions de la présente Convention.

(2)   L'alinéa 1er du présent article ne s'applique pas aux clauses concernant la perte ou le dommage résultant de la nature ou du vice propre des marchandises transportées.

Article 24

(1)   Dans le transport de passagers et de bagages, toute action en responsabilité, à quelque titre que ce soit, ne peut être exercée que dans les conditions et limites prévues par la présente Convention, sans préjudice de la détermination des personnes qui ont le droit d'agir et de leurs droits respectifs.

(2)   Dans le transport de marchandises, toute action en réparation introduite, à quelque titre que ce soit, que ce soit en vertu de la présente Convention, en raison d'un contrat ou d'un acte illicite ou pour toute autre cause, ne peut être exercée que dans les conditions et limites de responsabilité prévues par la présente Convention, sans préjudice de la détermination des personnes qui ont le droit d'agir et de leurs droits respectifs. Ces limites de responsabilité constituent un maximum et sont infranchissables quelles que soient les circonstances qui sont à l'origine de la responsabilité.

Article 25

Dans le transport de passagers et de bagages, les limites de responsabilité prévues a l'article 22 ne s'appliquent pas s'il est prouvé que le dommage résulte d'un acte ou d'une omission du transporteur ou de ses préposés fait, soit avec l'intention de provoquer un dommage, soit témérairement et avec conscience qu'un dommage en résultera probablement, pour autant que, dans le cas d'un acte ou d'une omission de préposés, la preuve soit également apportée que ceux-ci ont agi dans l'exercise de leurs fonctions.

303

Article 25A

(1)   Si une action est intentée contre un préposé du transporteur à la suite d'un dommage visé par la présente Convention, ce préposé, s'il prouve qu'il a agi dans l'exercice de ses fonctions, pourra se prévaloir des limites de responsabilité que peut invoquer ce transporteur en vertu de l'article 22.

(2)   Le montant total de la réparation qui, dans ce cas, peut être obtenu du transporteur et de ses préposés ne doit pas dépasser lesdites limites.

(3)   Dans le transport de passagers et de bagages, les dispositions des alinéas 1 et 2 du présent article ne s'appliquent pas s'il est prouvé que le dommage résulte d'un acte ou d'une omission du préposé fait, soit avec l'intention de provoquer un dommage, soit témérairement et avec conscience qu'un dommage en résultera probablement.

Article 26

(1)   La réception des bagages et marchandises sans protestation par le destinataire constituera présomption, sauf preuve contraire, que les marchandises ont été livrées en bon état et conformément au titre de transport.

(2)   En cas d'avarie, le destinataire doit adresser au transporteur une protestation immédiatement après la découverte de l'avarie et, au plus tard, dans un délai de sept jours pour les bagages et de quatorze jours pour les marchandises à dater de leur réception. En cas de retard, la protestation devra être faite au plus tard dans les vingt et un jours à dater du jour où le bagage ou la marchandise auront été mis à sa disposition.

(3)   Toute protestation doit être faite par réserve inscrite sur le titre de transport ou par un autre écrit expédié dans le délai prévu pour cette protestation.

(4)   A défaut de protestation dans les délais prévus, toutes actions contre le transporteur sont irrecevables, sauf le cas de fraude de celui-ci.

Article 27

En cas de décès du débiteur, l'action en responsabilité, dans les limites prévues par la présente Convention, s'exerce contre ses ayants droit.

Article 28

(1)   L'action en responsabilité devra être portée, au choix du demandeur, dans le territoire d'une des Hautes Parties Contractantes, soit devant le tribunal du domicile du transporteur, du siège principal de son exploitation ou du lieu où il possède un établissement par le soin duquel le contrat a été conclu, soit devant le tribunal du lieu de destination.

(2)   La procédure sera réglée par la loi du tribunal saisi.

Article 29

(1)   L'action en responsabilité doit être intentée, sous peine de déchéance, dans le délai de deux ans à compter de l'arrivée à destination ou du jour où l'aéronef aurait dû arriver, ou de l'arrêt du transport.

(2)   Le mode du calcul du délai est determiné par la loi du tribunal saisi.

Article 30

(1)   Dans les cas de transport régis par la définition du troisième alinéa de l'article 1er, à exécuter par divers transporteurs successifs, chaque transporteur acceptant des voyageurs, des bagages ou des marchandises est soumis aux règles par cette Convention, et est censé être une des parties contractantes du contrat de transport, pour autant que ce contrat ait trait à la partie du transport effectué sous son contrôle.

(2)   Au cas d'un tel transport, le voyageur ou ses ayants droit ne pourront recourir que contre le transporteur ayant effectué le transport au cours duquel l'accident ou le retard s'est produit, sauf dans le cas où, par stipulation expresse, le premier transporteur aura assuré la responsabilité pour tout le voyage.

(3)   S'il s'agit de bagages ou de marchandises, l'expéditeur aura recours contre le premier transporteur et le destinataire qui a le droit à la délivrance contre le dernier, et l'un et l'autre pourront, en outre, agir contre le transporteur ayant effectué le transport au cours duquel la destruction, la perte, l'avarie ou le retard se sont produits. Ces transporteurs seront solidairement responsables envers l'expéditeur et le destinataire.

Article 30A

La présente Convention ne préjuge en aucune manière la question de savoir si la personne tenue pour responsable en vertu de ses dispositions a ou non un recours contre toute autre personne.

Chapitre IV   Dispositions Relatives aux Transports Combinés

Article 31

(1)   Dans le cas de transports combinés effectués en partie par air et en partie par toute autre moyen de transport, les stipulations de la présente Convention ne s'appliquent qu'au transport aérien et si celui-ci répond aux conditions de l'article 1er.

(2)   Rien dans la présente Convention n'empêche les parties, dans le cas de transports combinés d'insérer dans le titre de transport aérien des conditions relatives à d'autres modes de transport, à condition que les stipulations de la présente Convention soient respectées en ce qui concerne le transport par air.

Chapitre V   Dispositions Générales et Finales

Article 32

Sont nulles toutes clauses du contrat de transport et toutes conventions particulières antérieures au dommage par lesquelles les parties dérogeraient aux règles de la présente Convention soit par une détermination de la loi applicable, soit par une modification des règles de compétence. Toutefois, dans le transport des marchandises, les clauses d'arbitrage sont admises, dans les limites de la présente Convention, lorsque l'arbitrage doit s'effectuer dans les lieux de compétence des tribunaux prévus à l'article 28, alinéa 1.

Article 33

Sous réserve des dispositions de l'alinéa 3 de l'article 5, rien dans la présente Convention ne peut empêcher un transporteur de refuser la conclusion d'un contrat de transport ou de formuler des règlements qui ne sont pas en contradiction avec les dispositions de la présente Convention.

Article 34

Les dispositions des articles 3 à 8 inclus relatives aux titres de transport ne sont pas applicables au transport effectué dans des circonstances extraordinaires en dehors de toute opération normale de l'exploitation aérienne.

Article 35

Lorsque dans la présente Convention il est question de jours, il s'agit de jours courants et non de jours ouvrables.

Article 36

La présente Convention est rédigée en français en un seul exemplaire qui restera déposé aux archives du Ministère des Affairs Etrangères de Pologne, et dont une copie certifiée conforme sera transmise par les soins du Gouvernement polonais au Gouvernement de chacune des Hautes Parties Contractantes.

Article 40A

(1)   . . .

(2)   Aux fins de la Convention, le mot territoire signifie non seulement le territoire métropolitain d'un Etat, mais aussi tous les territoires qu'il représente dans les relations extérieures.]

Appendix 2a

Carriage By Air (Supplementary Provisions) Act 1962

(1962 c 43)

An Act to give effect to the Convention, supplementary to the Warsaw Convention, for the unification of certain rules relating to international carriage by air performed by a person other than the contracting carrier; and for connected purposes

[19th July 1962]

1. Supplementary Convention to have force of law. (1) The provisions of the Convention, supplementary to the Warsaw Convention, for the unification of certain rules relating to international carriage by air performed by a person other than the contracting carrier, as set out in the Schedule to this Act, shall, so far as they relate to the rights and liabilities of carriers, carriers' servants and agents, passengers, consignors, consignees, and other persons, and subject to the provisions of this Act, have the force of law in the United Kingdom in relation to any carriage by air to which the Convention applies, irrespective of the nationality of the aircraft performing that carriage.

(2)   If there is any inconsistency between the text in English in Part I of the Schedule to this Act and the text in French in Part II of that Schedule, the text in French shall prevail.

2. Interpretation of Supplementary Convention. (1) In the Schedule to this Act "the Warsaw Convention" means:

(a)   before the day on which section one of the Carriage by Air Act 1961, comes into force, the Convention set out in the First Schedule to the Carriage by Air Act 1932, and

(b)   on and after that day, [whichever is applicable to the carriage in question of the Conventions set out in Schedules 1 and 1A] to the said Act of 1961,

but, in relation to rights or liabilities arising out of an occurrence before that day, "the Warsaw Convention" shall continue to have the same meaning as before that day.

(2)   In Articles VII and VIII in the Schedule to this Act "court" includes (in an arbitration allowed by the Conventions referred to in the foregoing subsection or by Article IX, 3 in the Schedule to this Act) an arbitrator.

(3)   . . .

Notes   Sub-s (1): in para (b) words from 'whichever is applicable' to 'Schedules 1 and 1A' in square brackets substituted by SI 1999/1312, art 3(1), (2). Date in force: 21 May 1999 (except in relation to rights and liabilities arising out of an occurrence which took place before that date): see SI 1999/1312, art 1.

Sub-s (3): applies to Scotland only.

---

3. Application of provisions of Acts of 1961 and 1932. (1) In . . . subsections (2) and (3) of section four of the said Act of 1961 (which explain the limitations on liability in Article 22 in [Schedule 1 or 1A] to that Act and enable a court to make appropriate orders and awards to give effect to those limitations) references to the said Article 22 shall include, subject to any necessary modifications, references to Article VI in the Schedule to this Act.

(2)   In section five of the said Act of 1961 (which limits the time for bringing proceedings against a carrier's servant or agent and to obtain contribution from a carrier) references to a carrier include references to an actual carrier as defined in paragraph (c) of Article I in the Schedule to this Act as well as to a contracting carrier as defined in paragraph (b) of that Article.

(3)   In section eight of the said Act of 1961 (which relates to actions against States brought in the United Kingdom in accordance with Article 28 in [Schedule 1 or 1A] to that Act) and in section two of the said Act of 1932 (which contains corresponding provisions) the reference to Article 28 shall include a reference to Article VIII in the Schedule to this Act.

Notes   Sub-s (1): words omitted repealed by the Civil Liability (Contribution) Act 1978, s 9(2), Sch 2.

Sub-s (1): words 'Schedule 1 or 1A' in square brackets substituted by SI 1999/1312, art 3(1), (3). Date in force: 21 May 1999 (except in relation to rights and liabilities arising out of an occurrence which took place before that date): see SI 1999/1312, art 1.

Sub-s (3): words 'Schedule 1 or 1A' in square brackets substituted by SI 1999/1312, art 3(1), (3). Date in force: 21 May 1999 (except in relation to rights and liabilities arising out of an occurrence which took place before that date): see SI 1999/1312, art 1.

---

4. Interim protection for carriers' servants and agents.   Article V in the Schedule to this Act, and so much of Article VI in that Schedule as limits the aggregate amount which can be recovered from a carrier and his servants and agents, shall, in relation to rights or liabilities arising out of an occurrence before the day on which Article 25A in the First Schedule to the said Act of 1961 [as originally enacted] (to which those provisions are supplementary) comes into force, apply not only in relation to carriage performed by an actual carrier and to the persons mentioned in those provisions but also in relation to any other carriage governed by the Convention set out in the First Schedule to the said Act of 1932 and to any carrier under that Convention and his servants and agents.

Notes   Words in square brackets prospectively inserted by the Carriage by Air and Road Act 1979, s 1(2), Sch 2, para 5, as from a day to be appointed.

[4A. Amendments consequential on revision of Supplementary Convention]   [(1) Section 8A of the said Act of 1961 (which among other things enables Her Majesty in Council to alter that Act and this Act in consequence of any revision of the convention to which that Act relates) shall have effect in relation to a revision of the Convention in the Schedule to this Act as it has effect in relation to a revision of the Convention mentioned in that section but as if the reference in that section to the said Act of 1961 were omitted.

(2) An order under the said section 8A may relate both to that Act and this Act; and in the preceding subsection "revision", in relation to the Convention in the Schedule to this Act, means an omission from, addition to or alteration of that Convention and includes replacement of that Convention or part of it by another convention.]

Notes Inserted by the Carriage by Air and Road Act 1979, s 3(2).

5. Application to British possessions, etc, and to carriage by air not governed by Supplementary Convention. (1) Section nine of the said Act of 1961 (which enables Her Majesty to extend that Act to British possessions and other territories) shall (except so far as it relates to United Kingdom trust territories) apply to this Act as it applies to that Act, and an order under that section may relate to both that Act and this Act.

(2) Section ten of the said Act of 1961 (which enables Her Majesty to apply [Schedules 1 and 1A] and other provisions of that Act to carriage by air which is not governed by [the Conventions set out in those Schedules]) shall apply to the Schedule and other provisions of this Act as it applies to that Act, and an order under that section may relate to both that Act and this Act.

(3) Before the day on which section one of the said Act of 1961 comes into force, in subsections (1) and (2) of this section the references to sections nine and ten of the said Act of 1961 shall be read respectively, subject to any necessary modifications, as references to sections three and four of the said Act of 1932 (which contain corresponding provisions).

(4) This section shall come into force on the passing of this Act.

Notes Sub-s (2): words 'Schedules 1 and 1A' in square brackets substituted by SI 1999/1312, art 3(1), (4)(a). Date in force: 21 May 1999 (except in relation to rights and liabilities arising out of an occurrence which took place before that date): see SI 1999/1312, art 1.
    Sub-s (2): words 'the Conventions set out in those Schedules' in square brackets substituted by SI 1999/1312, art 3(1), (4)(b). Date in force: 21 May 1999 (except in relation to rights and liabilities arising out of an occurrence which took place before that date): see SI 1999/1312, art 1.

6. Application to Crown. (1) This Act shall bind the Crown.

(2) This section shall not have effect before the day on which section one of the said Act of 1961 comes into force.

7. Short title, commencement and saving. (1) This Act may be cited as the Carriage by Air (Supplementary Provisions) Act 1962.

(2) Except as otherwise provided, this Act shall come into force on such day as Her Majesty may by Order in Council certify to be the day on which the Convention in the Schedule to this Act comes into force as regards the United Kingdom.

(3) This Act shall not apply so as to affect rights or liabilities arising out of an occurrence before the day mentioned in the last foregoing subsection; and nothing in this section shall prevent any provision of this Act having effect before that day by virtue of an order under subsection (2) of section five of this Act.

Appendix 2b

Guadalajara Convention 1961

Section 1

Part I   The English Text

This Convention supplementary to the Warsaw Convention, for the Unification of Certain Rules Relating to International Carriage by Air Performed by a Person other than the Contracting Carrier

Article I

In this Convention:

(a)   . . .

(b)   "contracting carrier" means a person who as a principal makes an agreement for carriage governed by the Warsaw Convention with a passenger or consignor or with a person acting on behalf of the passenger or consignor;

(c)   "actual carrier" means a person, other than the contracting carrier, who, by virtue of authority from the contracting carrier, performs the whole or part of the carriage contemplated in paragraph (b) but who is not with respect to such part a successive carrier within the meaning of the Warsaw Convention. Such authority is presumed in the absence of proof to the contrary.

Article II

If an actual carrier performs the whole or part of carriage which, according to the agreement referred to in Article I, paragraph (b), is governed by the Warsaw Convention, both the contracting carrier and the actual carrier shall, except as otherwise provided in this Convention, be subject to the rules of the Warsaw Convention, the former for the whole of the carriage contemplated in the agreement, the latter solely for the carriage which he performs.

Article III

1   The acts and omissions of the actual carrier and of his servants and agents acting within the scope of their employment shall, in relation to the carriage performed by the actual carrier, be deemed to be also those of the contracting carrier.

2   The acts and omissions of the contracting carrier and of his servants and agents acting within the scope of their employment shall, in relation to the carriage performed by the actual carrier, be deemed to be also those of the actual carrier.

Nevertheless, no such act or omission shall subject the actual carrier to liability exceeding the limits specified in Article 22 [or Article 22A] of the Warsaw Convention. Any special agreement under which the contracting carrier assumes obligations not imposed by the Warsaw Convention or any waiver of rights conferred by that Convention or any special declaration of interest in delivery at destination contemplated in Article 22 [or Article 22A] of the said Convention, shall not affect the actual carrier unless agreed to by him.

Article IV

Any complaint to be made or order to be given under the Warsaw Convention to the carrier shall have the same effect whether addressed to the contracting carrier or to the actual carrier. Nevertheless, orders referred to in Article 12 of the Warsaw Convention shall only be effective if addressed to the contracting carrier.

Article V

In relation to the carriage performed by the actual carrier, any servant or agent of that carrier or of the contracting carrier shall, if he proves that he acted within the scope of his employment, be entitled to avail himself of the limits of liability which are applicable under this Convention to the carrier whose servant or agent he is unless it is proved that he acted in a manner which, under the Warsaw Convention, prevents the limits of liability from being invoked.

Article VI

In relation to the carriage performed by the actual carrier, the aggregate of the amounts recoverable from that carrier and the contracting carrier, and from their servants and agents acting within the scope of their employment, shall not exceed the highest amount which could be awarded against either the contracting carrier or the actual carrier under this Convention, but none of the persons mentioned shall be liable for a sum in excess of the limit applicable to him.

Article VII

In relation to the carriage performed by the actual carrier, an action for damages may be brought, at the option of the plaintiff, against that carrier or the contracting carrier, or against both together or separately. If the action is brought against only one of those carriers, that carrier shall have the right to require the other carrier to be joined in the proceedings, the procedure and effects being governed by the law of the court seised of the case.

Article VIII

Any action for damages contemplated in Article VII of this Convention must be brought, at the option of the plaintiff, either before a court in which an action may be brought against the contracting carrier, as provided in Article 28 of the Warsaw Convention, or before the court having jurisdiction at the place where the actual carrier is ordinarily resident or has his principal place of business.

Article IX

1   Any contractual provision tending to relieve the contracting carrier or the actual carrier of liability under this Convention or to fix a lower limit than that which is

applicable according to this Convention shall be null and void, but the nullity of any such provision does not involve the nullity of the whole agreement, which shall remain subject to the provisions of this Convention.

2   In respect of the carriage performed by the actual carrier, the preceding paragraph shall not apply to contractual provisions governing loss or damage resulting from the inherent defect, quality or vice of the cargo carried.

3   Any clause contained in an agreement for carriage and all special agreements entered into before the damage occurred by which the parties purport to infringe the rules laid down by this Convention, whether by deciding the law to be applied, or by altering the rules as to jurisdiction, shall be null and void. Nevertheless, for the carriage of cargo arbitration clauses are allowed, subject to this Convention, if the arbitration is to take place in one of the jurisdictions referred to in Article VIII.

Article X

Except as provided in Article VII, nothing in this Convention shall affect the rights and obligations of the two carriers between themselves.

Articles XI–XVIII

. . .

Notes First words omitted define "Warsaw Convention"; words in square brackets prospectively inserted by the Carriage by Air and Road Act 1979, s 1(2), Sch 2, para 6, as from a day to be appointed; second words omitted deal with the coming into force of the Convention and provide that in the case of inconsistency the text in French shall prevail.

Appendix 3a

Carriage by Air Acts (Application of Provisions) Order 1967

SI 1967/480

Made   23rd March 1967

Authority: Carriage by Air Act 1961, s 10

1. Citation and Operation.   This Order may be cited as the Carriage by Air Acts (Application of Provisions) Order 1967 and shall come into operation on 1st June 1967.

2. Interpretation.   (1) In this Order, unless the context otherwise requires:

"the Act of 1961" means the Carriage by Air Act 1961;

"the Act of 1962" means the Carriage by Air (Supplementary Provisions) Act 1962;

["the 1955 amended Convention"] means the English text of the Warsaw Convention with the amendments made in it by the Hague Protocol, as set out in Schedule 1 to the Act of 1961, and includes the Additional Protocol to the Warsaw Convention as set out at the end of that Schedule;

["the MP4 amended Convention" means the English text of the Warsaw Convention with the amendments made in it by the Hague Protocol and as further amended by Protocol No 4 of Montreal, 1975 as set out in Schedule 1A to the Act of 1961;]

"the Guadalajara Convention" means the English text of the Convention, supplementary to the Warsaw Convention, for the Unification of Certain Rules relating to International Carriage by Air performed by a Person other than the Contracting Carrier, as set out in the Schedule to the Act of 1962.

(2)   The Interpretation Act 1889 shall apply for the interpretation of this Order as it applies for the interpretation of an Act of Parliament.

Notes   Paragraph (1): words 'the 1955 amended Convention' in square brackets substituted by SI 1999/1737, art 2(1), (2)(a). Date in force: 2 July 1999 (except in relation to rights and liabilities arising out of an occurrence which took place before that date): see SI 1999/1737, art 1.

Paragraph (1): definition 'the MP4 amended Convention' inserted by SI 1999/1737, art 2(1), (2)(b). Date in force: 2 July 1999 (except in relation to rights and liabilities arising out of an occurrence which took place before that date): see SI 1999/1737, art 1.

---

3. Application.   This Order shall apply to all carriage by air, not being carriage to which the [1955 amended Convention or the MP4 amended Convention] applies.

Notes   Words '1955 amended Convention or the MP4 amended Convention' in square brackets substituted by SI 1999/1737, art 2(1), (3). Date in force: 2 July 1999 (except in relation to rights and liabilities arising out of an occurrence which took place before that date): see SI 1999/1737, art 1.

4. Non-international carriage, and carriage of mail and postal packages.   Schedule 1 to this Order shall have effect in respect of carriage to which this Order applies, being either:

  (a)   carriage which is not international carriage as defined in Schedule 2 [or Schedule 3] to this Order, or

  (b)   carriage of mail or postal packages.

Notes   Words 'or Schedule 3' in square brackets inserted by SI 1998/1058, art 2(1). Date in force: 2 May 1998: see SI 1998/1058, art 1.

5. International carriage under the unamended Warsaw Convention.   (1) Schedule 2 to this Order shall have effect in respect of carriage to which this Order applies, being carriage which is international carriage as defined in that Schedule.

(2)   Section 2 of the Act of 1961 shall apply to such carriage as aforesaid with the following exceptions, adaptations and modifications:

  (a)   Before "Convention" where it first appears there shall be inserted "Warsaw";

  (b)   For "at the end of the Convention as set out in the First Schedule to this Act" there shall be substituted "to the Warsaw Convention".

(3)   Section 8 of the Act of 1961 shall apply to such carriage as aforesaid, with the following exceptions, adaptations and modifications:

  (a)   Before "Convention" where it first appears there shall be inserted "Warsaw";

  (b)   "As set out in the First Schedule to this Act" shall be omitted;

  (c)   The reference to "the said Schedule" shall be construed as a reference to the amended Convention as applied by Schedule 2 to this Order.

[5A].   [(1)   Schedule 3 to this Order shall have effect in respect of carriage to which this Order applies, being carriage which is international carriage as defined in that Schedule.

(2)   Section 2 of the Act of 1961 shall apply to such carriage as aforesaid with the following modifications to subsection (1):

  (a)   For "Convention" where it first appears there shall be substituted "Warsaw Convention as amended by Additional Protocol No 1 of Montreal 1975";

  (b)   For "at the end of the Convention as set out in the First Schedule to this Act" there shall be substituted "to the Warsaw Convention".

(3)   Section 8 of the Act of 1961 shall apply to such carriage as aforesaid, with the following adaptations and modifications:

(a) For "Convention" where it first appears there shall be inserted "Warsaw Convention as amended by Additional Protocol No 1 of Montreal 1975";

(b) The words "as set out in the First Schedule to this Act" shall be omitted;

(c) The reference to "the said Schedule" shall be construed as a reference to the amended Convention as applied by Schedule 3 to this Order.]

Notes   Inserted by SI 1998/1058, art 2(2). Date in force: 2 May 1998: see SI 1998/1058, art 1.

[5B. Application of the air carrier liability Regulation]   [(1)   In relation to Community air carriers:

(a) in respect of damages up to the equivalent in ecus of 100,000 SDR arising from the death, wounding or other bodily injury suffered by a passenger, Article 20 of Part III of Schedule 1 and Article 20(1) of Part B of Schedules 2 and 3 to this Order;

(b) in respect of damages arising from the death, wounding or other bodily injury suffered by a passenger Article 21 of Part III of Schedule 1 and of Part B of Schedules 2 and 3 to this Order; and

(c) in respect of damages arising from the death, wounding or other bodily injury suffered by a passenger Article 22(1) of Part III of Schedule 1 and of Part B of Schedules 2 and 3 to this Order,

do not have the force of law in the United Kingdom.]

Notes   Inserted by SI 1998/1058, art 4. Date in force: 17 October 1998: see SI 1998/1751, art 1.

6. Application of certain provisions of the Acts.   Sections 3, 4, 5, 6, 11 and 12 of the Act of 1961 and section 3(1) of the Act of 1962 shall apply to carriage to which this Order applies as if the references therein to the Conventions scheduled to those Acts and to the Schedules in which they are set forth were references to the amended Convention and to the Guadalajara Convention as they are applied by this Order.

7. Gratuitous carriage by the Crown.   The Acts of 1961 and 1962, and this Order, shall apply to gratuitous carriage by the Crown as they apply to carriage by the Crown for reward:
Provided that the Crown shall not be precluded by Article 3(2) of the [1955 amended Convention or the MP4 amended Convention] as so applied from availing itself of the provisions of Article 22 thereof (which provides for the limitation of the carrier's liability in the carriage of persons) by reason of a passenger ticket not having been delivered or of the ticket not including the required notice.

Notes   Words '1955 amended Convention or the MP4 amended Convention' in square brackets substituted by SI 1999/1737, art 2(1), (3). Date in force: 2 July 1999 (except in relation to rights and liabilities arising out of an occurrence which took place before that date): see SI 1999/1737, art 1.

8. Exemptions.   The Board of Trade may, subject to such conditions as they think fit, exempt any carriage or class of carriage or any person or class of person from any of the requirements imposed by this Order.

Appendix 3b

Schedule 1   Non-International Carriage and Carriage of Mail and Postal Packages

Article 4

[Part I   Application of the Warsaw Convention as Amended at the Hague and by Protocol No 4 of Montreal, 1975]

[The MP4 amended Convention as set out in Schedule 1A to the 1961 Act shall apply in respect of carriage described in Article 4 of this Order subject to the following exceptions, adaptations and modifications:

(1)   For "Convention", wherever it appears, there shall be substituted "Schedule".

(2)   In Article 1(1) the word "international" shall be omitted.

(3)   Article 1(2) and (3) shall not apply.

(4)   Article 2(2) and (3) shall not apply.

(5)   Chapter II shall not apply.

(6)   In Article 22(1) for "16,600 Special Drawing Rights" there shall be substituted "100,000 Special Drawing Rights".

(7)   Article 22(6) shall not apply and the following shall be inserted:

"(6)   The value on a particular day of one Special Drawing Right shall be treated as equal to such a sum in sterling as the International Monetary Fund have fixed as being the equivalent of one Special Drawing Right—

    (a)   for that day; or

    (b)   if no sum has been fixed for that day, for the last day before that day for which a sum has been so fixed.

(7)   A certificate given by or on behalf of the Treasury stating—

    (a)   that a particular sum in sterling has been fixed by the International Monetary Fund as referred to in paragraph (6) for a particular day; or

    (b)   that no sum has been so fixed for a particular day and that a particular sum in sterling has been so fixed for a day which is the last day for which a sum has been so fixed before the particular day, shall be conclusive evidence of those matters for the purposes of this article; and a document purporting to be such a certificate shall in any proceedings be received in evidence and, unless the contrary is proved, be deemed to be such a certificate.";

(8)   In Article 26(1) the words from "and" to the end shall be omitted.

(9)   In Article 26(3) the words from "upon" to "writing" shall be omitted.

(10)   Article 28 shall not apply.

(11)   In Article 30(1) the words from "and" where it first occurs to "Article 1" shall be omitted.

(12)   In Article 32 the words from "if" to the end shall be omitted.

(13)   Article 34 shall not apply.

(14)   Articles 36 to 41 shall not apply.

(15)   The Additional Protocol shall not apply.]

Notes   Substituted by SI 1999/1737, art 3(4), Schedule. Date in force: 2 July 1999 (except in relation to rights and liabilities arising out of an occurrence which took place before that date): see SI 1999/1737, art 1.

[Part II   Application of the Guadalajara Convention]

[The Guadalajara Convention shall apply in respect of carriage, described in Article 4 of this Order, subject to the following exceptions, adaptations and modifications:

(1)   For "the Convention" wherever it appears, there shall be substituted "the Guadalajara Convention as applied by this Schedule".

(2)   In Article 1, the following shall be added as paragraph (a):

""the Warsaw Convention" means the MP4 amended Convention as applied by this Schedule".

(3)   In Article II, the words from "according" to "paragraph (b)" shall be omitted.

(4)   In Article III.2 for "by that Convention" there shall be substituted "thereby" and for "of the said Convention" there shall be substituted "thereof".

(5)   In Article IV, the second sentence shall not apply.

(6)   In Article VII, the second sentence shall not apply.

(7)   Article VIII shall not apply.

(8)   In Article IX, the words from "if" to the end shall be omitted.

(9)   After Article X the following Article shall be added:

"Article XI

Nothing herein shall impose any liability on the Postmaster General or any authority for the time being established by or under any Act of Parliament to provide postal services".]

Notes Substituted by SI 1999/1737, art 3(4), Schedule. Date in force: 2 July 1999 (except in relation to rights and liabilities arising out of an occurrence which took place before that date): see SI 1999/1737, art 1.

[Part III]

[For convenience of reference the MP4 amended Convention and the Guadalajara Convention, with the exceptions, adaptations and modifications made by this Schedule are here set out:

A   The MP4 amended Convention, as applied by Schedule 1

Non-International Carriage and Carriage of Mail and Postal Packages

Chapter I   Scope—Definitions

Article 1

This Schedule applies to all carriage of persons, baggage or cargo performed by aircraft for reward. It applies equally to gratuitous carriage by aircraft performed by an air transport undertaking.

Article 2

This Schedule applies to carriage performed by the State or by legally constituted public bodies provided it falls within the conditions laid down in Article 1.

Chapter III   Liability of the Carrier

Article 17

The carrier is liable for damage sustained in the event of the death or wounding of a passenger or any other bodily injury suffered by a passenger, if the accident which caused the damage so sustained took place on board the aircraft or in the course of any of the operations of embarking or disembarking.

Article 18

(1)   The carrier is liable for damage sustained in the event of the destruction or loss of, or damage to, any registered baggage, if the occurrence which caused the damage so sustained took place during the carriage by air.

(2)   The carrier is liable for damage sustained in the event of the destruction or loss of, or damage to, cargo upon condition only that the occurrence which caused the damage so sustained took place during the carriage by air.

(3)   However, the carrier is not liable if he proves that the destruction, loss of, or damage to, the cargo resulted solely from one or more of the following:

(a)   inherent defect, quality or vice of that cargo;

(b)   defective packing of that cargo performed by a person other than the carrier or his servants or agents;

(c)   an act of war or an armed conflict;

(d)   an act of a public authority carried out in connection with the entry, exit or transit of the cargo.

(4)   The carriage by air within the meaning of the preceding paragraphs of this Article comprises the period during which the baggage or cargo is in the charge of the carrier, whether in an airport or on board an aircraft, or, in the case of a landing outside an airport, in any place whatsoever.

(5)   The period of the carriage by air does not extend to any carriage by land, by sea or by river performed outside an airport. If, however, such carriage takes place in the performance of a contract for carriage by air, for the purpose of loading, delivery or transhipment, any damage is presumed, subject to proof to the contrary, to have been the result of an event which took place during the carriage by air.

Article 19

The carrier is liable for damage occasioned by delay in the carriage by air of passengers, baggage or cargo.

Article 20

In the case of passengers and baggage, and in the case of damage occasioned by delay in the carriage of cargo, the carrier shall not be liable if he proves that he and his servants and agents have taken all necessary measures to avoid the damage or that it was impossible for them to take such measures.

Article 21

(1)   In the carriage of passengers and baggage, if the carrier proves that the damage was caused by or contributed to by the negligence of the person suffering the damage the Court may, in accordance with the provisions of its own law, exonerate the carrier wholly or partly from his liability.

(2)   In the carriage of cargo, if the carrier proves that the damage was caused by or contributed to by the negligence or other wrongful act or omission of the person claiming compensation, or the person from whom he derives his rights, the carrier shall be wholly or partly exonerated from his liability to the claimant to the extent that such negligence or wrongful act or omission caused or contributed to the damage.

Article 22

(1)   In the carriage of persons the liability of the carrier for each passenger is limited to the sum of 100,000 Special Drawing Rights. Where, in accordance with the law of the court seised of the case, damages may be awarded in the form of periodical

payments the equivalent capital value of the said payments shall not exceed this limit. Nevertheless, by special contract, the carrier and the passenger may agree to a higher limit of liability.

(2) (a) In the carriage of registered baggage, the liability of the carrier is limited to a sum of 17 Special Drawing Rights per kilogramme, unless the passenger or consignor has made, at the same time when the package was handed over to the carrier, a special declaration of interest in delivery at destination and has paid a supplementary sum if the case so requires. In that case the carrier will be liable to pay a sum not exceeding the declared sum, unless he proves that that sum is greater than the passenger's or the consignor's actual interest in delivery at destination.

(b) In the carriage of cargo, the liability of the carrier is limited to a sum of 17 Special Drawing Rights per kilogramme, unless the consignor has made, at the same time when the package was handed over to the carrier, a special declaration of interest in delivery at destination and has paid a supplementary sum, if the case so requires. In that case the carrier will be liable to pay a sum not exceeding the declared sum, unless he proves that that sum is greater than the consignor's actual interest in delivery at destination.

(c) In the case of loss, damage or delay of part of registered baggage or cargo, or of any object contained therein, the weight to be taken into consideration in determining the amount to which the carrier's liability is limited shall be only the total weight of the package or packages concerned. Nevertheless, when the loss, damage or delay of a part of the registered package or cargo, or of an object contained therein, affects the value of other packages covered by the same baggage check or the same air waybill, the total weight of such package or packages shall also be taken into consideration in determining the limit of liability.

(3) As regards objects of which the passenger takes charge himself the liability of the carrier is limited to 332 Special Drawing Rights per passenger.

(4) The limits prescribed in this Article shall not prevent the court from awarding, in accordance with its own law, in addition, the whole or part of the court costs and of the other expenses of the litigation incurred by the plaintiff. The foregoing provision shall not apply if the amount of the damages awarded, excluding court costs and other expenses of the litigation, does not exceed the sum which the carrier has offered in writing to the plaintiff within a period of six months from the date of the occurrence causing the damage, or before the commencement of the action, if that is later.

(5) The sums mentioned in terms of the Special Drawing Rights in this Article shall be deemed to refer to the Special Drawing Right as defined by the International Monetary Fund. Conversion of the sums into national currencies shall, in case of judicial proceedings, be made according to the value of such currencies in terms of the Special Drawing Right at the date of judgment.

(6) The value on a particular day of one Special Drawing Right shall be treated as equal to such a sum in sterling as the International Monetary Fund have fixed as being the equivalent of one Special Drawing Right:

(a) for that day; or

(b)   if no sum has been fixed for that day, for the last day before that day for which a sum has been so fixed.

(7)   A certificate given by or on behalf of the Treasury stating:

(a)   that a particular sum in sterling has been fixed by the International Monetary Fund as referred to in paragraph (6) for a particular day; or

(b)   that no sum has been so fixed for a particular day and that a particular sum in sterling has been so fixed for a day which is the last day for which a sum has been so fixed before the particular day,

shall be conclusive evidence of those matters for the purposes of this article; and a document purporting to be such a certificate shall in any proceedings be received in evidence and, unless the contrary is proved, be deemed to be such a certificate.

Article 23

(1)   Any provision tending to relieve the carrier of liability or to fix a lower limit than that laid down in this Schedule shall be null and void, but the nullity of any such provision does not involve the nullity of the whole contract, which shall remain subject to the provisions of this Schedule.

(2)   Paragraph (1) of this Article shall not apply to provisions governing loss or damage resulting from the inherent defect, quality or vice of the cargo carried.

Article 24

(1)   In the carriage of passengers and baggage, any action for damages, however founded, can only be brought subject to the conditions and limits set out in this Schedule, without prejudice to the question as to who are the persons who have the right to bring suit and what are their respective rights.

(2)   In the carriage of cargo, any action for damages, however founded, whether under this Schedule or in contract or in tort or otherwise, can only be brought subject to the conditions and limits of liability set out in this Schedule without prejudice to the question as to who are the persons who have the right to bring suit and what are their respective rights. Such limits of liability constitute maximum limits and may not be exceeded whatever the circumstances which give rise to the liability.

Article 25

In the carriage of passengers and baggage, the limits of liability specified in Article 22 shall not apply if it is proved that the damage resulted from an act or omission of the carrier, his servants or agents, done with intent to cause damage or recklessly and with knowledge that damage would probably result; provided that, in the case of such act or omission of a servant or agent, it is also proved that he was acting within the scope of his employment.

Article 25A

(1)   If an action is brought against a servant or agent of the carrier arising out of damage to which this Schedule relates, such servant or agent, if he proves that he acted within the scope of his employment, shall be entitled to avail himself of the limits of liability which that carrier himself is able to invoke under Article 22.

(2)   The aggregate of the amounts recoverable from the carrier, his servants or agents, in that case, shall not exceed the said limits.

(3)   In the carriage of passengers and baggage, the provisions of paragraphs (1) and (2) of this Article shall not apply if it is proved that the damage resulted from an act or omission of the servant or agent done with intent to cause damage or recklessly and with knowledge that damage would probably result.

Article 26

(1)   Receipt by the person entitled to delivery of baggage or cargo without complaint is prima facie evidence that the same has been delivered in good condition.

(2)   In the case of damage, the person entitled to delivery must complain to the carrier forthwith after the discovery of the damage, and, at the latest, within seven days from the date of receipt in the case of baggage and fourteen days from the date of receipt in the case of cargo. In the case of delay the complaint must be made at the latest within twenty-one days from the date on which the baggage or cargo has been placed at his disposal.

(3)   Every complaint must be made in writing despatched within the times aforesaid.

(4)   Failing complaint within the times aforesaid, no action shall lie against the carrier, save in the case of fraud on his part.

Article 27

In the case of the death of the person liable, an action for damages lies in accordance with the terms of this Schedule against those legally representing his estate.

Article 29

(1)   The right to damages shall be extinguished if an action is not brought within two years, reckoned from the date of arrival at the destination, or from the date on which the aircraft ought to have arrived, or from the date on which the carriage stopped.

(2)   The method of calculating the period of limitation shall be determined by the law of the Court seised of the case.

Article 30

(1)   In the case of carriage to be performed by various successive carriers, each carrier who accepts passengers, baggage or cargo is subjected to the rules set out in this Schedule, and is deemed to be one of the contracting parties to the contract of carriage in so far as the contract deals with that part of the carriage which is performed under his supervision.

(2)   In the case of carriage of this nature, the passenger or his representative can take action only against the carrier who performed the carriage during which the accident or the delay occurred, save in the case where, by express agreement, the first carrier has assumed liability for the whole journey.

(3)   As regards baggage or cargo, the passenger or consignor will have a right of action against the first carrier, and the passenger or consignee who is entitled to delivery will have a right of action against the last carrier, and further, each may take action against the carrier who performed the carriage during which the destruction, loss, damage or delay took place. These carriers will be jointly and severally liable to the passenger or to the consignor or consignee.

Article 30A

Nothing in this Schedule shall prejudice the question whether a person liable for damage in accordance with its provisions has a right of recourse against any other person.

Chapter IV   Provisions Relating to Combined Carriage

Article 31

(1)   In the case of combined carriage performed partly by air and partly by any other mode of carriage, the provisions of this Schedule apply only to carriage by air, provided that carriage by air falls within the terms of Article 1.

(2)   Nothing in this Schedule shall prevent the parties in the case of combined carriage from inserting in the document of air carriage conditions relating to other modes of carriage, provided that the provisions of this Schedule are observed as regards the carriage by air.

Chapter V   General and Final Provisions

Article 32

Any clause contained in the contract and all special agreements entered into before the damage occurred by which the parties purport to infringe the rules laid down by this Schedule, whether by deciding the law to be applied, or by altering the rules as to jurisdiction shall be null and void. Nevertheless for the carriage of cargo arbitration clauses are allowed subject to this Schedule.

Article 33

Except as provided in paragraph 3 of Article 5, nothing in this Schedule shall prevent the carrier either from refusing to enter into any contract of carriage or from making regulations which do not conflict with the provisions of this Schedule.

Article 35

The expression "days" when used in this Schedule means current days not working days.

B   The Guadalajara Convention as applied by Schedule 1

Non-International Carriage and Carriage of Mail and Postal Packages

Article I

In the Guadalajara Convention as applied by this Schedule:

(a) "the Warsaw Convention" means the MP4 amended Convention as applied by this Schedule;

(b) "contracting carrier" means a person who as a principal makes an agreement for carriage governed by the Warsaw Convention with a passenger or consignor or with a person acting on behalf of the passenger or consignor;

(c) "actual carrier" means a person, other than the contracting carrier, who by virtue of authority from the contracting carrier, performs the whole or part of the carriage contemplated in paragraph (b) but who is not with respect to such part a successive carrier within the meaning of the Warsaw Convention. Such authority is presumed in the absence of proof to the contrary.

Article II

If an actual carrier performs the whole or part of carriage which is governed by the Warsaw Convention, both the contracting carrier and the actual carrier shall, except as otherwise provided in the Warsaw Convention, be subject to the rules of the Warsaw Convention, the former for the whole of the carriage contemplated in the agreement and the latter solely for the carriage which he performs.

Article III

1. The acts and omissions of the actual carrier and of his servants and agents within the scope of their employment shall, in relation to the carriage performed by the actual carrier, be deemed to be also those of the contracting carrier.

2. The acts and omissions of the contracting carrier and of his servants and agents within the scope of their employment shall, in relation to the carriage performed by the actual carrier, be deemed to be also those of the actual carrier. Nevertheless, no such act or omission shall subject the actual carrier to liability exceeding the limits specified in Article 22 thereof. Any special agreement under which the contracting carrier assumes obligations not imposed thereby or any waiver of rights conferred thereby or any special declaration of interest in delivery at destination contemplated in Article 22 thereof, shall not affect the actual carrier unless agreed to by him.

Article IV

Any complaint to be made under the Warsaw Convention to the carrier shall have the same effect whether addressed to the contracting carrier or to the actual carrier.

Article V

In relation to the carriage performed by the actual carrier, any servant or agent of that carrier or of the contracting carrier shall, if he proves that he acted within the scope of his employment, be entitled to avail himself of the limits of liability which are applicable under the Guadalajara Convention as applied by this Schedule to the carrier whose servant or agent he is unless it is proved that he acted in a manner which, under the Warsaw Convention, prevents the limits of liability from being invoked.

Article VI

In relation to the carriage performed by the actual carrier, the aggregate of the amounts recoverable from that carrier and the contracting carrier, and from their servants and agents acting within the scope of their employment, shall not exceed the highest amount which could be awarded against either the contracting carrier or the actual carrier under the Guadalajara Convention as applied by this Schedule, but none of the persons mentioned shall be liable for a sum in excess of the limit applicable to him.

Article VII

In relation to the carriage performed by the actual carrier, an action for damages may be brought, at the option of the plaintiff, against that carrier or the contracting carrier or against both together or separately.

Article IX

1.   Any contractual provision tending to relieve the contracting carrier or the actual carrier of liability under the Guadalajara Convention as applied by this Schedule or to fix a lower limit than that which is applicable according to the Guadalajara Convention as applied by this Schedule shall be null and void, but the nullity of any such provision does not involve the nullity of the whole agreement, which shall remain subject to the provisions of the Guadalajara Convention as applied by this Schedule.

2.   In respect of the carriage performed by the actual carrier, the preceding paragraph shall not apply to contractual provisions governing loss or damage resulting from the inherent defect, quality or vice of the cargo carried.

3.   Any clause contained in an agreement for carriage and all special agreements entered into before the damage occurred by which the parties purport to infringe the rules laid down by the Guadalajara Convention as applied by this Schedule, whether by deciding the law to be applied or by altering the rules as to jurisdiction, shall be null and void. Nevertheless, for carriage of cargo arbitration clauses are allowed subject to the Guadalajara Convention as applied by this Schedule.

Article X

Except as provided in Article VII, nothing in the Guadalajara Convention as applied by this Schedule shall affect the rights and obligations of the two carriers between themselves.

Article XI

Nothing herein shall impose any liability on the Postmaster General or any authority for the time being established by or under any Act of Parliament with power to provide postal services.]

Notes   Substituted by SI 1999/1737, art 3(4), Schedule. Date in force: 2 July 1999 (except in relation to rights and liabilities arising out of an occurrence which took place before that date): see SI 1999/1737, art 1.

Appendix 3c

Schedule 2   International Carriage under the Unamended Warsaw Convention

Article 5

Part A

1.   [The 1955 amended Convention] and the Guadalajara Convention shall apply in respect of carriage which is "international carriage" as defined in paragraph 2 of this part of this Schedule, with the exceptions, adaptations and modifications set forth in paragraphs 3 and 4.

2.   For the purposes of Article 5 of this Order and of this Schedule "international carriage" shall have the meaning assigned to it by paragraph 3(2) of this part of this Schedule.

3.   [The 1955 amended Convention] shall apply to international carriage as aforesaid, with the following exceptions, adaptations and modifications:

> (1)   For "Convention", wherever it appears, there shall be substituted "Schedule".

> (2)   For Article 1(2) there shall be substituted the following:

""International carriage" means any carriage in which, according to the contract made by the parties, the place of departure and the place of destination, whether or not there be a break in the carriage or a transhipment, are situated either within the territories of two States Parties to the Convention for the Unification of Certain Rules relating to International Carriage by Air signed at Warsaw on behalf of His Majesty on 12th October 1929, or within the territory of a single such State, if there is an agreed stopping place within the territory subject to the sovereignty, suzerainty, mandate or authority of another State, even though that State is not a party to the said Convention of 1929."

> (3)   The following shall be substituted for Article 1(3):

"(3)   A carriage to be performed by several successive air carriers is deemed, for the purposes of this Schedule, to be one undivided carriage, if it has been regarded by the parties as a single operation, whether it had been agreed upon under the form of a single contract or of a series of contracts, and it does not lose its international character merely because one contract or a series of contracts is to be performed entirely within a territory subject to the sovereignty, suzerainty, mandate or authority of the same High Contracting Party."

> (4)   The following shall be substituted for Article 2:

"(1)   This Schedule applies to carriage performed by the State, not being a State which has availed itself of the Additional Protocol to the Warsaw Convention, or by legally constituted public bodies, provided it falls within the conditions laid down in Article 1.

(2)   This Schedule does not apply to carriage performed under the terms of any international postal Convention."

(5)   The following shall be substituted for Article 3:

"(1)   For the carriage of passengers the carrier must deliver a passenger ticket which shall contain the following particulars:—

(a)   the place and date of issue;

(b)   the place of departure and of destination;

(c)   the agreed stopping places, provided that the carrier may reserve the right to alter the stopping places in case of necessity, and that if he exercises that right, the alteration shall not have the effect of depriving the carriage of its international character;

(d)   the name and address of the carrier or carriers;

(e)   a statement that the carriage is subject to the rules relating to liability established by the Warsaw Convention.

(2)   The absence, irregularity or loss of the passenger ticket does not affect the existence or the validity of the contract of carriage, which shall none the less be subject to the rules of this Schedule. Nevertheless, if the carrier accepts a passenger without a passenger ticket having been delivered he shall not be entitled to avail himself of those provisions of this Schedule which exclude or limit his liability."

(6)   The following shall be substituted for Article 4:

"(1)   For the carriage of baggage, other than small personal objects of which the passenger takes charge himself, the carrier must deliver a baggage check.

(2)   The baggage check shall be made out in duplicate, one part for the passenger and the other part for the carrier.

(3)   The baggage check shall contain the following particulars:—

(a)   the place and date of issue;

(b)   the place of departure and of destination;

(c)   the name and address of the carrier or carriers;

(d)   the number of the passenger ticket;

(e)   a statement that delivery of the baggage will be made to the bearer of the baggage check;

(f)   the number and weight of the packages;

(g)   the amount of the value declared in accordance with Article 22(2);

(h)   a statement that the carriage is subject to the rules relating to liability established by the Warsaw Convention.

(4)   The absence, irregularity or loss of the baggage check does not affect the existence or the validity of the contract of carriage, which shall none the less be subject to the rules of this Schedule. Nevertheless, if the carrier accepts baggage without a baggage check having been delivered, or if the baggage check does not contain the particulars set out at (d) (f) and (h) above, the carrier shall not be entitled to avail himself of those provisions of this Schedule which exclude or limit his liability."

(7)   The following shall be substituted for Article 6(3):

"(3)   The carrier shall sign on acceptance of the [cargo]."

(8)   The following shall be substituted for Article 8:

"The air waybill shall contain the following particulars:—

(a)   the place and date of its execution;

(b)   the place of departure and of destination;

(c)   the agreed stopping places, provided that the carrier may reserve the right to alter the stopping places in case of necessity, and that if he exercises that right the alteration shall not have the effect of depriving the carriage of its international character;

(d)   the name and address of the consignor;

(e)   the name and address of the first carrier;

(f)   the name and address of the consignee, if the case so requires;

(g)   the nature of the cargo;

(h)   the number of the packages, the method of packing and the particular marks or numbers upon them;

(i)   the weight, the quantity and the volume or dimensions of the cargo;

(j)   the apparent condition of the cargo and of the packing;

(k)   the freight, if it has been agreed upon, the date and place of payment, and the person who is to pay it;

(l)   if the cargo is sent for payment on delivery, the price of the cargo, and, if the case so requires, the amount of the expenses incurred;

(m)   the amount of the value declared in accordance with Article 22(2);

(n)   the number of parts of the air waybill;

(o)   the documents handed to the carrier to accompany the air waybill;

(p)   the time fixed for the completion of the carriage and a brief note of the route to be followed, if these matters have been agreed upon;

(q) a statement that the carriage is subject to the rules relating to liability established by the Warsaw Convention."

(9) The following shall be substituted for Article 9:

"If the carrier accepts cargo without an air waybill having been made out, or if the air waybill does not contain all the particulars set out in Article 8(a) to (i) inclusive and (q), the carrier shall not be entitled to avail himself of the provisions of this Schedule which exclude or limit his liability."

(10) The following shall be substituted for Article 10(2):

"(2) The consignor will be liable for all damage suffered by the carrier or any other person by reason of the irregularity, incorrectness or incompleteness of the said particulars and statements."

[(10A) Article 15(3) shall not apply.]

(11) The following shall be inserted as Article 20(2):

"(2) In the carriage of cargo and baggage the carrier is not liable if he proves that the damage was occasioned by negligent pilotage or negligence in the handling of the aircraft or in navigation and that, in all other respects, he and his servants or agents have taken all necessary measurements to avoid the damage."

(12) The following shall be substituted for Article 22:

"(1) In the carriage of passengers the liability of the carrier for each passenger is limited to the sum of 125,000 francs. Where, in accordance with the law of the Court seised of the case, damages may be awarded in the form of periodical payments, the equivalent capital value of the said payments shall not exceed 125,000 francs. Nevertheless, by special contract, the carrier and the passenger may agree to a higher limit of liability.

(2) In the carriage of registered baggage and of cargo, the liability of the carrier is limited to a sum of 250 francs per kilogramme, unless the consignor has made, at the time when the package was handed over to the carrier, a special declaration of the value at delivery and has paid a supplementary sum if the case so requires. In that case the carrier will be liable to pay a sum not exceeding the declared sum, unless he proves that that sum is greater than the actual value to the consignor at delivery.

(3) As regards objects of which the passenger takes charge himself the liability of the carrier is limited to 5,000 francs per passenger.

(4) The sums mentioned above shall be deemed to refer to the French franc consisting of 65 1/2 milligrammes gold of millesimal fineness 900. These sums may be converted into any national currency in round figures."

(13) Article 23(2) shall not apply.

(14) The following shall be substituted for Article 25:

"(1) The carrier shall not be entitled to avail himself of the provisions of this Schedule which exclude or limit his liability, if the damage is caused by his wilful misconduct or by such default on his part as, in accordance with the law of the Court seised of the case, is considered to be equivalent to wilful misconduct.

(2)   Similarly the carrier shall not be entitled to avail himself of the said provisions, if the damage is caused as aforesaid by any servant or agent of the carrier acting within the scope of his employment."

[(14A)   Article 25A shall not apply.]

(15)   The following shall be substituted for Article 26(2):

"(2)   In the case of damage, the person entitled to delivery must complain to the carrier forthwith after the discovery of the damage, and, at the latest, within three days from the date of receipt in the case of baggage and seven days from the date of receipt in the case of cargo. In the case of delay the complaint must be made at the latest within fourteen days from the date on which the baggage or cargo has been placed at his disposal."

(16)   In Article 28(1), after "High Contracting Parties" there shall be added "to the Warsaw Convention".

(17)   The following shall be substituted for Article 34:

"This Schedule does not apply to international carriage by air performed by way of experimental trial by air navigation undertakings with the view to the establishment of a regular line of air navigation, nor does it apply to carriage performed in extraordinary circumstances outside the normal scope of an air carrier's business."

(18)   Articles 36 and 40A shall not apply.

(4)   The Guadalajara Convention shall apply to international carriage within the meaning of this Schedule, with the following exceptions, adaptations and modifications:

(1)   For "this Convention" wherever it appears there shall be substituted "the Guadalajara Convention as applied by this Schedule".

(2)   In Article I, the following shall be added as paragraph (a):

""the Warsaw Convention" means [the 1955 amended Convention] as applied by this Schedule."

Notes   Paragraph 1: words 'The 1955 amended Convention' in square brackets substituted by SI 1999/1737, art 2(1), (5). Date in force: 2 July 1999 (except in relation to rights and liabilities arising out of an occurrence which took place before that date): see SI 1999/1737, art 1.
Paragraph 2: words 'The 1955 amended Convention' in square brackets substituted by SI 1999/1737, art 2(1), (5). Date in force: 2 July 1999 (except in relation to rights and liabilities arising out of an occurrence which took place before that date): see SI 1999/1737, art 1.
Paragraph 3: in sub-para (7) word 'cargo' in square brackets substituted by SI 1998/1058, art 2(3)(a). Date in force: 2 May 1998: see SI 1998/1058, art 1.
Paragraph 3: sub-para (10A) inserted by SI 1998/1058, art 2(3)(b). Date in force: 2 May 1998: see SI 1998/1058, art 1.
Paragraph 3: sub-para (14A) inserted by SI 1998/1058, art 2(3)(c). Date in force: 2 May 1998: see SI 1998/1058, art 1.
Paragraph 4: words 'the 1955 amended Convention' in square brackets substituted by SI 1999/1737, art 2(1), (5). Date in force: 2 July 1999 (except in relation to rights and liabilities arising out of an occurrence which took place before that date): see SI 1999/1737, art 1.

Part B

Chapter 1   Scope—Definitions

Article 1

(1)   This Schedule applies to all international carriage of persons, baggage or cargo performed by aircraft for reward. It applies equally to gratuitous carriage by aircraft performed by an air transport undertaking.

(2)   "International carriage" means any carriage in which, according to the contract made by the parties, the place of departure and the place of destination, whether or not there be a break in the carriage or a transhipment, are situated either within the territories of two States Parties to the Convention for the Unification of Certain Rules relating to International Carriage by Air signed at Warsaw on behalf of His Majesty on 12th October 1929, or within the territory of a single such State, if there is an agreed stopping place within the territory subject to the sovereignty, suzerainty, mandate or authority of another State, even though that State is not a party to the said Convention of 1929.

(3)   A carriage to be performed by several successive air carriers is deemed, for the purposes of this Schedule, to be one undivided carriage, if it has been regarded by the parties as a single operation, whether it had been agreed upon under the form of a single contract or of a series of contracts, and it does not lose its international character merely because one contract or a series of contracts is to be performed entirely within a territory subject to the sovereignty, suzerainty, mandate or authority of the same High Contracting Party.

Article 2

(1)   This Schedule applies to carriage performed by the State, not being a State which has availed itself of the Additional Protocol to the Warsaw Convention, or by legally constituted public bodies, provided it falls within the conditions laid down in Article 1.

(2)   This Schedule does not apply to carriage performed under the terms of any international postal Convention.

Chapter II   Documents of Carriage

Section 1   Passenger Ticket

Article 3

(1)   For the carriage of passengers the carrier must deliver a passenger ticket which shall contain the following particulars:

(a)   the place and date of issue;

(b)   the place of departure and of destination;

(c)   the agreed stopping places, provided that the carrier may reserve the right to alter the stopping places in case of necessity, and that if he exercises that right, the alteration shall not have the effect of depriving the carriage of its international character;

(d)   the name and address of the carrier or carriers;

(e)   a statement that the carriage is subject to the rules relating to liability established by the Warsaw Convention.

(2)   The absence, irregularity or loss of the passenger ticket does not affect the existence or the validity of the contract of carriage, which shall none the less be subject to the rules of this Schedule. Nevertheless, if the carrier accepts a passenger without a passenger ticket having been delivered he shall not be entitled to avail himself of those provisions of this Schedule which exclude or limit his liability.

Section 2   Baggage Check

Article 4

(1)   For the carriage of baggage, other than small personal objects of which the passenger takes charge himself, the carrier must deliver a baggage check.

(2)   The baggage check shall be made out in duplicate, one part for the passenger and the other part for the carrier.

(3)   The baggage check shall contain the following particulars:

(a)   the place and date of issue;

(b)   the place of departure and of destination;

(c)   the name and address of the carrier or carriers;

(d)   the number of the passenger ticket;

(e)   a statement that delivery of the baggage will be made to the bearer of the baggage check;

(f)   the number and weight of the packages;

(g)   the amount of the value declared in accordance with Article 22(2);

(h)   a statement that the carriage is subject to the rules relating to liability established by the Warsaw Convention.

(4)   The absence, irregularity or loss of the baggage check does not affect the existence or the validity of the contract of carriage, which shall none the less be subject to the rules of this Schedule. Nevertheless, if the carrier accepts baggage without a baggage check having been delivered, or if the baggage check does not contain the particulars set out at (d) (f), and (h) above, the carrier shall not be entitled to avail himself of those provisions of this Schedule which exclude or limit his liability.

Section 3   Air Waybill

Article 5

(1)   Every carrier of cargo has the right to require the consignor to make out and hand over to him a document called an "air waybill"; every consignor has the right to require the carrier to accept this document.

(2)   The absence, irregularity or loss of this document does not affect the existence or the validity of the contract of carriage which shall, subject to the provisions of Article 9, be none the less governed by the rules of this Schedule.

Article 6

(1)   The air waybill shall be made out by the consignor in three original parts and be handed over with the cargo.

(2)   The first part shall be marked "for the carrier", and shall be signed by the consignor. The second part shall be marked "for the consignee"; it shall be signed by the consignor and by the carrier and shall accompany the cargo. The third part shall be signed by the carrier and handed by him to the consignor after the cargo has been accepted.

(3)   The carrier shall sign on acceptance of the cargo.

(4)   The signature of the carrier may be stamped; that of the consignor may be printed or stamped.

(5)   If, at the request of the consignor, the carrier makes out the air waybill, he shall be deemed, subject to proof to the contrary, to have done so on behalf of the consignor.

Article 7

The carrier of cargo has the right to require the consignor to make out separate waybills when there is more than one package.

Article 8

The air waybill shall contain the following particulars:

    (a)   the place and date of its execution;

    (b)   the place of departure and of destination;

    (c)   the agreed stopping places, provided that the carrier may reserve the right to alter the stopping places in case of necessity, and that if he exercises that right the alteration shall not have the effect of depriving the carriage of its international character;

    (d)   the name and address of the consignor;

    (e)   the name and address of the first carrier;

    (f)   the name and address of the consignee, if the case so requires;

(g)   the nature of the cargo;

(h)   the number of the packages, the method of packing and the particular marks or numbers upon them;

(i)   the weight, the quantity and the volume or dimensions of the cargo;

(j)   the apparent condition of the cargo and of the packing;

(k)   the freight, if it has been agreed upon, the date and place of payment, and the person who is to pay it;

(l)   if the cargo is sent for payment on delivery, the price of the cargo, and, if the case so requires, the amount of the expenses incurred;

(m)   the amount of the value declared in accordance with Article 22(2);

(n)   the number of parts of the air waybill;

(o)   the documents handed to the carrier to accompany the air waybill;

(p)   the time fixed for the completion of the carriage and a brief note of the route to be followed, if these matters have been agreed upon;

(q)   a statement that the carriage is subject to the rules relating to liability established by the Warsaw Convention.

Article 9

If the carrier accepts cargo without an air waybill having been made out, or if the air waybill does not contain all the particulars set out in Article 8(a) to (i) inclusive and (q), the carrier shall not be entitled to avail himself of the provisions of this Schedule which exclude or limit his liability.

Article 10

(1)   The consignor is responsible for the correctness of the particulars and statements relating to the cargo which he inserts in the air waybill.

(2)   The consignor will be liable for all damage suffered by the carrier or any other person by reason of the irregularity, incorrectness or incompleteness of the said particulars and statements.

Article 11

(1)   The air waybill is *prima facie* evidence of the conclusion of the contract, of the receipt of the cargo and of the conditions of carriage.

(2)   The statements in the air waybill relating to the weight, dimensions and packing of the cargo, as well as those relating to the number of packages, are *prima facie* evidence of the facts stated; those relating to the quantity, volume and condition of the cargo do not constitute evidence against the carrier except so far as they both have been, and are stated in the air waybill to have been, checked by him in the presence of the consignor, or relate to the apparent condition of the cargo.

Article 12

(1) Subject to his liability to carry out all his obligations under the contract of carriage, the consignor has the right to dispose of the cargo by withdrawing it at the aerodrome of departure or destination, or by stopping it in the course of the journey on any landing, or by calling for it to be delivered at the place of destination or in the course of the journey to a person other than the consignee named in the air waybill, or by requiring it to be returned to the aerodrome of departure. He must not exercise this right of disposition in such a way as to prejudice the carrier or other consignors and he must repay any expenses occasioned by the exercise of this right.

(2) If it is impossible to carry out the orders of the consignor the carrier must so inform him forthwith.

(3) If the carrier obeys the orders of the consignor for the disposition of the cargo without requiring the production of the part of the air waybill delivered to the latter, he will be liable, without prejudice to his right of recovery from the consignor, for any damage which may be caused thereby to any person who is lawfully in possession of that part of the air waybill.

(4) The right conferred on the consignor ceases at the moment when that of the consignee begins in accordance with Article 13. Nevertheless, if the consignee declines to accept the waybill or the cargo, or if he cannot be communicated with, the consignor resumes his right of disposition.

Article 13

(1) Except in the circumstances set out in the preceding Article, the consignee is entitled, on arrival of the cargo at the place of destination, to require the carrier to hand over to him the air waybill and to deliver the cargo to him, on payment of the charges due and on complying with the conditions of carriage set out in the air waybill.

(2) Unless it is otherwise agreed, it is the duty of the carrier to give notice to the consignee as soon as the cargo arrives.

(3) If the carrier admits the loss of the cargo, or if the cargo has not arrived at the expiration of seven days after the date on which it ought to have arrived, the consignee is entitled to put into force against the carrier the rights which flow from the contract of carriage.

Article 14

The consignor and the consignee can respectively enforce all the rights given them by Articles 12 and 13, each in his own name, whether he is acting in his own interest or in the interest of another, provided that he carries out the obligations imposed by the contract.

Article 15

(1) Articles 12, 13 and 14 do not affect either the relations of the consignor or the consignee with each other or the mutual relations of third parties whose rights are derived either from the consignor or from the consignee.

(2) The provisions of Articles 12, 13 and 14 can only be varied by express provision in the air waybill.

(3) . . .

Article 16

(1)   The consignor must furnish such information and attach to the air waybill such documents as are necessary to meet the formalities of customs, octroi or police before the cargo can be delivered to the consignee. The consignor is liable to the carrier for any damage occasioned by the absence, insufficiency or irregularity of any such information or documents, unless the damage is due to the fault of the carrier or his servants or agents.

(2)   The carrier is under no obligation to enquire into the correctness or sufficiency of such information or documents.

Chapter III   Liability of the Carrier

Article 17

The carrier is liable for damage sustained in the event of the death or wounding of a passenger or any other bodily injury suffered by a passenger, if the accident which caused the damage so sustained took place on board the aircraft or in the course of any of the operations of embarking or disembarking.

Article 18

(1)   The carrier is liable for damage sustained in the event of the destruction or loss of, or of damage to, any registered baggage or any cargo, if the occurrence which caused the damage so sustained took place during the carriage by air.

(2)   The carriage by air within the meaning of the preceding paragraph comprises the period during which the baggage or cargo is in charge of the carrier, whether in an aerodrome or on board an aircraft, or, in the case of a landing outside an aerodrome, in any place whatsoever.

(3)   The period of the carriage by air does not extend to any carriage by land, by sea or by river performed outside an aerodrome. If, however, such a carriage takes place in the performance of a contract for carriage by air, for the purpose of loading, delivery or transhipment, any damage is presumed, subject to proof to the contrary, to have been the result of an event which took place during the carriage by air.

Article 19

The carrier is liable for damage occasioned by delay in the carriage by air of passengers, baggage or cargo.

Article 20

(1)   The carrier is not liable if he proves that he and his servants or agents have taken all necessary measures to avoid the damage or that it was impossible for him or them to take such measures.

(2)   In the carriage of cargo and baggage the carrier is not liable if he proves that the damage was occasioned by negligent pilotage or negligence in the handling of the aircraft or in navigation and that, in all other respects, he and his servants or agents have taken all necessary measures to avoid the damage.

Article 21

If the carrier proves that the damage was caused by or contributed to by the negligence of the injured person the Court may, in accordance with the provisions of its own law, exonerate the carrier wholly or partly from his liability.

Article 22

(1)   In the carriage of passengers the liability of the carrier for each passenger is limited to the sum of 125,000 francs. Where, in accordance with the law of the Court seised of the case, damages may be awarded in the form of periodical payments, the equivalent capital value of the said payments shall not exceed 125,000 francs. Nevertheless, by special contract, the carrier and the passenger may agree to a higher limit of liability.

(2)   In the carriage of registered baggage and of cargo, the liability of the carrier is limited to a sum of 250 francs per kilogramme, unless the consignor has made, at the time when the package was handed over to the carrier, a special declaration of the value at delivery and has paid a supplementary sum if the case so requires. In that case the carrier will be liable to pay a sum not exceeding the declared sum, unless he proves that that sum is greater than the actual value to the consignor at delivery.

(3)   As regards objects of which the passenger takes charge himself the liability of the carrier is limited to 5,000 francs per passenger.

(4)   The sums mentioned above shall be deemed to refer to the French franc consisting of 65(1/2) milligrammes gold of millesimal fineness 900. These sums may be converted into any national currency in round figures.

Article 23

Any provision tending to relieve the carrier of liability or to fix a lower limit than that which is laid down in this Schedule shall be null and void, but the nullity of any such provision does not involve the nullity of the whole contract, which shall remain subject to the provisions of this Schedule.

Article 24

(1)   In the cases covered by Articles 18 and 19 any action for damages, however founded, can only be brought subject to the conditions and limits set out in this Schedule.

(2)   In the cases covered by Article 17 the provisions of the preceding paragraph also apply, without prejudice to the questions as to who are the persons who have the right to bring suit and what are their respective rights.

Article 25

(1)   The carrier shall not be entitled to avail himself of the provisions of this Schedule which exclude or limit his liability, if the damage is caused by his wilful misconduct or by such default on his part as, in accordance with the law of the Court seised of the case, is considered to be equivalent to wilful misconduct.

(2)   Similarly the carrier shall not be entitled to avail himself of the said provisions, if the damage is caused as aforesaid by any servant or agent of the carrier acting within the scope of his employment.

Article 25A

. . .

Article 26

(1)   Receipt by the person entitled to delivery of baggage or cargo without complaint is *prima facie* evidence that the same has been delivered in good condition and in accordance with the document of carriage.

(2)   In the case of damage, the person entitled to delivery must complain to the carrier forthwith after the discovery of the damage, and, at the latest, within three days from the date of receipt in the case of baggage and seven days from the date of receipt in the case of cargo. In the case of delay the complaint must be made at the latest within fourteen days from the date on which the baggage or cargo has been placed at his disposal.

(3)   Every complaint must be made in writing upon the document of carriage or by separate notice in writing despatched within the times aforesaid.

(4)   Failing complaint within the times aforesaid, no action shall lie against the carrier, save in the case of fraud on his part.

Article 27

In the case of the death of the person liable, an action for damages lies in accordance with the terms of this Schedule against those legally representing his estate.

Article 28

(1)   An action for damages must be brought, at the option of the plaintiff, in the territory of one of the High Contracting Parties to the Warsaw Convention, either before the Court having jurisdiction where the carrier is ordinarily resident, or has his principal place of business, or has an establishment by which the contract has been made or before the Court having jurisdiction at the place of destination.

(2)   Questions of procedure shall be governed by the law of the Court seised of the case.

Article 29

(1)   The right to damages shall be extinguished if an action is not brought within two years, reckoned from the date of arrival at the destination, or from the date on which the aircraft ought to have arrived, or from the date on which the carriage stopped.

(2)   The method of calculating the period of limitation shall be determined by the law of the Court seised of the case.

Article 30

(1)   In the case of carriage to be performed by various successive carriers and falling within the definition set out in the third paragraph of Article 1, each carrier who accepts passengers, baggage or cargo is subjected to the rules set out in this Schedule, and is deemed to be one of the contracting parties to the contract of carriage in so far

as the contract deals with that part of the carriage which is performed under his supervision.

(2)   In the case of carriage of this nature, the passenger or his representative can take action only against the carrier who performed the carriage during which the accident or the delay occurred, save in the case where, by express agreement, the first carrier has assumed liability for the whole journey.

(3)   As regards baggage or cargo, the passenger or consignor will have a right of action against the first carrier, and the passenger or consignee who is entitled to delivery will have a right of action against the last carrier, and further, each may take action against the carrier who performed the carriage during which the destruction, loss, damage or delay took place. These carriers will be jointly and severally liable to the passenger or to the consignor or consignee.

Chapter IV   Provisions Relating to Combined Carriage

Article 31

(1)   In the case of combined carriage performed partly by air and partly by any other mode of carriage, the provisions of this Schedule apply only to the carriage by air, provided that the carriage by air falls within the terms of Article 1.

(2)   Nothing in this Schedule shall prevent the parties in the case of combined carriage from inserting in the document of air carriage conditions relating to other modes of carriage, provided that the provisions of this Schedule are observed as regards the carriage by air.

Chapter V   General and Final Provisions

Article 32

Any clause contained in the contract and all special agreements entered into before the damage occurred by which the parties purport to infringe the rules laid down by this Schedule, whether by deciding the law to be applied, or by altering the rules as to jurisdiction, shall be null and void. Nevertheless, for the carriage of cargo arbitration clauses are allowed, subject to this Schedule, if the arbitration is to take place within one of the jurisdictions referred to in the first paragraph of Article 28.

Article 33

Nothing contained in this Schedule shall prevent the carrier either from refusing to enter into any contract of carriage, or from making regulations which do not conflict with the provisions of this Schedule.

Article 34

This Schedule does not apply to international carriage by air performed by way of experimental trial by air navigation undertakings with the view to the establishment of a regular line of air navigation, nor does it apply to carriage performed in extraordinary circumstances outside the normal scope of an air carrier's business.

Article 35

The expression "days" when used in this Schedule means current days not working days.

Additional Protocol to the Warsaw Convention

The High Contracting Parties reserve to themselves the right to declare at the time of ratification or of accession that the first paragraph of Article 2 of this Convention shall not apply to international carriage by air performed directly by the State, its colonies, protectorates or mandated territories or by any other territory under its sovereignty, suzerainty or authority.

B   The Guadalajara Convention as applied by Schedule 2

(International Carriage under the unamended Warsaw Convention)

Article I

In the Guadalajara Convention as applied by this Schedule:

(a)   "the Warsaw Convention" means [the 1955 amended Convention] as applied by this Schedule;

(b)   "contracting carrier" means a person who as a principal makes an agreement for carriage governed by the Warsaw Convention with a passenger or consignor or with a person acting on behalf of the passenger or consignor;

(c)   "actual carrier" means a person, other than the contracting carrier, who, by virtue of authority from the contracting carrier, performs the whole or part of the carriage contemplated in paragraph (b) but who is not with respect to such part a successive carrier within the meaning of the Warsaw Convention. Such authority is presumed in the absence of proof to the contrary.

Article II

If an actual carrier performs the whole or part of carriage which, according to the agreement referred to in Article I, paragraph (b), is governed by the Warsaw Convention, both the contracting carrier and the actual carrier shall, except as otherwise provided in the Guadalajara Convention as applied by this Schedule, be subject to the rules of the Warsaw Convention, the former for the whole of the carriage contemplated in the agreement, the latter solely for the carriage which he performs.

Article III

(1)   The acts and omissions of the actual carrier and of his servants and agents acting within the scope of their employment shall, in relation to the carriage performed by the actual carrier, be deemed to be also those of the contracting carrier.

(2)   The acts and omissions of the contracting carrier and of his servants and agents acting within the scope of their employment shall, in relation to the carriage

performed by the actual carrier, be deemed to be also those of the actual carrier. Nevertheless, no such act or omission shall subject the actual carrier to liability exceeding the limits specified in Article 22 of the Warsaw Convention. Any special agreement under which the contracting carrier assumes obligations not imposed by the Warsaw Convention or any waiver of rights conferred by that Convention or any special declaration of interest in delivery at destination contemplated in Article 22 of the said Convention, shall not affect the actual carrier unless agreed to by him.

Article IV

Any complaint to be made or order to be given under the Warsaw Convention to the carrier shall have the same effect whether addressed to the contracting carrier or to the actual carrier. Nevertheless, orders referred to in Article 12 of the Warsaw Convention shall only be effective if addressed to the contracting carrier.

Article V

In relation to the carriage performed by the actual carrier, any servant or agent of that carrier or of the contracting carrier shall, if he proves that he acted within the scope of his employment, be entitled to avail himself of the limits of liability which are applicable under the Guadalajara Convention as applied by this Schedule to the carrier whose servant or agent he is unless it is proved that he acted in a manner which, under the Warsaw Convention, prevents the limits of liability from being invoked.

Article VI

In relation to the carriage performed by the actual carrier, the aggregate of the amounts recoverable from that carrier and the contracting carrier, and from their servants and agents acting within the scope of their employment, shall not exceed the highest amount which could be awarded against either the contracting carrier or the actual carrier under the Guadalajara Convention as applied by this Schedule, but none of the persons mentioned shall be liable for a sum in excess of the limit applicable to him.

Article VII

In relation to the carriage performed by the actual carrier, an action for damages may be brought, at the option of the plaintiff, against that carrier or the contracting carrier, or against both together or separately. If the action is brought against only one of those carriers, that carrier shall have the right to require the other carrier to be joined in the proceedings, the procedure and effects being governed by the law of the Court seised of the case.

Article VIII

Any action for damages contemplated in Article VII of the Guadalajara Convention as applied by this Schedule must be brought, at the option of the plaintiff, either before a Court in which any action may be brought against the contracting carrier, as provided in Article 28 of the Warsaw Convention, or before the Court having jurisdiction at the place where the actual carrier is ordinarily resident or has his principal place of business.

Article IX

(1)   Any contractual provision tending to relieve the contracting carrier or the actual carrier of liability under the Guadalajara Convention as applied by this Schedule or to fix a lower limit than that which is applicable according to the Guadalajara Convention as applied by this Schedule shall be null and void, but the nullity of any such provision does not involve the nullity of the whole agreement, which shall remain subject to the provisions of the Guadalajara Convention as applied by this Schedule.

(2)   In respect of the carriage performed by the actual carrier, the preceding paragraph shall not apply to contractual provisions governing loss or damage resulting from the inherent defect, quality or vice of the cargo carried.

(3)   Any clause contained in an agreement for carriage and all special agreements entered into before the damage occurred by which the parties purport to infringe the rules laid down by the Guadalajara Convention as applied by this Schedule, whether by deciding the law to be applied, or by altering the rules as to jurisdiction, shall be null and void. Nevertheless, for the carriage of cargo arbitration clauses are allowed, subject to the Guadalajara Convention as applied by this Schedule, if the arbitration is to take place in one of the jurisdictions referred to in Article VIII.

Article X

Except as provided in Article VII, nothing in the Guadalajara Convention as applied by this Schedule shall affect the rights and obligations of the two carriers between themselves.

Notes   Article 15: para (3) revoked by SI 1998/1058, art 2(4). Date in force: 2 May 1998: see SI 1998/1058, art 1.
      Article 25A: revoked by SI 1998/1058, art 2(4). Date in force: 2 May 1998: see SI 1998/1058, art 1.
      Article I: in definition 'the Warsaw Convention' words 'the 1955 amended Convention' in square brackets substituted by SI 1999/1737, art 2(1), (5). Date in force: 2 July 1999 (except in relation to rights and liabilities arising out of an occurrence which took place before that date): see SI 1999/1737, art 1.

[Schedule 3   International Carriage Under the Warsaw Convention as Amended by Additional Protocol No 1 of Montreal 1975]

[Article 5A]

[Part A]

[1.   [The 1955 amended Convention] and the Guadalajara Convention shall apply in respect of carriage which is "international carriage" as defined in paragraph 2 of this part of this Schedule, with the exceptions, adaptations and modifications set forth in paragraphs 3 and 4.

2.   For the purposes of Article 5A of this Order and of this Schedule "international carriage" shall have the meaning assigned to it by paragraph 3(2) of this part of this Schedule.

3. [The 1955 amended Convention] shall apply to international carriage as aforesaid, with the following exceptions, adaptations and modifications:

(1)   For "Convention", wherever it appears, there shall be substituted "Schedule".

(2)   The following shall be substituted for Article 1(2):

"(2)   "International carriage" means any carriage in which, according to the contract made by the parties, the place of departure and the place of destination, whether or not there be a break in the carriage or a transhipment, are situated either within the territories of two States Parties to the Convention for the Unification of Certain Rules relating to International Carriage by Air signed at Warsaw on behalf of His Majesty on 12th October 1929 as amended by Additional Protocol No 1 of Montreal 1975, or within the territory of a single such State, if there is an agreed stopping place within the territory subject to the sovereignty, suzerainty, mandate or authority of another State, even though that State is not a party to the said Convention of 1929 as so amended.".

(3)   The following shall be substituted for Article 1(3):—

"(3)   A carriage to be performed by several successive air carriers is deemed for the purposes of this Schedule, to be one undivided carriage, if it has been regarded by the parties as a single operation, whether it had been agreed upon under the form of a single contract or of a series of contracts, and it does not lose its international character merely because one contract or a series of contracts is to be performed entirely within a territory subject to the sovereignty, suzerainty, mandate or authority of the same High Contracting Party.".

(4)   The following shall be substituted for Article 2:

"Article 2
(1)   This Schedule applies to carriage performed by the State, not being a State which has availed itself of the Additional Protocol to the Warsaw Convention, or by legally constituted public bodies, provided it falls within the conditions laid down in Article 1.

(2)   This Schedule does not apply to carriage performed under the terms of any international postal Convention.".

(5)   The following shall be substituted for Article 3:

"Article 3
(1)   For the carriage of passengers the carrier must deliver a passenger ticket which shall contain the following particulars:—

     (a)   the place and date of issue;

     (b)   the place of departure and of destination;

     (c)   the agreed stopping places, provided that the carrier may reserve the right to alter the stopping places in case of necessity, and that if he exercises that right, the alteration shall not have the effect of depriving the carriage of its international character;

(d) the name and address of the carrier or carriers;

(e) a statement that the carriage is subject to the rules relating to liability established by the Warsaw Convention.

(2) The absence, irregularity or loss of the passenger ticket does not affect the existence or the validity of the contract of carriage, which shall none the less be subject to the rules of this Schedule. Nevertheless, if the carrier accepts a passenger without a passenger ticket having been delivered he shall not be entitled to avail himself of those provisions of this Schedule which exclude or limit his liability.".

(6) The following shall be substituted for Article 4:

"Article 4

(1) For the carriage of baggage, other than small personal objects of which the passenger takes charge himself, the carrier must deliver a baggage check.

(2) The baggage check shall be made out in duplicate, one part for the passenger and the other part for the carrier.

(3) The baggage check shall contain the following particulars:—

(a) the place and date of issue;

(b) the place of departure and of destination;

(c) the name and address of the carrier or carriers;

(d) the number of the passenger ticket;

(e) a statement that delivery of the baggage will be made to the bearer of the baggage check;

(f) the number and weight of the packages;

(g) the amount of the value declared in accordance with Article 22(2);

(h) a statement that the carriage is subject to the rules relating to liability established by the Warsaw Convention.

(4) The absence, irregularity or loss of the baggage check does not affect the existence or the validity of the contract of carriage, which shall none the less be subject to the rules of this Schedule. Nevertheless, if the carrier accepts baggage without a baggage check having been delivered, or if the baggage check does not contain the particulars set out at (d), (f) and (h) above, the carrier shall not be entitled to avail himself of those provisions of this Schedule which exclude or limit his liability.".

(7) The following shall be substituted for Article 6(3):—

"(3) The carrier shall sign on acceptance of the cargo.".

(8) The following shall be substituted for Article 8:—

"Article 8

The air waybill shall contain the following particulars:—

(a)   The place and date of its execution;

(b)   the place of departure and of destination;

(c)   the agreed stopping places, provided that the carrier may reserve the right to alter the stopping places in case of necessity, and that if he exercises that right the alteration shall not have the effect of depriving the carriage of its international character;

(d)   the name and address of the consignor;

(e)   the name and address of the first carrier;

(f)   the name and address of the consignee, if the case so requires;

(g)   the nature of the cargo;

(h)   the number of the packages, the method of packing and the particular marks or numbers upon them;

(i)   the weight, the quantity and the volume or dimensions of the cargo;

(j)   the apparent condition of the cargo and of the packing;

(k)   the freight, if it has been agreed upon, the date and place of payment, and the person who is to pay it;

(l)   if the cargo is sent for payment on delivery, the price of the cargo, and, if the case so requires, the amount of the expenses incurred;

(m)   the amount of the value declared in accordance with Article 22(2);

(n)   the number of parts of the air waybill;

(o)   the documents handed to the carrier to accompany the air waybill;

(p)   the time fixed for the completion of the carriage and a brief note of the route to be followed, if these matters have been agreed upon;

(q)   a statement that the carriage is subject to the rules relating to liability established by the Warsaw Convention.".

(9)   The following shall be substituted for Article 9:

"Article 9

If the carrier accepts cargo without an air waybill having been made out, or if the air waybill does not contain all the particulars set out in Article 8(a) to (i) inclusive and (q), the carrier shall not be entitled to avail himself of the provisions of this Schedule which exclude or limit his liability.".

(10)   The following shall be substituted for Article 10(2):

"(2) The consignor will be liable for all damage suffered by the carrier or any other person by reason of the irregularity, incorrectness or incompleteness of the said particulars and statements.".

(11) Article 15(3) shall not apply.

(12) The following shall be substituted for Article 20(2):

"(2) In the carriage of cargo and baggage the carrier is not liable if he proves that the damage was occasioned by negligent pilotage or negligence in the handling of the aircraft or in navigation and that, in all other respects, he and his servants or agents have taken all necessary measures to avoid the damage.".

(13) The following shall be substituted for Article 22:

"Article 22

(1)   In the carriage of passengers the liability of the carrier for each passenger is limited to the sum of 8,300 Special Drawing Rights. Where, in accordance with the law of the court seised of the case, damages may be awarded in the form of periodic payments, the equivalent capital value of the said payments shall not exceed this limit. Nevertheless, by special contract, the carrier and the passenger may agree to a higher limit of liability.

(2)   In the carriage of registered baggage and of cargo, the liability of the carrier is limited to a sum of 17 Special Drawing Rights per kilogramme, unless the consignor has made, at the time when the package was handed over to the carrier, a special declaration of interest in delivery at destination and has paid a supplementary sum if the case so requires. In that case the carrier will be liable to pay a sum not exceeding the declared sum, unless he proves that the sum is greater than the consignor's actual interest in delivery at destination.

(3)   As regards objects of which the passenger takes charge himself the liability of the carrier is limited to 332 Special Drawing Rights per passenger.

(4)   The sums mentioned in terms of the Special Drawing Right in this Article shall be deemed to refer to the Special Drawing Right as defined by the International Monetary Fund. Conversion of the sums into national currencies shall, in case of judicial proceedings, be made according to the value of such currencies in terms of the Special Drawing Right at the date of the judgement. The value of a national currency, in terms of the Special Drawing Right, of a High Contracting Party which is a Member of the International Monetary Fund, shall be calculated in accordance with the method of valuation applied by the International Monetary Fund, in effect at the date of the judgement, for its operations and transactions. The value of a national currency, in terms of the Special Drawing Right, of a High Contracting Party which is not a Member of the International Monetary Fund, shall be calculated in a manner determined by that High Contracting Party.

Nevertheless, those States which are not Members of the International Monetary Fund and whose law does not permit the application of the provisions of paragraphs 1, 2 and 3 of Article 22 may at the time of ratification or accession or at any time thereafter declare that the limit of liability of the carrier in judicial proceedings in their territories is fixed at a sum of 125,000 monetary units per passenger with respect to paragraph 1 of Article 22; 250 monetary units per kilogramme with respect to paragraph 2 of Article 22; and 5,000 monetary units per passenger with respect to paragraph 3 of Article 22. This monetary unit corresponds to sixty-five and a half milligrammes of gold of millesimal fineness nine hundred. These sums may be converted into the national currency concerned in round figures. The conversion of these sums into national currency shall be made according to the law of the State concerned.".

(14)   Article 23(2) shall not apply.

(15)   The following shall be substituted for Article 25:

"Article 25
(1)   The carrier shall not be entitled to avail himself of the provisions of this Schedule which exclude or limit his liability, if the damage is caused by his wilful misconduct or by such default on his part as, in accordance with the law of the Court seised of the case, is considered to be equivalent to wilful misconduct.

(2)   Similarly the carrier shall not be entitled to avail himself of the said provisions, if the damage is caused as aforesaid by any servant or agent of the carrier acting within the scope of his employment.".

(16)   Article 25A shall not apply.

(17)   The following shall be substituted for Article 26(2):

"(2)   In the case of damage, the person entitled to delivery must complain to the carrier forthwith after the discovery of the damage, and, at the latest, within three days from the date of receipt in the case of baggage and seven days from the date of receipt in the case of cargo. In the case of delay the complaint must be made at the latest within fourteen days from the date on which the baggage or cargo has been placed at his disposal.".

(18)   In Article 28(1), after "High Contracting Parties" there shall be added "to the Warsaw Convention as amended by Additional Protocol No 1 of Montreal 1975".

(19)   The following shall be substituted for Article 34:

"Article 34
This Schedule does not apply to international carriage by air performed by way of experimental trial by air navigation undertakings with the view to the establishment of a regular line of air navigation, nor does it apply to carriage performed in extraordinary circumstances outside the normal scope of an air carrier's business.".

(20)   Articles 36 and 40A shall not apply.

4.   The Guadalajara Convention shall apply to international carriage within the meaning of this Schedule, with the following exceptions, adaptations and modifications:—

(1)   For "this Convention" wherever it appears there shall be substituted "the Guadalajara Convention as applied by this Schedule".

(2)   In Article 1, the following shall be added as paragraph (a):—

""the Warsaw Convention" means [the 1955 amended Convention] as applied by this Schedule.".]

Notes   Inserted by SI 1998/1058, art 2(5). Date in force: 2 May 1998: see SI 1998/1058, art 1.

Paragraph 1: words 'The 1955 amended Convention' in square brackets substituted by SI 1999/1737, art 2(1), (5). Date in force: 2 July 1999 (except in relation to rights and liabilities arising out of an occurrence which took place before that date): see SI 1999/1737, art 1.

Paragraph 3: words 'The 1955 amended Convention' in square brackets substituted by SI 1999/1737, art 2(1), (5). Date in force: 2 July 1999 (except in relation to rights and liabilities arising out of an occurrence which took place before that date): see SI 1999/1737, art 1.

Paragraph 4: words 'the 1955 amended Convention' in square brackets substituted by SI 1999/1737, art 2(1), (5). Date in force: 2 July 1999 (except in relation to rights and liabilities arising out of an occurrence which took place before that date): see SI 1999/1737, art 1.

[Part B]

[For convenience of reference [the 1955 amended Convention] and the Guadalajara Convention, with the exceptions, adaptations and modifications by this Schedule, are here set out:

A   The amended Warsaw Convention, as applied by Schedule 3

(International Carriage Under the Unamended Warsaw Convention as Amended by Additional Protocol No 1 of Montreal 1975)

Chapter I   Scope—Definitions

Article 1

(1)   This Schedule applies to all international carriage of persons, baggage or cargo performed by aircraft for reward. It applies equally to gratuitous carriage by aircraft performed by an air transport undertaking.

(2)   "International carriage" means any carriage in which, according to the contract made by the parties, the place of departure and the place of destination, whether or not there be a break in the carriage or a transhipment, are situated either within the territories of two States Parties to the Convention for the Unification of Certain Rules relating to International Carriage by Air signed at Warsaw on behalf of His Majesty on 12th October 1929 as amended by Additional Protocol No 1 of Montreal 1975, or within the territory of a single such State, if there is an agreed stopping place within the territory subject to the sovereignty, suzerainty, mandate or authority of another State, even though that State is not a party to the said Convention of 1929 as so amended.

(3)   A carriage to be performed by several successive air carriers is deemed, for the purposes of this Schedule, to be one undivided carriage, if it has been regarded by the parties as a single operation, whether it had been agreed upon under the form of a single contract or of a series of contracts, and it does not lose its international character merely because one contract or a series of contracts is to be performed entirely within a territory subject to the sovereignty, suzerainty, mandate or authority of the same High Contracting Party.

Article 2

(1)   This Schedule applies to carriage performed by the State, not being a State which has availed itself of the Additional Protocol to the Warsaw Convention, or by legally constituted public bodies, provided it falls within the conditions laid down in Article 1

(2)   This Schedule does not apply to carriage performed under the terms of any international postal Convention .

Chapter II   Documents of Carriage

Section I   Passenger Ticket

Article 3

(1)   For the carriage of passengers the carrier must deliver a passenger ticket which shall contain the following particulars:

    (a)   the place and date of issue;

    (b)   the place of departure and of destination;

    (c)   the agreed stopping places, provided that the carrier may reserve the right to alter the stopping places in case of necessity, and that if he exercises that right, the alteration shall not have the effect of depriving the carriage of its international character;

    (d)   the name and address of the carrier or carriers;

    (e)   a statement that the carriage is subject to the rules relating to liability established by the Warsaw Convention.

(2)   The absence, irregularity or loss of the passenger ticket does not affect the existence or the validity of the contract of carriage, which shall none the less be subject to the rules of this Schedule. Nevertheless, if the carrier accepts a passenger without a passenger ticket having been delivered he shall not be entitled to avail himself of those provisions of this Schedule which exclude or limit his liability.

Section 2   Baggage Check

Article 4

(1)   For the carriage of baggage, other than small personal objects of which the passenger takes charge himself, the carrier must deliver a baggage check.

(2)   The baggage check shall be made out in duplicate, one part for the passenger and the other part for the carrier.

(3)   The baggage check shall contain the following particulars:

    (a)   the place and date of issue;

    (b)   the place of departure and of destination;

(c)   the name and address of the carrier or carriers;

(d)   the number of the passenger ticket;

(e)   a statement that delivery of the baggage will be made to the bearer of the baggage check;

(f)   the number and weight of the packages;

(g)   the amount of the value declared in accordance with Article 22(2);

(h)   a statement that the carriage is subject to the rules relating to liability established by the Warsaw Convention.

(4)   The absence, irregularity or loss of the baggage check does not affect the existence or the validity of the contract of carriage, which shall none the less be subject to the rules of this Schedule. Nevertheless, if the carrier accepts baggage without a baggage check having been delivered, or if the baggage check does not contain the particulars set out at (d), (f) and (h) above, the carrier shall not be entitled to avail himself of those provisions of this Schedule which exclude or limit his liability.

Section 3   Air Waybill

Article 5

(1)   Every carrier of cargo has the right to require the consignor to make out and hand over to him a document called an "air waybill"; every consignor has the right to require the carrier to accept this document.

(2)   The absence, irregularity or loss of this document does not affect the existence or the validity of the contract of carriage which shall, subject to the provisions of Article 9, be none the less governed by the rules of this Schedule.

Article 6

(1)   The air waybill shall be made out by the consignor in three original parts and be handed over with the cargo.

(2)   The first part shall be marked "for the carrier", and shall be signed by the consignor. The second part shall be marked "for the consignee"; it shall be signed by the consignor and by the carrier and shall accompany the cargo. The third part shall be signed by the carrier and handed by him to the consignor after the cargo has been accepted.

(3)   The carrier shall sign on acceptance of the cargo.

(4)   The signature of the carrier may be stamped; that of the consignor may be printed or stamped.

(5)   If, at the request of the consignor, the carrier makes out the air waybill, he shall be deemed, subject to proof to the contrary, to have done so on behalf of the consignor.

Article 7

The carrier of cargo has the right to require the consignor to make out separate way-bills when there is more than one package.

Article 8

The air waybill shall contain the following particulars:

(a)   the place and date of its execution;

(b)   the place of departure and of destination;

(c)   the agreed stopping places, provided that the carrier may reserve the right to alter the stopping places in case of necessity, and that if he exercises that right the alteration shall not have the effect of depriving the carriage of its international character;

(d)   the name and address of the consignor;

(e)   the name and address of the first carrier;

(f)   the name and address of the consignee, if the case so requires;

(g)   the nature of the cargo;

(h)   the number of the packages, the method of packing and the particular marks or numbers upon them;

(i)   the weight, the quantity and the volume or dimensions of the cargo;

(j)   the apparent condition of the cargo and of the packing;

(k)   the freight, if it has been agreed upon, the date and place of payment, and the person who is to pay it;

(l)   if the cargo is sent for payment on delivery, the price of the cargo, and, if the case so requires, the amount of the expenses incurred;

(m)   the amount of the value declared in accordance with Article 22(2);

(n)   the number of parts of the air waybill;

(o)   the documents handed to the carrier to accompany the air waybill;

(p)   the time fixed for the completion of the carriage and a brief note of the route to be followed, if these matters have been agreed upon;

(q)   a statement that the carriage is subject to the rules relating to liability established by the Warsaw Convention.

Article 9

If the carrier accepts cargo without an air waybill having been made out, or if the air waybill does not contain all the particulars set out in Article 8(a) to (i) inclusive and (q), the carrier shall not be entitled to avail himself of the provisions of this Schedule which exclude or limit his liability.

Article 10

(1)   The consignor is responsible for the correctness of the particulars and statements relating to the cargo which he inserts in the air waybill.

(2)   The consignor will be liable for all damage suffered by the carrier or any other person by reason of the irregularity incorrectness or incompleteness of the said particulars and statements.

Article 11

(1)   The air waybill is prima facie evidence of the conclusion of the contract, of the receipt of the cargo and of the conditions of carriage.

(2)   The statements in the air waybill relating to the weight, dimensions and packing of the cargo, as well as those relating to the number of packages, are prima facie evidence of the facts stated; those relating to the quantity, volume and condition of the cargo do not constitute evidence against the carrier except so far as they both have been, and are stated in the air waybill to have been, checked by him in the presence of the consignor, or relate to the apparent condition of the cargo.

Article 12

(1)   Subject to his liability to carry out all his obligations under the contract of carriage, the consignor has the right to dispose of the cargo by withdrawing it at the aerodrome of departure or destination, or by stopping it in the course of the journey on any landing, or by calling for it to be delivered at the place of destination or in the course of the journey to a person other than the consignee named in the air waybill, or by requiring it to be returned to the aerodrome of departure. He must not exercise this right of disposition in such a way as to prejudice the carrier or other consignors and he must repay any expenses occasioned by the exercise of this right.

(2)   If it is impossible to carry out the orders of the consignor the carrier must so inform him forthwith.

(3)   If the carrier obeys the orders of the consignor for the disposition of the cargo without requiring the production of the part of the air waybill delivered to the latter, he will be liable, without prejudice to his right of recovery from the consignor, for any damage which may be caused thereby to any person who is lawfully in possession of that part of the air waybill

(4)   The right conferred on the consignor ceases at the moment when that of the consignee begins in accordance with Article 13. Nevertheless, if the consignee declines to accept the waybill or the cargo, or if he cannot be communicated with, the consignor resumes his right of disposition.

Article 13

(1)   Except in the circumstances set out in the preceding Article, the consignee is entitled, on arrival of the cargo at the place of destination, to require the carrier to hand over to him the air waybill and to deliver the cargo to him, on payment of the charges due and on complying with the conditions of carriage set out in the air waybill.

(2)   Unless it is otherwise agreed, it is the duty of the carrier to give notice to the consignee as soon as the cargo arrives.

(3)   If the carrier admits the loss of the cargo, or if the cargo has not arrived at the expiration of seven days after the date on which it ought to have arrived, the consignee is entitled to put into force against the carrier the rights which flow from the contract of carriage.

Article 14

The consignor and the consignee can respectively enforce all the rights given them by Articles 12 and 13, each in his own name, whether he is acting in his own interest or in the interest of another, provided that he carries out the obligations imposed by the contract.

Article 15

(1)   Articles 12, 13 and 14 do not affect either the relations of the consignor or the consignee with each other or the mutual relations of third parties whose rights are derived either from the consignor or from the consignee.

(2)   The provisions of Articles 12, 13 and 14 can only be varied by express provision in the air waybill.

Article 16

(1)   The consignor must furnish such information and attach to the air waybill such documents as are necessary to meet the formalities of customs, octoroon or police before the cargo can be delivered to the consignee. The consignor is liable to the carrier for any damage occasioned by the absence, insufficiency or irregularity of any such information or documents, unless the damage is due to the fault of the carrier or his servants or agents.

(2)   The carrier is under no obligation to enquire into the correctness or sufficiency of such information or documents.

Chapter III   Liability of the Carrier

Article 17

The carrier is liable for damage sustained in the event of the death or wounding of a passenger or any other bodily injury suffered by a passenger, if the accident which caused the damage so sustained took place on board the aircraft or in the course of any of the operations of embarking or disembarking.

Article 18

(1)   The carrier is liable for damage sustained in the event of the destruction or loss of, or of damage to, any registered baggage or any cargo, if the occurrence which caused the damage so sustained took place during the carriage by air.

(2)   The carriage by air within the meaning of the preceding paragraph comprises the period during which the baggage or cargo is in charge of the carrier, whether in an aerodrome or on board an aircraft, or, in the case of a landing outside an aerodrome in any place whatsoever.

(3)   The period of the carriage by air does not extend to any carriage by land, by sea or by river performed outside an aerodrome. If, however, such a carriage takes place in the performance of a contract for carriage by air, for the purpose of loading, delivery or transhipment, any damage is presumed, subject to proof to the contrary, to have been the result of an event which took place during the carriage by air.

Article 19

The carrier is liable for damage occasioned by delay in the carriage by air of passengers, baggage or cargo.

Article 20

(1)   The carrier is not liable if he proves that he and his servants or agents have taken all necessary measures to avoid the damage or that it was impossible for him or them to take such measures.

(2)   In the carriage of cargo and baggage the carrier is not liable if he proves that the damage was occasioned by negligent pillage or negligence in the handling of the aircraft or in navigation and that, in all other respects, he and his servants or agents have taken all necessary measures to avoid the damage.

Article 21

If the carrier proves that the damage was caused by or contributed to by the negligence of the injured person the Court may, in accordance with the provisions of its own law, exonerate the carrier wholly or partly from his liability.

Article 22

(1)   In the carriage of passengers the liability of the carrier for each passenger is limited to the sum of 8,300 Special Drawing Rights. Where, in accordance with the law of the court seized of the case, damages may be awarded in the form of periodic payments, the equivalent capital value of the said payments shall not exceed this limit. Nevertheless, by special contract, the carrier and the passenger may agree to a higher limit of liability.

(2)   In the carriage of registered baggage and of cargo, the liability of the carrier is limited to a sum of 17 Special Drawing Rights per kilogram, unless the consignor has made, at the time when the package was handed over to the carrier, a special declaration of interest in delivery at destination and has paid a supplementary sum if the case so requires. In that case the carrier will be liable to pay a sum not exceeding the declared sum, unless he proves that that sum is greater than the consignor's actual interest in delivery at destination.

(3)   As regards objects of which the passenger takes charge himself the liability of the carrier is limited to 332 Special Drawing Rights per passenger.

(4)   The sums mentioned in terms of the Special Drawing Right in this Article shall be deemed to refer to the Special Drawing Right as defined by the International Monetary Fund. Conversion of the sums into national currencies shall, in case of judicial proceedings, be made according to the value of such currencies in terms of the Special Drawing Right at the date of the judgement. The value of a national currency, in terms of the Special Drawing Right, of a High Contracting Party which is a Member of the Monetary Fund, shall be calculated in accordance with the method of valuation

applied by the International Monetary Fund, in effect at the date of the judgement, for its operations and transactions. The value of national currency, in terms of the Special Drawing Right, of a High Contracting Party which is not a Member of the International Monetary Fund, shall be calculated in a manner determined by that High Contracting Party.

Nevertheless, those States which are not Members of the International Monetary Fund and whose law does not permit the application of the provisions of paragraphs 1, 2 and 3 of Article 22 may at the time of ratification or accession or at any time thereafter declare that the limit of liability of the carrier in judicial proceedings in their territories is fixed at a sum of 125,000 monetary units per passenger with respect to paragraph 1 of Article 22; 250 monetary units per kilogram with respect to paragraph 2 of Article 22; and 5,000 monetary units per passenger with respect to paragraph 3 of Article 22. This monetary unit corresponds to sixty-five and a half milligrams of gold of millesimal fineness nine hundred. These sums may be converted into the national currency concerned in round figures. The conversion of these sums into national currency shall be made according to the law of the State concerned.

Article 23

Any provision tending to relieve the carrier of liability or to fix a lower limit than that which is laid down in this Schedule shall be null and void, but the nullity of any such provision does not involve the nullity of the whole contract, which shall remain subject to the provisions of this Schedule.

Article 24

(1)   In the cases covered by Articles 18 and 19 any action for damages, however founded, can only be brought subject to the conditions and limits set out in this Schedule.

(2)   In the cases covered by Article 17 the provisions of the preceding paragraph also apply, without prejudice to the questions as to who are the persons who have the right to bring suit and what are their respective rights.

Article 25

(1)   The carrier shall not be entitled to avail himself of the provisions of this Schedule which exclude or limit his liability, if the damage is caused by his wilful misconduct, or by such default on his part as, in accordance with the law of the Court seised of the case, is considered to be equivalent to wilful misconduct.

(2)   Similarly the carrier shall not be entitled to avail himself of the said provisions, if the damage is caused as aforesaid by any servant or agent of the carrier acting within the scope of his employment.

Article 26

(1)   Receipt by the person entitled to delivery of baggage or cargo without complaint is prima facie evidence that the same has been delivered in good condition and in accordance with the document of carriage.

(2)   In the case of damage, the person entitled to delivery must complain to the carrier forthwith after the discovery of the damage, and, at the latest, within three days from the date of receipt in the case of baggage and seven days from the date of receipt

in the case of cargo. In the case of delay the complaint must be made at the latest within fourteen days from the date on which the baggage or cargo has been placed at his disposal.

(3)   Every complaint must be made in writing upon the document of carriage or by separate notice in writing despatched within the times aforesaid.

(4)   Failing complaint within the times aforesaid, no action shall lie against the carrier, save in the case of fraud on his part.

Article 27

In the case of the death of the person liable, an action for damages lies in accordance with the terms of this Schedule against those legally representing his estate.

Article 28

(1)   An action for damages must be brought, at the option of the plaintiff, in the territory of one of the High Contracting Parties to the Warsaw Convention as amended by Additional Protocol No 1 of Montreal 1975, either before the Court having jurisdiction where the carrier is ordinarily resident, or has his principal place of business, or has an establishment by which the contract has been made or before the Court having jurisdiction at the place of destination.

(2)   Questions of procedure shall be governed by the law of the Court seised of the case.

Article 29

(1)   The right to damages shall be extinguished if an action is not brought within two years, reckoned from the date of arrival at the destination, or from the date on which the aircraft ought to have arrived, or from the date on which the carriage stopped.

(2)   The method of calculating the period of limitation shall be determined by the law of the Court seised of the case.

Article 30

(1)   In the case of carriage to be performed by various successive carriers and falling within the definition set out in the third paragraph of Article 1, each carrier who accepts passengers, baggage or cargo is subjected to the rules set out in this Schedule, and is deemed to be one of the contracting parties to the contract of carriage in so far as the contract deals with that part of the carriage which is performed under his supervision.

(2)   In the case of carriage of this nature, the passenger or his representative can take action only against the carrier who performed the carriage during which the accident or the delay occurred, save in the case where, by express agreement, the first carrier has assumed liability for the whole journey.

(3)   As regards baggage or cargo, the passenger or consignor will have a right of action against the first carrier, and the passenger or consignee who is entitled to delivery will have a right of action against the last carrier, and further, each may take action against the carrier who performed the carriage during which the destruction,

loss, damage or delay took place. These carriers will be jointly and severally liable to the passenger or to the consignor or consignee.

Chapter IV   Provisions Relating to Combined Carriage

Article 31

(1)   In the case of combined carriage performed partly by air and partly by any other mode of carriage, the provisions of this Schedule apply only to the carriage by air, provided that the carriage by air falls within the terms of Article 1.

(2)   Nothing in this Schedule shall prevent the parties in the case of combined carriage from inserting in the document of air carriage conditions relating to other modes of carriage, provided that the provisions of this Schedule are observed as regards the carriage by air.

Chapter V   General and Final Provisions

Article 32

Any clause contained in the contract and all special agreements entered into before the damage occurred by which the parties purport to infringe the rules laid down by this Schedule, whether by deciding the law to be applied, or by altering the rules as to jurisdiction, shall be null and void. Nevertheless, for the carriage of cargo arbitration clauses are allowed, subject to this Schedule, if the arbitration is to take place within one of the jurisdictions referred to in the first paragraph of Article 28.

Article 33

Nothing contained in this Schedule shall prevent the carrier either from refusing to enter into any contract of carriage, or from making regulations which do not conflict with the provisions of this Schedule.

Article 34

This Schedule does not apply to international carriage by air performed by way of experimental trial by air navigation undertakings with the view to the establishment of a regular line of air navigation, nor does it apply to carriage performed in extraordinary circumstances outside the normal scope of an air carrier's business.

Article 35

The expression "days" when used in this Schedule means current days not working days.

B   The Guadalajara Convention as applied by Schedule 3

(International Carriage Under the Unamended Warsaw Convention as Amended by Additional Protocol No 1 of Montreal 1975)

Article I

In the Guadalajara Convention as applied by this Schedule:

(a)   "The Warsaw Convention" means [the 1955 amended Convention] as applied by this Schedule;

(b)   "contracting carrier" means a person who as a principal makes an agreement for carriage governed by the Warsaw Convention with a passenger or consignor or with a person acting on behalf of the passenger or consignor;

(c)   "actual carrier" means a person, other than the contracting Carrier, who, by virtue of authority from the contracting carrier, performs the whole or part of the carriage contemplated in paragraph (b) but who is not with respect to such part a successive carrier within the meaning of the Warsaw Convention. Such authority is presumed in the absence of proof to the contrary.

Article II

If an actual carrier performs the whole or part of carriage which, according to the agreement referred to in Article I, paragraph (b), is governed by the Warsaw Convention, both the contracting carrier and the actual carrier shall, except as otherwise provided in the Guadalajara Convention as applied by this Schedule, be subject to the rules of the Warsaw Convention, the former for the whole of the carriage contemplated in the agreement, the latter solely for the carriage which he performs.

Article III

1.   The acts and omissions of the actual carrier and of his servants and agents acting within the scope of their employment shall, in relation to the carriage performed by the actual carrier, be deemed to be also those of the contracting carrier.

2.   The acts and omissions of the contracting carrier and of his servants and agents acting within the scope of their employment shall, in relation to the carriage performed by the actual carrier, be deemed to be also those of the actual carrier. Nevertheless, no such act or omission shall subject the actual carrier to liability exceeding the limits specified in Article 22 of the Warsaw Convention. Any special agreement under which the contracting carrier assumes obligations not imposed by the Warsaw Convention or any waiver of rights conferred by that Convention or any special declaration of interest in delivery at destination contemplated in Article 22 of the said Convention, shall not affect the actual carrier unless agreed to by him.

Article IV

Any complaint to be made or order to be given under the Warsaw Convention to the carrier shall have the same effect whether addressed to the contracting carrier or to the actual carrier. Nevertheless, orders referred to in Article 12 of the Warsaw Convention shall only be effective if addressed to the contracting carrier.

Article V

In relation to the carriage performed by the actual carrier, any servant or agent of that carrier or of the contracting carrier shall, if he proves that he acted within the scope of his employment be entitled to avail himself of the limits of liability which are applicable under the Guadalajara Convention as applied by this Schedule to the carrier whose servant or agent he is unless it is proved that he acted in a manner which, under the Warsaw Convention, prevents the limits of liability from being invoked.

Article VI

In relation to the carriage performed by the actual carrier, the aggregate of the amounts recoverable from that carrier and the contracting carrier, and from their servants and agents acting within the scope of their employment, shall not exceed the highest amount which could be awarded against either the contracting carrier or the actual carrier under the Guadalajara Convention as applied by this Schedule, but none of the persons mentioned shall be liable for a sum in excess of the limit applicable to him.

Article VII

In relation to the carriage performed by the actual carrier, an action for damages may be brought at the option of the plaintiff, against that carrier or the contracting carrier, or against both together or separately. If the action is brought against only one of those carriers, that carrier shall have the right to require the other carrier to be joined in the proceedings, the procedure and effects being governed by the law of the Court seised of the case.

Article VIII

Any action for damages contemplated in Article VII of the Guadalajara Convention as applied by this Schedule must be brought, at the option of the plaintiffs either before a Court in which an action may be brought against the contracting carrier, as provided in Article 28 of the Warsaw Convention, or before the Court having jurisdiction at the place where the actual carrier is ordinarily resident or has his principal place of business.

Article IX

1.   Any contractual provision tending to relieve the contracting carrier or the actual carrier of liability under the Guadalajara Convention as applied by this Schedule or to fix a lower limit than that which is applicable according to the Guadalajara Convention as applied by this Schedule shall be null and void, but the nullity of any such provision does not involve the nullity of the whole agreement, which shall remain subject to the provisions of the Guadalajara Convention as applied by this Schedule.

2.   In respect of the carriage performed by the actual carrier, the preceding paragraph shall not apply to contractual provisions governing loss or damage resulting from the inherent defect, quality or vice of the cargo carried.

3. Any clause contained in an agreement for carriage and all special agreements entered into before the damage occurred by which the parties purport to infringe the rules laid down by the Guadalajara Convention as applied by this Schedule, whether by deciding the law to be applied, or by altering the rules as to jurisdiction, shall be null and void. Nevertheless, for the carriage of cargo arbitration clauses are allowed, subject to the Guadalajara Convention as applied by this Schedule, if the arbitration is to take place in one of the jurisdictions referred to in Article VIII.

Article X

Except as provided in Article VII, nothing in the Guadalajara Convention as applied by this Schedule shall affect the rights and obligations of the two carriers between themselves.]

Notes   Inserted by SI 1998/1058, art 2(5). Date in force: 2 May 1998: see SI 1998/1058, art 1.

Words 'the 1955 amended Convention' in square brackets in both places they occur substituted by SI 1999/1737, art 2(1), (5). Date in force: 2 July 1999 (except in relation to rights and liabilities arising out of an occurrence which took place before that date): see SI 1999/1737, art 1.

Appendix 4

Carriage by Air (Parties to Convention) Order 1999

SI 1999/1313

Made   11th May 1999

Her Majesty, in exercise of the powers conferred upon Her by section 2(1) of the Carriage by Air Act 1961 (which provides that Her Majesty may by Order in Council from time to time certify who are the High Contracting Parties to the Warsaw Convention as amended at The Hague, 1955, relating to international carriage by air, in respect of what territories they are respectively parties and to what extent they have availed themselves of the provisions of the Additional Protocol to the said Convention), by section 2(4) of that Act (which provides that an Order in Council under section 2 may contain such transitional and other consequential provisions as appear to Her Majesty to be expedient) and by those subsections as applied to international carriage under the unamended Warsaw Convention by article 5 of the Carriage by Air Acts (Application of Provisions) Order 1967 and to international carriage under the Warsaw Convention as amended by Additional Protocol No 1 of Montreal 1975 by article 5A of that Order, is pleased, by and with the advice of Her Privy Council, to order, and it is hereby ordered, as follows:

1.   This Order may be cited as the Carriage by Air (Parties to Convention) Order 1999.

2.   It is hereby certified that the High Contracting Parties to the Warsaw Convention, 1929, to the Warsaw Convention as amended at The Hague, 1955, and to the Warsaw Convention as amended by Additional Protocol No 1 of Montreal, 1975, and the territories in respect of which they are respectively parties are as specified in Schedule 1 to this Order.

3.   In the said Schedule 1 an asterisk means that this Order does not certify that a State is a party, in respect of that territory, to the Convention named at the head of the column.

4.   It is hereby certified that the High Contracting Parties specified in Schedule 2 to this Order have availed themselves of the provisions of the Additional Protocol to the Convention to which they are hereby certified as Parties, by declaring that the first paragraph of article 2 of the Convention shall not apply to international carriage by air performed directly by the State or any territory or possession under its jurisdiction.

5.   The Carriage by Air (Parties to Convention) Order 1988 is hereby revoked.

Schedule 1 High Contracting Parties to the Warsaw Convention, 1929, to the Warsaw Convention as Amended at The Hague, 1955 and to the Warsaw Convention as Amended by Additional Protocol No 1 of Montreal, 1975

Articles 2 and 3

High Contracting Parties	Territories in respect of which they are respectively parties	Dates on which the Warsaw Convention, 1929 came into force	Dates on which the Warsaw Convention as amended at The Hague, 1955 came into force	Dates on which the Warsaw Convention as amended by Protocol No 1 of Montreal, 1975 came into force
The United Kingdom of Great Britain and Northern Ireland	Great Britain and Northern Ireland	15th May 1933	1st June 1967	15th February 1996
	The Channel Islands	15th May 1933	1st June 1967	15th February 1996
	The Isle of Man	15th May 1933	1st June 1967	15th February 1996
	Anguilla	3rd March 1935	*	15th February 1996
	Bermuda	3rd March 1935	1st June 1967	15th February 1996
	British Antarctic Territory	3rd March 1935	1st June 1967	15th February 1996
	British Indian Ocean Territory	3rd March 1935	1st June 1967	15th February 1996
	British Virgin Islands	3rd March 1935	1st June 1967	15th February 1996
	Cayman Islands	3rd March 1935	1st June 1967	15th February 1996
	Falkland Islands	3rd March 1935	1st June 1967	15th February 1996
	Gibraltar	3rd March 1935	1st June 1967	15th February 1996
	Montserrat	3rd March 1935	1st June 1967	15th February 1996
	Pitcairn, Henderson, Ducie and Oeno Islands	*	*	15th February 1996
	St Helena	3rd March 1935	1st June 1967	15th February 1996

High Contracting Parties	Territories in respect of which they are respectively parties	Dates on which the Warsaw Convention, 1929 came into force	Dates on which the Warsaw Convention as amended at The Hague, 1955 came into force	Dates on which the Warsaw Convention as amended by Protocol No 1 of Montreal, 1975 came into force
	St Helena Dependencies	3rd March 1935	1st June 1967	15th February 1996
	South Georgia and the South Sandwich Islands	3rd March 1935	1st June 1967	15th February 1996
	The Sovereign Base Areas of Akrotiri and Dhekelia	3rd March 1935	1st June 1967	15th February 1996
	Turks and Caicos Islands	3rd March 1935	1st June 1967	15th February 1996
The Islamic State of Afghanistan	Afghanistan	21st May 1969	21st May 1969	*
The Democratic and Popular Republic of Algeria	Algeria	31st August 1964	31st August 1964	*
The Republic of Angola	Angola	8th June 1998	8th June 1998	*
Antigua and Barbuda	Antigua and Barbuda		3rd March 1935	* *
The Argentine Republic	Argentina	19th June 1952	10th September 1969	15th February 1996
The Commonwealth of Australia	Australia and all external territories for whose international affairs of which Australia is responsible	30th October 1935	1st August 1963	*
The Republic of Austria	Austria	27th December 1961	24th June 1971	*
The Commonwealth of the Bahamas	Bahamas	3rd March 1935	1st June 1967	*

High Contracting Parties	Territories in respect of which they are respectively parties	Dates on which the Warsaw Convention, 1929 came into force	Dates on which the Warsaw Convention as amended at The Hague, 1955 came into force	Dates on which the Warsaw Convention as amended by Protocol No 1 of Montreal, 1975 came into force
The State of Bahrain	Bahrain	10th June 1998	10th June 1998	10th June 1998
The People's Republic of Bangladesh	Bangladesh	18th February 1935	1st August 1963	*
Barbados	Barbados	3rd March 1935	*	*
The Republic of Belarus	Belarus	25th December 1959	1st August 1963	*
The Kingdom of Belgium	Belgium	11th October 1936	25th November 1963	*
Belize	Belize	3rd March 1935	1st June 1967	*
The Republic of Benin	Benin	13th February 1933	1st August 1963	*
Bosnia and Herzegovina	Bosnia and Herzegovina	13th February 1933	1st August 1963	15th February 1996
The Republic of Botswana	Botswana	1st December 1952	*	*
The Federal Republic of Brazil	Brazil	13th February 1933	14th September 1964	15th February 1996
Brunei Darussalam	Brunei	2nd October 1936	*	*
The Republic of Bulgaria	Bulgaria	23rd September 1949	13th March 1964	*
The Republic of Burkina	Burkina Faso	9th March 1962	*	*
The Kingdom of Cambodia	Cambodia	13th February 1933	12th March 1997	*
The Republic of Cameroon	Cameroon	13th February 1933	1st August 1963	*

High Contracting Parties	*Territories in respect of which they are respectively parties*	*Dates on which the Warsaw Convention, 1929 came into force*	*Dates on which the Warsaw Convention as amended at The Hague, 1955 came into force*	*Dates on which the Warsaw Convention as amended by Protocol No 1 of Montreal, 1975 came into force*
Canada	Canada	8th September 1947 (except for the Province of Newfoundland) 5th July 1939 (for Newfoundland)	17th July 1964	15th February 1996
The Republic of Chad	Chad	13th February 1933	11th September 1964	*
The Republic of Chile	Chile	31st May 1979	31st May 1979	15th February 1996
The People's Republic of China	China	18th October 1958 (except for HKSAR) 3rd March 1935 (for HKSAR)	18th November 1975 (except for HKSAR) 1st June 1967 (for HKSAR)	*
The Republic of Colombia	Colombia	13th November 1966	13th November 1966	15th February 1996
The Federal Islamic Republic of the Comoros	The Comoros	9th September 1991	*	*
The Republic of the Congo	Congo (Brazzaville)	13th February 1933	1st August 1963	*
The Democratic Republic of the Congo	Congo (Democratic Republic)	11th October 1936	*	*
The Republic of Costa Rica	Costa Rica	8th August 1984	8th August 1984	*
The Republic of Côte d'Ivoire	Ivory Coast	13th February 1933	1st August 1963	*
The Republic of Croatia	Croatia	13th February 1933	1st August 1963	15th February 1996
The Republic of Cuba	Cuba	19th October 1964	28th November 1965	20th July 1998

High Contracting Parties	Territories in respect of which they are respectively parties	Dates on which the Warsaw Convention, 1929 came into force	Dates on which the Warsaw Convention as amended at The Hague, 1955 came into force	Dates on which the Warsaw Convention as amended by Protocol No 1 of Montreal, 1975 came into force
The Republic of Cyprus	The territory of the Republic of Cyprus	3rd March 1935	21st October 1970	15th February 1996
The Czech Republic	The Czech Republic	15th February 1935	1st August 1963	*
The Kingdom of Denmark	Denmark, Greenland and the Faroe Islands	1st October 1937	1st August 1963	15th February 1996 (for Denmark only)
The Commonwealth of Dominica	Dominica	3rd March 1935	*	*
The Dominican Republic	Dominican Republic	25th May 1972	25th May 1972	*
The Republic of Ecuador	Ecuador	1st March 1970	1st March 1970	*
The Arab Republic of Egypt	Egypt	5th December 1955	1st August 1963	15th February 1996
The Republic of El Salvador	El Salvador	*	1st August 1963	*
The Republic of Equatorial Guinea	Equatorial Guinea	19th March 1989	*	*
The Republic of Estonia	Estonia	14th June 1998	14th June 1998	14th June 1998
The Federal Democratic Republic of Ethiopia	Ethiopia	12th November 1950	*	15th February 1996
The Republic of Fiji	Fiji	3rd March 1935	1st June 1967	*
The Republic of Finland	Finland	1st October 1937	23rd August 1977	15th February 1996

High Contracting Parties	Territories in respect of which they are respectively parties	Dates on which the Warsaw Convention, 1929 came into force	Dates on which the Warsaw Convention as amended at The Hague, 1955 came into force	Dates on which the Warsaw Convention as amended by Protocol No 1 of Montreal, 1975 came into force
The French Republic	France and all Overseas Departments and territories subject to the sovereignty or authority of the French Republic	13th February 1933	1st August 1963	15th February 1996
The Gabonese Republic	Gabon	16th May 1969	16th May 1969	*
The Republic of The Gambia		The Gambia	3rd March 1935	* *
The Federal Republic of Germany	Germany	29th December 1933	1st August 1963	*
The Republic of Ghana	Ghana	3rd March 1935	9th November 1997	9th November 1997
Grenada	Grenada	3rd March 1935	13th November 1985	*
The Republic of Guatemala	Guatemala	4th May 1997	26th October 1971	4th May 1997
The Republic of Guinea	Guinea	10th December 1961	7th January 1991	*
The Co-operative Republic of Guyana	Guyana	3rd March 1935	*	*
The Hellenic Republic	Greece	11th April 1938	21st September 1965	15th February 1996
The Republic of Honduras	Honduras	25th September 1994	*	15th May 1996
The Republic of Hungary	Hungary	27th August 1936	1st August 1963	*
The Republic of Iceland	Iceland	19th November 1948	1st August 1963	*

High Contracting Parties	Territories in respect of which they are respectively parties	Dates on which the Warsaw Convention, 1929 came into force	Dates on which the Warsaw Convention as amended at The Hague, 1955 came into force	Dates on which the Warsaw Convention as amended by Protocol No 1 of Montreal, 1975 came into force
The Republic of India	India	18th February 1935	15th May 1973	*
The Republic of Indonesia	Indonesia	29th September 1933	*	*
The Islamic Republic of Iran	Iran	6th October 1975	6th October 1975	*
The Republic of Iraq	Iraq	26th September 1972	26th September 1972	*
The Republic of Ireland	The territory of the Republic of Ireland	19th December 1935	1st August 1963	15th February 1996
The State of Israel	Israel	6th January 1950	3rd November 1964	15th February 1996
The Italian Republic	Italy	15th May 1933	2nd August 1963	15th February 1996
Jamaica	Jamaica	3rd March 1935	*	*
Japan	Japan	18th August 1953	8th November 1967	*
The Hashemite Kingdom of Jordan	Jordan	17th March 1938	13th February 1974	*
The Republic of Kenya	Kenya	3rd March 1935	*	*
The Republic of Kiribati	Kiribati	3rd March 1935	1st June 1967	*
The Republic of Korea	South Korea	*	11th October 1967	*
The State of Kuwait	Kuwait	9th November 1975	9th November 1975	6th February 1997
The Laos People's Democratic Republic	Laos	13th February 1933	1st August 1963	*

High Contracting Parties	Territories in respect of which they are respectively parties	Dates on which the Warsaw Convention, 1929 came into force	Dates on which the Warsaw Convention as amended at The Hague, 1955 came into force	Dates on which the Warsaw Convention as amended by Protocol No 1 of Montreal, 1975 came into force
The Republic of Latvia	Latvia	13th February 1933 *		*
The Republic of Lebanon	Lebanon	24th January 1934	8th August 1978	*
The Kingdom of Lesotho	Lesotho	1st December 1952	15th January 1976	*
The Republic of Liberia	Liberia	31st July 1942	*	*
The Great Socialist People's Libyan Arab Jamahiriya	Libya	14th August 1969	14th August 1969	*
The Principality of Liechtenstein	Liechtenstein	7th August 1934	3rd April 1966	*
The Republic of Lithuania	Lithuania	*	19th February 1997	*
The Grand Duchy of Luxembourg	Luxembourg	5th January 1950	1st August 1963	*
The Republic of Madagascar	Madagascar	13th February 1933	1st August 1963	*
The Republic of Malawi	Malawi	25th January 1978	7th September 1971	*
Malaysia	Malaysia	2nd October 1936 (except for Malacca and Penang) 3rd March 1935 (for Malacca and Penang)	19th December 1974	*
The Republic of the Maldives	The Maldives	11th November 1996	11th November 1996	*
The Republic of Mali	Mali	13th February 1933	29th March 1964	*

High Contracting Parties	Territories in respect of which they are respectively parties	Dates on which the Warsaw Convention, 1929 came into force	Dates on which the Warsaw Convention as amended at The Hague, 1955 came into force	Dates on which the Warsaw Convention as amended by Protocol No 1 of Montreal, 1975 came into force
The Republic of Malta	Malta	3rd March 1935	*	*
The Islamic Republic of Mauritania	Mauritania	13th February 1933	*	*
The Republic of Mauritius	Mauritius	3rd March 1935	1st June 1967	*
The United Mexican States	Mexico	15th May 1933	1st August 1963	15th February 1996
The Republic of Moldova	Moldova	19th June 1997	19th June 1997	*
The Principality of Monaco	Monaco	*	8th July 1979	*
Mongolia	Mongolia	29th July 1962	*	*
The Kingdom of Morocco	Morocco	5th April 1958	15th February 1976	*
The Union of Myanmar	Burma	18th February 1935	*	*
The Republic of Namibia	Namibia	22nd March 1955	17th December 1967	*
The Republic of Nauru	Nauru	30th October 1935	1st August 1963	*
The Kingdom of Nepal	Nepal	13th May 1966	13th May 1966	*
The Kingdom of the Netherlands	The Netherlands and all territories subject to the sovereignty or authority of the Kingdom of the Netherlands	29th September 1933	1st August 1963	15th February 1996 (except for Aruba)

High Contracting Parties	Territories in respect of which they are respectively parties	Dates on which the Warsaw Convention, 1929 came into force	Dates on which the Warsaw Convention as amended at The Hague, 1955 came into force	Dates on which the Warsaw Convention as amended by Protocol No 1 of Montreal, 1975 came into force
New Zealand	New Zealand (including the Cook Islands and the Tokelau Islands)	5th July 1937	14th June 1967	*
The Republic of Niger	Niger	13th February 1933	1st August 1963	*
The Federal Republic of Nigeria	Nigeria	3rd March 1935	29th September 1969	*
The Kingdom of Norway	Norway and all territories subject to the sovereignty or authority of the Kingdom of Norway	1st October 1937	1st August 1963	15th February 1996 (for Norway only)
The Sultanate of Oman	Oman	4th November 1976	2nd November 1987	*
The Islamic Republic of Pakistan	Pakistan	18th February 1935	1st August 1963	*
The Republic of Panama	Panama	10th January 1997	10th January 1997	*
The Independent State of Papua New Guinea	Papua New Guinea	30th October 1935	1st August 1963	*
The Republic of Paraguay	Paraguay	26th November 1969	26th November 1969	*
The Republic of Peru	Peru	3rd October 1988	3rd October 1988	2nd October 1997
The Republic of Philippines	The Philippines	7th February 1951	28th February 1967	*
The Republic of Poland	Poland	13th February 1933	1st August 1963	*

High Contracting Parties	Territories in respect of which they are respectively parties	Dates on which the Warsaw Convention, 1929 came into force	Dates on which the Warsaw Convention as amended at The Hague, 1955 came into force	Dates on which the Warsaw Convention as amended by Protocol No 1 of Montreal, 1975 came into force
The Portuguese Republic	Portugal and all territories subject to the sovereignty or authority of the Portuguese Republic	18th June 1947	15th December 1963	15th February 1996
The State of Qatar	Qatar	21st March 1987	21st March 1987	*
Romania	Romania	13th February 1933	1st August 1963	*
The Russian Federation	Russia	18th November 1934	1st August 1963	*
The Rwandese Republic	Rwanda	11th October 1936	27th March 1991	*
The Federation of Saint Christopher and Nevis	Saint Christopher and Nevis	3rd March 1935	*	*
Saint Lucia	Saint Lucia	3rd March 1935	*	*
Saint Vincent and the Grenadines	Saint Vincent and the Grenadines		3rd March 1935	* *
The Independent State of Samoa	Samoa	5th July 1937	14th January 1973	*
The Kingdom of Saudi Arabia	Saudi Arabia	27th April 1969	27th April 1969	*
The Republic of Senegal	Senegal	13th February 1933	17th September 1964	*
The Republic of Seychelles	Seychelles	22nd September 1980	22nd September 1980	*
The Republic of Sierra Leone	Sierra Leone	3rd March 1935	*	*
The Republic of Singapore	Singapore	3rd December 1971	4th February 1968	*

High Contracting Parties	Territories in respect of which they are respectively parties	Dates on which the Warsaw Convention, 1929 came into force	Dates on which the Warsaw Convention as amended at The Hague, 1955 came into force	Dates on which the Warsaw Convention as amended by Protocol No 1 of Montreal, 1975 came into force
The Slovak Republic	Slovakia	13th February 1935	1st August 1963	*
Solomon Islands	Solomon Islands	3rd March 1935	1st June 1967	*
The Republic of South Africa	South Africa	22nd March 1955	17th December 1967	*
The Kingdom of Spain	Spain and all territories subject to the sovereignty or authority of the Kingdom of Spain	13th February 1933	6th March 1966	15th February 1996
The Democratic Socialist Republic of Sri Lanka	Sri Lanka	3rd March 1935	22nd May 1997	*
The Republic of Sudan	Sudan	12th May 1975	12th May 1975	*
The Republic of Suriname	Surinam	29th September 1933		1st August 1963 *
The Kingdom of Swaziland	Swaziland	1st December 1952	18th October 1971	*
The Kingdom of Sweden	Sweden	1st October 1937	1st August 1963	15th February 1996
The Swiss Confederation	Switzerland	7th August 1934	1st August 1963	15th February 1996
The Syrian Arab Republic	Syria	2nd March 1959	1st August 1963	*
The Republic of Tajikistan	Tajikistan	4th May 1994	*	*
The United Republic of Tanzania	Tanzania	3rd March 1935	*	*
The Former Yugoslav Republic of Macedonia	Macedonia	13th February 1933	1st August 1963	15th February 1996

High Contracting Parties	Territories in respect of which they are respectively parties	Dates on which the Warsaw Convention, 1929 came into force	Dates on which the Warsaw Convention as amended at The Hague, 1955 came into force	Dates on which the Warsaw Convention as amended by Protocol No 1 of Montreal, 1975 came into force
The Republic of Togo	Togo	30th September 1980	30th September 1980	15th February 1996
The Kingdom of Tonga	Tonga	2nd October 1936	22nd May 1977	*
The Republic of Trinidad and Tobago	Trinidad and Tobago	3rd March 1935	8th August 1983	*
The Tunisian Republic	Tunisia	13th February 1933	13th February 1964	15th February 1996
The Republic of Turkey	Turkey	23rd June 1978	23rd June 1978	*
Turkmenistan	Turkmenistan	20th March 1995	*	*
Tuvalu	Tuvalu	3rd March 1935	1st June 1967	*
The Republic of Uganda	Uganda	3rd March 1935	*	*
Ukraine	Ukraine	12th November 1959	1st August 1963	*
United Arab Emirates	United Arab Emirates	3rd July 1986	16th January 1994	*
The United States of America	The United States of America and all territories subject to the sovereignty or authority of the United States of America	29th October 1934	*	*
The Oriental Republic of Uruguay	Uruguay	2nd October 1979	*	*
The Republic of Uzbekistan	Uzbekistan	28th May 1997	*	28th May 1997
The Republic of Vanuatu	Vanuatu	24th January 1982	24th January 1982	*

High Contracting Parties	Territories in respect of which they are respectively parties	Dates on which the Warsaw Convention, 1929 came into force	Dates on which the Warsaw Convention as amended at The Hague, 1955 came into force	Dates on which the Warsaw Convention as amended by Protocol No 1 of Montreal, 1975 came into force
The Republic of Venezuela	Venezuela	13th September 1955	1st August 1963	15th February 1996
The Socialist Republic of Vietnam	Vietnam	13th February 1933	9th January 1983	*
The Republic of Yemen	Yemen	4th August 1982	4th August 1982	*
The Federal Republic of Yugoslavia	Yugoslavia	13th February 1933	1st August 1963	15th February 1996
The Republic of Zambia	Zambia	3rd March 1935	23rd June 1970	*
The Republic of Zimbabwe	Zimbabwe	3rd April 1935	25th January 1981	*

Schedule 2   High Contracting Parties which have Availed Themselves of the Provisions of the Additional Protocol to the Convention to which they are Certified as Parties in Schedule 1

Article 4

Canada
The Republic of Chile
The Republic of the Congo
The Republic of Cuba
The Federal Democratic Republic of Ethiopia
The Republic of the Philippines
The United States of America

Explanatory Note

(This note is not part of the Order)

The Carriage by Air Act 1961 gives effect in the United Kingdom to the Warsaw Convention as amended at The Hague, 1955, relating to international carriage by air, and the Carriage by Air Acts (Application of Provisions) Order 1967 makes transitional provision for the application of that Act to carriage still governed by the unamended Warsaw Convention, to which the United Kingdom remains a party, and to carriage governed by the Warsaw Convention as amended by Additional Protocol No 1 of Montreal 1975.

Under section 2(1) of the Act and articles 5 and 5A of that Order, Her Majesty may by Order in Council from time to time certify, among other things, who are the High Contracting Parties to the Warsaw Convention as amended at The Hague, to the unamended Warsaw Convention, and to the Warsaw Convention as amended by Additional Protocol No 1 of Montreal 1975, and such an Order is conclusive evidence of the matters so certified.

This Order, which supersedes the Carriage by Air (Parties to Convention) Order 1988, certifies the High Contracting Parties to the Convention as amended at The Hague, the unamended Convention, and the Convention as amended by Additional Protocol No 1 of Montreal 1975, the territories in respect of which they are parties and the extent to which they have availed themselves of the provisions of the Additional Protocol to the Convention.

Appendix 5

Council Regulation (EC) No 2027/97 of 9 October 1997 on air carrier liability in the event of accidents

OJ L 285/97

The Council of The European Union,

Having regard to the Treaty establishing the European Community, and in particular Article 84 (2) thereof,
Having regard to the proposal from the Commission (1),
Having regard to the opinion of the Economic and Social Committee (2),

Acting in accordance with the procedure laid down in Article 189 (c) of the Treaty (3),

(1)   Whereas, in the framework of the common transport policy, it is necessary to improve the level of protection of passengers involved in air accidents;

(2)   Whereas the rules on liability in the event of accidents are governed by the Convention for the Unification of Certain Rules Relating to International Carriage by Air, signed at Warsaw on 12 October 1929, or that Convention as amended at The Hague on 28 September 1955 and the Convention done at Guadalajara on 18 September 1961, whichever may be applicable each being hereinafter referred to, as applicable, as the 'Warsaw Convention`; whereas the Warsaw Convention is applied worldwide for the benefit of both passengers and air carriers;

(3)   Whereas the limit set on liability by the Warsaw Convention is too low by today's economic and social standards and often leads to lengthy legal actions which damage the image of air transport; whereas as a result Member States have variously increased the liability limit, thereby leading to different terms and conditions of carriage in the internal aviation market;

(4)   Whereas in addition the Warsaw Convention applies only to international transport; whereas, in the internal aviation market, the distinction between national and international transport has been eliminated; whereas it is therefore appropriate to have the same level and nature of liability in both national and international transport;

(5)   Whereas a full review and revision of the Warsaw Convention is long overdue and would represent, in the long term, a more uniform and applicable response, at an international level, to the issue of air carrier liability in the event of accidents; whereas efforts to increase the limits of liability imposed in the Warsaw Convention should continue through negotiation at multilateral level;

(6)   Whereas, in compliance with the principle of subsidiarity, action at Community level is desirable in order to achieve harmonization in the field of air carrier liability and could serve as a guideline for improved passenger protection on a global scale;

(7)   Whereas it is appropriate to remove all monetary limits of liability within the

meaning of Article 22 (1) of the Warsaw Convention or any other legal or contractual limits, in accordance with present trends at international level;

(8) Whereas, in order to avoid situations where victims of accidents are not compensated, Community air carriers should not, with respect of any claim arising out of the death, wounding or other bodily injury of a passenger under Article 17 of the Warsaw Convention, avail themselves of any defence under Article 20 (1) of the Warsaw Convention up to a certain limit;

(9) Whereas Community air carriers may be exonerated from their liability in cases of contributory negligence of the passenger concerned;

(10) Whereas it is necessary to clarify the obligations of this Regulation in the light of Article 7 of Council Regulation (EEC) No 2407/92 of 23 July 1992 on licensing of air carriers (4); whereas, in this regard, Community air carriers should be insured up to a certain limit laid down in this Regulation;

(11) Whereas Community air carriers should always be entitled to claim against third parties;

(12) Whereas prompt advance payments can considerably assist the injured passengers or natural persons entitled to compensation in meeting the immediate costs following an air accident;

(13) Whereas the rules on the nature and limitation of liability in the event of death, wounding or any other bodily injury suffered by a passenger form part of the terms and conditions of carriage in the air transport contract between carrier and passenger; whereas, in order to reduce the risk of distorting competition, third-country carriers should adequately inform passengers of their conditions of carriage;

(14) Whereas it is appropriate and necessary that the monetary limits expressed in this Regulation be reviewed in order to take into account economic developments and developments in international fora;

(15) Whereas the International Civil Aviation Organization (ICAO) is at present engaged in a review of the Warsaw Convention; whereas, pending the outcome of such review, actions on an interim basis by the Community will enhance the protection of passengers; whereas the Council should review this Regulation as soon as possible after the review by ICAO, HAS ADOPTED THIS REGULATION:

Article 1

This Regulation lays down the obligations of Community air carriers in relation to liability in the event of accidents to passengers for damage sustained in the event of death or wounding of a passenger or any other bodily injury suffered by a passenger, if the accident which caused the damage so sustained took place on board an aircraft or in the course of any of the operations of embarking or disembarking.

This Regulation also clarifies some insurance requirements for Community air carriers. In addition, this Regulation sets down some requirements on information to be provided by air carriers established outside the Community which operate to, from or within the Community.

Article 2

1. For the purpose of this Regulation:

(a) 'air carrier` shall mean an air transport undertaking with a valid operating licence;
(b) 'Community air carrier` shall mean an air carrier with a valid operating licence granted by a Member State in accordance with the provisions of Regulation (EEC) No 2407/92;
(c) 'person entitled to compensation` shall mean a passenger or any person entitled to claim in respect of that passenger, in accordance with applicable law;
(d) 'ecu` shall mean the unit of account in drawing up the general budget of the European Communities in accordance with Articles 207 and 209 of the Treaty;
(e) 'SDR` shall mean a Special Drawing Right as defined by the International Monetary Fund;
(f) 'Warsaw Convention` shall mean the Convention for the Unification of Certain Rules Relating to International Carriage by Air, signed at Warsaw on 12 October 1929, or the Warsaw Convention as amended at The Hague on 28 September 1955 and the Convention supplementary to the Warsaw Convention done at Guadalajara on 18 September 1961 — whichever is applicable to the passenger contract of carriage, together with all international instruments which supplement, and are associated with, it and are in force.

2. Concepts contained in this Regulation which are not defined in paragraph 1 shall be equivalent to those used in the Warsaw Convention.

Article 3

1. (a) The liability of a Community air carrier for damages sustained in the event of death, wounding or any other bodily injury by a passenger in the event of an accident shall not be subject to any financial limit, be it defined by law, convention or contract.
(b) The obligation of insurance set out in Article 7 of Regulation (EEC) No 2407/92 shall be understood as requiring that a Community air carrier shall be insured up to the limit of the liability required under paragraph 2 and thereafter up to a reasonable level.

2. For any damages up to the sum of the equivalent in ecus of 100 000 SDR, the Community air carrier shall not exclude or limit his liability by proving that he and his agents have taken all necessary measures to avoid the damage or that it was impossible for him or them to take such measures.

3. Notwithstanding the provisions of paragraph 2, if the Community air carrier proves that the damage was caused by, or contributed to by, the negligence of the injured or deceased passenger, the carrier may be exonerated wholly or partly from its liability in accordance with applicable law.

Article 4

In the event of death, wounding or any other bodily injury suffered by a passenger in the event of an accident, nothing in this Regulation shall
(a) imply that a Community air carrier is the sole party liable to pay damages; or
(b) restrict any rights of a Community air carrier to seek contribution or indemnity from any other party in accordance with applicable law.

Article 5

1. The Community air carrier shall without delay, and in any event not later than fifteen days after the identity of the natural person entitled to compensation has been

established, make such advance payments as may be required to meet immediate economic needs on a basis proportional to the hardship suffered.

2.   Without prejudice to paragraph 1, an advance payment shall not be less than the equivalent in ecus of 15 000 SDR per passanger in the event of death.

3.   An advance payment shall not constitute recognition of liability and may be offset against any subsequent sums paid on the basis of Community air carrier liability, but is not returnable, except in the cases prescribed in Article 3 (3) or in circumstances where it is subsequently proved that the person who received the advance payment caused, or contributed to, the damage by negligence or was not the person entitled to compensation.

Article 6

1.   The provisions contained in Articles 3 and 5 shall be included in the Community air carrier's conditions of carriage.

2.   Adequate information on the provisions contained in Articles 3 and 5 shall, on request, be available to passengers at the Community air carrier's agencies, travel agencies and check-in counters and at points of sale. The ticket document or an equivalent shall contain a summary of the requirements in plain and intelligible language.

3.   Air carriers established outside the Community operating to, from or within the Community and not applying the provisions referred to in Articles 3 and 5 shall expressly and clearly inform the passengers thereof, at the time of purchase of the ticket at the carrier's agencies, travel agencies or check-in counters located in the territory of a Member State. Air carriers shall provide the passengers with a form setting out their conditions. The fact that only a liability limit is indicated on the ticket document or an equivalent shall not constitute sufficient information.

Article 7

No later than two years after the entry into force of this Regulation, the Commission shall draw up a report on the application of the Regulation which, inter alia, takes into account economic developments and developments in international fora. Such report may be accompanied by proposals for a revision of this Regulation.

Article 8

This Regulation shall enter into force one year after the date of its publication in the Official Journal of the European Communities.

This Regulation shall be binding in its entirety and directly applicable in all Member States.

Notes
(1) OJ C 104, 10. 4. 1996, p. 18 and OJ No C 29, 30. 1. 1997, p. 10.
(2) OJ C 212, 22. 7. 1996, p. 38.
(3) Opinion of the European Parliament of 17 September 1996 (OJ No C 320, 28. 10. 1996, p. 30), Council Common Position of 24 February 1997 (OJ No C 123, 21. 4. 1997, p. 89) and Decision of the European Parliament of 29 May 1997 (OJ C 182, 16. 6. 1997).
(4) OJ L 240, 24. 8. 1992, p. 1.

Appendix 6

Air Carrier Liability Order 1998

SI 1998/1751

Made 21st July 1998

Citation and commencement

1.   This Order may be cited as the Air Carrier Liability Order 1998 and shall come into force on 17th October 1998.

Interpretation

2.   In this Order:

"Council Regulation" means Council Regulation (EC) No 2027/97 of 9th October 1997 on air carrier liability in the event of accidents;

"non-Community air carrier" means an air carrier established outside the Community operating to, from or within the Community; and

other expressions have, in so far as the context admits, the same meaning as in the Council Regulation.

Amendments

3.   The Carriage by Air Act 1961 shall be amended as follows:

(1)   After section 1(1) there shall be inserted the following subsection:

"(1A)   In relation to Community air carriers—

(a)   in respect of damages up to the equivalent in ecus of 100,000 SDR arising from the death, wounding or other bodily injury suffered by a passenger, the provisions of Article 20 of the Convention; and

(b)   in respect of damages arising from the death, wounding or other bodily injury suffered by a passenger the provisions of Articles 21 and 22(1) of the Convention,

do not have the force of law in the United Kingdom.".

(2)   For section 14(2) there shall be substituted the following:

"(2)   In this Act—

"the Council Regulation" means Council Regulation (EC) No 2027/97 of 9th October 1997 on air carrier liability in the event of accidents;

"Community air carrier", "SDR" and "ecu" have the meaning given by Article 2 of the Council Regulation; and

"court" includes (in an arbitration allowed by the Convention) an arbitrator.".

4. In the Carriage by Air Acts (Application of Provisions) Order 1967, after article 5A there shall be inserted the following article:

"Application of the air carrier liability Regulation

5B

(1) In relation to Community air carriers:

(a) in respect of damages up to the equivalent in ecus of 100,000 SDR arising from the death, wounding or other bodily injury suffered by a passenger, Article 20 of Part III of Schedule 1 and Article 20(1) of Part B of Schedules 2 and 3 to this Order;

(b) in respect of damages arising from the death, wounding or other bodily injury suffered by a passenger Article 21 of Part III of Schedule 1 and of Part B of Schedules 2 and 3 to this Order; and

(c) in respect of damages arising from the death, wounding or other bodily injury suffered by a passenger Article 22(1) of Part III of Schedule 1 and of Part B of Schedules 2 and 3 to this Order,

do not have the force of law in the United Kingdom.".

5. In the Licensing of Air Carriers Regulations 1992, regulation 11(1)(b) shall be deleted.

Offences

6. (1) A Community air carrier which fails to include the provisions contained in Articles 3 and 5 of the Council Regulation in its conditions of carriage in accordance with Article 6.1 of that Regulation shall be guilty of an offence.

(2) A Community air carrier which fails to ensure that:

(a) the information required to be made available on request to passengers by paragraph 2 of Article 6 of the Council Regulations is so made available; or

(b) its ticket document or an equivalent contains the summary of the requirements contained in Articles 3 and 5 of the Council Regulation as required by paragraph 2 of Article 6 of that Regulation,

shall be guilty of an offence unless it proves that the failure to do so occurred without its consent or connivance and that it exercised all due diligence to prevent the failure.

(3)   A non-Community carrier which does not apply the provisions in Articles 3 and 5 of the Council Regulations and which fails to ensure that the information or the form required to be provided by passengers by paragraph 3 of Article 6 of the Council Regulations is so provided shall be guilty of an offence unless it proves that the failure to do so occurred without its consent or connivance and that it exercised all due diligence to prevent failure.

7.   (1)   A person guilty of an offence under this Order shall be liable:

    (a)   on summary conviction, to a fine not exceeding level 5 on the standard scale, and

    (b)   on conviction on indictment, to a fine.

(2)   Where an offence under these Regulations has been committed by a body corporate and is proved to have been committed with the consent or connivance of or to be attributable to any neglect on the part of any director, manager, secretary or other similar officer of the body corporate or any such person who was purporting to act in such capacity, he, as well as the body corporate, shall be guilty of that offence and be liable to be proceeded against and punished accordingly.

(3)   Where the affairs of a body corporate are managed by its members, paragraph (2) above shall apply in relation to the acts and defaults of a member in connection with his functions of management as if he were a director of the body corporate.

(4)   Where a Scottish partnership is guilty of an offence under these Regulations in Scotland and that offence is proved to have been committed with the consent or connivance of or to be attributable to any neglect on the part of a partner, he, as well as the partnership, shall be guilty of that offence and shall be liable to be proceeded against and punished accordingly.

Explanatory note

(This note is not part of the Regulations)

This Order implements Council Regulation (EC) No 2027/97 of 9th October 1997 on air carrier liability in the event of accidents.

The principal provisions are as follows:

(1)   The limits on carrier liability imposed by the Warsaw Convention (the Convention for the Unification of Certain Rules relating to International Carriage by Air signed at Warsaw on 12th October 1929), the Warsaw Convention as amended at The Hague on 28th September 1955 and the Convention supplementary to the Warsaw Convention done at Guadalajara on 18th September 1961 in the event of passenger death, wounding or bodily injury are removed in relation to Community air carriers from the Carriage by Air Act 1961 and the Carriage by Air Acts (Application of Provisions) Order 1967 (articles 3 and 4 respectively).

(2)   The minimum liability limit required by regulation 11(1)(b) of the Licensing of Air Carriers Regulations 1992 is deleted (article 5).

(3)   Community air carriers are no longer entitled to rely on the defence in Article 20(1) of the Warsaw Convention (or that Convention as amended) (taking all necessary

measures to avoid the damage or that it was impossible to take such measures) in relation to damages for passenger death, wounding or bodily injury of up to 100,000 Special Drawing Rights (articles 3 and 4).

(4)   Criminal offences are created for the breach of certain requirements set out in Article 6 of the Council Regulation (article 6).

Index

Accident, 7.32–7.43
  burden of proof, 7.43
  deliberate conduct, 7.38
  events not constituting, 7.39
  examples, 7.37
  injuries caused by fellow
      passengers, 7.40–7.42
  meaning, 7.32–7.43
Air carrier liability for passenger
    injury: EU regulation, 12.1–12.43
  advance payments, 12.34–12.40
    difficulties in practical application,
        12.40
    'immediate economic needs', 12.38
  background, 12.1–12.6
  contributory negligence, 12.29–12.33
  direct effect, 12.8–12.13
  disposing with limits on
      compensation, 12.20–12.24
  implementation in UK, 12.8–12.13
  information and documents of
      carriage, 12.41–12.43
  limiting defences available to
      Community air carriers,
      12.25–12.28
  measure of damages, 12.23
  procedure, 12.10
  scheme, 12.18, 12.19
  scope, 12.14–12.17
  Warsaw Convention, and,
      12.14–12.17
Air Carrier Liability Order 1998, 1.45
Air waybill, 6.1–6.37
  conditions of carriage contained in,
      6.34–6.37
    inaccuracy, 6.26
    incompleteness, 6.26
    irregularity, 6.26
  contents, 6.6, 6.14–6.20
    evidential status, 6.21–6.25
    responsibility for accuracy,
        6.21–6.25
  creation, 6.7–6.11
  customary form, 6.7
  document of title, 6.27–6.33
  evidence of contract, 6.12

Air waybill *contd*
  form, 6.3, 6.7–6.11
  function, 6.2
  'made out', 6.8
  Montreal Protocol No 4, 6.19
    Warsaw Hague Amendment, 6.19
  nature, 6.12, 6.13
  negotiability, 6.27–6.33
  particulars, 6.15
    effect of non-inclusion, 6.16–6.18
    Montreal Convention 1999, 6.19
  role, 6.5
  separate, 6.11
  standard form, 6.9, 6.10
  transfer, 6.4
  Unfair Contract Terms Act 1977,
      and, 6.37
Aircraft
  meaning, 4.3, 4.4
All necessary measures
  approach of US courts, 9.38, 9.39
  bad weather, 9.26
  burden of proof, 9.29, 9.30
  causation, 9.32
  defective construction, 9.24
  delay, 9.27, 9.28
  force majeure, 9.25, 9.26
  foreseeabiity of risk of damage, 9.31
  general principles, 9.14–9.22
  impossibility, 9.33–9.37
  meaning, 9.9–9.13
  nature of risk, 9.20
  particular instances, 9.23–9.42
  reasonableness, 9.10–9.13
  servants or agents, 9.40–9.42
  standard carrier practice, 9.21–9.22
  state of knowledge, 9.15
  warnings, 9.16–9.19
All necessary measures/impossibility
    defence, 9.3–9.42
  all necessary measures. *See* All
      necessary measures
  drafting background, 9.5, 9.6
  Montreal Convention 1999, 9.8
  subsequent changes and proposals,
      9.7

389